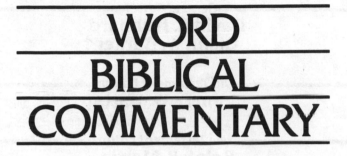

WORD BIBLICAL COMMENTARY

General Editors
David A. Hubbard
Glenn W. Barker †

Old Testament Editor
John D. W. Watts

New Testament Editor
Ralph P. Martin

WORD
BIBLICAL
COMMENTARY

VOLUME 45

1&2 Thessalonians

F. F. BRUCE

WORD BOOKS, PUBLISHER • WACO, TEXAS

Word Biblical Commentary:
1 AND 2 THESSALONIANS
Copyright © 1982 by Word, Incorporated

Library of Congress Cataloging in Publication Data
Main entry under title:

Word biblical commentary.

  Includes bibliographies.
  1. Bible—Commentaries—Collected works.
BS491.2.W67   220.7'7   81-71769
ISBN 0-8499-0244-4 (v. 45)   AACR2

Printed in the United States of America

Unless otherwise indicated, Scripture quotations in the body of the commentary are from
the Revised Standard Version of the Bible, copyright 1946 (renewed 1973), 1956, and ©
1971 by the Division of Christian Education of the National Council of the Churches of
Christ in the USA, and are used by permission. Those marked NIV are from New International
Version of the Bible, copyright © 1973 by New York Bible Society International. The author's
own translation of the text appears in italic type under the heading "Translation."

5 6 7 8 9 LBM 7 6 5

To

Arnold Anderson

colleague and friend

Contents

Editorial Preface

The launching of the *Word Biblical Commentary* brings to fulfillment an enterprise of several years' planning. The publishers and the members of the editorial board met in 1977 to explore the possibility of a new commentary on the books of the Bible that would incorporate several distinctive features. Prospective readers of these volumes are entitled to know what such features were intended to be; whether the aims of the commentary have been fully achieved time alone will tell.

First, we have tried to cast a wide net to include as contributors a number of scholars from around the world who not only share our aims, but are in the main engaged in the ministry of teaching in university, college and seminary. They represent a rich diversity of denominational allegiance. The broad stance of our contributors can rightly be called evangelical, and this term is to be understood in its positive, historic sense of a commitment to scripture as divine revelation, and to the truth and power of the Christian gospel.

Then, the commentaries in our series are all commissioned and written for the purpose of inclusion in the *Word Biblical Commentary*. Unlike several of our distinguished counterparts in the field of commentary writing, there are no translated works, originally written in a non-English language. Also, our commentators were asked to prepare their own rendering of the original biblical text and to use those languages as the basis of their own comments and exegesis. What may be claimed as distinctive with this series is that it is based on the biblical languages, yet it seeks to make the technical and scholarly approach to a theological understanding of scripture understandable by—and useful to—the fledgling student, the working minister as well as to colleagues in the guild of professional scholars and teachers.

Finally, a word must be said about the format of the series. The layout in clearly defined sections has been consciously devised to assist readers at different levels. Those wishing to learn about the textual witnesses on which the translation is offered are invited to consult the section headed "Notes." If the readers' concern is with the state of modern scholarship on any given portion of scripture, then they should turn to the sections on "Bibliography" and "Form/Structure/Setting." For a clear exposition of the passage's meaning and its relevance to the ongoing biblical revelation, the "Comment" and concluding "Explanation" are designed expressly to meet that need. There is therefore something for everyone who may pick up and use these volumes.

If these aims come anywhere near realization, the intention of the editors will have been met, and the labor of our team of contributors rewarded.

General Editors: *David A. Hubbard*
Glenn W. Barker†
Old Testament: *John D. W. Watts*
New Testament: *Ralph P. Martin*

Author's Preface

The invitation to contribute the volume on 1 and 2 Thessalonians to the Word Biblical Commentary has provided a welcome incentive to examine these two short documents in greater depth than I have previously done. The exercise has been rewarding.

The letters to the Thessalonians, if not absolutely the earliest Christian writings to have survived (as is widely believed) are certainly among the earliest. They were written not more than twenty years after the death and resurrection of Jesus, at a time when the gospel was already making headway in the Gentile world. They claim to have been sent by three missionaries—Paul, Silvanus and Timothy—to the church of Thessalonica a few months after its foundation. The names of Silvanus and Timothy are not added to Paul's in the prescripts of the two letters simply as a gesture of courtesy: internal evidence suggests that Silvanus at least played a fully responsible part in the authorship along with Paul. The letters reflect basic Christian teaching of the period—teaching maintained both in the church of Jerusalem and in the Gentile mission.

While difficulties are raised when an attempt is made to establish the relationship of 2 Thessalonians to 1 Thessalonians, the greatest difficulties are those involved in arguments that 2 Thessalonians is pseudonymous. Both letters are here treated as authentic.

Any commentator must stand on the shoulders of his predecessors. Among commentators on Thessalonians to whom I am conscious of being especially indebted, G. Wohlenberg, G. Milligan, B. Rigaux and E. Best are outstanding.

The Greek text followed in this commentary, except where there is a clear indication to the contrary, is that of the new (twenty-sixth) edition of the Nestle-Aland *Novum Testamentum Graece*. For the Greek Old Testament the text of A. Rahlfs's *Septuaginta* has been followed.

August 1981   F. F. Bruce

Abbreviations

	schaft vom Alten und Neuen Testament
BZ	Biblische Zeitschrift
BZNW	Beihefte zur Zeitschrift für die neutestamentliche Wissenschaft
C.Ap.	Contra Apionem (Josephus)
CBC	Cambridge Bible Commentary on the New English Bible
CBQ	Catholic Biblical Quarterly
Cels.	Contra Celsum (Origen)
CGT	Cambridge Greek Testament
CIL	Corpus Inscriptionum Latinarum
Claud.	Divus Claudius (Suetonius)
CNT	Commentaire du Nouveau Testament
Comm. in Matt.	Commentary on Matthew (Origen)
ConB	Coniectanea Biblica
CPI	Corpus Papyrorum Iudaicarum
CTM	Concordia Theological Monthly
Cyr.	Cyropaedia (Xenophon)
De resurr. carn.	De resurrectione carnis (Tertullian)
Dial.	Dialogue with Trypho (Justin)
Diss.	Dissertation
EBib	Etudes Bibliques
EGT	Expositor's Greek Testament. 5 volumes (London: Hodder & Stoughton, 1900–1910).
EKKNT	Evangelisch-Katholischer Kommentar zum Neuen Testament
Ep. (Epp.)	Epistle(s)
EstBib	Estudios Bíblicos
EstEcl	Estudios Eclesiásticos
Eth. Nic.	Nicomachean Ethics (Aristotle)
ETL	Ephemerides Theologicae Lovanienses
EvQ	The Evangelical Quarterly
ExpB	The Expositor's Bible
ExpTim	The Expository Times
FRLANT	Forschungen zur Religion und Literatur des Alten und Neuen Testaments
Geog.	Geography (Strabo)
Gnom. Byz.	Gnomologium Byzantinum
Gos. Thom.	Gospel of Thomas (from Nag Hammadi)
HCNT	Handcommentar zum Neuen Testament
HDB	Hastings' Dictionary of the Bible, 5 volumes
HE	Historia Ecclesiastica (Eusebius)
Hist.	Historia(e) (Herodotus, Thucydides, Polybius, Diodorus, Livy, Tacitus, Dio Cassius)
HNT	Handbuch zum Neuen Testament (ed. Lietzmann, H.)
HNTC	Harper's New Testament Commentaries
Hom.	Homiliae (Chrysostom)
HTR	Harvard Theological Review
HUCA	Hebrew Union College Annual
IB	Interpreter's Bible. 12 volumes (Nashville/New York; Abingdon, 1952–57).
ICC	International Critical Commentary
Id.	Idyllia (Theocritus)
IDB	Interpreter's Dictionary of the Bible. 5 volumes (Nashville/New York: Abingdon, 1962–76).
IG	Inscriptiones Graecae
Il.	Iliad (Homer)

INT	Introduction to the New Testament	MNTC	Moffatt New Testament Commentary
Iph. in Taur.	Iphigenia in Tauris (Euripides)	MT	Masoretic Text
IrBibSt(ud)	Irish Biblical Studies	NCB	New Century Bible
JBL	Journal of Biblical Literature	NClarB	New Clarendon Bible
		NEB	New English Bible
JBLMS	Journal of Biblical Literature Monograph Series	NedTTs	Nederlands Theologisch Tijdschrift
JETS	Journal of the Evangelical Theological Society	Nestle-Aland ²⁶	Nestle, E., Aland, K. & B., etc., Novum Testamentum Graece (Stuttgart: Deutsche Bibelstiftung, 1979)
JHS	Journal of Hellenic Studies	NF	Neutestamentliche Forschungen
JRS	Journal of Roman Studies	N.F.	Neue Folge
JRStatSoc	Journal of the Royal Statistical Society	NICNT	New International Commentary on the New Testament
JSS	Journal of Semitic Studies		
JTS	Journal of Theological Studies	NIDNTT	New International Dictionary of New Testament Theology, ed. Brown, C., 3 volumes (Grand Rapids, MI: Zondervan, 1975–78)
LD	Lectio Divina		
Leg.	De Legatione ad Gaium (Philo)		
LouvStud	Louvain Studies		
LSB	La Sacra Bibbia	NKZ	Neue kirchliche Zeitschrift
LXX	Septuagint	NovT	Novum Testamentum
Mart. Isa.	Martyrdom of Isaiah	NovTSup	Novum Testamentum Supplements
Med.	Meditationes (Marcus Aurelius)	n.s.	new series
Mem.	Memorabilia (Xenophon)	NTC	New Testament Commentary (Hendriksen, W.)
MeyerK	Kritisch-Exegetischer Kommentar (ed. Meyer, H. A. W.)	NTD	Das Neue Testament Deutsch
MHT	Moulton, J. H., Howard, W. F., Turner, N., Grammar of New Testament Greek. 4 volumes (Edinburgh: T. & T. Clark, 1906–76).	NTS	New Testament Studies
		NTSR	New Testament for Spiritual Reading
		Oed. Col.	Oedipus Coloneus (Sophocles)
		Olynth.	Olynthiaca (Demosthenes)
MM	Moulton, J. H., Milligan, G., The Vocabulary of the Greek Testament (London: Hodder & Stoughton, 1930).	Or. Sib.	Oracula Sibyllina
		Pers.	Persae (Aeschylus)
		Plant.	De Plantis (? Aristotle)
		P. Lond.	London Papyri
		P. Oxy.	Oxyrhynchus Papyri
		PW	von Pauly, A. F., Wissowa, G., Realencyclo-

	pädie für die klassische	*TJ*	*Theologische Jahrbücher*
	Altertumswissenschaft	*TQ*	*Theologische Quartal-*
RB	*Revue Biblique*		*schrift*
RÉGr	*Revue des Études*	*TS*	*Theological Studies*
	Grecques	*TSK*	*Theologische Studien und*
RestQ	*Restoration Quarterly*		*Kritiken*
RHPR	*Revue d'Histoire et de*	TU	Texte und Unter-
	Philosophie Religieuses		suchungen
RivB	*Rivista Biblica*	*TZ*	*Theologische Zeitschrift*
RNT	Regensburger Neues	UBS³	*The Greek New Testa-*
	Testament		*ment.* United Bible
RSR	*Recherches de Science Re-*		Societies, 3rd edi-
	ligieuse		tion, 1975.
RSV	Revised Standard Ver-	*VD*	*Verbum Domini*
	sion	*Vis.*	*Vision (in Shepherd of*
RTR	*Reformed Theological Re-*		*Hermas)*
	view	VS	Verbum Salutis
SAB	*Sitzungsberichte der köni-*	*VT*	*Vetus Testamentum*
	glichen preussischen	WC	Westminster Com-
	Akademie der Wissen-		mentaries
	schaften zu Berlin	WMANT	Wissenschaftliche
SBL	Society of Biblical Lit-		Monographien zum
	erature		Alten und Neuen
SBS	Stuttgarter Bibelstu-		Testament
	dien	WSB	Wuppentaler Studien-
SBT	Studies in Biblical		Bibel
	Theology	*ZAW*	*Zeitschrift für die alttesta-*
Scorp.	*Scorpiace* (Tertullian)		*mentliche Wissenschaft*
SD	Studies and Docu-	ZBK	Zürcher Bibelkom-
	ments		mentare
SE	*Studia Evangelica*	ZK	Zahn-Kommentar
SIG	*Sylloge Inscriptionum*	*ZNW*	*Zeitschrift für die neutes-*
	Graecarum (ed. W.		*tamentliche Wissen-*
	Dittenberger)		*schaft*
SJT	*Scottish Journal of Theol-*	*ZST*	*Zeitschrift für systema-*
	ogy		*tische Theologie*
SNT	Studien zum Neuen	*ZTK*	*Zeitschrift für Theologie*
	Testament		*und Kirche*
SNTSMS	Society for New Testa-	*ZWT*	*Zeitschrift für wissen-*
	ment Studies Mono-		*schaftliche Theologie*
	graph Series		
ST	*Studia Theologica*		
TB	*Tyndale Bulletin*		
TBl	*Theologische Blätter*	**(b) Ancient Authors**	
TDNT	Theological Dictionary of	Aesch.	Aeschylus
	the New Testament.	Clem.	Clement (of Rome)
	Tr. Bromiley, G. W.	Eurip.	Euripides
	10 volumes (Grand	Euseb.	Eusebius
	Rapids, MI: Eerd-	Herm.	Hermas
	mans, 1964–76)	Soph.	Sophocles
Theod.	The Greek OT of	Thuc.	Thucydides
	Theodotion	Xen.	Xenophon
Tim.	*Timaeus* (Plato)		

(c) Jewish literature

bSanh.	Babylonian Talmud: tractate *Sanhedrin*
Gen. Rab.	*Genesis Rabba*
Mur	Wadi Murabba'at texts
QL	Qumran Literature
1Q27	Text 27 from Qumran Cave 1
1QpHab	Pesher (commentary) on Habakkuk from Qumran Cave 1
Tg. Isa	Targum on Isaiah
Tg. Neof.	Targum Neofiti 1 (Vatican Library) on the Pentateuch
T. Jos.	Testament of Joseph
T. Levi	Testament of Levi (from Testaments of the Twelve Patriarchs)

(d) Textual notes

The letters and numbers used to indicate individual manuscripts are those commonly found in *apparatus critici*. Other abbreviations are:

byz	Byzantine text (exhibited by majority of manuscripts)
cop	Coptic versions
cop^{bo}	Bohairic version
cop^{sa}	Sahidic version
lat	Latin versions
lat^{vet}	Old Latin
lat^{vg}	Latin Vulgate
lat$^{vg.cl}$	Latin Vulgate, Clementine edition (1592)
lat$^{vg.st}$	Latin Vulgate, Stuttgart edition (^{2}1975)
syr	Syriac versions
syr^{Pesh}	Peshiṭta version
syr^{hcl**}	Harclean Syriac, asterisked reading
syr$^{hcl.mg}$	Harclean Syriac, marginal reading
TR	Textus Receptus (text of early printed editions of the Greek New Testament)
*	after the siglum of a manuscript indicates the original hand (later corrected)
c	correction by later hand
^{1}	first corrector
^{2}	second corrector
cod	reading of one codex
codd	reading of some codices
p^t	The witness cited shows this reading partly (*partim*) or . some times when he reproduces the text; at other times he shows a different reading.
vid	The witness cited seems (*videtur*) to show this reading (it may be too obscure or mutilated for certainty)
al	Other (*alii*) codices also show this reading.
pc	A few (*pauci*) codices show this reading.
pm	Very many (*permulti*) codices show this reading.

Names of patristic authorities cited in the textual notes are abbreviated as follows:

Ambst	"Ambrosiaster" (Latin, 4th century)
Aug	Augustine (Latin, 4th/5th century)
Clem.Al	Clement of Alexandria (Greek, late 2nd century)
Did	Didymus of Alexandria (Greek, late 4th century)
Euseb	Eusebius of Caesarea (Greek, early 4th century)

Iren^{lat}   Latin translation (4th century) of Irenaeus of Lyons (Greek, late 2nd
            century)
Mcion   Marcion (Greek, mid-2nd century)
Pelag   Pelagius (Latin, 4th/5th century)
Spec   Speculum (Pseudo-Augustinian compilation, Latin, 5th century)
Tert   Tertullian (Latin, 2nd/3rd century)

(e) Others

The usual literary abbreviations (such as *ad loc.*, "at the place" referred to)
are self-explanatory; so are the abbreviations for books of the Bible and the better
known apocrypha and pseudepigrapha.

Commentaries on Thessalonians (see list on pp. xxviii, xxix) are cited by authors'
names; so occasionally are other works where reference to the appropriate sectional
bibliography rules out the possibility of ambiguity. More often short titles are used.

Introduction

I. Background to the Thessalonian Letters

Bibliography

Bauman, R. A. *The Crimen Maiestatis in the Roman Republic and Augustan Principate.* Johannesburg: Witwatersrand University Press, 1967. **Bauman, R. A.** *Impietas in Principem.* München: Beck, 1974. **Bell, H. I.** *Jews and Christians in Egypt.* London: British Museum, 1924. **Bornkamm, G.** *Paul.* Tr. D. M. G. Stalker. London: Hodder & Stoughton, New York: Harper and Row, 1971. **Bruce, F. F.** "The Romans through Jewish Eyes." In *Paganisme, Judaïsme, Christianisme: Mélanges offerts à Marcel Simon,* ed. A. Benoit, M. Philonenko, C. Vogel. Paris: E. de Boccard, 1978, 3–12. **Burton, E. D.** "The Politarchs." *AJT* 2 (1898) 598–632. **Cadbury, H. J.** *The Book of Acts in History.* New York: Harper, 1955. **Davies, P. E.** "The Macedonian Scene of Paul's Journeys." *BA* 26 (1963) 91–106. **Edson, C.** "Macedonica," I ("A Dedication of Philip V"), II ("State Cults of Thessalonica"), *Harvard Studies in Classical Philology* 51 (1940), 125–126, 127–136; III ("Cults of Thessalonica"), *HTR* 41 (1948) 153–204. **Eisler, R.** *The Messiah Jesus and John the Baptist.* Ed. A. H. Krappe. London: Methuen, 1931. **Geyer, F.** *Mazedonien bis zur Thronbesteigung Philipps II.* Beihefte der historischen Zeitschrift, 19. München: Oldenbourg, 1930. **Geyer, F., and Hoffmann, O.** "Makedonia." *PW* xiv.1 (1928) 638–771. **Hammond, N. G. L.** *History of Macedonia,* i–ii. Oxford: Clarendon Press, 1972–79. **Hammond, N. G. L.** "The Western Part of the Via Egnatia." *JRS* 64 (1974) 185–194. **Harnack, A.** *The Mission and Expansion of Christianity in the First Three Centuries,* i–ii. Tr. J. Moffatt. London: Williams and Norgate, 1908. **Harnack, A.** "Probabilia über die Adresse und den Verfasser des Hebräerbriefs." *ZNW* 1 (1900) 16–41. **Hemer, C. J.** "Alexandria Troas." *TB* 26 (1975) 79–112. **Hengel, M.** *Acts and the History of Earliest Christianity.* Tr. J. Bowden. London: SCM Press, 1979. **Jewett, R.** "The Agitators and the Galatian Congregation." *NTS* 17 (1970–71) 198–212. **Judge, E. A.** "The Decrees of Caesar at Thessalonica." *RTR* 30 (1971) 1–7. **Judge, E. A.** *The Social Pattern of the Christian Groups in the First Century.* London: Tyndale Press, 1960. **Judge, E. A., and Thomas, G. S. R.** "The Origin of the Church at Rome: A New Solution." *RTR* 25 (1966) 81–94. **Lake, K.** *The Earlier Epistles of St. Paul.* London: Rivingtons, ²1914. **Laourdas, B., and Makaronas, C.** (ed.), *Ancient Macedonia.* Thessaloniki: Institute for Balkan Studies, 1970. **Larsen, J. A. O.** *Greek Federal States.* Oxford: Clarendon Press, 1968. **Larsen, J. A. O.** "Roman Greece." In T. Frank (ed.), *An Economic Survey of Ancient Rome,* iv. Baltimore: Johns Hopkins Press, 1938, 259–498. **Morgan, M. G.** "Metellus Macedonicus and the Province Macedonia." *Historia* 18 (1969) 422–446. **Oberhummer, E.** "Thessalonike." *PW,* 2te Reihe, vi.1 (1936) 143–163. **O'Sullivan, F.** *The Egnatian Way.* Newton Abbot: David and Charles, 1972. **Papazoglu, F.** "Quelques aspects de l'histoire de la province Macédoine." In *ANRW* ii.7.1 (1979), 302–369. **Smallwood, E. M.** *Documents illustrating the Principates of Gaius, Claudius and Nero.* Cambridge: Cambridge University Press, 1967. **Tarn, W. W., and Griffith, G. T.** *Hellenistic Civilisation.* London: E. Arnold, ³1952. **Vacalopoulos, A.** *History of Thessaloniki.* Thessaloniki: Institute for Balkan Studies, 1963. **Vickers,**

H. J. "Hellenistic Thessaloniki." *JHS* 92 (1972) 156–170. **Walbank, F. W.** *Philip V of Macedon.* Cambridge: Cambridge University Press, 1940.

1. *Macedonia*

Macedonia was an ancient kingdom in the Balkan peninsula, to the north of the Greek states. When the Persians invaded Europe in the early fifth century B.C., the Macedonian kings collaborated with them and so preserved their position; nevertheless Alexander I gave covert aid to the Greeks who were attacked by Xerxes in 480 B.C. (Herodotus, *Hist.* 5.17, 18; 7.173; 9.45). Alexander I and his successors patronized Greek art and letters; indeed, Alexander as a young man was allowed to compete in the footrace at the Olympian games, perhaps because his family claimed Argive descent (Herodotus, *Hist.* 5.22; 8.137). By the fourth century Macedonia was for most practical purposes part of the Greek world. Philip II (356–336 B.C.) made himself master of the formerly independent city-states of Greece; after his assassination his son Alexander III (the Great) made this united Graeco-Macedonian dominion the base for his conquest of Western Asia and Egypt. With the division of Alexander's empire after his death (323 B.C.), Macedonia soon became a separate kingdom again.

The Macedonian kingdom first clashed with the Romans when Philip V (221–179 B.C.) made a treaty with Hannibal during the Second Punic War (Polybius, *Hist.* 7.9). The Romans, however, stirred up sufficient trouble for him east of the Adriatic to keep him occupied, and his treaty with Hannibal remained ineffective. When the Second Punic War was over, and with Hannibal safely out of the way, the Romans invented a pretext for declaring war on Philip. This Second Macedonian War, as it is called (200–197 B.C.), ended with Philip's defeat at Cynoscephalae (Polybius, *Hist.* 28.22–28). He was obliged henceforth to confine his rule to Macedonia, and Rome proclaimed herself the liberator and protector of the city-states of Greece (Plutarch, *Flamininus* 10).

Philip's son Perseus in his turn excited Rome's suspicions, which were further fomented by his enemy the king of Pergamum, Rome's ally. The ensuing Third Macedonian War (171–168 B.C.) ended with the Roman victory at Pydna (Polybius, *Hist.* 31.29). The royal dynasty of Macedonia was abolished; the kingdom was divided by the Romans into four republics (Livy, *Hist.* 45.29.5 ff.; Larsen, *States*, 295 ff.). But in 149 B.C. an adventurer named Andriscus, claiming to be a son of Perseus, reunited Macedonia under his rule for a short time (Diodorus, *Hist.* 32.9b, 15; Florus, *Epitome* 1.30). When he was put down in 148 B.C., the Romans decided that the only course to take with Macedonia was to annex it as a province (Florus, *Epitome* 1.32.3; cf. Morgan, "Metellus Macedonicus . . ."). The four republics set up twenty years before remained as geographical divisions, but retained little political significance. To consolidate their hold on the new province, the Romans built a military highway, the Via Egnatia, from Apollonia and Dyrrhachium on the Adriatic coast of Macedonia to Thessalonica; it was in due course extended farther east to Philippi and its port Neapolis, and later still to Byzantium (Strabo, *Geog.* 7.7.4; cf. Hammond, "The Western Part . . . ," and, for a good popular account of recent date, O'Sullivan, *The Egnatian Way*). As may be gathered from 1 Maccabees 8:1–16, the story of the overthrow of the Macedonian kings, losing nothing in the telling, made a deep impression on the inhabitants of Syria and Palestine as they learned more and more about those invincible Romans from the distant west (cf. Bruce, "The Romans through Jewish Eyes").

Macedonia thus became a base for the further extension of Roman power. Augustus made it a senatorial province in 27 B.C. In A.D. 15 it was combined with Achaia and Moesia to form one imperial province (Tacitus, *Ann.* 1.76.4; 80.1), but was handed back to the senate in A.D. 44, with Thessalonica as the seat of provincial administration (cf. also Papazoglu, "Macédoine").

2. *The Gospel Comes to Macedonia*

The gospel reached Macedonia less than twenty years after the death of Christ. One of the earliest Christian documents (if not absolutely the earliest extant)—the first Pauline letter to the Thessalonians—was sent, probably toward the end of A.D. 50, to the Christian community in Thessalonica. From this letter it appears that the community owed its existence to a missionary visit paid to the city by Paul and two of his colleagues not long before. That visit had been preceded by a visit to Philippi, where the missionaries had been "shamefully treated" (1 Thess 2:2). Their sojourn in Thessalonica had also been attended by trouble, and their converts there had endured some measure of persecution (1 Thess 1:6; 2:14). From Thessalonica they—or at least Paul himself—had gone on to Athens (1 Thess 3:1); attempts to return to Thessalonica had been frustrated (1 Thess 2:17, 18). The letter had to serve in lieu of a personal visit.

This outline of events, gathered from 1 Thessalonians, agrees so well with the fuller record of Acts 16:6–18:5 that the record, though it is substantially later than 1 Thessalonians, may confidently be accepted as providing a historical framework within which the data of 1 Thessalonians can be read with greater understanding (on Acts as a historical source cf. Hengel, *Acts*).

According to the narrative of Acts, shortly after the Council of Jerusalem (Acts 15:5–29), Paul set out with his colleague Silas (called Silvanus in the Pauline letters) to traverse Asia Minor from the Cilician Gates westward. Macedonia played no part in their planned itinerary. So far as can be inferred from the record, they were making for Ephesus. But they were prevented from continuing their journey in that direction and found themselves (accompanied now by Timothy, who had joined them at Lystra) obliged to turn northwest from Iconium or Pisidian Antioch until they reached the Aegean Sea at the port of Alexandria Troas (cf. Hemer, "Alexandria Troas"). At this point the first of the "we" passages of Acts begins:

A vision appeared to Paul in the night: a man of Macedonia was standing beseeching him and saying: "Come over to Macedonia and help us." And when

he had seen the vision, immediately we sought to go on into Macedonia, concluding that God had called us to preach the gospel to them (Acts 16:9, 10).

The missionary party, now increased to four by the addition of the
narrator himself (as the transition from "they" to "we" suggests), crossed
by sea to Neapolis (modern Kavalla) and traveled along the Via Egnatia
for about ten miles to the Roman colony of Philippi. There they made
several converts and established a promising church, but they ran into
trouble with the city authorities. Their two leaders, Paul and Silas/Silvanus,
suffered an official beating with the lictors' rods, followed by a night's
imprisonment in the city jail. When the authorities discovered that the
men to whom they had meted out this summary treatment were Roman
citizens like themselves, they were alarmed and begged them to leave Philippi: they did not feel strong enough to be responsible for their safety
(Acts 16:11–40).
Leaving the narrator behind in Philippi (it appears), the three others
continued their westward journey along the Via Egnatia until they reached
Thessalonica, about ninety miles distant from Philippi (Acts 17:1).

3. Christianity at Thessalonica
Thessalonica, founded about 315 B.C. by the Macedonian king Cassander
and named after his wife (a half-sister of Alexander the Great) had as its
original residents the former inhabitants of Therme and some twenty-five
neighboring towns or villages, whom Cassander forcibly settled in his new
foundation. It was made the seat of provincial administration when Macedonia was annexed by Rome in 167 B.C. From 42 B.C. it enjoyed the status
of a free city, governed by its own politarchs (five or six in number). The
term "politarchs" is well attested epigraphically as the designation of the
chief magistrates of Macedonian cities, but Acts 17:6 is the only place
where it occurs in Greek literature (cf. Burton, "The Politarchs").
In Thessalonica there was a sizeable Jewish community with its synagogue, which Paul and his friends attended according to their custom.
Paul in particular participated animatedly in the services, especially in the
exposition of the scripture lessons, arguing that the Scriptures foretold a
suffering Messiah, and that this Messiah had come in the person of Jesus
(Acts 17:2, 3). Some members of the congregation were persuaded—Jason,
for example, whose hospitality the missionary party enjoyed in Thessalonica, and Aristarchus, later to be Paul's traveling companion and fellow-
prisoner (cf. Col 4:10; Phlm 24; Acts 19:29; 20:4; 27:2). Several converts
were also made among the fringe of Gentile God-fearers who attended
the synagogue; these included several ladies of good family, wives of leading
citizens.
These adherents formed the nucleus of the church in Thessalonica.
Their numbers were soon augmented by an even greater body of converts
won from outright paganism. After three sabbath days the synagogue authorities decided that they had had enough of the missionaries and their

message. The missionaries therefore made a direct approach to the rank and file of the citizens, many of whom "turned to God from idols, to serve a living and true God" (1 Thess 1:9).

The church of Thessalonica was thus established, comprising a majority of former pagans. Paul and his colleagues gave the members of the young church such instruction in the Christian faith and way of life as they were accustomed to give their converts elsewhere. But their stay in Thessalonica was interrupted.

A demonstration was staged against them by the first-century counterparts of our modern "Rentamob"—in the delightful idiom of King James's translators, "certain lewd fellows of the baser sort" (τῶν ἀγοραίων ἄνδρας τινὰς πονηρούς, Acts 17:5; Lake, *Epistles* 69 n. 1, translates ἀγοραῖοι as "agitators," citing Plutarch, *Aemil. Paul.* 38: ἀνθρώπους ἀγεννεῖς καὶ δεδουλευκότας, ἀγοραίους δὲ καὶ δυναμένους ὄχλον συναγαγεῖν, "ignoble and servile fellows, agitators adept at gathering a crowd"). The "lewd fellows" themselves were incited by parties that had an interest in the missionaries' enforced departure from Thessalonica. Unable to lay hands on the missionaries themselves, the demonstrators seized Jason and others who had befriended them and dragged them before the politarchs: "These men who have subverted the civilized world (οἱ τὴν οἰκουμένην ἀναστατώσαντες) have come here too," they protested, "and Jason has harbored them. Their practices are clean contrary to Caesar's decrees; they are proclaiming a rival emperor, Jesus" (Acts 17:6, 7).

A militant messianism was spreading among the Jewish communities throughout the Roman Empire (cf. Jewett, "The Agitators and the Galatian Congregation"). It was just about this time that Claudius expelled the Jews from Rome because of their persistent rioting. If (as is most probable) the "Chrestus" at whose instigation, according to Suetonius (*Claudius* 25.4), this rioting had broken out was identical with the Jesus whom Paul proclaimed to be Christ, the case against Paul and his associates was clear. If he was some other messianic figure, possibly alive and active in Rome in A.D. 49—Simon Magus has been implausibly suggested by Eisler (*The Messiah Jesus*, 581) and, more guardedly, by Judge and Thomas ("The Origin . . . ," 87)—the custodians of law and order in the Roman world were not likely to see any material difference between him and the one for whom Paul made messianic claims. The trouble in Rome had not been spontaneously generated there; it had been carried by visitors from the east. It was from the east, too, that these alleged troublemakers had come to Thessalonica, carriers of what the emperor himself had described a few years earlier as "a general plague which infests the whole world" (Claudius, *Letter to the Alexandrines*, P. Lond. 1912, *CPI* 2.153, line 99).

The fact that the rival emperor whom Paul and the others were accused of proclaiming had been sentenced to death by a Roman judge on a charge of sedition—as any one could ascertain who took the trouble to inquire—spoke for itself. The "decrees (δόγματα) of Caesar" which they were said to contravene have formed the subject of a study by Judge ("The Decrees of Caesar"). He points out that, while the demonstrators had intended to bring Paul and the other missionaries before the "popular assembly" (δῆμος), it was before the politarchs that they dragged Jason and his companions, and suggests that the charges before the one body need not have been identical with those actually pressed before the other. (This presupposes that the author of Acts, true to his custom, uses his terms here with precision and does not simply mean that the demonstrators wished to expose the missionaries to the violence of the mob.)

Evidently the proclamation of another emperor was the most serious respect in which the missionaries were accused of contravening the decrees of Caesar. But such sedition (*maiestas*) was an offense against public law and required no specific decree of Caesar to make it illegal (for the *lex Iulia de maiestate* see Bauman, *The Crimen Maiestatis* . . . , and *Impietas in principem*). It is plain, however, from the two Thessalonian letters that there was a prominent eschatological note in the apostolic preaching in Thessalonica. It affirmed not only that the Messiah foretold by the prophets of Israel had appeared in the person of Jesus, but also that this Jesus—crucified, risen and exalted—would reappear on earth as universal judge (cf. 2 Thess 1:7–10). "It would not have been hard to interpret such announcements as predictions of a change of ruler" (Judge, "Decrees," 3). Both Augustus and Tiberius had been very sensitive about the activities of astrologers and other prognosticators. Augustus in A.D. 11 issued a decree forbidding, among other things, the forecasting of anyone's death (Dio Cassius, *Hist.* 56.25.5, 6); five years later this prohibition was reaffirmed and extended by Tiberius (Dio Cassius, *Hist.* 57.15.8). The practice of magic and divination in general was banned as well as of astrology; in particular, consultation about the emperor's health or about high matters of state was apparently forbidden under the severest penalties (cf. Tacitus, *Ann.* 2.27–32; Paulus, *Sententiae* 5.21).

There is also the possibility that Claudius's disapproval of Jewish militancy, which found expression in his letter to the people of Alexandria at the beginning of his principate (A.D. 41), found further expression in an official decree. If so, the terms of the indictment against Paul and his party would naturally imply their disobedience to such a decree.

It has been argued, moreover, that city magistrates and other local authorities throughout the provinces were responsible (possibly under oath) to enforce the decrees of Caesar and to take appropriate action in the face of any threat to his personal or political well-being (Judge, "Decrees," 5–7; *The Social Pattern*, 34, 35).

In these circumstances, one can only admire the wisdom of the Thessalonian politarchs in keeping cool heads and refusing to take panic action. Perhaps Jason and the others brought before them were known to be men of substance who would not readily encourage troublemakers. At any rate the politarchs contented themselves with "taking security" (λαβεῖν τὸ ἱκανόν, cf. Latin *satis accipere*) from them (Acts 17:9)—making them responsible for the missionaries' good behavior, which meant their guaranteeing that they, and in particular Paul, would leave the city quietly.

To protect his friends, Paul had no option but to leave, but he left most reluctantly. He believed that the new Christians in Thessalonica had received insufficient instruction to prepare them for the life which they would henceforth have to lead, but successive attempts which he made to return to them were thwarted (1 Thess 2:18). He well knew the kind of treatment they would have to put up with, and he felt for them acutely. What would the leading citizens say to their wives who had joined this new and suspect society? "A fine lot these Jewish spellbinders are! They come here and persuade you to join their following, but as soon as trouble blows up, off they go and leave their dupes to face the music!" That was hard enough to bear, but both letters to the Thessalonians make it plain that some of the converts had to endure worse than ridicule: they are commended for their "steadfastness and faith" in all their "persecutions and . . . afflictions" (2 Thess 1:4).

Paul and Silvanus were spirited away quietly by night and escorted to Beroea, a city lying some way south of the Via Egnatia—*oppidum deuium,* "a town off the main road," as Cicero calls it (*In Pisonem* 89). In Beroea as in Thessalonica they visited the synagogue and used the reading of the Scripture lessons as an occasion for communicating the gospel to the congregation. The Jews of Beroea gave them unprejudiced attention and showed themselves willing to study the sacred text carefully to see if it could reasonably be interpreted along the lines indicated by the two visitors. A number of them were convinced. One is known to us by name—Sopater the son of Pyrrhus (probably identical with the Sosipater of Rom 16:21), who seven years later accompanied Paul to Judea with other delegates from his Aegean mission-field who were taking their respective churches' contributions to the Jerusalem relief fund (Acts 20:4). In addition, the converts at Beroea, as at Thessalonica, included several "Greek women of high standing" (Acts 17:12).

Throughout Paul's Macedonian mission, then, women of substance appear to have played an influential part among his converts, beginning with Lydia, his first convert in Philippi (Acts 16:14). This is in keeping with the traditional status of women in Macedonian society. "If Macedonia produced perhaps the most competent group of men the world had yet seen, the women were in all respects the men's counterparts; they played a large part in affairs, received envoys and obtained concessions from them for their husbands, built temples, founded cities, engaged mercenaries, commanded armies, held fortresses, and acted on occasion as regents or even co-rulers" (Tarn and Griffith, *Hellenistic Civilisation,* 98, 99). This example, set by women of the ruling classes, was evidently followed by their freeborn sisters in lower social ranks.

But some of Paul's and Silvanus's opponents in Thessalonica, learning of their activity in Beroea, made their way there and stirred up the same

kind of agitation as they had done at home. Once again Paul had to be
spirited away for his own safety and that of his converts. His Beroean
friends conveyed him to Athens, and from Athens, after a short stay, he
went on to Corinth, where he arrived, as he says, "in weakness and in
much fear and trembling" (1 Cor 2:3).

He had been virtually expelled as a troublemaker from one Macedonian
city after another. Had he and his companions been mistaken when they
crossed the sea from Asia Minor to Macedonia under a conviction of divine
guidance? Had the Macedonian mission proved abortive? In each Macedonian city they visited they had established a community of believers. But
the missionaries had been forced to leave these young converts abruptly,
quite inadequately equipped with the instruction and encouragement necessary to enable them to stand firm in the face of determined opposition.
Would their immature faith prove equal to the challenge? It did, outstandingly so, but this could not have been foreseen. The first gospel campaign
in Macedonia, in the light of the sequel, can be recognized as an illustrious
success, but at the time when Paul was compelled to leave the province
it must have been felt as a heartbreaking failure.

4. Paul's Plan of Action

Paul is not said in our records to have had any definite plan of action
in mind when he landed in Macedonia. But perhaps, as he and his companions journeyed westward along the Via Egnatia, a plan of action began
to take shape in his thinking. It was not by his own choice that he left
the Via Egnatia at Thessalonica and turned south to Beroea. If no obstacles
had been placed in his path, he could have continued to its western terminus
on the Adriatic. But the western terminus of the Via Egnatia would have
been no goal in itself; its importance lay in its being a stage on the road
to Rome. A short sea-crossing over the Straits of Otranto would have
taken him to Brundisium (Brindisi), and from there the Via Appia led to
Rome.

Some seven years later Paul tells the Roman Christians that he has frequently been prevented from carrying out a longstanding intention of pay-
ing them a visit (Rom 1:13; 15:22). His first steps along the Via Egnatia
might certainly have moved him to conceive such an intention. So Bornkamm judges: "We can be perfectly sure that, at the latest, in Asia Minor
and on the journey through Macedonia to Thessalonica, Rome was present
in Paul's mind as a far-off objective" (Paul, 51; cf. Harnack, Mission and
Expansion, 74–75; Cadbury, Book of Acts, 60–61; Judge and Thomas, "Origin," 90). But he was "hindered" from realizing it at the time, partly by
the agitation in Thessalonica which compelled him to turn south, partly
by his involvement in the formation and building up of Christian communities in Corinth and other places in Achaia after his enforced departure
from Macedonia and partly, perhaps, because news of Claudius's recent
expulsion of Jews from Rome showed him that he need not think of going
there at that time. He certainly learned of the expulsion edict at the latest

when he came to Corinth and met Priscilla and Aquila, who had been obliged to leave Rome because of that edict (Acts 18:2). But he may have learned of it earlier. If Jews who were expelled from Rome headed for the east, the Via Egnatia offered itself as a major highway along which they might travel. News of the edict (which is probably to be dated A.D. 49), and possibly some of those who had been evicted because of it, could have reached Thessalonica while Paul was still there. If so, this would help to fill in more of the background against which the charges against Paul and his colleagues at Thessalonica are to be evaluated.

5. *Paul and the Churches of Macedonia*

Paul's continuing relations with the Thessalonian and other Macedonian churches can be followed to some extent in the letters to the Thessalonians and the Philippians; he alludes to them further in writing to the Corinthians and the Romans. From these references we gather that his relations with them were outstandingly happy. He commends them for their steadfastness in faith and witness even under severe persecution and for their consistently generous giving—not only to himself personally but also to the Jerusalem relief fund—in circumstances of deep poverty (cf. 2 Cor 8:1–5; 11:9; Rom 15:26).

Five years after Paul's enforced departure from Macedonia he was able to revisit the province, and this time no great difficulties appear to have arisen for him. With the accession of Nero in October, A.D. 54, some of the hindrances imposed in the principate of Claudius may have lapsed. Toward the end of his Ephesian ministry (in the spring of A.D. 55) Paul planned to pass through Macedonia and continue south to see his friends in Corinth (1 Cor 16:5) and, although troubles in the Corinthian church caused some modification in his plans (2 Cor 1:15–2:13), he did spend a considerable time in Macedonia. It is indicated also by the narrative of Acts (19:21; 20:1, 2) that he visited Macedonia at this time, but a careful reading of the evidence suggests that his stay in the province was longer than might appear on the surface of the Acts narrative—that, in fact, he was able to travel farther west along the Via Egnatia than he had been allowed to do on his first visit.

This conclusion is dictated by the wording of Romans 15:19 where Paul, at the end of his apostolic program in the eastern Mediterranean, says that he has completed the preaching of the gospel "from Jerusalem and as far round as Illyricum." The mention of Illyricum, as the farthest west area where he has preached hitherto, implies that he has traveled along the Via Egnatia possibly as far as its terminus at Dyrrhachium and then turned north to cross the frontier separating Macedonia from Illyricum.

It was not his intention on this occasion to take ship across the Straits of Otranto. He hoped to visit Rome on the way to Spain in the near future (perhaps he crossed into Illyricum to gain some experience in preaching the gospel in Latin, the language which he would be obliged to use in Spain); meanwhile, he planned to visit Jerusalem with those delegates of his Gentile churches who were to carry their contributions to the fund for the relief of the mother church.

He returned from Illyricum in (probably) the late summer of A.D. 56 and traveled back east along the Via Egnatia; then he moved south from eastern Macedonia to Corinth to spend the winter there. About the beginning of the navigation season in A.D. 57 he was joined by the delegates of the Gentile churches, who were to sail with him from Cenchreae to Judea (cf. Acts 20:4; they represented "all the churches of Christ" from which greetings are sent to the Roman Christians in Rom 16:16). They did indeed sail from Cenchreae but Paul, learning of a plot against his life, changed his traveling plans, went north to Macedonia by land and took ship from the port of Philippi to Alexandria Troas, where he found his fellow-travelers awaiting him. At Philippi he was rejoined by the author of the "we" narrative, who journeyed to Jerusalem with him (Acts 20:5, 6). This brief and unplanned visit to Philippi (on which he no doubt passed through Thessalonica) was the last occasion spent by Paul on Macedonian soil. But the churches of Macedonia never forgot him, and his apostolic achievement in the province has endured in vigor to the present day.

II. THE THESSALONIAN LETTERS

Bibliography

(a) Commentaries

Alford, H. *The Greek Testament,* iii. London: Rivingtons, [5]1871, 43–69, 248–299. **Amiot, F.** *S. Paul, Epître aux Galates: Epîtres aux Thessaloniciens.* VS. Paris: Beauchesne, 1946. **Bailey, J. W.** "The First and Second Epistles to the Thessalonians." *IB.* xi. Nashville: Abingdon, 1955, 243–329. **Bengel, J. A.** *Gnomon Novi Testamenti* (Tübingen, 1773). London/Edinburgh: Williams and Norgate, [3]1862, 746–764. **Best, E.** *The First and Second Epistles to the Thessalonians.* HNTC. New York: Harper, 1972. **Bicknell, E. J.** *The First and Second Epistles to the Thessalonians.* WC. London: Methuen, 1932. **Boor, W. de.** *Die Briefe des Paulus an die Thessalonicher.* WSB. Wuppertal: Brockhaus, 1960. **Bornemann, W.** *Die Thessalonicherbriefe.* MeyerK. Göttingen: Vandenhoeck & Ruprecht, [5/6]1894. **Calvin, J.** *The Epistles of Paul the Apostle to the Romans and to the Thessalonians* (Strasbourg, 1540). Tr. R. Mackenzie. Edinburgh: Oliver & Boyd, 1960, 329–423. **Denney, J.** *The Epistles to the Thessalonians.* ExpB. London: Hodder & Stroughton, 1892. **Dewailly, L.-M.** *La Jeune Eglise de Thessalonique.* LD 37. Paris: Cerf, 1963. **Dibelius, M.** *An die Thessalonicher I–II. An die Philipper.* HNT 11. Tübingen: Mohr, [3]1937. **Dobschütz, E. von.** *Die Thessalonicherbriefe.* MeyerK Göttingen: Vandenhoeck & Ruprecht, [7]1909. **Donfried, K. P.** *The Epistles to the Thessalonians.* ICC. Edinburgh: T. & T. Clark, forthcoming. **Eadie, J.** *A Commentary on the Greek Text of the Epistles of Paul to the Thessalonians.* London: Griffin, 1877. **Ellicott, C. J.** *St. Paul's Epistles to the Thessalonians.* London: Longmans, [4]1880. **Findlay, G. G.** *The Epistles to the Thessalonians.* CGT. Cambridge: Cambridge University Press, 1925. **Frame, J. E.** *The Epistles of St. Paul to the Thessalonians.* ICC. Edinburgh: T. & T. Clark, 1912. **Grayston, K.** *The Letters of Paul to the Philippians and to the Thessalonians.* CBC. Cambridge: Cambridge University Press, 1967. **Hendriksen, W.** *I & II Thessalonians.* NTC. Grand Rapids, MI: Baker, 1955. **Hiebert, D. E.** *The*

Thessalonian Epistles: A Call to Readiness. Chicago: Moody Press, 1971. **Hobbs, H. H.** "1–2 Thessalonians." *BBC* xi. Nashville: Broadman Press, 1972, 257–298. **Hogg, C. F.,** and **Vine, W. E.** *The Epistles of Paul the Apostle to the Thessalonians.* Glasgow: Pickering & Inglis, 1914. **Holtz, T.** *Der erste Brief an die Thessalonicher,* EKKNT 13 Neukirchen-Vluyn: Neukirchener Verlag, forthcoming. **Hubbard, D. A.** *Thessalonians,* Waco, TX: Word, 1977. **Jowett, B.** *The Epistles of St. Paul to the Thessalonians, Galatians, Romans.* 2 volumes. London: John Murray, ³1894. **Kelly, W.** *The Epistles of Paul the Apostle to the Thessalonians.* London: C. A. Hammond, ³1953. **Lightfoot, J. B.** *Notes on the Epistles of St. Paul.* London: Macmillan, 1895, 1–136. **Lünemann, G.** *Critical and Exegetical Commentary on the NT: The Epistles to the Thessalonians.* Tr. P. J. Gloag. Edinburgh: T. & T. Clark, 1880. **Marxsen, W.** *Der erste Brief an die Thessalonicher.* ZBK:NT 11.1. Zürich: Theologischer Verlag, 1979. **Marxsen, W.** *Der zweite Brief an die Thessalonicher.* ZBK:NT 11.2. Zürich: Theologischer Verlag, forthcoming. **Masson, C.** *Les deux Epîtres de Saint Paul aux Thessaloniciens.* CNT xia. Neuchâtel/Paris: Delachaux et Niestlé, 1957. **Milligan, G.** *St. Paul's Epistles to the Thessalonians.* London: Macmillan, 1908. **Moffatt, J.** "The First and Second Epistles of Paul the Apostle to the Thessalonians." *EGT* iv. London: Hodder & Stoughton, 1910, 1–54. **Moore, A. L.** *I and II Thessalonians.* NCB. London: Nelson, 1969. **Morris, L.** *The First and Second Epistles to the Thessalonians.* NICNT. Grand Rapids, MI: Eerdmans, 1959. **Neil, W.** *The Epistle[s] of Paul to the Thessalonians.* MNTC. London: Hodder & Stoughton, 1950. **Oepke, A.** "Die Briefe an die Thessalonicher." In *Die kleineren Briefe des Apostels Paulus.* NTD 8. Göttingen: Vandenhoeck & Ruprecht, ³1953. **Plummer, A.** *A Commentary on St. Paul's First Epistle to the Thessalonians.* London: R. Scott, 1918. **Plummer, A.** *A Commentary on St. Paul's Second Epistle to the Thessalonians.* London: R. Scott, 1918. **Reese, J. M.** *1 and 2 Thessalonians.* NT Message 16, Wilmington, DE, Glazier, 1979. **Rigaux, B.** *Saint Paul: Les Epîtres aux Thessaloniciens.* EB. Paris: Gabalda, 1956. **Rossano, P.** *Lettere ai Tessalonicesi.* LSB. Torino: Marietti, 1965. **Schlatter, A.** *Die Briefe an die Thessalonicher, Philipper, Timotheus und Titus.* Stuttgart: Calwer Verlag, 1950. **Schlier, H.** *Der Apostel und seine Gemeinde. Auslegung des ersten Briefes an die Thessalonicher.* Freiburg: Herder, 1972. **Schmiedel, P. W.** *Die Briefe an die Thessalonicher und an die Korinther.* HCNT. Freiburg: Mohr, 1892. **Schürmann, H.,** and **Egenholf, H. A.** *The Two Epistles to the Thessalonians.* NTSR. London: Sheed and Ward, 1981. **Staab, K.** *Die Thessalonicherbriefe.* RNT. Regensburg: Pustet, 1965. **Trilling, W.** *Der zweite Briefe an die Thessalonicher,* EKKNT 14 Neukirchenr-Vluyn: Neukirchener Verlag, 1980. **Walvoord, J. F.** *The Thessalonian Epistles.* Grand Rapids, MI: Zondervan, 1967. **Ward, R. A.** *Commentary on 1 & 2 Thessalonians.* Waco, TX: Word, 1973. **Whiteley, D. E. H.** *Thessalonians in the RSV.* NClarB. Oxford: Clarendon Press, 1969. **Wohlenberg, G.** *Der erste und zweite Thessalonicherbrief.* ZK. Leipzig: Deichert, 1909.

(b) Other Works

Askwith, E. H. " 'I' and 'We' in the Thessalonian Epistles." *Expositor,* series 8, 1 (1911) 149–159. **Bacon, B. W.** *Introduction to the New Testament.* New York: Macmillan, 1900. **Barnett, A. E.** *The New Testament: its Making and Meaning.* New York: Abingdon-Cokesbury, 1946. **Baur, F. C.** *Paul: his Life and Works.* 2 volumes. Tr. A. Menzies. London: Williams and Norgate, 1875–76. Appendix III of Volume II of the English edition is a translation of Baur's "Die beiden Briefe an die Thessalonicher," *TJ* 14 (1855) 141–167. **Beare, F. W.** "Thessalonians, First Letter to the" and "Thessalonians, Second Letter to the." In *IDB* iv, 621–629. **Bornkamm, G.** *Paul.* Tr. D. M. G. Stalker. New York: Harper, 1971. **Brassac, A.** "Une inscription de Delphes et la chronologie de Saint Paul." *RB* 10 (1913) 36–53, 207–217. **Buck, C. H.,** and **Taylor, G.** *St. Paul: A Study of the Development of his Thought.* New York: Scribners, 1969. **Bultmann, R.** *Theology of the New Testament.* 2 volumes. Tr. K. Grobel. London: SCM Press, 1952–55. **Burkitt, F. C.** *Christian Beginnings.* London: University of London Press, 1924. **Collins, R. F.** "The Theology of Paul's First Letter to the Thessalonians." *LouvStud* 6 (1977) 315–337. **Collins, R. F.** "A propos the Integrity of 1 Thessalonians." *ETL* 55 (1979) 67–106. **Collins, R. F.** "1 Thessalonians and the Liturgy of the Early Church." *BTB* 10 (1980) 51–64. **Davies, J. G.** "The Genesis of Belief in an Imminent Parousia." *JTS* n.s. 14 (1963) 104–107. **Day, P.** "The practical purpose of 2 Thessalonians." *ATR* 45 (1963) 203–206. **Eckart, K. G.** "Der zweite echte Brief des Apostels Paulus an die Thessalonicher." *ZTK* 58 (1961) 30–44. **Ellingworth, P.,** and **Nida, E. A.** *A Translator's Handbook on Paul's Letters to the Thessalonians.* Stuttgart: United Bible Societies, 1975. **Ellis, E. E.** "Paul and his Co-Workers." *NTS* 17 (1970–71) 437–452. **Faw, C. E.** "On the Writing of First Thessalonians." *JBL* 71 (1952) 217–225. **Fuller, R. H.** *A Critical Introduction to the New Testament.* London: Duckworth, 1966. **Giblin, C. H.** *The Threat to Faith.* AnBib 31. Rome: Pontifical Biblical Institute, 1967. **Goguel, M.** *Introduction au Nouveau Testament.* iv. 1 Paris: Leroux, 1925. **Gregson, R. G.** "A Solution to the Problems of the Thessalonian Epistles." *EvQ* 38 (1966) 76–80. **Grotius, H.** *Annotationes in Novum Testamentum,* i. Amsterdam: Blaev, 1641; ii. Paris, 1646. **Hadorn, W.** *Die Abfassung der Thessalonicherbriefe in der Zeit der dritten Missionsreise des Paulus.* BFCT 24, 3–4. Gütersloh: Bertelsmann, 1919. **Hadorn, W.** "Die Abfassung der Thessalonicherbriefe auf der dritten Missionsreise und der Kanon des Marcion." *ZNW* 19 (1919–20) 67–72. **Harnack, A. von** "Das Problem des zweiten Thessalonicherbriefs." *SAB* 31 (1910) 560–578. **Henneken, B.** *Verkündigung und Prophetie im ersten Thessalonicherbrief.* SBS 29. Stuttgart: Katholisches Bibelwerk, 1969. **Hilgenfeld, A.** "Die beiden Briefe an die Thessalonicher, nach Inhalt und Ursprung." *ZWT* 5 (1862) 225–264. **Hort, F. J. A.** *The Christian Ecclesia.* London: Macmillan, 1897. **Jewett, R.** "The Agitators and the Galatian Congregation." *NTS* 17 (1970–71) 198–212. **Jewett, R.** *Paul's Anthropological Terms. A Study of their Use in Conflict Settings.* AGJU 10. Leiden: Brill, 1971. **Jewett, R.** *Dating Paul's Life.* London: SCM Press, 1979. **Kaye, B. N.** "Eschatology and Ethics in 1 and 2 Thessalonians." *NovT* 17 (1975) 47–57. **Kemmler, D. W.** *Faith and Human Reason. A Study of Paul's Method of Preaching as illustrated by 1–2 Thessalonians and Acts 17, 2–4.* NovTSup 40. Leiden: Brill, 1975. **Knox, J.** "A Conjecture as to the Original Status of II Corinthians and II Thessalonians in the Pauline Corpus." *JBL* 55 (1936) 145–153. **Koester, H.** "1 Thessalonians—Experiment in Christian Writing" in *Continuity and Discontinuity in Church History: Essays presented to G. H. Williams,* ed. Church, F. F. and George, T. Studies in the History of Christian Thought, 19. Leiden: Brill, 1979, 33–44. **Kümmel, W. G.** *Introduction to the New Testament.* Tr. A. J. Mattill. London: SCM Press, 1965. **Kümmel, W. G.** "Das literarische und geschichtliche Problem des ersten Thessalonicherbriefes." *Neotestamentica und Patristica: Eine Freundesgabe O. Cullmann . . . überreicht,* ed. W. C. van Unnik. NovTSup 6. Leiden: Brill, 1962, 213–227. **Lake, K.** *The Earlier Epistles of St. Paul.* London: Rivingtons, ²1914. **Levison, M., Morton, A. Q., Wake, W. C.** "On Certain Statistical Features of the Pauline Epistles." *Philosophical Journal* 3 (1966), 129–148. **Lightfoot, J. B.** *Biblical Essays.* London: Macmillan, 1893, 235–250 ("The Churches of Macedonia"), 251–269 ("The Church of Thessalonica"). **Lindemann, A.** "Zum Abfassungszweck des Zweiten Thessalonicherbriefes." *ZNW* 68 (1977) 35–47. **Lipsius, R. A.** "Über Zweck und Veranlassung des ersten Thessalonicherbriefs." *TSK* 27 (1854) 903–934. **Lüde-**

mann, G. *Paulus, der Heidenapostel.* Band 1: *Studien zur Chronologie.* FRLANT 123. Göttingen: Vandenhoeck & Ruprecht, 1980. **Lütgert, W.** *Die Vollkommenen im Philipperbrief und die Enthusiasten in Thessalonich.* BFCT 13.6. Gütersloh: Bertelsmann, 1909. **Lütgert, W.** *Freiheitspredigt und Schwarmgeister in Korinth.* BFCT 12.3. Gütersloh: Bertelsmann, 1908. **Lütgert, W.** *Gesetz und Geist. Eine Untersuchung zur Vorgeschichte des Galaterbriefs.* BFCT 22.6. Gütersloh: Bertelsmann, 1919. **Manson, T. W.** *Studies in the Gospels and Epistles,* ed. M. Black. Manchester: Manchester University Press, 1962, 259–278 ("The Letters to the Thessalonians," reprinted from *BJRL* 35, 1952–53, 428–447). **Martin, R. P.** *New Testament Foundations.* 2 volumes. Grand Rapids, MI: Eerdmans, 1975–78. **Marxsen, W.** *Introduction to the New Testament.* Tr. G. Buswell. Oxford: Blackwell, 1968. **Mearns, C. L.** "Early Eschatological Development in Paul: the Evidence of I and II Thessalonians." *NTS* 27 (1980–81) 137–157. **Michaelis, W.** *Die Gefangenschaft des Paulus in Ephesus und das Itinerar des Timotheus.* NF 1.3. Gütersloh: Bertelsmann. 1925. **Michaelis, W.** "Der zweite Thessalonicherbrief kein Philipperbrief." *TZ* 1 (1945) 282–286. **Moffatt, J.** *Introduction to the Literature of the New Testament.* Edinburgh: T. & T. Clark, ³1918. **Morton, A. Q.** "The Authorship of Greek Prose." *JRStatSoc* series A 127 (1965), 169–233. **Morton, A. Q.,** "The Authorship of the Pauline Corpus" in *The New Testament in Historical and Contemporary Perspective. Essays in Memory of G. H. C. Macgregor,* ed. W. Barclay and H. Anderson. Oxford: Blackwell, 1965, 209–235. **Morton, A. Q.** *The Integrity of the Pauline Epistles.* Manchester: Manchester Statistical Society, 1965. **Nellessen, E.** *Untersuchungen zur altlateinischen Überlieferung des 1. Thessalonicherbriefes.* BBB 22. Bonn: Hanstein, 1965. **Ogg, G.** *The Chronology of the Life of Paul.* London: Epworth, 1968. **Orchard, J. B.** "Thessalonians and the Synoptic Gospels." *Bib* 19 (1938) 19–42. **Plassart, A.** "L'inscription de Delphes mentionnant le Proconsul Gallion." *RÉGr* 80 (1967) 372–378. **Rigaux, B.** "Vocabulaire chrétien antérieure à la première épître aux Thessaloniciens." *BETL* 13 (1959) 380–389. **Robinson, J. A. T.** *Redating the New Testament.* London: SCM Press, 1975. **Schade, H.-H.** *Apokalyptische Christologie bei Paulus.* Göttingen: Vandenhoeck & Ruprecht, 1981. **Schmidt, J. E. C.** *Vermutungen über die beiden Briefe an die Thessalonicher.* Bibliothek für Kritik und Exegese des Neuen Testaments. Hadamer, 1801, 385–386. **Schmidt, J. E. C.** *Einleitung in das Neue Testament.* Giessen, 1804, 256–257. **Schmithals, W.** *Paul and the Gnostics.* Tr. J. E. Steely. Nashville/New York: Abingdon, 1972, 123–218 ("The Historical Situation of the Thessalonian Letters"). **Schmithals, W.** *Der Römerbrief als historisches Problem.* SNT 9. Gütersloh: Mohn, 1975. **Schmithals, W.** "Die Thessalonicherbriefe als Briefkompositionen." In *Zeit und Geschichte: Dankesgabe an Rudolf Bultmann,* ed. E. Dinkler. Tübingen: Mohr, 1964, 295–315. **Schrader, C.** *Der Apostel Paulus,* Teil 5. Leipzig: 1836. **Schwank, B.** "Der sogenannte Brief an Gallio und die Datierung des 1 Thess." *BZ* 15 (1971) 265–266. **Schweizer, E.** "Der zweite Thessalonicherbrief ein Philipperbrief?" *TZ* 1 (1945) 90–105. **Schweizer, E.** "Replik." *TZ* 1 (1945) 286–289. **Schweizer, E.** "Zum Problem des zweiten Thessalonicherbriefes." *TZ* 2 (1946) 74–75. **Smallwood, E. M.** *Documents illustrating the Principates of Gaius, Claudius and Nero.* Cambridge: Cambridge University Press, 1967. **Smith, D.** *The Life and Letters of St. Paul.* London: Hodder & Stoughton, 1919. **Suhl, A.** *Paulus und seine Briefe: Eine Beitrag zur Paulinischen Chronologie* SNT 11. Gütersloh: Mohn, 1975. **Thieme, K.** *Die Struktur des Ersten Thessalonicher-Briefes.* In *Abraham unser Vater . . . Festschrift für Otto Michel,* ed. O. Betz, M. Hengel, P. Schmidt, Leiden: Brill, 1963, 450–458. **Trilling, W.** *Untersuchungen zum zweiten Thessalonicherbrief.* Leipzig: St. Benno, 1972. **Uprichard, R. E. H.** "The Person and Work of Christ in 1 Thessalonians." *IrBibStud* 1 (1979) 19–27 = *EvQ* 53 (1981) 108–114. **Ware, P.** "The Coming of the Lord: Eschatology and 1 Thessalonians." *RestQ* 22 (1979) 109–120. **Weiss, J.** *Earliest Christianity.* Tr. F. C. Grant and others. 2 volumes. New York: Harper (Torchbooks), 1959. **West, J. C.** :"The Order of 1 and 2 Thessalonians." *JTS* 15 (1913–14) 66–74. **Wrede, W.** *Die Echtheit des zweiten Thessalonicherbriefs.* TU 24.2. Leipzig: Hinrichs, 1903.

1. *Authorship*

Two letters addressed to "the church of the Thessalonians" have been preserved to us in the NT canon. They are included in the *corpus Paulinum,* but in fact each of them is superscribed in the names of "Paul, Silvanus and Timothy." Both Silvanus (Silas) and Timothy (at least by inference) appear in the record of Acts as Paul's companions during his first visit to Thessalonica (Acts 17:1–9). For a short time after Paul's departure from Thessalonica the three were separated, but they were reunited in Corinth (Acts 18:5; cf. 2 Cor 1:19). Corinth thus suggests itself as the place from which the letters to the Thessalonian church were sent.

Since Paul, Silvanus and Timothy are named together as joint-authors of the letters, it is *prima facie* conceivable that Silvanus and Timothy played a responsible part along with Paul in the composition. Timothy indeed was Paul's aide-de-camp and is named along with Paul in the prescript of some other letters (2 Corinthians, Philippians, Colossians, Philemon), certainly because he was in Paul's company when these were written and possibly because he served Paul as amanuensis. Silvanus, on the other hand, occupied a more independent status in relation to Paul. He was not a convert of Paul's (as Timothy was); he was a member of the church of Jerusalem, enjoying the confidence of the leaders of that church, being himself one of the "leading men among the brethren" there (Acts 15:22). The *a priori* likelihood that such a man would be joint-author of letters in which he is named as one of the senders, in a substantial and not a merely nominal sense, is borne out by internal evidence.

The teaching of these two letters is that which (so far as can be judged) was common in primitive Christianity. It was received and imparted by Paul among others, but there is little here that is *distinctively* Pauline. F. C. Burkitt in particular maintained that both letters were the work of Silvanus (*Christian Beginnings,* 130–133). This, to his mind, explained their "archaic features" (not least in comparison with Galatians, which he judged on independent grounds to be the earliest of Paul's extant letters). He recognized in them "a monument of not quite the earliest stage of Jerusalemite Christianity," adding, "If I may hazard a final guess, I should say that Silas had heard St. Stephen gladly."

When Paul in other letters expresses his thanks to God for those to whom he writes, he usually does so in the first person singular ("I give thanks . . ."), even when others are associated with him in the prescript (cf. 1 Cor 1:4; Phil 1:3; Phlm 4). (Colossians, sent in the name of himself and Timothy to a church not personally known to him, is an exception. Col 1:3 begins, "We always thank God. . . .") In both the Thessalonian letters the first person plural is used: "We give thanks to God always . . ."

(1 Thess 1:2); "We are bound to give thanks to God always . . ." (2 Thess 1:3). This use of the first person plural is maintained throughout both letters, apart from certain places where the singular suddenly appears (1 Thess 2:18; 3:5; 5:27; 2 Thess 2:5; 3:17). In two of these five places the first personal pronoun is accompanied by the name "Paul" (1 Thess 2:18; 2 Thess 3:17). All of them are best explained by the supposition that they are Paul's personal additions, whether inserted by him orally as the letters were being dictated or appended—possibly in his own hand—when they were being read over after completion (see comments on each). The inclusion of his name in the prescripts and especially his signature at the end of the second letter would provide evidence enough that the contents as a whole were approved by him, whoever was responsible for the actual composition.

The authenticity of both letters, and especially of 2 Thessalonians, has been questioned from time to time, although both appear in the earliest lists of the Pauline writings. The first scholar to cast doubts on the authenticity of 2 Thessalonians appears to have been J. E. C. Schmidt, in a succession of works published between 1798 and 1804. F. C. Baur regarded himself as a pioneer in doubting the authenticity of 1 Thessalonians which, he wrote in 1845, "has as yet excited no suspicions" (it seems, however, that he was anticipated by C. Schrader in 1836). The absence of anything in 1 Thessalonians on which criticism can easily lay hold has been for many critics a powerful argument for its authenticity. Baur, however, saw in this "a criterion adverse to a Pauline origin" (implying, perhaps, that the authentic Paul provides no lack of material for criticism to lay hold of—which, in one sense, is true enough). In Baur's eyes, 1 Thessalonians was based on the narrative of Acts (itself, as he reckoned, a second-century work), and contains reminiscences of genuine Pauline letters (especially 1 and 2 Corinthians). Moreover, the statement in 1 Thessalonians 2:16 that retribution has overtaken the Jews εἰς τέλος "finally" presupposes the fall of Jerusalem in A.D. 70 (*Paul: His Life and Works*, ii, 85–92).

Whereas 1 Thessalonians appeared to Baur to reflect Paul's eschatological views (at second hand, to be sure), he found in 2 Thessalonians the eschatology of a very different school of thought. In an article published in 1855 he argued that 2 Thessalonians was composed under the influence of the Johannine Apocalypse: the "man of lawlessness" of 2 Thessalonians 2:3–10 is modeled on the "beast" of Revelation 13:1–9. Paul's alleged signature at the end of 2 Thessalonians is a mark of pseudonymity: in Paul's day there was no need to guarantee the authenticity of his letters; only with the circulation of pseudepigrapha did this become necessary ("Die beiden Briefe an die Thessalonicher").

One of Baur's disciples, R. A. Lipsius, found it possible to accept the authenticity of 1 Thessalonians while remaining true to his master's general position: by detecting an anti-judaizing tendency in the letter he was able to fit it into Baur's historical reconstruction of primitive Christianity ("Über Zweck und Veranlassung des ersten Thessalonicherbriefs").

More recently Morton's statistical analysis of the style of 1 and 2 Thessalonians has led to the conclusion that neither of these letters comes from the author of the Roman, Corinthian and Galatian correspondence. The data which he adduces could be satisfied simply if Silvanus were held to have had a major part in the composition of the two letters.

More will be said about the authenticity of 2 Thessalonians. At present, it may be observed that of the two letters 1 Thessalonians is much more informative about the movements of Paul and his companions after their departure from Thessalonica.

2. *Date and Occasion*

It is commonly agreed that 1 Thessalonians, together with 2 Thessalonians, if its authenticity is accepted, should be dated shortly after the first evangelization of Thessalonica, during what is traditionally (but imprecisely) called Paul's "second missionary journey"—about A.D. 50. The proposal has sometimes been made, because of the supposed reference in 2 Thessalonians 2:4 to the Emperor Gaius's attempt to set up his statue in the Jerusalem temple, to date the evangelization of Thessalonica and the writing of at least 2 Thessalonians several years earlier. Hugo Grotius in the seventeenth century dated 2 Thessalonians in A.D. 40, the year of that attempt (*Annotationes* i, 1032; ii, 651). More recently Buck and Taylor, identifying the "restrainer" of 2 Thessalonians 2:6, 7 with the Emperor Claudius, who replaced Gaius in A.D. 41, have dated the evangelization of Thessalonica early in that year (before Gaius's assassination) and the writing of 2 Thessalonians in the later part of A.D. 44 (*St. Paul*, 150–162). But the exegesis of 2 Thessalonians 2:1–12 is too debatable to provide the basis for chronological calculations. (Buck and Taylor identify the "wrath" of 1 Thess 2:16 with the Judean famine of A.D. 46.)

Others have argued for a later dating of one or both epistles, in the course of the "third missionary journey" (cf. Michaelis, *Gefangenschaft*, 60–67). This later dating is generally (though not in Michaelis) bound up with the view that the problems with which Paul and his colleagues take issue in the Thessalonian correspondence were essentially the same as those which manifested themselves in the Corinthian church in the period of Paul's Ephesian ministry—problems arising from a gnosticizing tendency. The arguments for this dating put forward by Hadorn in 1919 (*Die Abfassung der Thessalonicherbriefe in der Zeit der dritten Missionsreise des Paulus*) have been amplified by Schmithals (*Paul and the Gnostics*, 123–218). He maintains that the apostolic movements of 1 Thessalonians 3:1–10 should not be correlated with those of Acts 17: the reference to Athens in v 1, for example, is to be understood not of the famous stop-over in Athens of Acts 17:15–34 but of a later, otherwise unrecorded, stop-over made in the course of Paul's "painful visit" from Ephesus to Corinth (2 Cor 2:1). It is not clear why Paul should spend time in Athens when his business in Corinth was so urgent. There is no hint, either in Acts or in Paul's letters, that the situation in Thessalonica caused him special concern at that later time. Nor is there any indication, either in Acts or in Paul's letters, that Silvanus was in his company at that later time, as he manifestly was when the Thessalonian letters were written. Nor is there anything in either of the Thessalonian letters which requires a gnosticizing tendency at Thessalonica for its explanation.

After being expelled from Thessalonica, and then in turn from Beroea, Paul was taken to Athens, where he waited for his companions to rejoin him (Acts 17:15, 16). When they did so, he sent Timothy back to Thessalonica to see how the new converts there were faring and to report on their well-being. Timothy was personally attached to Paul, so it was by Paul's authority that he went to Thessalonica (1 Thess 3:5), but Silvanus concurred in his mission (1 Thess 3:1–4). Timothy returned with good news, and it was the receipt of his news that prompted the sending of 1 Thessalonians.

By the time Timothy returned, Paul had moved on to Corinth, and Silvanus was also there, having come back from a visit which he also had paid to some place in Macedonia (Acts 18:5). We may confidently date 1 Thessalonians in the earlier part of Paul's stay in Corinth, and 2 Thessalonians not long afterward.

If we wish to date 1 Thessalonians more precisely, our main piece of evidence is the Delphi inscription (*SIG* ii³, 801), reproducing a letter from Claudius to that city, apparently confirming the citizens in certain privileges and making reference to Gallio, proconsul of Achaia (cf. Smallwood, *Documents* § 376; Brassac, "Une inscription de Delphes et la chronologie de Saint Paul"). The letter is dated in the period of Claudius's twenty-sixth acclamation as *imperator*—a period known from other inscriptions (*CIL* iii.476, vi.1256) to have covered the first seven months of A.D. 52. It has usually been supposed that the letter mentions Gallio as current proconsul of Achaia; in that case, since proconsuls normally entered on their tour of duty on 1 July, it would follow that Gallio arrived in Achaia as proconsul on 1 July, A.D. 51 or (less probably) 1 July, A.D. 52. It would follow further that Paul's eighteen months in Corinth (Acts 18:11–17) lasted from the late summer of A.D. 50 to the spring of A.D. 52 or (less probably) from the late summer of A.D. 51 to the spring of A.D. 53, so that the later part of A.D. 50 or (less probably) A.D. 51 would be the date of 1 Thessalonians.

But it has been argued by Plassart ("L'inscription de Delphes") that Claudius in the letter refers to Gallio not as the current proconsul but as having been proconsul in the recent past. If this is so (lacunae in the inscription make certainty impossible), then he cannot have entered on his proconsulship later than July, A.D. 51, and may have done so a year earlier. The later part of A.D. 50 would in that case be the latest date for the sending of 1 Thessalonians (cf. Schwank, "Der sogenannte Brief").

3. *Early Christian Experience at Thessalonica*

The report brought back by Timothy from the church of Thessalonica was so generally encouraging that the missionaries sent off a letter there and then, expressing their joy and relief. If they had feared that the Thessalonian converts were disillusioned or discouraged by the turn of events attending and following their hasty departure from the city—which, in the eyes of less well-disposed people, might have seemed like leaving them in the lurch—they were assured that, on the contrary, their converts were enthusiastically propagating the new faith on their own initiative.

Even so, Paul in particular felt it necessary to explain his failure to return after his hurried leave-taking. If the converts did not blame him, some of their relatives and neighbors did; and it would be well if the converts had the necessary information to answer any criticisms. Besides, questions had been asked about the missionaries' conduct during their stay in Thessalonica: they were being charged with mercenary motives and worse. Happily, they were able in this regard to appeal to their converts' knowledge of the facts. The missionaries did not behave like parasites, but earned their own living by manual work. The new believers could thus learn by example as well as by precept how Christians ought to live.

If the Thessalonian Christians found themselves enduring persecution because of their new faith and way of life, let them reflect that this was the common lot of Christians. In this respect they stood in the noble succession of the churches of Judea.

But Timothy brought news not only of their faith and charity, and of their steadfastness under persecution, but also of the failure of some of them to grasp the ethical implications of the gospel. Sexual relations, for example, should be confined within the frontiers of marriage; a life consecrated to the service of God could make no room for fornication. And for a member of the church to be guilty of a sexual trespass against the family circle of a fellow-Christian would be an appalling denial of the brotherly love which ought to prevail among them, and which was actually manifesting itself among them in so many desirable ways. The earnestness with which the writers warn them against sexual laxity suggests they had learned that such a warning was necessary.

Another warning was called for because some of them, whether from an over-enthusiastic expectation of the imminent Advent of Christ or from some other cause, thought that it was pointless to go on working, and so were inevitably becoming a burden to others. This too was a denial of brotherly love, and it made a very unfavorable impression on non-Christians. The writers therefore urge on each of them the importance of earning an honest living.

4. *Eschatology at Thessalonica*

The eschatological interest in the Thessalonian church is reflected in the relatively large amount of space devoted to eschatology in these two epistles.

Early Christian eschatology is closely related to a pattern of expectation widely held among Jews at the time. In this pattern the present age (characterized by some, as by the Qumran community, as "the age of wickedness") was in due course to be superseded by the age to come, the resurrection age. This view of the two ages finds expression in the synoptic Gospels, as in Luke 20:34–36, where "the sons of this age" are set in contrast with "those who are accounted worthy to attain to that age and to the resurrection from the dead." The "days of the Messiah" in some forms of this expectation would mark a transition between the two ages, representing possibly the climax of "this age" or the dawn of "that age," or intervening as an intermediate age between the two.

The early Christians took over this general pattern. For them, however, the pattern underwent a crucial modification in the fact that the Messiah had come, in the person of Jesus. The days of the Messiah had therefore begun. Not only so: Jesus had died and been raised from the dead. In him the first installment (ἀπαρχή) of the resurrection had already taken place. The "age to come," the resurrection age, had thus invaded this age; this age was on its way out but had not yet disappeared, while that age had broken in but was not yet fully manifested. This doctrine of the overlapping of the two ages (the "already" and the "not yet") is highly germane to Paul's distinctive teaching about the Spirit as the "guarantee" or "initial down payment" (ἀρραβών) of the coming heritage of glory (cf. 2 Cor 1:22; 5:5; Eph 1:13, 14; Gal 5:5; Rom 8:23) which, however, is not made explicit in the Thessalonian correspondence.

The Thessalonians had received some eschatological instruction while the missionaries were with them. They were taught to expect the Advent from heaven of the Son of God who had been raised from the dead; by his Advent they would be saved from the end-time retribution to be experienced by the ungodly (1 Thess 1:9, 10; 5:9, 10) and would receive a share in his kingdom and glory (1 Thess 2:12). But the missionaries had to leave the city before the teaching necessary for their converts' equipment had been completed; some questions therefore were left unanswered in their minds. What would be the relation of the Lord's Advent to the condition of "the dead in Christ"? Would believers who died before the Advent be at some disadvantage as compared with those who survived to witness the great event? And what relation did the Advent bear to the last great rebellion against God which also figured in the general pattern of expectation?

The end of the present age, it was held in some strands of Jewish thought, would be a time of severe distress for the people of God in which only a minority would stand firm: apart from that minority there would be a large-scale apostasy. The leader of the apostasy and persecutor of the faithful would be a sinister personage sometimes envisaged as a demonic power, sometimes as a human tyrant, modeled on Antiochus Epiphanes (175–164 B.C.) and, later, on the Emperor Gaius (A.D. 37–41), both of whom, in one way or another, demanded the worship which was due to the true God alone. In the Olivet discourse of the synoptic Gospels it is probably this sinister personage who is referred to as "the abomination of desolation standing where he ought not" (τὸ βδέλυγμα τῆς ἐρημώσεως ἑστηκότα ὅπου οὐ δεῖ, Mark 13:14). At the height of his power he would be overthrown by an act of God.

In Christian thought, the act of God by which the great rebel would be overthrown was identified with the Advent of Christ. Both orally and in writing the missionaries (and especially Paul) taught the Thessalonians this. But if the great rebel was to be consumed in the blaze of Christ's Advent-glory, it followed that the Advent would not take place before the great rebel had made his appearance and played his brief but frightful part on the stage of history.

At his Advent, Christ would gather his people to himself to give them their reward for faithfulness and recompense for suffering; their manifestation with him would indeed enhance his glory, and from then on they would be with him forever. For unrepentant rebels and apostates, on the other hand, and especially for persecutors of his people, his Advent would be an occasion for retribution and destruction. (There is nothing particularly Pauline in this outline of expected events: Paul received it as part of the Christian tradition and developed it along distinctive lines, but there is little if any trace of his distinctive development in the Thessalonian letters.)

The Thessalonian letters present the first literary evidence for the use of παρουσία (Parousia) in the sense of the future Advent of Christ: it occurs in this sense six times in the two letters. The event is depicted repeatedly in language borrowed from portrayals of OT theophanies. But it is the ethical implications that are chiefly stressed: the writers look forward to the Parousia especially as the time when their service will be reviewed and rewarded by the Lord who commissioned them, and they will be content, they say, to have it assessed by the quality of their converts.

In the relatively short interval since the missionaries' departure from Thessalonica some members of the church had died. The others were concerned about the status of these departed friends at the Parousia. Would they in some way forfeit the glory of being associated with their returning Lord? Apparently they had not been told that the resurrection of departed believers in Christ would coincide with his Advent: they are now given this assurance, and that on the highest authority—"by the word of the Lord" (1 Thess 4:15). In fact, the first thing to happen at the Parousia is that "the dead in Christ will rise."

It is implied, but not expressly stated, that the Parousia is expected within the lifetime of most Christians then living, including the writers. At a later stage in Paul's career he expected rather to be among those who would be raised from the dead (2 Cor 4:14; 5:1–10). But this shift of perspective—the so-called "delay of the Parousia"—does not appear to have occasioned any material change in his theology in general or his eschatology in particular. The apostolic doctrine of the Parousia is independent of its timing.

No more positive indication of the timing of the Parousia is given than that, as Jesus had spoken of the Son of Man coming when he was least expected (Mark 13:33–37), so "the day of the Lord will come like a thief in the night" (1 Thess 5:2). It is on the ungodly, however, that the day will break with such unwelcome suddenness: believers will be prepared

for it—not because they know when it will come (they do not know) but
because to live the Christian life is to be permanently ready for the great
day. Others may remain in the darkness and fall asleep; believers live in
the light and stay awake (1 Thess 5:1–11). Unhealthy excitement is discouraged; moral alertness and sobriety are enjoined.

The enjoining of moral alertness and sobriety includes those practical
exhortations with which 1 Thessalonians ends. These exhortations cover
general principles of Christian ethics; some of them reflect the part which
prophesying played in the church. Prophesying is encouraged, but not
everything that claims to be the product of prophetic inspiration is to be
accepted uncritically. What matters is *what* is said rather than *how* it is
said, and what is said must be weighed by the hearers to make sure that
it is consistent with what is already known to be true.

5. *Relation between the Two Letters*

If only 1 Thessalonians had come down to us, the Thessalonian correspondence would present no great problem. The authenticity of 2:13–16
would have to be discussed (see p. 43 below) and it would be necessary
to consider arguments for discerning two distinct letters in this short document (see p. xliv below); but in general the letter could be accepted without
serious question as one sent by Paul and his associates to their converts
in Thessalonica shortly after they were forced to leave the city, and from
it we could fill in various details about the evangelization of Thessalonica
and the fortunes of the church there after the missionaries' departure.

Again, if only 2 Thessalonians had been preserved, its genuineness would
be "scarcely contested" (Harnack, "Problem," 562). From it we could not
reconstruct the course of events as can be done from 1 Thessalonians,
but it could be gathered that the church was in good heart, so that the
writers are prompted to give God spontaneous thanks for it as well as to
impart further encouragement. It stood in need of further instruction about
the coming Day of the Lord, and those members who, because of eschatological excitement or something similar, were idle and becoming a burden
to their friends, required plain and stern admonition.

It is the fact that both letters have come down to us that raises questions
which demand an answer—questions, in particular, about their relation
to one another.

In general, 2 Thessalonians covers much the same ground as 1 Thessalonians, if more perfunctorily. Again there is thanksgiving to God for the
Thessalonian Christians' faith and love, amid the persecutions which they
are enduring. These persecutions, it is remarked, are a means of fitting
them for the kingdom of God, while they are equally certain tokens of
the doom of their persecutors when the Lord comes "to be glorified in
his holy ones" (1:10).

The one outstanding feature which distinguishes 2 Thessalonians is the
eschatological section in 2:1–12. This is followed by exhortation of a general
kind, including a severe warning against idleness. Again the readers are

reminded, as in 1 Thessalonians 2:9–12, how the missionaries had set them an example in this respect. This example, coupled with teaching to the same effect—"If any one refuses to work, let him not eat" (2 Thess 3:10)—formed part of the "traditions" to which the Thessalonians are urged to hold fast (2 Thess 2:15; 3:16).

If both letters are authentic, they were evidently sent within a brief interval, one after the other. (Those who view them as sent to distinct groups within the Thessalonian church might conclude that they were sent simultaneously.) Why then should there be so much repetition and overlapping between them? And why, at the same time, should there be a different eschatological outlook in the one as against the other?

One of the boldest answers to this double question has been given by Lindemann ("Zum Abfassungszweck"), following in part lines laid down in 1862 by Hilgenfeld ("Die beiden Briefe an die Thessalonicher"). He argues that 2 Thessalonians was written as a deliberate replacement for 1 Thessalonians by someone who did not approve of the eschatological perspective of 1 Thessalonians. This person reproduced the substance of 1 Thessalonians in the matter of thanksgiving, encouragement and admonition, in a somewhat abridged and impersonal form, but he replaced the eschatological teaching of 1 Thessalonians, with its emphasis on the imminence of the Parousia, with a new section (2 Thess 2:1–12) in which he insisted that the Parousia would be preceded by certain events—in particular by the rise of the "man of lawlessness"—and that not until the man of lawlessness was entrenched in supreme power would Christ appear in glory and deal him his deathblow.

That we have to do with a deliberate replacement, Lindemann maintains, is shown, first, by the writer's suggestion in 2 Thessalonians 2:2 that any eschatological teaching in Paul's name which disagrees with that about to be set forth should be treated as a forgery and, second, by the explicit signature of Paul in 2 Thessalonians 3:17. In Lindemann's view, 2 Thessalonians is not an example of conventional deutero-Pauline pseudepigraphy (in which a devoted disciple of Paul tries to apply to a new situation the treatment which he believes Paul would have given it); the writer wants his readers to reject the genuine 1 Thessalonians as spurious and sets himself to substitute for it a composition of his own. He was only partially successful in his aim; the church did not reject 1 Thessalonians but it did accept the new composition and thus saddled itself with the problem of reconciling the two.

Mearns explains the different eschatological perspectives in the two letters by Paul's having changed his teaching so as to mitigate "the enthusiastic excesses of an extreme imminentistic hope which followed his expounding of the apocalyptic scheme in I Thessalonians" ("Early Eschatological Development," 157).

Another attempt to solve the problem of the relation between the two letters is the suggestion that they were sent to distinct groups in the Thessalonian church.

Harnack ("Problem") thought that 2 Thessalonians was addressed more particularly to the Jewish-Christian membership of the church, 1 Thessalonians having been sent to the Gentile Christians. This view found favor with Lake (*Epistles*, 82–95) and Burkitt (*Christian Beginnings*, 133). But it is difficult to reconcile it with Paul's policy of integrating former Jews and former Gentiles in the new fellowship. Anything calculated to encourage the maintenance of a sense of separateness between the two groups would have been resisted by him. While 1 Thessalonians is expressly addressed to those who have "turned to God from idols" (1:9), there is nothing in 2 Thessalonians which appears to be intended distinctively for Jewish members of the church.

Ellis ("Paul and his Co-Workers") recognizes positive substance in Harnack's observation that a distinct group is addressed in 2 Thessalonians, but thinks that the distinct group was Paul's Thessalonian co-workers, the responsible leaders of the congregation. It is they who are in a position to deal authoritatively with idlers and others who disregard the apostolic injunctions (2 Thess 3:6–15). In 1 Thessalonians the readers are urged to give recognition and esteem to their leaders; then follows a one-sentence exhortation to the leaders to care for the others (1 Thess 5:12–14). What is compressed into one sentence in 1 Thess 5:14 is expanded in 2 Thessalonians as a whole. This interpretation does not lie open to the fundamental objections which Harnack's thesis invites.

The suggestion that 2 Thessalonians was earlier than 1 Thessalonians was first put forward, it appears, by Hugo Grotius in 1641 (*Annotationes* i, 1032; ii.051). It has been made also by Manson ("The Letters to the Thessalonians"), Weiss (*Earliest Christianity*, i, 289–291), West ("The Order of 1 and 2 Thessalonians"), Buck and Taylor (*St. Paul*, 150–162), and Gregson ("A Solution to the Problems of the Thessalonian Epistles").

There is nothing antecedently improbable in dating 2 Thessalonians before 1 Thessalonians. The traditional sequence of Pauline letters to churches is based on length, not on date. If 2 Thessalonians is indeed the earlier of the two, this does not affect what has been said above about the occasion of 1 Thessalonians. It would simply have to be assumed that when Timothy was sent back from Athens to Thessalonica (1 Thess 3:2), he carried with him a letter for the church—our 2 Thessalonians. Then, when he returned with good news from Thessalonica, 1 Thessalonians was written in response to that good news.

The main arguments for the priority of 2 Thessalonians are these:

(*a*) At the beginning of 2 Thessalonians (1:4, 5) the readers are said to be currently enduring persecution for their faith; in 1 Thessalonians (2:14) the persecution is referred to in the past tense.

(*b*) The deplorable idleness of some members of the church has just come to the writers' attention in 2 Thessalonians (3:11, 12); in 1 Thessalonians (4:10–12; 5:14) it is mentioned as something well known to writers and readers.

(c) The personal signature at the end of 2 Thessalonians, with its explanatory note (3:17), is pointless except in the first letter to a new addressee or addressees.

(d) If the people addressed had already received the eschatological teaching of 2 Thessalonians 2:1–12, then the statement in 1 Thessalonians 5:1 that they had no need of instruction about "times and seasons" would be very much to the point.

(e) The two sections in 1 Thessalonians which begin with the words "Now concerning . . ." (περὶ δέ . . .) take up topics already touched on *(ex hypothesi)* in 2 Thessalonians—brotherly love (1 Thess 4:9; cf. 2 Thess 3:6–15) and the times and seasons (1 Thess 5:1; cf. 2 Thess 2:1–12). (Quite apart from the chronological sequence of the two letters, Faw, "On the Writing of First Thessalonians," argues that, as in 1 Corinthians, the sections in 1 Thessalonians beginning περὶ δέ introduce apostolic answers to questions which the Thessalonian church had put in a letter.)

These arguments are of varying cogency; they receive further notice below in the commentary proper. On the other side, it must be said that there is no explicit mention in 1 Thessalonians of a previous letter sent to the church, whereas in 2 Thessalonians 2:15 there is what could well be a reference to an earlier letter: "Hold fast the traditions which you were taught, whether by word of mouth or by a letter from us."

In particular, the eschatological teaching of the two letters is easier to understand if 1 Thessalonians is the earlier. In 1 Thessalonians the Parousia is spoken of as if it were likely to take place in the lifetime of most of the readers (and writers); it will come when least expected, "like a thief in the night" (1 Thess 5:2). This may have led some readers to conclude that it was so imminent that there was no point in going on with the ordinary concerns of daily life; perhaps, indeed, it had already arrived. To correct this error the writers say in 2 Thessalonians 2:1–12, "The Parousia is imminent indeed, but not so imminent as all that. Do not be misled into thinking that the great day is already with us. It will come soon enough, but certain things must first take place—the climax of world rebellion against God and the appearance of the man who incarnates the spirit of rebellion and claims for himself the worship due to God. When he has reached the summit of his power, then the Parousia of Christ will come and with its coming the rebellion will collapse."

If it be thought that the idea of certain well-defined events preceding the Day of the Lord is inconsistent with the idea of its arrival like a thief by night, let it be considered, first, that the same ambivalence is found in the synoptic tradition of Jesus' eschatological teaching. True, in the gospels source analysis can be applied to the tradition: it is in Q that the day of the Son of Man's revelation overtakes the world with the suddenness of Noah's flood or the destruction of Sodom and Gomorrah (Luke 17:26–30), whereas in Mark's account of the Olivet discourse "wars and rumors of wars" will be rife, but "the end is not yet"; "the gospel must first be preached to all the nations," and not until the abomination of desolation is seen "standing where he ought not" will the Son of Man come (Mark 13:7, 10, 14, 26). Luke and Matthew do not appear to have been conscious of inconsistency between these two perspectives: Luke incorporates both separately—the Q material in Luke 17:22–37 and the Markan material in Luke 21:5–36—while Matthew interweaves the two in one composite discourse (Matt 24:1–51). Moreover, in the two separate strands it is Mark who includes the urgent call to be on the alert, "for you do not know when the time will come" (Mark 13:32–37), while Q not only says that first the Son of Man "must suffer many things and be rejected by this generation" (Luke 17:25)—this could be regarded as Luke's insertion of a Markan motif in a Q context—but suggests that when the spiritually alert recognize a situation ripe for judgment, they may expect the judgment to fall: "where the body is, there the eagles will be gathered together" (Luke 17:37; cf. Matt 24:28).

Let it be considered, again, that the eschatological teaching of 1 Thessalonians is mainly on a personal level: it is given in response to questions about the lot of believers who have died before the Parousia. This is followed by a brief reference to the Day of the Lord as it affects men and women in general: it will take the ungodly by surprise, but believers, being children of light, will be awake and prepared for it.

In 2 Thessalonians believers are told further how they may be prepared for the great day: they will recognize the events which signal its approach. Personal eschatology belongs more to the realm of individual piety and is largely unrelated to world happenings; a cosmic perspective on the Day of the Lord calls for some account to be taken of the course of history. Paul's consuming urge for the evangelization of the world did not blind him to the significance of world events; on the contrary, his missionary strategy would have been less effective had he not paid attention to them.

He had been able thus far to exploit the peaceful conditions of the Roman world in the interests of his Gentile mission, but there were disquieting straws in the wind. There was mounting unrest in Judea, and this unrest had repercussions elsewhere, as he and his colleagues learned in Thessalonica, where they were branded as men who had "subverted the world." By the time they arrived in Corinth, they had heard of the expulsion of Jews from Rome. The troubles which had driven him from one Macedonian city after another were fresh in Paul's mind when 2 Thessalonians was written. Probably Gallio's encouraging judgment at Corinth had not yet been given. Roman law and order were still in control, but it was only too clear that the "hidden power of lawlessness" was already at work, and it would probably continue to work until it erupted violently and swept all before it. When the Thessalonians are told that the Day of the Lord cannot arrive until the great rebellion has broken out, the Day is not being postponed to the indefinite future: the great rebellion might well break out within a few years. If they paid heed to what they were being told, they would be ready—well informed as well as morally alert.

Gallio's judgment may have modified Paul's perspective, but it was not radically changed. Although in his later letters he does not use the apocalyptic terms of the Thessalonian correspondence, the substance of his outlook remained unchanged, as may be seen even in the maturity of his letter to the Romans. Shortly after the very positive assessment of the powers that be in Romans 13:1–7, he goes on to say, "Recognize this critical season: it is already high time for you to wake up from sleep, for our deliverance is nearer now than when we first believed. The night is far advanced; the day is at hand. Let us then put off the works of darkness and put on the armor of light. Let our conduct be seemly, fit for the light of day . . ." (Rom 13:11–13).

6. *Miscellaneous Solutions*

(a) One or two scholars have argued that 2 Thessalonians was sent not to the church of Thessalonica but to one of the other Macedonian churches, about the same time as 1 Thessalonians was sent to Thessalonica. This, it is said, would account for the large proportion of material common to both.

Goguel, for example, suggested that 2 Thessalonians was originally intended for the newly formed church in Beroea (*Introduction au NT* iv.1, 335). Schweizer has thought of it as originally a letter to Philippi ("Der zweite Thessalonicherbrief ein Philipperbrief?"; cf. Michaelis's reply, "Der zweite Thessalonicherbrief kein Philipperbrief," and Schweizer's "Replik"). A copy of this letter to Philippi was preserved in the Thessalonian church and cherished by it to the point where the original greeting to Philippi was replaced by one borrowed from the prescript of 1 Thessalonians. It would in that case be the first letter to the Philippians, our present Epistle to the Philippians being the second. Polycarp, it is pointed out, in his letter to the church of Philippi, knows of more than one letter sent to that church by Paul (*Ep.* 3:2); he says, too (*Ep.* 11:3), that Paul in his letters praises the Philippians to all the churches (an inference which could be made more readily from 2 Thess 1:4 than from anything in our Philippians).

But if Paul wrote a letter to the Philippians at the same time as 1 Thessalonians, we might expect it to contain the same kind of warm personal references to the people addressed as we find in 1 Thessalonians—and, for that matter, several years later in our Philippians.

(b) Mention must be made also of attempts to analyze the Thessalonian correspondence into more documents than the two letters in our textual and canonical tradition.

Eckart's argument that 1 Thessalonians consists of two letters (along with certain non-Pauline additions), editorially joined at 3:5 ("Der zweite echte Brief"), was rebutted by Kümmel ("Das literarische und geschichtliche Problem"). A more elaborate analysis, based on the recognition of epistolary protocols and "eschatocols" as well as on internal evidence, has been defended by Schmithals (*Paul and the Gnostics*, 211, 213). He distinguishes four separate letters to the Thessalonians, each of them authentic, in the following chronological order:

Thessalonians A = 2 Thessalonians 1:1–12 + 3:6–16
Thessalonians B = 1 Thessalonians 1:1–2:12 + 4:2–5:28
Thessalonians C = 2 Thessalonians 2:13–14 + 2:1–12 + 2:15–3:5 + 3:17–18
Thessalonians D = 1 Thessalonians 2:13–4:1

He points out that each of the four ends with an "eschatocol" introduced by αὐτὸς δὲ ὁ κύριος/θεός (2 Thess 3:16; 1 Thess 5:23; 2 Thess 2:16; 1 Thess 3:11).

Some features of this analysis are reviewed at appropriate points in the commentary below.

In a later study (*Der Römerbrief*) Schmithals argues that Romans 5:(1)2–11 and 13:11–14 (quoted above, p. xliv) also belong originally to Paul's Thessalonian correspondence.

(c) Schmithals's arrangement of the sequence of the Thessalonian letters, like his dating of them to the same period as the Corinthian correspondence, is bound up with his identification of gnosticism as the root of the trouble in the Thessalonian church with which the letters deal.

Schmithals is not the first to explain the admonitions of 1 and 2 Thessalonians in terms of gnosticism or some form of enthusiasm. In 1909 Lütgert (*Die Vollkommenen in Philipperbrief*) envisaged the writers taking issue with enthusiastic tendencies of the same kind as those which (he believed) caused Paul such concern in the churches of Corinth (*Freiheitspredigt und Schwarmgeister in Korinth*) and Galatia (*Gesetz und Geist*). Ten years later Hadorn argued that in writing to the Thessalonians Paul was rebutting a libertine heresy such as was rife at Corinth (and which, as at Corinth, involved a denial of the doctrine of resurrection).

More recently, Marxsen (*INT* 37–40) expressed the view that 2 Thessalonians—not, in his judgment, a Pauline epistle—was written to counter a form of gnosticism. The warning in 2 Thessalonians 2:2 against supposing the Day of the Lord to have arrived is compared with Paul's ironical reply in 1 Corinthians 4:8–13 to those "men of the Spirit" in the church of Corinth whose conduct suggested that they had already entered the coming kingdom of glory. But the persecuted Christians of Thessalonica (as they are presumed to be in 2 Thess 1:4) are not likely to have entertained this particular form of overrealized eschatology. Even if they did hold some form of overrealized eschatology, it was possible in the apostolic age, as it is manifestly possible today, to embrace such an outlook and yet have nothing to do with gnosticism.

Schmithals, however, has presented the most detailed case for a gnostic background to the Thessalonian correspondence. No doubt, when a gnostic background is postulated, many features of the letters can be explained in terms of it, such as the apostolic apologia of 1 Thessalonians 2:3–12 (cf. 2 Cor 11:21–29; Phil 3:4–7). But the apostles' motives might be queried by a variety of critics, while their reply to the critics' queries would remain essentially the same. There is, in fact, nothing in the Thessalonian letters which requires explanation in terms of gnosticism; gnosticism can be read out of them only if it be first read into them.

7. *Christian Doctrine in Thessalonians*

The eschatology of the Thessalonian letters has been outlined above (pp. xxxvi–xxxix); it was suggested that it is not distinctively Pauline but that which was generally accepted in the primitive church, by Paul and others alike. The same may be said of the other areas of Christian doctrine which are covered in these two letters; what we have here is the common tradition of the earliest apostolic teaching. Perhaps even at this early date diversity was manifesting itself together with the unity: not all, for example, might have been happy to express their hope of glory by means of the apocalyptic imagery found in both 1 and 2 Thessalonians. But this would have been a question of language rather than of substance: all would have agreed in acknowledging Christ as their hope of glory.

(a) God. God is the "living and true God" to whom former pagans turned in faith from their idolatry (1 Thess 1:9). He is thus identical with the God of Israel, who would have been referred to by his Jewish worshipers in the same terms. But he is also "God the Father" (1 Thess 1:1), "our God and Father" (1 Thess 1:3)—not only because he is *ipso facto* the Father of his children but because he is primarily the Father of Jesus Christ "his Son" (1 Thess 1:10) and therefore also the Father of all those who are believers in Christ.

God has chosen his people (1 Thess 1:4); he is the object of their faith (1 Thess 1:8). He bestows the authority underlying the apostles' bold confidence (1 Thess 2:2); it is he who has entrusted them with the gospel (1 Thess 2:4); it is his pleasure that they seek and his witness that they invoke to the purity of their motives and conduct (1 Thess 2:5–10). It is his guidance that must be followed (1 Thess 3:11), his will that must be obeyed (1 Thess 4:3; 5:18). He has called his people to lead holy lives (1 Thess 4:7) and he is able to bring to its consummation the holiness to which he has called them (1 Thess 5:23). It is he who raised up Jesus from the dead (1 Thess 1:10) and will, with him, bring back his people from the dead (1 Thess 4:14), thus finally accomplishing the salvation to which he has appointed them (1 Thess 5:9).

(b) Christ. The spontaneous and repeated association of Christ with God in these letters bears witness to the exalted place which he occupied, alongside God, in the thought and worship of the writers, as of other early Christians. The church has its being "in God the Father and the Lord Jesus Christ" (1 Thess 1:1; 2 Thess 1:1); it is from them both that grace and peace are invoked on the readers (2 Thess 1:2; cf. also 2 Thess 1:12, "the grace of our God and the Lord Jesus Christ"). When guidance is sought for the writers or spiritual help for the readers, the prayer is directed to "our God and Father himself and our Lord Jesus" (1 Thess 3:11) or

"our Lord Jesus Christ and God our Father" (2 Thess 2:16)—the very indifference of the sequence in which the two are named is significant. If the Father is God, θεός, the Son is Lord, κύριος, and much that is said of God can be said equally well of the Lord: alongside "the God of peace" (1 Thess 5:23) we have "the Lord of peace" (2 Thess 3:16). If believers are "loved by God" (1 Thess 1:4), they are also "loved by the Lord" (2 Thess 2:13).

Jesus is the Son of God (1 Thess 1:9). His Word carries unsurpassed authority (1 Thess 4:15). He "died for us, in order that we . . . might live together with him" (1 Thess 5:10). He was raised from the dead by God and is at present with him in heaven, from which his people expect him to come as their deliverer from the end-time retribution (1 Thess 1:10). His coming, at which "the dead in Christ will rise first" (1 Thess 4:16), will bring relief and glory to his people and final judgment to the ungodly (1 Thess 5:9; 2 Thess 1:5–10). This is in keeping with his portrayal as "judge of the living and the dead" (Acts 10:42).

(c) *The Spirit.* The Spirit is all-pervasive in the Christian life, which is indeed his creation. It is by his power that the gospel is proclaimed effectively (1 Thess 1:5); not only is his joy imparted to those who believe it (1 Thess 1:6) but he himself is given to them as the *Holy* Spirit (1 Thess 4:8) to perform his sanctifying work in their lives (2 Thess 2:13). In church life, too, he plays his part by communicating the divine will through prophetic utterances; to ignore or inhibit such utterances is to "quench the Spirit" (1 Thess 5:19).

(d) *Christian living.* Christians manifest the new life which the gospel has brought them by spreading the gospel abroad in their turn (1 Thess 1:8). Their lives should be consistent with the gospel, marked by "work of faith and labor of love and steadfastness of hope in our Lord Jesus Christ" (1 Thess 1:3). Some particular aspects of Christian ethics are alluded to as the occasion arises: endurance under trials (1 Thess 2:14; 2 Thess 1:4), love for one another (1 Thess 3:12; 2 Thess 1:3), chastity (1 Thess 4:3–8), honesty in everyday living (1 Thess 4:11; 2 Thess 3:6–13) and doing good to all (1 Thess 5:15).

Again, these ethical commendations and admonitions are couched in general Christian and not in distinctively Pauline terms. If nothing is said expressly in these letters of the antithesis between flesh and Spirit, that is not because Paul did not yet have "in his repertoire" the flesh-Spirit categories on which he drew in other letters (Jewett, *Paul's Anthropological Terms,* 111), but because those categories did not figure in the thinking of the other authors of the Thessalonian letters, more particularly Silvanus.

The First Letter
to the Thessalonians

STRUCTURE

1. PRESCRIPT (1:1)

2. THANKSGIVING (1:2–10)

3. APOSTOLIC DEFENSE (2:1–12)
   (a) *The Missionaries' Visit* (2:1–4)
   (b) *The Missionaries' Behavior* (2:5–8)
   (c) *The Missionaries' Example* (2:9–12)

4. FURTHER THANKSGIVING (2:13–16)

5. PLANS FOR A SECOND VISIT (2:17–3:13)
   (a) *Out of Sight, Not Out of Mind* (2:17–20)
   (b) *Mission of Timothy* (3:1–5)
   (c) *Joy and Thanksgiving at Timothy's Report* (3:6–10)
   (d) *First Wish-Prayer for the Thessalonian Christians* (3:11–13)

6. EXHORTATION (4:1–5:24)
   (a) *On Keeping the Traditions* (4:1, 2)
   (b) *On Sexual Purity* (4:3–8)
   (c) *On Brotherly Love* (4:9–12)
   (d) *On the Faithful Departed* (4:13–18)
   (e) *On Times and Seasons* (5:1–11)
   (f) *On Recognition of Leaders* (5:12, 13)
   (g) *On Various Christian Duties* (5:14–22)
   (h) *Second Wish-Prayer for the Thessalonian Christians* (5:23, 24)

7. LETTER CLOSING (5:25–28)

Prescript (1 Thess 1:1)

Bibliography

Lohmeyer, E. "Probleme paulinischer Theologie. I. Briefliche Grussüberschriften." *ZNW* 26 (1927) 158–173; with Friedrich, G. "Lohmeyers These über'das paulinische Briefpräskript'kritisch beleuchtet." *ZNW* 46 (1955) 272–274. **Roller, O.** *Das Formular der paulinischen Briefe: Ein Beitrag zur Lehre vom antiken Briefe.* BWANT 4/6 (58). Stuttgart: Kohlhammer, 1933. **White, J. L.** *The Form and Function of the Body of the Greek Letter.* SBL Dissertation Series, 2. Missoula, MT: Scholars Press, 1972.

Translation

[1] *Paul, Silvanus and Timothy to the church of the Thessalonians in God the* [a] *Father and the Lord Jesus Christ: grace to you and peace.* [b]

Notes

[a] ἡμῶν ("our") added by A 81 *pc* lat[a r vg.codd] cop[sa.codd].

[b] ἀπὸ θεοῦ πατρὸς ἡμῶν καὶ κυρίου Ἰησοῦ Χριστοῦ added by א Λ I byz lat[vg codd] syr[hcl**] (from 2 Thess 1:2).

Form/Structure/Setting

The standard form of the initial salutation or prescript in ancient letters was "A to B, greetings." Cf. Ezra 7:12, "Artaxerxes, king of kings, . . . to Ezra the priest, greetings"); Cicero, *Epistulae ad Quintum fratrem*, 1.2 (*M. Cicero Q. fratri* s[alutem], "Marcus Cicero to Quintus his brother, health"); P. Oxy. 119.1 (Θέων Θέωνι τῷ πατρὶ χαίρειν, "Theon to Theon his father, greetings"). Here A comprises the three names Paul, Silvanus and Timothy; B is "the church of the Thessalonians . . ."; the greetings take the form "grace to you and peace." This is the shortest prescript among the Pauline *homologoumena*.

Comment

1:1. Παῦλος καὶ Σιλουανὸς καὶ Τιμόθεος, "Paul and Silvanus and Timothy." The same three names appear in the prescript of 2 Thessalonians. It is not unusual to find Paul's name combined with others in the prescripts of the Pauline letters; cf. Παῦλος . . . καὶ Σωσθένης ὁ ἀδελφός, "Paul . . . and Sosthenes the brother" (1 Cor 1:1); Παῦλος . . . καὶ Τιμόθεος (2 Cor 1:1; similarly Phil 1:1; Col. 1:1; Phlm 1); Παῦλος . . . καὶ οἱ σὺν ἐμοὶ πάντες ἀδελφοί, "Paul . . . and all the brothers with me" (Gal. 1:1, 2). Only in

Romans, Ephesians and the Pastoral Letters does Paul's name stand unaccompanied in the prescript.

Here the sequence of names may reflect seniority. But while Paul was the senior partner, the inclusion of the other two names need not be a matter of courtesy only: both Silvanus and Timothy, and especially Silvanus (see 3:2, with comment), may have participated responsibly in the composition of the letter.

Silvanus is mentioned in 2 Cor 1:19 as having shared with Paul and Timothy in the evangelization of Corinth, and the implication of the repeated "we" in this letter is that he similarly shared in the evangelization of Thessalonica. It is uncertain if he is identical with the Silvanus of 1 Pet 5:12. But it is certain that he is identical with the Silas of Acts. Silas was associated with Paul and Timothy in the evangelization of Thessalonica (Acts 17:1–9) and Corinth (Acts 18:5).

If further evidence may be adduced from Acts to fill in our knowledge of Silvanus, Silas was a member of the Jerusalem church, deputed (along with one Judas Barsabbas) to convey the letter containing the apostolic decree to Antioch (Acts 15:22, 27, 32). Not long afterward, he was coopted by Paul as his colleague for a missionary journey which took them from Antioch through Asia Minor to Alexandria Troas on the northwest coast of the peninsula and from there by sea to Macedonia, where he was involved in the evangelization of Philippi, Thessalonica and Beroea; later he rejoined Paul in Corinth. If it is a reasonable inference from Acts 16:37, where Paul describes Silas and himself as Ῥωμαῖοι, "Romans," that Silas was a Roman citizen as well as Paul, then Silvanus might be his Roman cognomen, while Silas is a hypocoristic (as Epaphras to Epaphroditus) or else represents his Aramaic name (cf. Talmudic שִׁילָא, Palmyrene שאילא).

Timothy receives more frequent mention in Paul's letters. He was plainly an associate in whom Paul had complete confidence, entrusting him with responsible missions, e.g. to Thessalonica (3:2, 6), to Corinth (1 Cor 4:17; 16:10) and to Philippi (Phil 2:19). According to Acts he was a native of a South Galatian city (probably Lystra), the son of a Jewish mother and a Greek father, and was converted to Christianity during Barnabas and Paul's first visit to that region. When Paul later revisited the region with Silas, he circumcised Timothy and took him along as a junior colleague. Timothy accompanied Paul and Silas on their journey to Macedonia (Acts 16:1–10; 17:14, 15) and later rejoined Paul in Corinth (Acts 18:5). The picture of his companionship with Paul in Acts is confirmed by Paul's own account in Phil 2:20–22: "I have no one like him, who will be genuinely anxious for your welfare. . . . But Timothy's worth you know, how as a son with a father he has served with me in the gospel."

τῇ ἐκκλησίᾳ Θεσσαλονικέων, "to the church of the Thessalonians." Paul's earlier letters are explicitly addressed to churches (cf. 2 Thess 1:1; Gal 1:2; 1 Cor 1:2; 2 Cor 1:1), but his later letters to churches are variously addressed to "all God's beloved . . . , called to be saints" (Rom 1:7); "all the saints" (Phil 1:1); "the saints and faithful brethren in Christ" (Col

1:2); "the saints who are also faithful in Christ Jesus" (Eph 1:1). For "saints" see comment on 2 Thess 1:10.

ἐν θεῷ πατρὶ καὶ κυρίῳ Ἰησοῦ Χριστῷ, "in God the Father and the Lord Jesus Christ." This phrase probably qualifies τῇ ἐκκλησίᾳ Θεσσαλονικέων. Classical usage would require τῇ to be repeated before ἐν θεῷ to maintain the phrase in the attributive position, but Hellenistic usage is less strict. The church of the Thessalonians has its being "in God the Father and the Lord Jesus Christ" (cf. 2 Thess 1:1). We may compare the collocation of God and Christ in a similar expression in 2:14, τῶν ἐκκλησιῶν τοῦ θεοῦ . . . ἐν Χριστῷ Ἰησοῦ "the churches of God . . . in Christ Jesus").

The noun ἐκκλησία, "church, assembly" would not have any sacral association in the minds of recent converts from paganism: hence it is qualified by words which declare plainly whose "assembly" it is to which the converts now belong. Gk. ἐκκλησία was quickly specialized among Gentile Christians to designate a company of believers in Jesus; its synonym συναγωγή, "synagogue" was increasingly reserved to denote a Jewish congregation. The phrase ἐκκλησία κυρίου is found occasionally in LXX to denote the people of Israel as "the assembly of the LORD" (Heb. קְהַל יהוה)—repeatedly so in the early part of Deut 23. But God's ἐκκλησία in the New Testament age has no national frontiers; it comprises Jewish and Gentile believers without distinction.

Here, however, the believing community in Thessalonica is not called the church of God, but the church "in God." This is an unusual expression in the Pauline corpus, where otherwise "in God" is used of boasting in God (Rom 2:17; 5:11) or of being hidden in God (Eph 3:9; Col 3:3). On the other hand, "in Christ," "in Christ Jesus" or "in the Lord" is a characteristic Pauline expression, especially when it has "incorporative" force, pointing to believers' participation in Christ's risen life or their membership in his body. If this is the force of the words "in . . . the Lord Jesus Christ" here, then "in God the Father" must be understood in the same way. This is so uncharacteristic of Paul that Best (62) thinks the preposition ἐν must have instrumental force: "the Christian community brought into being by God the Father and our Lord Jesus Christ." (The affirmation of Acts 17:28, "in him we live and move and have our being," perhaps quoted from Epimenides of Crete, refers to the old creation and not to the new order of grace.) Possibly Silvanus rather than Paul is responsible for the present wording, which designates God and Christ as the sphere in which the church exists.

In any case, the spontaneous joining of "God the Father" and "the Lord Jesus Christ" under a single preposition bears witness to the exalted place which the risen Christ occupies in the thoughts of Paul and his colleagues (cf. 3:11). In resurrection Christ wears a heavenly humanity as "a life-giving spirit" (1 Cor 15:45–49) and has been invested by God with the title κύριος, "lord," "the name which is above every name" (Phil 2:9). God and Christ are entirely at one in the salvation of believers and in their maintenance in a spiritual fellowship.

χάρις ὑμῖν καὶ εἰρήνη, "grace and peace to you." "Peace" (Heb. שלום)
was (and is) the normal Jewish greeting, as "rejoice" (χαίρειν, χαῖρε, χαίρετε)
was the normal Greek greeting. It is very doubtful if, as has often been
suggested, χάρις in the prescript of Pauline letters is a Christian adaptation
of the greeting χαίρειν. The double form χάρις καὶ εἰρήνη is rather a variant
on "mercy and peace" current in some Jewish circles (cf. 2 Bar 78:2). E.
Lohmeyer (*Probleme*, 159) argues that the formula χάρις καὶ εἰρήνη was primarily liturgical and only secondarily epistolary. "Χάρις is the source of
all real blessings, εἰρήνη their end and issue" (Lightfoot, 8).

To χάρις ὑμῖν καὶ εἰρήνη Paul habitually adds ἀπὸ θεοῦ πατρὸς [ἡμῶν] καὶ
κυρίου Ἰησοῦ Χριστοῦ—another instance of the joining of "God the Father"
and "the Lord Jesus Christ" under a single preposition. The omission of
these words (as here) is exceptional, and may perhaps be due to the heavi-
ness of style which their inclusion would impart after ἐν θεῷ πατρὶ καὶ κυρίῳ
Ἰησοῦ Χριστῷ in the preceding phrase (although that does not stand in
the way of their inclusion in 2 Thess 1:2).

Explanation

Paul, Silvanus (Silas) and Timothy, the three missionaries who had first
brought the gospel to Thessalonica and planted the church there, now
send a letter to that church a few weeks or, at most, a few months after
their departure from the city. They greet the church as "the church of
the Thessalonians in God the Father and the Lord Jesus Christ," perhaps
in recognition of the fact that it consisted for the most part of former
pagans who, as they are reminded below (vv 9, 10), had abandoned their
false gods not only "to serve the living and true God" but also "to wait
for his Son from heaven, whom he raised from the dead, Jesus."

Thanksgiving (1 Thess 1:2-10)

Bibliography

Ahern, B. M. "Fellowship of his Sufferings." *CBQ* 22 (1960) 1–32. **Betz, H.-D.** *Nachfolge und Nachahmung Jesu Christi im Neuen Testament.* BHT 37. Tübingen: Mohr, 1967. **Charpentier, É.** "L'action de grâce du pasteur. 1 Th 1, 1–5b." *AsSeign* n.s. No. 60 (1975) 10–15. **De Boer, W. P.** *The Imitation of Paul.* Kampen: Kok, 1962. **Friedrich, G.** "Ein Tauflied hellenistischer Judenchristen, 1 Thess. 1, 9 f." *TZ* 21 (1965) 502–516. **Giblin, C. H.** *In Hope of God's Glory.* New York: Herder, 1970. **Hanson, A. T.** *The Wrath of the Lamb.* London: SPCK, 1957. **Harris, J. R.** "A Study in Letter-Writing." *Expositor,* Series 5, 8 (1898), 161–180. **Hunter, A. M.** *Paul and his Predecessors.* London: SCM Press, ²1961. **Kamlah, E.** "Wie beurteilt Paulus seine Leiden? Ein Beitrag zur Untersuchung seiner Denkstruktur." *ZNW* 54 (1963) 217–232. **Käsemann, E.** *Commentary on Romans.* Tr. G. W. Bromiley. Grand Rapids, MI: Eerdmans, 1980. **Kemmler, D. W.** *Faith and Human Reason. A Study of Paul's Method of Preaching as Illustrated by 1–2 Thessalonians and Acts 17, 2–4.* NovT Sup 40. Leiden: Brill, 1975, 149–168 ("1 Th. 1, 3"). **Langevin, P.-É.** *Jésus Seigneur et l'eschatologie. Exégèse de textes prépauliniens.* Bruges/Paris: Desclée et Brouwer, 1967, 64–99 ("Exégèse de 1 Th 1, 9–10"). **Laub, F.** *Eschatologische Verkündigung und Lebensgestaltung nach Paulus. Eine Untersuchung zum Wirken des Apostels beim Aufbau der Gemeinde in Thessalonike.* Biblische Untersuchungen, 10. Regensburg: Pustet, 1973. **Mattern, L.** *Das Verständnis des Gerichtes bei Paulus.* ATANT 47. Zürich: Zwingli, 1966, 82–86 ("1 Thess 1, 10"). **Mearns, C. L.** "Early Eschatological Development in Paul: the evidence of I and II Thessalonians." *NTS* 27 (1980–81) 137–157. **Morris, L.** "The Wrath of God." *ExpTim* 63 (1951–52) 142–145. **Munck, J.** "I Thess. 1.9–10 and the Missionary Preaching of Paul." *NTS* 9 (1962–63) 95–110. **O'Brien, P. T.** *Introductory Thanksgivings in the Letters of Paul.* NovT Sup 49. Leiden: Brill, 1977. **Rigaux, B.** *Dieu l'a ressuscité. Exégèse et théologie biblique.* Gembloux: Duculot, 1973. **Robinson, W. C., Jr.** "Word and Power." In *Soli Deo Gloria. New Testament Studies in Honor of William Childs Robinson,* ed. J. McD. Richards. Richmond, VA: John Knox Press, 1968, 68–82. **Rossano, P.** "La Parola e lo Spirito. Riflessioni su 1 Tess 1, 5 e 1 Cor 2, 4–5." In *Mélanges Bibliques en hommage au R. P. Béda Rigaux,* ed. A. Descamps et A. de Halleux. Gembloux: Duculot, 1970, 437–444. **Sanders, J. T.** "The Transition from Opening Epistolary Thanksgiving to Body in the Letters of the Pauline Corpus." *JBL* 81 (1962) 348–362. **Schneider, G.** "Urchristliche Gottesverkündigung in hellenistischer Umwelt." *BZ* 13 (1969) 59–75. **Schubert, P.** *Form and Function of the Pauline Thanksgivings.* BZNW 20. Berlin: Töpelmann, 1939. **Schulz, A.** *Nachfolgen und Nachahmen. Studien über das Verhältnis der neutestamentlichen Jüngerschaft zur urchristlichen Vorbildethik.* München: Kösel, 1962. **Stanley, D. M.** " 'Become Imitators of me.' The Pauline Conception of Apostolic Tradition." *Bib* 40 (1959) 859–877. **Tannehill, R. C.** *Dying and Rising with Christ.* BZNW 32. Berlin: Töpelmann, 1967, 100–104 ("1 Thessalonians 1, 5–8 and 2, 13–16"). **Tasker, R. V. G.** *The Biblical Doctrine of the Wrath of God.* London: Tyndale Press, 1951. **Weir, T. H.** "1 Th i.3." *ExpTim* 34 (1922–23) 525. **Weir, T. H.** "Notes on 1 and 2 Thessalonians." *ExpTim* 35 (1923–24) 140. **Wilckens, U.** *Die Missionsreden der Apostelgeschichte. Form- und traditionsgeschichtliche Untersuchungen.* WMANT 5. Neukirchen-

Vluyn: Neukirchener Verlag, 1974, 80–86 ("1 Thess 1, 9.10 und Hebr 5, 11–6, 2"). **Wiles, G. P.** *Paul's Intercessory Prayers. The Significance of the Intercessory Prayer Passages in the Letters of St. Paul.* SNTSMS 24. Cambridge: Cambridge University Press, 1974.

2 *We give thanks to God continually for you all as we mention you* ᵃ *in our prayers,* 3 *unceasingly calling to mind your work of faith and labor of love and patience of hope in* ᵇ *our Lord Jesus Christ, in the presence of our God and Father,* 4 *knowing as we do (the genuineness of) your election, brothers so dear to God.* 5 *Our* ᶜ *gospel indeed did not come* ᵈ *to you in word only but also in power—in the Holy Spirit and in fullest conviction. You for your part know what kind of persons we were among* ᵉ *you for your sakes.*

6 *As for you, you became imitators of us and of the Lord, when you accepted* ᶠ *the word amid much tribulation, with joy inspired by* ᵍ *the Holy Spirit.* 7 *So you became an example* ʰ *to all the believers in Macedonia and in Achaia.* 8 *From you the word of the Lord has sounded out not only in Macedonia and in* ⁱ *Achaia, but* ʲ *in every place your faith toward God has gone forth, so that we have no need to speak a word.* 9 *They themselves report concerning us* ᵏ *what kind of entrance we had among you, and how*

you turned to God from your idols
to serve the living and true God
10 *and to wait for his Son from heaven,*
the one whom he raised from the ˡ *dead,*
Jesus, our deliverer
from the coming wrath.

Notes

ᵃ ὑμῶν ("you") is implied; it is expressly read by ℵ² C D F G Ψ byz latᵛᵉᵗ syr Ambst.

ᵇ This translation treats τοῦ κυρίου ἡμῶν Ἰησοῦ Χριστοῦ as objective genitive after the verbal idea implicit in ἐλπίδος ("hope").

ᶜ For ἡμῶν ("our") τοῦ θεοῦ ("God's") is substituted in ℵ² C; the conflated τοῦ θεοῦ ἡμῶν is read by ℵ*.

ᵈ ἐγενήθη, aorist of γίνεσθαι in default of an aorist of εἶναι (cf. ἐγενήθημεν later in v 5).

ᵉ ἐν is omitted before ὑμῖν (yielding the meaning "to you") in ℵ A C P 048 33 81 1739 *pc* latᵛᵍ·ˢᵗ.

ᶠ δεξάμενοι, simultaneous aorist participle.

ᵍ καί is read before πνεύματος ("with joy and the Holy Spirit") in B latᵛᵍ·ᶜᵒᵈᵈ.

ʰ τύπους ("examples") is read for τύπον by ℵ A C F G Ψ byz syrʰᵉˡ.

ⁱ ἐν τῇ ("in") is omitted by B K *al.*

ʲ ἀλλὰ καί ("but also") is read for ἀλλά ("but") by ℵ² D² byz latᵛᵍ·ᶜˡ Ambst.

ᵏ ὑμῶν ("you") is read for ἡμῶν ("us") by B 81 *al* latᵃ ᵈ ᵛᵍ·ᶜᵒᵈᵈ (Best prefers ἡμῶν as *lectio difficilior*).

ˡ τῶν is omitted before νεκρῶν by A C K *al.*

Form/Structure/Setting

The thanksgiving following the prescript, attested occasionally in Greek epistolography, was developed as a special feature of Paul's epistolary style. The present thanksgiving report, which begins in v 2, appears to be interrupted by the apologia of 2:1–12 and the "apostolic parousia" of 2:17–3:8, but is resumed in 2:13 and again in 3:9. The note of thanksgiving permeates the first part of the letter as far as 3:10 at least; indeed, O'Brien (*Thanksgiving*, 144), following Schubert (*Form*, 17–27), sees "good reasons for considering that Paul's introductory thanksgiving stretches from chaps. 1:2 to 3:13."

The thanksgiving report includes a brief prayer report (vv 2b–4), which is mainly concerned with the Thessalonians' faith and which exhibits a rhythmical pattern marked by the three participial constructions μνείαν ποιούμενοι . . . μνημονεύοντες . . . εἰδότες . . . ("mentioning . . . calling to mind . . . knowing"). Within the second of these three constructions we note the triple beat of τοῦ ἔργου τῆς πίστεως / τοῦ κόπου τῆς ἀγάπης / τῆς ὑπομονῆς τῆς ἐλπίδος ("your work of faith . . . labor of love . . . patience of hope," v 3).

The report of the Thessalonians' conversion in vv 9b–10 comprises two tristichs, beginning respectively with ἐπεστρέψατε "you turned" and ὃν ἤγειρεν, "whom he raised" (see translation above).

Comment

1:2. Εὐχαριστοῦμεν, "we give thanks." The plural form implies that all three missionaries were in a real sense joint authors of the letter. In other letters where the name of one of Paul's companions is conjoined with his own in the prescript (e.g. Sosthenes in 1 Corinthians or Timothy in Philippians) the use of the singular εὐχαριστῶ, "I give thanks," makes it plain that Paul himself is the author (1 Cor 1:4; Phil 1:3; in Col 1:3 εὐχαριστοῦμεν may indicate that Timothy is in some degree joint author). In 2 Thess 1:3, εὐχαριστοῦμεν is replaced by εὐχαριστεῖν ὀφείλομεν, "we are bound to give thanks." In Rom 1:8 (πρῶτον μὲν εὐχαριστῶ), Paul indicates the importance which he attaches to thanksgiving. In 2 Cor 1:3 and Eph 1:3, the thanksgiving takes the form εὐλογητὸς ὁ θεός (cf. also 1 Pet 1:3). Only in Galatians is the note of thanksgiving absent; the news from the Galatian churches gave Paul nothing to be thankful about.

περὶ πάντων ὑμῶν, "concerning you all," may be construed either with εὐχαριστοῦμεν τῷ θεῷ or with μνείαν ποιούμενοι (if ὑμῶν be omitted after μνείαν; see note a). If it is construed with μνείαν ποιούμενοι then the balance of the sentence requires that ἀδιαλείπτως, "unceasingly," be construed with μνημονεύοντες (as in Nestle-Aland[26]). (For ἀδιαλείπτως cf. 2:13; 5:17.)

μνείαν ποιούμενοι, "making mention" (cf. Rom 1:9; Eph 1:16; Phlm 4). In Plato (*Phaedrus* 254a; *Protagoras* 317e) and other Attic writers μνείαν ποιεῖσθαι means "to mention" and it probably has the same meaning in Paul. Cf. 3:6 for μνείαν ἔχειν.

2. μνημονεύοντες, "remembering (ἀδιαλείπτως, 'unceasingly')." In the Pauline corpus μνημονεύειν regularly means "remember" (cf. 2:9; 2 Thess 2:5; Gal 2:10; Eph 2:11; Col 4:18; 2 Tim 2:8). Here the object of the verb is the threefold genitive ἔργου . . . κόπου . . . ὑπομονῆς.

ὑμῶν, "your"—genitive in dependence on ἔργου . . . κόπου . . . ὑπομονῆς ("your work of faith . . .").

τοῦ ἔργου τῆς πίστεως καὶ τοῦ κόπου τῆς ἀγάπης καὶ τῆς ὑπομονῆς τῆς ἐλπίδος. For the triad of graces, "faith, love, hope" (πίστις, ἀγάπη, ἐλπίς), cf. 5:8; Gal 5:5, 6; Rom 5:1–5; Col 1:4, 5, in addition to the well-known 1 Cor 13:13. (Instances outside the Pauline corpus are Heb 10:22–24; 1 Pet 1:21, 22.) The writers rejoice that these graces are manifested in the life and activity of the Thessalonian Christians. "The triad of faith, hope and love is the quintessence of the God-given life in Christ" (Bornkamm, *Paul*, 219). Hunter (33–35) and others have maintained that the triad belongs to the vocabulary of pre-Pauline Christianity. Faith is based on the assurance that God has acted for his people's salvation in Christ; love is the present (and continuing) relationship between God and his people through Christ; hope is bound up with the conviction that "he who has begun a good work" in them "will complete it until the day of Jesus Christ" (Phil 1:6).

Faith shows itself in work (cf. Gal 5:6, πίστις δι' ἀγάπης ἐνεργουμένη, "faith working through love") and love in labor, but the distinction between ἔργον and κόπος here is more rhetorical than substantial. As for τῆς ὑπομονῆς τῆς ἐλπίδος, while it is formally parallel to τοῦ ἔργου τῆς πίστεως and τοῦ κόπου τῆς ἀγάπης, it "more likely expresses subjectively the patient hope which accompanies active faith . . . and laboring love" (BDF § 163).

τοῦ κυρίου ἡμῶν Ἰησοῦ Χριστοῦ, "of our Lord Jesus Christ," is objective genitive after ἐλπίδος. It is in him that his people's hope is placed, and their hope will be realized at his Parousia. Cf. 5:8, ἐλπίδα σωτηρίας, "hope of salvation," the "salvation" being that to which God has appointed his people "through our Lord Jesus Christ" (5:9). The same hope is described in Rom 5:2 as "hope of the glory of God" (cf. Col 1:27, Χριστὸς ἐν ὑμῖν, ἡ ἐλπὶς τῆς δόξης, "Christ in you, the hope of glory"). Perhaps "hope" has the emphatic position at the end of the triad here because of the eschatological note of the whole letter (just as the context of 1 Cor 13:13 requires that "love" should occupy that emphatic position there).

For the nouns which respectively govern the three graces in the genitive cf. Rev 2:2, where the Lord says to the church of Ephesus, οἶδα τὰ ἔργα σου καὶ τὸν κόπον καὶ τὴν ὑπομονήν σου ("I know your works, your labor and your enduring").

ἔμπροσθεν τοῦ θεοῦ καὶ πατρὸς ἡμῶν, "in the presence of our God and Father." It is uncertain how much of the preceding construction is to be taken together with this phrase. It is too distant from μνημονεύοντες to be construed with that participle; it is more natural to suppose that the

Thessalonians' work, labor and patient hope are exercised in the presence of God—not only in awareness of their responsibility to him but also in view of the Parousia (cf. 3:13, where the same phrase, ἔμπροσθεν τοῦ θεοῦ καὶ πατρὸς ἡμῶν, is closely associated with "the Parousia of our Lord Jesus").

4. εἰδότες, "knowing," like the preceding participles ποιούμενοι (v 2) and μνημονεύοντες (v 3), refers to the missionaries, the subject of the principal verb εὐχαριστοῦμεν. They know that the Thessalonian believers are truly among the elect people of God because the unmistakable signs of the new life have become apparent in them, including their ready response to the gospel—a vital as well as a verbal response. This knowledge (εἰδότες, "because we know") enhances the writers' sense of gratitude to God.

ἀδελφοὶ ἠγαπημένοι ὑπὸ [τοῦ] θεοῦ, "brothers beloved by God." This form of address is repeated with a slight variation in 2 Thess 2:13, ἀδελφοὶ ἠγαπημένοι ὑπὸ κυρίου. Cf. Deut 33:12 (ἠγαπημένος ὑπὸ κυρίου, "beloved by the Lord"); Sir 45:1 (ἠγαπημένον ὑπὸ θεοῦ καὶ ἀνθρώπων Μωϋσῆν, "Moses, beloved by God and men").

τὴν ἐκλογὴν ὑμῶν, "your election." The writers had recognized the genuineness of the Thessalonians' faith by their eager acceptance of the gospel when first they heard it, and this recognition was now confirmed by the news which Timothy had brought back about them (cf. 3:6). It was thus made doubly evident that God had chosen them.

In the OT God chooses Abraham (Neh 9:7) and his offspring, the people of Israel, after him (Deut 4:37; 1 Kings 3:8; Isa 41.8, 9; 43.10, 44.1, 2; 45:4; 49:7), in order to make himself known through them to the rest of humankind. In the NT the chosen people are confined within no national frontiers: they are chosen "in Christ"—by faith-union with him who is the elect one of God *par excellence*—whether they are Jews or Gentiles. Believers in Christ from the people of Israel form "a remnant according to election of grace" (Rom 11:5), but the same election of grace embraces believers from every nation. There is no distinction in the Pauline letters, as there is in the gospels (cf. Matt 22:14), between the called and the chosen. The choosing and the calling are alike the act of God: he chose his people in Christ "before the world's foundation" (Eph 1:4) and called them in time (cf. 2 Thess 2:13, 14) in order that they might reproduce his character by being "conformed to the image of his Son" (Rom 8:29). While the act of election took place in God's eternal counsel, its effects are seen in the lives of the elect, as they were seen now in the lives of the Thessalonian Christians. See Col 3:12 (with J. B. Lightfoot's note *ad loc.*) for the graces which characterize the elect; cf. also Rom 8:33; 1 Cor 1:27, 28; 2 Tim 2:10; Tit 1:1.

5. ὅτι, either "because . . ." ("we recognize your election by God because . . .") or "namely, that . . ." ("we recognize your election by God—we recognize, namely, that . . .").

τὸ εὐαγγέλιον ἡμῶν, "our gospel," i.e. "the gospel which we preached"; cf. 2 Thess 2:14; 2 Cor 4:3; also τὸ εὐαγγέλιόν μου, "my gospel"—"the gospel which I preach" (Rom 2:16; 16:25; 2 Tim 2:8).

οὐκ ἐγενήθη εἰς ὑμᾶς ἐν λόγῳ μόνον ἀλλὰ καὶ ἐν δυνάμει, "did not come to you in word alone, but also in power." "Word alone" here means speech unaccompanied by the convincing power of the Holy Spirit. Such speech, however eloquent and moving, would be ineffective in evoking faith from the hearers. Cf. 2:13; also 1 Cor 2:4, 5, where Paul's λόγος ("word") and κήρυγμα ("preaching") are marked not by the persuasive techniques of rhetoric but by "demonstration of the Spirit and power" (ἐν ἀποδείξει πνεύματος καὶ δυνάμεως), in order that the hearers' faith might be securely based in the power of God, not in human wisdom.

The writers speak of "our gospel" in the sense that it has been entrusted to them to proclaim it, but its author is God, whose Spirit is active both in those who declare it and in those who receive it. By the accepted standards of secular wisdom the gospel had nothing to commend it to the pagans of Thessalonica and other Greek cities: the message of salvation through a crucified Savior was more likely to arouse derision than admiration. But the fact of its divine origin was demonstrated by its power to liberate those who believed it and make them new men and women.

The origin of the term εὐαγγέλιον, "glad tidings," to designate the Christian message is still a disputed question, but no more probable account is given than that which points to the use of the cognate verb εὐαγγελίζεσθαι in Isa 40:9; 52:7; 60:6; 61:1 LXX of the announcement of Zion's restoration after the Babylonian exile. The whole context (Isa 40–66) in which these occurrences are found is interpreted in the NT with reference to the Christian salvation (Isa 52:7 is quoted in this sense in Rom 10:15 and Isa 61:1 in Luke 4:18).

ἐν πνεύματι ἁγίῳ, "in (the) Holy Spirit." The absence of the article need not imply that the personal Holy Spirit is not in view here (cf. v 6; Rom 5:5; 9:1; 15:13, 16, 19; 1 Cor 12:3; 2 Cor 6:6, together with instances of the anarthrous πνεῦμα θεοῦ "Spirit of God" in Rom 8:9, etc.). The position of ἐν πνεύματι ἁγίῳ in the midst of such phrases as ἐν δυνάμει, "in power," and [ἐν] πληροφορίᾳ "[in] conviction" is paralleled in 2 Cor 6:6. The δύναμις is the power of the Spirit's working; the πληροφορία is the conviction which he produces in the receptive hearer.

[ἐν] πληροφορίᾳ πολλῇ, "in fullest conviction." While "fullness" is a possible translation of πληροφορία (so Rigaux even here), its NT and early Christian usage (Col 2:2; Heb 6:11; 10:22; 1 Clement 42:3), like that of the verb πληροφορεῖν in Paul (Rom 4:21; 14:5; Col 4:12), points to "full assurance," "full conviction" as the meaning. The reference is to the Thessalonians' deep inward persuasion of the truth of the gospel, a token of the Holy Spirit's work in their hearts, more impressive and more lasting than the persuasion produced by spectacular or miraculous signs. Such signs there no doubt were in the earliest stages of their new life, as there were in other Pauline churches (cf. Gal 3:5), but it is not to them that appeal is made here.

καθὼς οἴδατε οἷοι ἐγενήθημεν, "even as you know what kind of persons we were." The conjunction καθώς links the following words with the preceding so as to imply: "we know what kind of people you turned out to be when you received the gospel *as* you know what kind of people we were when we brought it to you." The spiritual power and conviction with which the message was received matched the spiritual power and conviction with which it was delivered.

This use of οἴδατε, "you know," with reference to the converts' knowledge of the example shown and the teaching given by Paul and his colleagues appears elsewhere in the Pauline correspondence (cf. Gal 4:13; Phil 4:15; 2 Thess 2:6; 3:7) but nowhere so frequently as in this letter (cf. 2:1, 2, 5, 11; 3:3, 4; 4:2; 5:2). The appeal to the Thessalonians' knowledge of the missionaries' behavior among them is amplified in 2:1–12; here the emphasis lies more particularly on their presentation of the gospel to them, although it is clearly implied that the gospel was presented not only in their words but in their lives. A message designed to change its hearers' lives would lack all effectiveness if the preachers' conduct was manifestly inconsistent with it. It was important, when the gospel was brought to people who had never heard it before, that those people should see Christianity in action—and where would they see it, if not in the conduct of those who brought it? The preachers were conscious of this responsibility, and paid special attention to their "ways in Christ" (1 Cor 4:17) for the sake of those whom they were evangelizing (δι' ὑμᾶς), so that to follow their example would be tantamount to following the example of the Lord (v 6).

6. Καὶ ὑμεῖς μιμηταὶ ἡμῶν ἐγενήθητε καὶ τοῦ κυρίου, "and you became imitators of us and of the Lord." For the close collocation of the apostolic example with the example of Christ see 1 Cor 11:1 (with special reference to the duty of promoting the interests of others rather than one's own). (Cf. also Gal 4:12; Phil 3:17; 4:9.)

The Thessalonian church was an apostolic fellowship because its members not only accepted the apostles' teaching but also followed the apostles' example. They followed the apostles' example more especially by gladly enduring persecution for the gospel's sake and also (v 8) by sharing the gospel with others.

δεξάμενοι τὸν λόγον ἐν θλίψει πολλῇ μετὰ χαρᾶς πνεύματος ἁγίου, "accepting the word in much tribulation with joy of the Holy Spirit." Joy in the midst of persecution was a familiar Christian grace in the apostolic age, and was directly imparted by the Holy Spirit (cf. Gal 5:22, ὁ δὲ καρπὸς τοῦ πνεύματός ἐστιν . . . χαρά, "the fruit of the Spirit is . . . joy." So in Rom 5:3, 5 Paul says that "we rejoice amid our tribulations (ἐν ταῖς θλίψεσιν) . . . because the love of God is poured out in our hearts through the Holy Spirit who has been given to us." That tribulation is the normal lot of Christians is taken for granted by most NT writers: in Acts 14:22 Paul and Barnabas tell the churches of South Galatia that it is "through many tribulations" (διὰ πολλῶν θλίψεων) that "we must enter into the kingdom of God," and in John 16:33 Jesus' last word to his disciples before leaving the upper room is: "In the world you have tribulation (θλῖψις); but take courage: I have overcome the world."

Tribulation (θλῖψις) is a term applicable to the various kinds of hardship which Christians have to endure because of their faith and witness. In 2 Thess 1:4 tribulations and persecutions (διωγμοί) are conjoined. Nothing is said in Acts 17:1–9 about persecution directed against the Thessalonian converts in general; it is against the missionaries and secondarily against their hosts ("Jason and some of the brethren") that the rabble is stirred up by disapproving Jews. It might be expected that, when the missionaries got away safely, resentment against them would be turned against their followers; according to 2:14, it was at the hands of their compatriots that they met with persecution. Thus they shared the lot not only of the missionaries but of the Lord himself: as Paul might have put it, they experienced "the fellowship of his sufferings" (cf. Phil 3:10).

7. ὥστε γενέσθαι ὑμᾶς τύπον πᾶσιν τοῖς πιστεύουσιν, "so that you became an example for all the believers." From following the example of the missionaries, the Thessalonian Christians became in turn an example to other believers, both in their courageous acceptance of suffering for Christ's sake and in their fearless proclamation of the message which had brought salvation to themselves.

ἐν τῇ Μακεδονίᾳ καὶ ἐν τῇ Ἀχαΐᾳ, "in Macedonia and in Achaia." Their example was observed not only in their own province of Macedonia but also in the province of Achaia (comprising central and southern Greece) which adjoined it on the south. For Macedonia as a Roman province see p. xx; as for Achaia, it was constituted a separate province under Augustus in 27 B.C., being administered by a proconsul from then until A.D. 15 and again from A.D. 44 onward (cf. Acts 18:12). In Corinth, a Roman colony (since 44 B.C.) and the seat of administration of the province of Achaia, the writers now found themselves; they were thus in an advantageous position to assess the wide-ranging impact of the Thessalonians' example.

The repetition of ἐν τῇ before Ἀχαΐᾳ is strictly correct, since Macedonia and Achaia were two distinct provinces. A less precise construction occurs in Acts 19:21 (τὴν Μακεδονίαν καὶ Ἀχαΐαν); cf. also the variant reading in v 8.

Paul seems regularly to envisage the Christian community in a city as representing the province to which that city belongs: the Philippian church in Macedonia (Phil 4:15), the Corinthian church in Achaia (1 Cor 16:15; 2 Cor 1:1), the Ephesian church in Asia (1 Cor 16:19; 2 Cor 1:8 (?); Rom 16:5).

8. ἀφ' ὑμῶν γὰρ ἐξήχηται ὁ λόγος τοῦ κυρίου, "for from you the word of the Lord has sounded out." Having received the gospel, the Thessalonian Christians had no thought of keeping it to themselves; by word and life they made it known to others. From the beginning they functioned as a missionary church.

"The word of the Lord" (used similarly of the gospel in 2 Thess 3:1) is a common OT locution: τοῦ κυρίου, "of the Lord," is subjective genitive because the Lord is the author of the word. For Paul and his associates the κύριος is regularly Jesus. The verb ἐξηχεῖν (here only in NT) denotes a loud ringing sound, as of a trumpet blast.

ἀλλ᾽ ἐν παντὶ τόπῳ, "but in every place" ἀλλά has the force of ἀλλὰ καί ("but also"): "not only in Macedonia and Achaia" but even farther afield the news of their faith and witness had penetrated. How did the missionaries know this? Had Priscilla and Aquila heard the news before they left Rome? Chronologically, this is perhaps hardly likely, but they could certainly have heard it as they traveled east along the Egnatian Way, and told Paul and his friends about it when they met them in Corinth.

ἐν παντὶ τόπῳ. For the hyperbole cf. 2 Cor 2:14; also Rom 1:8 (ἐν ὅλῳ τῷ κόσμῳ, "in all the world," more apt in the case of Rome); Col 1:6 (ἐν παντὶ τῷ κόσμῳ).

ἡ πίστις ὑμῶν ἡ πρὸς τὸν θεόν, "your faith toward God" with the repetition of the article marking πρὸς τὸν θεόν as being in attributive relation to πίστις —the classical construction. Moreover, the repeated article prevents ambiguity here (it rules out the rendering "your faith has gone out to God").

ὥστε μὴ χρείαν ἔχειν ἡμᾶς λαλεῖν τι, "so that we have no need to speak a word." On a later occasion Paul thought fit to boast to the Corinthian Christians about the achievement of the churches of Macedonia (including Thessalonica), with special reference to their generous giving (2 Cor 8:1–5). At this earlier stage, however, he and his companions had no need to boast at Corinth or elsewhere about the Thessalonians' faith: the news had gone ahead of them. But see 2 Thess 1:4. (For χρείαν ἔχειν with infinitive cf. 4:9; 5:1.)

9. αὐτοὶ γὰρ περὶ ἡμῶν ἀπαγγέλλουσιν, "they themselves report concerning us." By αὐτοί we are to understand the people of Macedonia and Achaia (not to mention those ἐν παντὶ τόπῳ) who had heard the news: the faith of the Thessalonians had become a topic of general conversation. There is no basis for Harris's conjectural emendation of ἀπαγγέλλουσιν to ἀπαγγέλλετε, "(you yourselves) report," as though the writers were referring to a letter sent by the Thessalonian church ("A Study . . . ," 170, 171).

ὁποίαν εἴσοδον ἔσχομεν πρὸς ὑμᾶς, "what kind of entrance we had to you"— i.e. how you welcomed us and our message.

ἐπεστρέψατε πρὸς τὸν θεὸν ἀπὸ τῶν εἰδώλων δουλεύειν θεῷ ζῶντι καὶ ἀληθινῷ, "you turned to God from idols to serve the living and true God." This phrase is commonly supposed to reproduce a form of language current in preaching to pagans: there is a noteworthy parallel in Acts 14:15, where Paul and Barnabas call on the people of Lystra "to turn from these vanities (i.e. idolatrous practices) to the living God" (ἀπὸ τούτων τῶν ματαίων ἐπιστρέφειν ἐπὶ θεὸν ζῶντα). The verb ἐπιστρέφειν is common in Acts in the sense of evangelical conversion; it is not characteristic of Paul, who uses it once only of turning to the Lord (2 Cor 3:16, in a quotation from the OT) and once of turning back from the faith of the gospel (Gal 4:9).

It is plain that the community addressed in such terms as these consisted predominantly of converted pagans. From the record of Acts 17:1–9 the impression might be gained that the Thessalonian converts were mainly Jews and God-fearers; but evidently more evangelization was carried on in the city than Luke reports: the missionaries must have stayed longer than the two or three weeks during which they were granted the hospitality of the synagogue.

This summary of what constituted the Thessalonians' conversion experience lacks some distinctive notes of Paul's teaching. We note the absence of any mention of *theologia crucis* (contrast, e.g., Gal 3:1; 6:14; 1 Cor 2:2; Rom 3:25)—it features in the Thessalonian correspondence only at 1 Thess 5:10—and the absence of any reference to God's justifying grace. This, combined with the rhythmical structure of the passage, suggests that we are dealing with a pre-Pauline formula, which has left its mark also on Acts 14:15. Turning to God from idols to serve a living and true God would characterize proselytes from paganism to Judaism as much as converts to Christianity: it is the words that follow, about Jesus the Son of God, that impart a distinctively Christian note to the formula.

θεῷ ζῶντι καί ἀληθινῷ. For the anarthrous construction cf. Acts 14:15 (quoted above); Rom 9:26; 2 Cor 3:3; 6:16; 1 Tim 3:15; 4:10; Heb 3:12; 9:14 (reminiscent of our present formula); 10:31; 12:22; 1 Pet 1:23. There is only one God who, by contrast with idols, can be described as "a living (and true) God"; hence there is no danger of misunderstanding in the absence of the article. Because he alone is the "living God," he alone is "real" (ἀληθινός) over against the multiplicity of false gods (cf. 1 Cor 8:4–6). This is the only occurrence of ἀληθινός in the Pauline corpus. When God is called ἀληθής in Rom 3:4, the meaning is that he always speaks the truth.

10. ἀναμένειν τὸν υἱὸν αὐτοῦ ἐκ τῶν οὐρανῶν, "to wait for his Son from heaven." The expectation of the coming of Christ is a constant element in the early Christian message. Plainly it had been emphasized in the preaching at Thessalonica (cf. 2:19; 3:13; 4:13–18; 5:1–11); while further instruction about it is given in the course of 1 (and 2) Thessalonians, the writers take it for granted that their readers are familiar with the essential outline.

In the primitive eschatology of Acts 3:19–21 the hope is held out that "times of refreshing" will come from God when he sends Jesus to Israel as *Messias designatus,* "whom heaven must receive until the time for establishing all that God spoke by the mouth of his holy prophets from of old." The Advent *(Parousia)* of Christ in glory is not treated in the early church simply as the consummating event due to take place in the indefinite end-time but as something to be actively expected in the near future: it is assumed rather than asserted in these early letters that Christians of that generation may hope to witness it. While this is the only NT occurrence of ἀναμένειν ("to wait"), the same thought is expressed in other Pauline letters by the verb ἀπεκδέχεσθαι, as in 1 Cor 1:7, "waiting for the revelation (ἀπεκδεχομένους τὴν ἀποκάλυψιν) of our Lord Jesus Christ"; Phil 3:20, "from heaven we await (ἀπεκδεχόμεθα) a Savior, the Lord Jesus Christ." Even where this personal note is less prominent, the same event is referred to with the verb ἀπεκδέχεσθαι in Rom 8:23, where "we wait for (ἀπεκδεχόμενοι) instatement as sons, the redemption of the body," and in Gal 5:5, where "through the Spirit, by faith, we wait for (ἀπεκδεχόμεθα) the hope of righteousness."

There is no firm ground for the view that this part of "Paul's report is influenced by the second adventist terms in which, if he had thought then as he now did, he would have preached the gospel on his founding mission at Thessalonica" (Mearns, "Early Eschatological Development," 143). This is not exclusively Paul's report; it summarizes the Thessalonian Christians' response to the preaching of his colleagues and himself together, and represents teaching which they held in common with other Christian leaders of the first generation.

With ἐκ τῶν οὐρανῶν (the plural "from the heavens" reflects Semitic usage) cf. 4:16 (καταβήσεται ἀπ' οὐρανοῦ, singular); 2 Thess 1:7 (ἐν τῇ ἀποκαλύψει τοῦ κυρίου Ἰησοῦ ἀπ' οὐρανοῦ); also Phil 3:20, quoted above (ἐν οὐρανοῖς . . . ἐξ οὗ). Christ is at present exalted with God; it is from the presence of God that he will be revealed in glory. To wait for him has ethical implications; those who wait are bound to live holy lives so as to be ready to meet him (cf. 5:6–8, 23).

This is the only place in the Thessalonian letters where Jesus is called the Son of God.

ὃν ἤγειρεν ἐκ [τῶν] νεκρῶν, "whom he raised from the dead." The preaching at Lystra, mentioned in the comment on v 9, has close affinities with the preaching at Athens (Acts 17:22–31) where, after pointing out to his hearers the folly of idolatry, Paul warns them of the urgent need for repentance (of their idolatry) in view of the fact that God "has fixed a day on which he will judge the world in righteousness by a man whom he has appointed, and of this he has given a pledge to all by raising him from the dead." There we find the same correlation as here between the resurrection of Jesus and the judgment to come; but, whereas the Athenians are warned that on that appointed Day Jesus, the risen one, will function as universal judge (cf. 2 Thess 1:7, 8), the Thessalonians have learned to recognize in Jesus their "deliverer from the coming wrath."

In the Pauline corpus ἐγείρειν, "to raise", whether in the active voice (with God as subject) or in the passive, is the most common verb denoting resurrection, whether Christ's or his people's. The transitive forms of ἀνιστάναι are not found in Paul; for intransitive forms (frequent in this sense in Acts) see 4:14, 16 below.

Ἰησοῦν τὸν ῥυόμενον ἡμᾶς ἐκ τῆς ὀργῆς τῆς ἐρχομένης, "Jesus, our deliverer from the coming wrath." The name Ἰησοῦς underscores the identity of the risen and coming Lord with Jesus of Nazareth, who only twenty years before had been put to death in Judea. The present tense of ῥυόμενον carries no implication of realized eschatology with it (Mearns, "Early Eschatological Development," 143): the participle plays the part of a *nomen agentis*, "our deliverer" (cf. Rom 11:26, in a quotation from Isa 59:20 LXX, where ὁ ῥυόμενος, "the Deliverer," is practically a divine title).

ἐκ τῆς ὀργῆς τῆς ἐρχομένης. The coming wrath is the divine judgment to be poured out on the wicked at the time of the end (cf. ἀπὸ τῆς μελλούσης ὀργῆς in the preaching of John the Baptist, Matt 3:7; Luke 3:7). In Rom 1:18 God's ὀργή is already being revealed on earth as evildoers reap in their present lives the natural fruit of their misconduct; it will be consummated on the "day of wrath and revelation of God's righteous judgment"— the day, says Paul, "when, according to my gospel, God judges the secrets of human beings through Christ Jesus" (Rom 2:5, 16). It is the judgment of that day that is denoted here by "the coming wrath."

The tendency of some modern exegetes (e.g. Dodd, *Romans,* 20–24; Hanson, *Wrath*) to treat the wrath of God as an impersonal process of retribution operating in the universe does insufficient justice to Paul's thought. For Paul, God is personal, and his wrath must be as personal as his grace, even if his wrath be his "strange work" (cf. Isa 28:21) in contrast to his proper and congenial work of justifying the ungodly (Rom 4:5). Even "in the apparently purely immanent causal connection" of Rom 1:18–32 "God himself is at work in a hidden way, so that his ὀργή does not become an impersonal nemesis nor even . . . a human condition" (Käsemann, *Romans,* 37; see also Morris "Wrath"; Tasker, *Biblical Doctrine*).

To the objection that personal ὀργή is unworthy of the God of love the response might be made which Paul makes elsewhere to a rather different objection: "What shall we say? That God is unjust to inflict wrath? . . . By no means! For then how could God judge the world?" (Rom 3:5, 6).

How the people of Christ are delivered by him from the coming wrath (cf. Rom 5:9, σωθησόμεθα δι᾽ αὐτοῦ ἀπὸ τῆς ὀργῆς) is discussed further in the comment on 5:9, 10 below.

Explanation

For the Thessalonian Christians, as for the recipients of all the Pauline letters (with the significant exception of Galatians), Paul and his colleagues pour out unceasing thanks and prayer to God. They had been compelled to leave Thessalonica before their new converts, as they judged, were sufficiently grounded in the principles of Christian faith and life. They knew that the converts would be exposed to persecution of one sort or another— to mockery for being such fools as to be taken in by those dubious visitors, if not to positive violence—and it was natural to wonder how they would stand up to such treatment. The missionaries could hope that the memory of their preaching and the impact of their personal example would help the converts to stand firm. They could reassure themselves by recalling how the genuine marks of the new life were shown in the Thessalonians' response to the gospel; the Holy Spirit manifested his presence and power among them.

The Spirit's activity was evident in the "work of faith and labor of love and steadfast hope" in Christ which characterized the Thessalonian believers' lives from their first reception of the gospel. The Christian graces—faith, love and hope—displayed themselves in such a way as to leave no doubt that those believers had been enrolled by God among his chosen people.

While salvation is received by faith and not by works, the reality of saving faith is attested by its practical effect, "the work of faith." James's position is not so far removed from this—"I by my works will show you my faith" (Jas 2:18)—although his emphasis is different. In Gal 5:6 saving faith is described as "faith working through love"; so here the Thessalonians' "work of faith" is accompanied by their "labor of love." Their energy in Christian service bore witness to their faith and love alike. And their "steadfastness of hope in our Lord Jesus Christ" was their response to the prospect of his coming, which was an essential part of the apostolic message. Whereas in Galatians there is one reference only to this prospect—"through the Spirit, by faith, we wait for the hope of righteousness" (Gal 5:5)—it pervades the whole of 1 Thessalonians (cf. v 10).

The "power" in which the gospel came to the Thessalonians (v 5) was something which they could remember as well as the missionaries. They would not readily forget the signs of divine activity among them—not only the enthusiasm and conviction produced by the preaching and the joy that more than outweighed the persecution, but those mighty works that regularly accompanied the reception of the gospel in the apostolic age. The phenomena which accompanied the outpouring of the Spirit in Jerusalem on the first Christian Pentecost had reproduced themselves in Thessalonica, and carried their own persuasion with them. Similarly, when the churches of Galatia were disposed to fall back from the faith of the gospel to legalistic reliance on works, they were reminded how it was by "the hearing of faith" and not by works that they received the Spirit and experienced the mighty works which attended his coming among them (Gal 3:2–5). Nor was it only in Jerusalem and on the Pauline mission field that such things were experienced: the Christians to whom the letter to the Hebrews was sent could recall how, when the saving message was first brought to them, God "bore witness by signs and wonders and various mighty works and by gifts of the Holy Spirit distributed according to his own will" (Heb 2:4). Those early Christians did not need to be taught the doctrine of the Holy Spirit as part of a program of theological education, his person and power were matters of living experience to them. As far as Thessalonica was concerned, prophecy appears to have been a familiar gift of the Spirit, if one may judge from references to it later in this letter (cf. 5:19–22).

By the time these words were written, Timothy had been sent back by his colleagues to Thessalonica to find out how the infant church was faring, and had returned to them with good news. The members of the church were standing firm indeed: the initial joy with which the Holy Spirit had filled them had not begun to wane. On the contrary, it seemed to flourish in the midst of the severe persecution which they had to endure. More than that: they had begun spontaneously to propagate their faith. It was not only Timothy who reported this: news of the Thessalonians' conversion had spread not only in their own province of Macedonia and in the neighboring province of Achaia, but it had reached more distant parts. "Have you heard about those new Christians in Thessalonica?" people were asking one another. "They gave Paul and his companions a great welcome, and they have taken to their new faith in a big way; they cannot keep it to themselves but must let everybody know about it. Not only have they themselves turned from pagan idolatry to serve the living and true God; not only are they eagerly awaiting for the risen Christ to be revealed from heaven, but they are telling others how the same faith and hope may be theirs too."

With news like that reaching them, it is not surprising that the missionaries' hearts were filled with joyful thanksgiving to God.

Apostolic Defense (1 Thess 2:1–12)

(a) The Missionaries' Visit (2:1–4)

Bibliography

Boers, H. "The Form-Critical Study of Paul's Letters: I Thessalonians as a Case Study." *NTS* 22 (1975–76) 140–158. **Cranfield, C. E. B.** "A Study of 1 Thessalonians 2." *IrBibSt* 1 (1979) 215–226. **Denis, A. -M.** "L'apôtre Paul, prophète messianique des Gentiles." *ETL* 33 (1957) 245–318. **Kemmler, D. W.** *Faith and Human Reason.* NovT Sup 40. Leiden: Brill, 1975, 168–177 ("1 Th 2, 2 f."). **Malherbe, A. J.** " 'Gentle as a Nurse': The Stoic Background to 1 Thess. II." *NovT* 12 (1970) 203–217. **Mearns, C. L.** "Early Eschatological Development in Paul: the evidence of I and II Thessalonians." *NTS* 27 (1980–81) 137–157. **Pfitzner, V. C.** *Paul and the Agon Motif.* NovT Sup 16. Leiden: Brill, 1967, 109–129. **Rossano, P.** "Preliminari all' esegesi di 1 Tess., cap. 2." *BibOr* 7 (1965) 117–122. **Sanders, J. T.** "The Transition from Opening Epistolary Thanksgiving to Body in Letters of the Pauline Corpus." *JBL* 81 (1962) 348–462. **Schmithals, W.** *Paul and the Gnostics.* Tr. J. E. Steely. Nashville/New York: Abingdon, 1972. **Unnik, W. C. van** "The Christian's Freedom of Speech in the New Testament." *BJRL* 44 (1962) 166–188. **White, J. L.** *The Form and Function of the Body of the Greek Letter.* SBL Dissertation Series, 2. Missoula, MT: Scholars Press, 1972. **Zimmer, F.** "I Thess. 2, 3–8 erklärt." In *Theologische Studien Herrn . . . Professor D. Bernard Weiss zu seinem 70. Geburtstage dargebracht.* Göttingen: Vandenhoeck & Ruprecht, 1897, 248–273.

Translation

¹ *Brothers, you know yourselves that our coming in among you has not proved ineffectual.* ² *We had previously endured suffering and been shamefully treated, as you know, in Philippi, but we were emboldened in our God to declare the word of God to you amid great conflict.* ³ *Our appeal to you arose from no motives of deceit or impurity nor* ᵃ *was it made by way of guile.* ⁴ *No: as we have been approved by God to be entrusted with the gospel, so we speak: it is not human beings that we aim to please, but God,* ᵇ *who tests our hearts.*

Notes

ᵃ οὐδέ, for which D² byz read οὔτε.
ᵇ θεῷ, to which the article τῷ is prefixed by ℵ² A D² F G Ψ byz.

Form/Structure/Setting

With 2:1 we come to "the transition from opening epistolary thanksgiving to body" in this letter (Sanders, "Transition," 348, 355–356). The "body" or central section, which begins at 2:1, is variously reckoned as

ending with 2:12 or as going on to 3:8, to 3:13 or even to 4:12. Much
depends on the definition of terms used. It might be expected that the
"body" of the letter would contain its main substance or express its main
purpose. It is by no means evident that this is done in 2:1–12, so it seems
best to designate this section by the character of its contents: "apostolic
defense." The section falls naturally into three subsections, dealing respectively with the missionaries' reception at Thessalonica (2:1–4), with their
conduct while they remained there (2:5–8) and with the example they left
their converts (2:9–12). For each of these three aspects they can appeal
confidently to their readers' personal knowledge.

Comment

2:1. αὐτοὶ γὰρ οἴδατε, "for you yourselves know," sometimes called (as
by White, 69) a "disclosure formula," although here nothing is being disclosed (as in 4:13); an appeal is rather being made to what the Thessalonians
already know (as in 1:5; see comment ad loc.). The connecting γάρ harks
back to a previous mention of the missionaries' conduct in Thessalonica—
either to καθὼς οἴδατε οἷοι ἐγενήθημεν ἐν ὑμῖν (1:5) or to ὁποίαν εἴσοδον ἔσχομεν
πρὸς ὑμᾶς (1:9). The wording of the latter clause is caught up here in τὴν
εἴσοδον ἡμῶν τὴν πρὸς ὑμᾶς "our coming in among you" (note the classical
repetition of τὴν before πρὸς ὑμᾶς, preserving that phrase in the attributive
relation to τὴν εἴσοδον). Here, however, it is not so much the missionaries'
reception by the Thessalonians as their personal conduct that is emphasized.

οὐ κενὴ γέγονεν, "has not proved empty." Lightfoot argues that κενή
here means "hollow, empty, wanting in purpose and earnestness" rather
than "fruitless, ineffective" (μάταιος), since it is the character of the preaching, not its result, that is in question: the writers repeat in different terms
their οὐκ ἐν λόγῳ μόνον ἀλλά καὶ ἐν δυνάμει of 1:5. In fact, the character
and result of the preaching cannot be separated: the latter as much as
the former is denoted in the δύναμις of 1:5. The Thessalonians' positive
response to the gospel and subsequent energy in spreading it abroad bore
sufficient testimony both to the quality of the preaching and to the power
that accompanied it.

The apologia introduced in these words may be a recurring feature of
epistolary style, but there is nothing merely formal or "stylistic" about
it. Paul and his colleagues found themselves repeatedly obliged to defend
their motives and behavior against those who impugned the purity of the
former and the integrity of the latter. They knew themselves to be as
much under this necessity in Corinth, from which they now wrote, as they
had been in Thessalonica.

2. προπαθόντες καὶ ὑβρισθέντες, καθὼς οἴδατε, ἐν Φιλίπποις, "having endured suffering and having been shamefully treated, as you know, in Philippi," a reference to the illegal beating and imprisonment endured by
Paul and Silvanus not long before their arrival at Thessalonica (Acts 16:19–

24). It is implied in καθὼς οἴδατε that the Thessalonians had heard about this, probably from Paul and Silvanus themselves. The outrage (ὑβρίζεσθαι) lay not so much in their being subjected, Roman citizens though they were, to treatment from which Roman citizens were legally exempt, as to their being publicly stripped and flogged without any inquiry into the charges brought against them—outrageous treatment whether they were Roman citizens or not.

ἐπαρρησιασάμεθα . . . λαλῆσαι, "we spoke out freely." They do not say, "Having been ill-treated at Philippi, we were more circumspect in Thessalonica" but rather: "we were emboldened in God to preach the gospel there too." In Greek democratic parlance παρρησία meant "freedom of speech" and something of this sense attaches to it and its derivative verb παρρησιάζεσθαι as used in the NT, together with the sense of "courage." Here the writers imply, "We took courage (ingressive aorist) and 'declared the gospel of God to you frankly and fearlessly' (NEB)." "Undoubtedly Paul is reacting here against all sorts of religious propagandists of his day. His preaching does not aim at pleasing men, not even himself, but pleasing God: his gospel is not 'according to man' (Gal 1:11) and therefore provokes opposition; but he has not adulterated the gospel. The word 'freedom of speech' has here its place in the missionary-practice of the apostle: it comprises both the full truth of the gospel and full freedom towards the judgement of men" (van Unnik, "Freedom of Speech," 473).

Malherbe ("Gentle," 208) draws a parallel between this passage and Dio Chrysostom, *Oration* 32 (early 2nd century A.D.), in which there is a description of various types of Cynic and Stoic and an insistence that, while the right and duty of παρρησία must be maintained, it should not involve λοιδορία (verbal abuse): Dio distinguishes his own discharge of his divine commission in language quite similar to this.

ἐν τῷ θεῷ ἡμῶν. For the divine source of their courage and strength cf. 2 Cor 3:12; 4:7; 12:9f.

τὸ εὐαγγέλιον τοῦ θεοῦ, "the gospel of God," probably denoting God as the author of the gospel (as in vv 8, 9); cf. Rom 1:1; 15:16; 2 Cor 11:7. For other genitives depending on εὐαγγέλιον see 1:5 (ἡμῶν); 3:2 (τοῦ Χριστοῦ).

ἐν πολλῷ ἀγῶνι, "amid great conflict"; again, the narrative of Acts 17:5–9, telling of the agitation stirred up against the missionaries, provides an eloquent commentary. In Phil 1:30, Paul refers both to his previous imprisonment in Philippi and to his current *libera custodia* in Rome as an ἀγών. The word implies that there is opposition against which it is necessary to contend. This is so even in Col 2:1 (ἡλίκον ἀγῶνα ἔχω), where the conflict is inward and spiritual: the opposition is the false teaching to which the churches of the Lycus valley are exposed.

3. ἡ . . . παράκλησις ἡμῶν, probably "our appeal (to you)"; cf. 2 Cor 5:20, ὡς τοῦ θεοῦ παρακαλοῦντος δι' ἡμῶν, "God appealing through us." The noun παράκλησις is capable of all the variations of meaning found with the verb παρακαλεῖν (to appeal, exhort, strengthen).

οὐκ ἐκ πλάνης οὐδὲ ἐξ ἀκαθαρσίας οὐδὲ ἐν δόλῳ, "neither from motives of deceit or impurity nor by way of guile." So many wandering charlatans (γόητες) made their way about the Greek world, peddling their religious or philosophical nostrums, and living at the expense of their devotees (like Lucian's false prophet Alexander), that it was necessary for Paul and his friends to emphasize the purity of their motives and actions by contrast with these. The same kind of contrast is made by Dio Chrysostom in *Oration* 32 (mentioned in comment on v 2 above). "The normal heathen 'missionaries' . . . were itinerant apostles and miracle-workers of the most varied persuasions, heralds of heathen gods, and dispensers of salvation, adroit and eloquent, ardent and evoking ardor, but also smart and conceited in extolling the mighty acts of their gods and fooling the masses. . . . There can be no doubt that they constituted dangerous rivals of the gospel and that general popular opinion expected the Christian missionaries to be able to vie with them" (Bornkamm, *Paul*, 64).

ἐκ πλάνης, according to Lightfoot, means "from error" rather than "from deceit"—the defect envisaged being intellectual rather than moral. More probably, however, the writers mean that they were neither deceivers nor deceived (cf. 2 Tim 3:13, πλανῶντες καὶ πλανώμενοι). By ἀκαθαρσία sexual impurity is probably denoted, *pace* Schmithals (145), who thinks it refers to the "lack of integrity" with which Paul was charged for springing a demand for contributions to the Jerusalem relief fund on his converts without warning, after ostentatiously refusing to live at their expense. Schmithals compares ἐν δόλῳ here with 2 Cor 12:16 (ὑπάρχων πανοῦργος δόλῳ ὑμᾶς ἔλαβον), where a charge of craftiness and guile is brought against Paul at Corinth in this specific connection. But the Jerusalem relief fund can be read out of the Thessalonian correspondence only if it first be read into it. Equally unconvincing is Mearns's explanation ("Development," 145) of ἀκαθαρσία as denoting the lack of integrity shown by Paul in his alleged eschatological *volte-face* between leaving Thessalonica and sending this letter (see p. xl above). It is much more satisfactory to regard πλάνη, ἀκαθαρσία and δόλος as characteristic of the traveling mountebanks with whom Paul and his friends contrast themselves here.

4. δεδοκιμάσμεθα, "we have been approved" (after testing, δοκιμασία). πιστευθῆναι τὸ εὐαγγέλιον, "to be entrusted with the gospel"; cf. Gal 2:7 (πεπίστευμαι τὸ εὐαγγέλιον); 1 Cor 9:17 (οἰκονομίαν πεπίστευμαι).

οὕτως λαλοῦμεν, "so we speak (as those thus commissioned)." Only if they conducted themselves in a manner worthy of the gospel which they proclaimed could they reasonably expect their converts to live in a manner worthy of the gospel which they received (cf. Phil 1:27, μόνον ἀξίως τοῦ εὐαγγελίου τοῦ Χριστοῦ πολιτεύεσθε, "only conduct yourselves worthily of the gospel of Christ").

οὐχ ὡς ἀνθρώποις ἀρέσκοντες, "not as seeking to please human beings." Cf. Gal 1:10; Col 3:22. Paul's versatility, his readiness to "become all things to all men" for the gospel's sake (1 Cor 9:22), could easily have been misrepresented as the policy of a fence-sitter, who adapted his message to suit his varying audiences. Indeed, he himself could go so far as to say that he pleased everyone in everything (πάντα πᾶσιν ἀρέσκω), but in the sense of seeking their advantage in preference to his own (1 Cor 10:33). Basically, he insists that it is God, not human beings, whom he aims to please. Cf. Col 1:10, περιπατῆσαι ἀξίως τοῦ κυρίου εἰς πᾶσαν ἀρέσκειαν ("to conduct oneself in a manner worthy of the Lord, to please him in everything").

Every clause and phrase here expresses the sense of responsibility which Paul constantly felt with regard to his apostolic commission; cf. Rom 1:14; 1 Cor 4:1–4; 9:16, 17; 15:9, 10; 2 Cor 2:17; 4:1–15; Gal 1:15–17; 2:7–10; Eph 3:7–13; Col 1:23–2:5. He was frequently charged with altering his message to please his constituency, with being "all things to all men" in an unworthy sense; here is his answer.

The charge persisted even after the apostolic age: in the *Clementine Homilies* 18.10 Paul (thinly disguised as Simon Magus) is rebuked by Peter for speaking ἀρεσκόντως τοῖς παροῦσιν ὄχλοις, "in a manner pleasing to the crowds that are present."

θεῷ τῷ δοκιμάζοντι τὰς καρδίας ἡμῶν, "God who tests our hearts." Cf. Rom 8:27, where God is ὁ . . . ἐραυνῶν τὰς καρδίας (also Acts 1:24, σὺ κύριε καρδιόγνωστα πάντων, and 15:8, ὁ καρδιογνώστης θεός, with Rev 2:23, where the risen Lord speaks as ὁ ἐραυνῶν νεφροὺς καὶ καρδίας). The idea of God as the searcher and tester of hearts is common in the OT; cf. Pss 7:9; 139 (LXX 138):23; Prov 17:3; Jer 11:20; 12:3; 17:10; 1 Chr 28:9; 29:7. The writers are in effect invoking God as witness to the integrity of their motives, which are viewed as having their source in the "heart" (cf. 3:13, with comment).

Explanation

Perhaps the conduct or motives of Paul and his companions had been represented in an unfavorable light to their converts in Thessalonica. Religious charlatans have been common in every age and some people, forgetting that hypocrisy is the tribute which vice pays to virtue, conclude that everyone who is active in a religious cause is in it for the money or the prestige or some other ulterior consideration. There are cynics who cannot believe that public or private action, involving sacrifice of time, money, comfort and even reputation, is ever undertaken purely with a view to the well-being of others.

Paul and his friends had been targets for such criticism, and the circumstances of their stay in Thessalonica and of their departure from the city lent some point to it. Their preaching had provoked an outburst of rioting and, when they were forced to leave, the hostility which had been aimed at them was turned against their supporters and converts. What was the outcome of their visit to Thessalonica? Nothing but trouble, some people said; it was a pity that they had ever come. The sooner they were forgotten, the better for all concerned.

The missionaries defend themselves against such criticism or, rather, they appeal to their converts' lively recollection of the facts. The outcome of their visit to Thessalonica had been the establishment of the Thessalonian church, which had begun in its turn to spread the gospel abroad. Their approach to the people of Thessalonica had nothing deceitful or morally suspect about it: they had no recourse to underhanded methods nor did they adapt their message to their hearers' tastes. Their presentation of the message might vary in accordance with the background knowledge of varying audiences—a Jewish audience, for example, could be presumed to know much that would be unfamiliar to a pagan audience—but the message itself was a sacred trust committed to them and must not be adulterated. Not only could the gospel be neutralized by inadequacies or distortions in the language in which it was communicated; it could be neutralized by conduct on the preachers' part which was inconsistent with its character or unworthy of the God whose gospel it was. Not for nothing is it repeatedly emphasized that it is *the gospel of God.* The preachers knew themselves to be responsible to God—the tester of hearts—for their conduct, language and thought-life.

To the Thessalonians, in short, as later to the Corinthians, Paul and the others could say, "We have renounced disgraceful, underhanded ways; we refuse to practice cunning or to tamper with God's word, but by the open statement of the truth we would commend ourselves to everyone's conscience in the sight of God" (2 Cor 4:2).

(b) *The Missionaries' Behavior (2:5–8)*

Bibliography

Crawford, C. "The 'Tiny' Problem of 1 Thessalonians 2, 7: The case of the curious vocative." *Bib* 54 (1973) 69–72. **Dungan, D. L.** *The Sayings of Jesus in the Churches of Paul. The Use of the Synoptic Tradition in the Regulation of Early Church Life.* Philadelphia: Fortress, 1971. **Gibbins, H. J.** "1 Thessalonians ii.6." *ExpTim* 14 (1902–3) 527. **Malherbe, A. J.** " 'Gentle as a Nurse': The Stoic Background to 1 Thess. II." *NovT* 12 (1970) 203–217.

Translation

⁵ *We never had recourse to flattering talk, as you know, nor did we make use of any pretext for covetousness, as God is our witness;* ⁶ *neither did we seek applause from human beings, whether from you or from others.* ⁷ *We might have required you to support us, as apostles of Christ, but were gentle* ᵃ *among you, like* ᵇ *a nurse cherishing her own children.* ⁸ *Such was our affection* ᶜ *for you that we chose* ᵈ *rather to share with you not only the gospel of God* ᵉ *but our very selves, so dear had you become to us.*

Notes

ᵃ For ἤπιοι ("gentle"), the reading of ℵᶜ A C² D² Ψ ᶜ byz latᵛᵉ·ˢᵗ copˢᵃ·ᶜᵒᵈᵈ there is a strongly attested variant νήπιοι ("infants") read by P⁶⁵ ℵ* B C* D* F G I Ψ* *pc* latᵛᵉᵗ ᵛᵉ·ʷʷ copˢᵃ·ᶜᵒᵈ ᵇᵒ Clem.Al. The variation is due either to haplography or dittography of ν. It is the sense that is decisive for ἤπιοι, although νήπιοι is preferred by Nestle-Aland ²⁶· Crawford retains νήπιοι but construes it (unconvincingly) as vocative, addressed to the Thessalonian Christians. (See comment below.)

ᵇ ὡς ἐὰν . . . θάλπῃ, indefinite construction. In Hellenistic Greek (especially in LXX, NT and papyri) ἐὰν frequently replaces ἄν in relative clauses (see BDF § 107).

ᶜ ὁμειρόμενοι ("ardently desiring"), for which ἱμειρόμενοι is read in a number of minuscules. ὁμείρεσθαι is a Hellenistic verb (also spelled with a smooth breathing); it has the meaning of classical ἱμείρεσθαι (but the two are not etymologically related).

ᵈ For εὐδοκοῦμεν (which is to be understood as imperfect, though it has not the augmented spelling ηὐδοκοῦμεν), a few minuscules have the aorist εὐδοκήσαμεν. (Cf. 3:1.)

ᵉ For τοῦ θεοῦ ("of God") a few minuscules have τοῦ Χριστοῦ ("of Christ"); cf. 3:2.

Form/Structure/Setting

The apostolic defense is continued. The missionaries disown all self-seeking considerations and affirm that their consuming passion was the well-being of their converts, as the converts themselves can testify. In this subsection, as in those preceding and following, there is an appeal to the readers' knowledge of the facts (v 5; cf. vv 1, 11) and an insistence that the gospel which they preach is God's (v 8; cf. vv 2, 9).

Comment

2:5. Οὔτε γάρ ποτε ἐν λόγῳ κολακείας ἐγενήθημεν, "for neither did we ever have recourse to language of flattery." The κόλαξ, "the flatterer," a stock character in the literature of ethics and manners, habitually employs flattery to gain some advantage for himself. He trades on the fact that people naturally like to hear things which set them in a favorable light, and by telling them such things he expects to gain a following. According to Aristotle, "the man who joins in gratifying people . . . for the sake of getting something for himself in the way of money or money's worth is a flatterer" (*Eth. Nic.* 4.6.9). "Flattery," says Theophrastus, "might be regarded as converse (ὁμιλία) which is base, but advantageous to the flatterer" (*Characters,* 2). Dio Chrysostom (*Oration* 32) condemns the use of flattery in public speech. La Fontaine sums the situation up in a well-known couplet:

Apprenez que tout flatteur
Vit au dépens de celui qui l'écoute.

Learn that every flatterer
Lives at the flattered listener's cost.

καθὼς οἴδατε, "as you know" as in 1:5; 2:2, etc.

οὔτε ἐν προφάσει πλεονεξίας, "nor (did we make use of) any pretext for covetousness." Ostensibly the language might be above suspicion, but if its real purpose is the speaker's advantage, it is but a pretext (πρόφασις) for covetousness (πλεονεξία). That this was not so with Paul and his companions is known both to their converts (καθὼς οἴδατε) and to God (θεὸς μάρτυς, "God is witness"); cf. v 10.

Covetousness or cupidity, πλεονεξία, the desire to get more (πλεονεκτεῖν, as in 4:6), is a vice especially reprobated in the NT. In Mark 7:22 it is included, along with fornication, adultery, murder and the like, among the "evil things" which come from within the human heart and convey real defilement (cf. 1 Cor 5:10, 11; 6:10). In Luke 12:15–21 the parable of the rich fool is told to encourage hearers to "beware of all covetousness" and to realize that "a man's life does not consist in the abundance of his possessions." In Col 3:5 and Eph 5:5 πλεονεξία is a form of idolatry. It is not merely the desire to possess more than one has, but to possess more than one ought to have, especially that which belongs to someone else. It "is the sin of the man who has allowed full play to the desire to have what he should not have, who thinks his desires and appetites and lusts are the most important thing in the world, who sees others as things to be exploited, who has no god except himself and his desires" (W. Barclay, *A New Testament Wordbook*, London: SCM Press, 1955, 99).

In 2 Cor 9:5; 12:17, 18 Paul rebuts the charge of πλεονεξία against himself and his colleagues in reference to the gathering of the Jerusalem relief fund, but there is nothing in the present context to suggest such a reference here.

θεὸς μάρτυς, "God is witness" (cf. Roman 1:9; 2 Cor 1:23; Phil 1:8).

6. οὔτε ζητοῦντες . . . δόξαν, "nor seeking . . . applause." Some propagandists stood on their dignity and required respectful attention and subservience. Paul could not esteem too highly the glory of the message with which he was entrusted (cf. 2 Cor 3:7–11), but he himself and his colleagues were but "earthen vessels" in which the treasure of the gospel was placed (2 Cor 3:7). Far from demanding service and deference from their converts, they presented themselves as their converts' "servants for Jesus' sake" (2 Cor 4:5).

ἐξ ἀνθρώπων . . . ἀφ᾽ ὑμῶν . . . ἀπ᾽ ἄλλων. It would be hypercritical to press a distinction between ἐξ and ἀπό here. Cf. Rom 2:29, οὗ ὁ ἔπαινος οὐκ ἐξ ἀνθρώπων ἀλλ᾽ ἐκ τοῦ θεοῦ, with 1 Cor 4:5, καὶ τότε ὁ ἔπαινος γενήσεται ἑκάστῳ ἀπὸ τοῦ θεοῦ. To gain a reputation as successful evangelists or as leaders of a school which could boast a large number of disciples was not the aim of Paul or his friends. He set no store by the recognition or assessment of men: he was content to abide the Lord's judgment (1 Cor 4:3, 4). On the worthlessness of δόξα παρὰ ἀνθρώπων, "the praise of men," cf. John 5:41–44.

7. δυνάμενοι ἐν βάρει εἶναι, "being able to make demands," refers to the right which preachers of the gospel had, according to Paul, to be maintained

by their converts and others to whose spiritual welfare they ministered—a right which Paul chose not to exercise (cf. 2 Thess 3:7–9; 1 Cor 9:3–18; 2 Cor 11:7–11). This right (as Paul points out in 1 Cor 9:14) was conferred by Jesus on those whom he sent out (ἀπέστειλεν) on a preaching and healing mission in his name in the course of his Galilean ministry (Mark 6:7–13; Matt 10:5–15; Luke 9:1–6; 10:1–12): "the laborer," he said to them, "deserves his pay" (μισθός, Luke 10:7) or "his food" (τροφή, Matt 10:10). Paul took the Lord's instructions to mean that his servants were entitled to their maintenance but not compelled to require it (cf. Dungan, *Sayings*, 27–40).

With this use of βάρος cf. ἐπιβαρεῖν in v 9 and 2 Thess 3:8, καταβαρεῖν in 2 Cor 12:16 and ἀβαρής in 2 Cor 11:9. In this matter of refusing to be a financial burden on the churches, Paul's colleagues may well have been influenced by his example. His reasons for forgoing the right to material support may have been manifold: partly his rabbinical upbringing which forbade him to make religious teaching a means of livelihood (cf. *Pirqe 'Abot* 1.13; 4.7), partly his native independence of spirit, which made it embarrassing for him even to acknowledge a voluntary gift (cf. Phil 4:10–20), and in large measure his desire to set his converts a good example (cf. 2 Thess 3:9; Acts 20:34, 35).

ὡς Χριστοῦ ἀπόστολοι, "as Christ's messengers." Here ἀπόστολος is used in a rather general sense: Paul associates his companions with his own apostolic ministry—in which indeed they shared. Paul normally gives ἀπόστολος a wider range of meaning than does Luke (who, apart from the reference to Paul and Barnabas in Acts 14:4, 14, restricts it to the twelve), but the special sense in which he uses the term—e.g. when he groups James the Lord's brother with "all the apostles" in 1 Cor 15:7 (cf. Gal 1:19) or refers in Rom 16:7 to Andronicus and Junia(s), who were "in Christ" before himself, as "noteworthy among the apostles"—can scarcely be stretched to include Timothy, his own "son in the faith" (1 Tim 1:2), whatever may be said of Silvanus. If one may judge from Paul's account of the origin of his own apostleship, he appears to use the term of one who had seen the risen Lord and had been commissioned by him (whether alone or in a company with others).

ἀλλὰ ἐγενήθημεν ἤπιοι ἐν μέσῳ ὑμῶν, "but we showed ourselves gentle among you." The variant νήπιοι, "infants," is well attested (see notes above) but is due probably to dittography of the final letter of ἐγενήθημεν. It is inappropriate in the immediate context, where the writers go on to compare themselves not to infants but to a nurse or a parent caring for her children. "Being gentle" also provides a fitting contrast to "being burdensome" in the preceding clause.

ὡς ἐὰν τροφὸς θάλπῃ τὰ ἑαυτῆς τέκνα, "as a nurse cherishes her own children." Since they are "her own children," the τροφός may be a nursing mother; on the other hand, τὰ ἑαυτῆς τέκνα may mean "the children entrusted to her personal care," but this is rather less likely. We may compare Paul's maternal metaphor in Gal 4:19, τέκνα μου, οὓς πάλιν ὠδίνω ("my children, for whom I suffer birthpangs all over again"). Cf. the paternal figure in v 11 below (and note the parallel τέκνα ἑαυτοῦ).

With ἐν μέσῳ ὑμῶν cf. Luke 22:27, "I am in your midst (ἐν μέσῳ ὑμῶν) as the one who serves." For the general idea of the simile cf. Num 11:12, where Moses speaks of himself as directed by Yahweh to take the people of Israel into his bosom (κόλπος), "as a nurse takes up a sucking child" (ὡσεὶ ἄραι τιθηνὸς τὸν θηλάζοντα).

Malherbe ("Gentle," 211) suggests that the ἠπιότης to which the writers appeal here forms a designed contrast to the harshness (σκληρότης) characteristic of one type of itinerant Cynic, who could not distinguish scurrilous reproach (ὀνειδισμός) from admonition (νουθεσία) and had recourse to the former when the latter was required (he quotes Gnom. Byz., ed. C. Wachsmuth, 59, 176). By contrast Crates, who "rebuked not with harshness but with grace" (ἐπετίμα οὐ μετὰ πικρίας ἀλλὰ μετὰ χάριτος, Plutarch, Quaestiones Conviviales 632E; Julian, Oration 6.201B), Musonius, Demonax and Dio Chrysostom (cf. comment on v 2 above) were well-known for gentleness.

8. οὕτως ὁμειρόμενοι ὑμῶν, "having such an affection for you." The verb (see notes above) is not found elsewhere in the NT; it is used in Job 3:21 LXX of "longing for" death (Heb. חָכָה).

εὐδοκοῦμεν μεταδοῦναι ὑμῖν, "we were resolved to share with you"; μεταδοῦναι has two objects, but the sharing of the one (τὸ εὐαγγέλιον τοῦ θεοῦ, for which cf. v 2) is not on the same footing as the sharing of the other. They could share the gospel with their converts without any diminution in their own enjoyment of its benefits, but to share their own lives involved utter self-denial, "spending and being spent" in the interest of others (cf. 2 Cor 12:15).

τὰς ἑαυτῶν ψυχάς, "our own selves." The reflexive pronoun which originally belonged to the third person is here extended in scope to cover the first person (cf. 2 Thess 3:9; 2 Cor 4:5; for its extension to cover the second person cf. 5:13). The ψυχή is here the seat of affection and will (cf. μιᾷ ψυχῇ, Phil 1:27; σύμψυχος, Phil 2:2; ἰσόψυχος, Phil 2:19). The meaning is not simply "we were willing to give (lay down) our lives for you" but "we were willing to give ourselves to you, to put ourselves at your disposal, without reservation." Those addressed seem to have followed and reciprocated the apostolic example, to judge from 2 Cor 8:5, where it is said that the Macedonian churches "first gave themselves (ἑαυτούς) to the Lord and to us (Paul and his companions) by the will of God."

διότι ἀγαπητοὶ ἡμῖν ἐγενήθητε, "so dear you had become to us." This repeats the sense of οὕτως ὁμειρόμενοι ὑμῶν and in doing so emphasizes the warmth of the missionaries' outgoing love for their converts.

Explanation

When the missionaries disclaim the use of flattery to disguise an underlying ambition to secure wealth, power and high repute, we are not surprised that they appeal to the Thessalonians' knowledge that such a disclaimer is well founded. All the evidence at our disposal indicates that Paul and his friends spoke the simple truth. If they had indeed aimed at wealth, power and high repute, they would have to be dismissed as men who signally failed to achieve their aim. By secular standards they were marked to the end of their days by poverty, weakness, disrepute and all sorts of tribulation; but they assessed their lot by other than secular standards—"as having nothing, and yet possessing everything" (2 Cor 6:10).

But more impressive than their disclaimer of unworthy motives and actions is the assertion of their loving care for their converts. The note of maternal affection in v 7 comes from the heart of Paul. Far from seeking any material help from their converts, they were eager to share with them all that they had, and indeed all that they were. No other attitude would befit the preachers of a gospel which proclaimed as Lord and Savior one who "emptied himself" (Phil 2:7) for the enrichment of others.

Jesus conducted himself among his disciples as a servant; from his example they were expected to learn that they in turn should be servants one to another and to their fellow men and women. Any doctrine of the Christian ministry which presents the minister as a ruler in the church is unworthy of the precedent set by the church's Lord and Master; in accordance with that precedent he is not a ruler but a servant. The Pope himself has no more honorable designation than "servant of the servants of God."

The extent and nature of the tradition which Paul and his colleagues had received about the life and teaching of Jesus may be debated, but this is not in dispute: in that tradition (independently preserved in the canonical Gospels) Jesus came to serve, not to be served, and taught his followers accordingly: not that lowly service will be rewarded by promotion to a position of greatness but that, in his kingdom, lowly service *is* true greatness.

(c) *The Missionaries' Example (2:9–12)*

Bibliography

De Boer, W. P. *The Imitation of Paul.* Kampen: Kok, 1962. **Gutierrez, P.** *La paternité spirituelle selon saint Paul.* EB. Paris: Gabalda, 1968, 87–117. **Hock, R. F.** "Paul's Tentmaking and the Problem of his Social Class." *JBL* 97 (1978) 555–564. **Hock, R. F.** "The Workshop as a Social Setting for Paul's Missionary Preaching," *CBQ* 41 (1979) 438–450. **Hock, R. F.** *The Social Context of Paul's Ministry: Tentmaking and Apostleship.* Philadelphia: Fortress, 1980. **Vos, G.** *The Pauline Eschatology.* Grand Rapids: Eerdmans, 1952. **Wiederkehr, D.** *Die Theologie der Berufung in den Paulusbriefen.* Freiburg: Universitätsverlag, 1963.

Translation

[9] *You remember, brothers, our labor and toil. We* [a] *worked by night and day so as not to become burdensome to any of you when we preached the gospel of*

God to you. [10] *You are witnesses, and so is God, how devout, just and blameless our behavior was toward you believers* b—[11] *how, as you know, we treated each one of you as a father would treat his own children.* c [12] *Thus we exhorted you,* d *encouraged you and charged* e *you to conduct yourselves in a manner worthy of God, the one who calls* f *you into his own kingdom and glory.*

Notes

a The sentence begins with νυκτός ("by night") to which γάρ ("for") is added by D¹ byz syr^hcl.mg.

b For the present participle πιστεύουσιν ("believers") P⁶⁵ lat (cf. vg *qui credidistis*) read the aorist participle πιστεύσασιν, "(who) have believed."

c The ὡς before ἕνα ἕκαστον ("each one"), like ὡς before ὁσίως κτλ in v 10, depends on ὑμεῖς μάρτυρες κτλ ("you are witnesses . . . how . . ."), but the clause introduced by the second ὡς has no principal verb corresponding to ἐγενήθημεν in the clause introduced by the former ὡς. The ὡς before πατήρ is the comparative particle meaning "as" or "like."

d After παρακαλοῦντες ("exhorting") ὑμᾶς ("you") is omitted by א lat^vg.cod.

e For μαρτυρόμενοι ("charging") D* F G byz read μαρτυρούμενοι ("being witnessed to"), which is inappropriate in this context.

f For τοῦ καλοῦντος, present participle ("who calls"), τοῦ καλέσαντος, aorist participle ("who called") is read by א A and a few minuscules with lat^a f vg syr cop.

Form/Structure/Setting

This paragraph completes the apostolic defense with a further appeal to the readers' recollection of the missionaries' conduct.

Schmithals (*Paul and the Gnostics*, 212, 213) argues that "Thessalonians B" (1:1–2:12 + 4:2–5:28) is editorially interrupted after 2:12 by the insertion of "Thessalonians D" (2:13–4:1), to be resumed at 4:2.

Comment

2:9. Μνημονεύετε, "you remember" (indicative rather than imperative). As the missionaries remembered the Thessalonians' "work of faith and labor of love" (1:3), so they expected that the Thessalonians would remember how they too had labored while they were with them.

τὸν κόπον ἡμῶν καὶ τὸν μόχθον, "our toil and moil" (Lightfoot), with a suggestion of hardship and fatigue.

νυκτὸς καὶ ἡμέρας ἐργαζόμενοι, presumably in tentmaking (σκηνοποιΐα, perhaps more generally "leather working"), so far as Paul himself was concerned (cf. Acts 18:3). A later teacher, Rabban Gamaliel III, gave voice to a traditional principle when he said that study of the Torah was excellent if it were combined with a secular occupation (*Pirqe 'Abot* 2.2), and this principle, in accordance with which Paul had been brought up, was carried over by him into his apostolic ministry. In Thessalonica, then, as later in Corinth (1 Cor 4:12) and Ephesus (Acts 19:12; 20:34), Paul maintained himself by manual labor, and his companions evidently did the same. A stay of several weeks in Thessalonica is implied. The phrase recurs in 2

Thess 3:8. Cf. 3:10, νυκτὸς καὶ ἡμέρας, "night and day," also Acts 20:31, νύκτα καὶ ἡμέραν . . . νουθετῶν, "admonishing all night and all day."

The question arises why nothing is said here of financial help received from Philippi during the mission in Thessalonica. In Phil 4:15, 16, Paul reminds the Christians in Philippi that when he left Macedonia, after his first gospel preaching there, they were the only church to communicate with him "in respect of giving and receiving" and adds that already in Thessalonica they sent to relieve his need καὶ ἅπαξ καὶ δίς (which may mean "and that more than once" or, less probably, "and more than once" elsewhere; for the Greek phrase cf. v 18 below). It may be that the money sent from Philippi was not sufficient to remove completely the need for manual labor in Thessalonica; it may be, too, that there was a desire not to embarrass the Thessalonian Christians by mentioning gifts received from other Christians. There was no occasion to make the Thessalonian Christians feel ashamed of themselves by using the kind of language which Paul uses to the church of Corinth in 2 Cor 11:8, 9.

πρὸς τὸ μὴ ἐπιβαρῆσαί τινα ὑμῶν (repeated in 2 Thess 3:8), "so as not to burden any of you"—i.e. financially (see comment on ἐν βάρει εἶναι, v 7 above). Other traveling preachers, both Christian (cf. 2 Cor 11:20) and non-Christian, did make themselves burdensome financially and in other ways. Paul in particular made it his policy to be different from them and to shut the mouths of those who would have liked to say that he, like others, was in this preaching business for what he could get out of it (cf. 2 Cor 11:12).

ἐκηρύξαμεν εἰς ὑμᾶς, "we proclaimed to you." For εἰς denoting the recipients of such a proclamation cf. Mark 14:9; Luke 24:47; Acts 17:15. The verb κηρύσσειν is frequently used in the NT for preaching the gospel (cf. Mark 1:14; 1 Cor 1:23, etc.); the noun κῆρυξ, "herald," from which it is derived, is used of Paul in 1 Tim 2:7; 2 Tim 1:11, and its own derivative κήρυγμα is used of the content of the preaching in Rom 16:25 (τὸ κήρυγμα Ἰησοῦ Χριστοῦ) and some other places.

τὸ εὐαγγέλιον τοῦ θεοῦ, "the gospel of God" as in vv 2, 8.

10. ὑμεῖς μάρτυρες καὶ ὁ θεός. This collocation of the Thessalonians' testimony and God's is repeated from v 5 (καθὼς οἴδατε . . . θεὸς μάρτυς). For a similar coincidence of divine and human testimony cf. John 15:26, 27, "But when the Counselor comes . . . he will bear witness to me; and you also are witnesses" (ἐκεῖνος μαρτυρήσει . . . καὶ ὑμεῖς δὲ μαρτυρεῖτε); Acts 5:32, "And we are witnesses to these things, and so is the Holy Spirit. . . ." (καὶ ἡμεῖς ἐσμεν μάρτυρες . . . καὶ τὸ πνεῦμα τὸ ἅγιον).

ὡς ὁσίως καὶ δικαίως καὶ ἀμέμπτως . . . ἐγενήθημεν. This use of adverbs rather than adjectives (ὅσιοι καὶ δίκαιοι καὶ ἄμεμπτοι) with γίνομαι is unusual (cf. Acts 20:18 in a similar context, πῶς . . . ἐγενόμην). For the regular adjectival construction cf. v 7, ἐγενήθημεν ἤπιοι. If (as Lightfoot would have it on the basis of classical usage) ὁσίως refers to the Godward aspect of the missionaries' conduct and δικαίως to its manward aspect, then ἀμέμπτως may imply that in neither aspect could any fault be found with it. But in fact it is their conduct and attitude to the Thessalonian Christians (ὑμῖν τοῖς πιστεύουσιν, "to you who believe,") that are in view throughout. Their δικαιοσύνη "righteousness" in dealings with men and women was ὁσιότης "holiness" in the sight of God. That the classical distinction between the two terms was blurred in Hellenistic Greek appears, e.g., from Wisd Sol 9:3, where God is said to govern the world "in holiness and righteousness (ἐν ὁσιότητι καὶ δικαιοσύνῃ)"; the same phrase occurs in Luke 1:75, where Zechariah speaks of God's promise that the children of Abraham should serve him "in holiness and righteousness."

ὑμῖν τοῖς πιστεύουσιν, "to you believers." The precise force of the dative has been disputed: Wohlenberg (following Theodoretus) takes the meaning to be "in the sight of you believers" and Rigaux understands "among you believers"; however, "in relation to (or 'toward') you believers" seems more natural.

11. καθάπερ οἴδατε, "just as you know"—a further appeal to the Thessalonians' personal knowledge of the facts (cf. vv 1, 2, 5, 9, 10).

ἕνα ἕκαστον ὑμῶν. Cf. Acts 20:31, νουθετῶν ἕνα ἕκαστον, "(for three years I did not cease night or day) to admonish every one (with tears.)"

ὡς πατὴρ τέκνα ἑαυτοῦ, "as a father with his own children." Chrysostom, Pelagius and others after them have pointed out that, while Paul compares himself to a nurse or mother when he speaks of cherishing his converts, he compares himself to a father when he speaks of instructing them. In 1 Cor 4:14, 15 he claims the privilege of giving his Corinthian converts fatherly admonition because it was he who "became their father in Christ Jesus through the gospel." Lightfoot, who accepts the reading νήπιοι in v 7, agrees that ἤπιοι "makes very excellent sense" and compares Homer, Odyssey 2.47, πατὴρ δ᾽ ὡς ἤπιος ἦεν, "he (Odysseus) was gentle as a father," and Iliad 24.770, ἑκυρὸς δὲ πατὴρ ὡς ἤπιος αἰεί, "my father-in-law (Priam) has always been gentle as a father."

Both the maternal and paternal figures are used of the God of Israel in the OT; cf. Isa 66:13 ("as one whom his mother comforts, so I will comfort you") and Ps. 103:13 ("as a father pities his children, so the Lord pities those who fear him").

12. παρακαλοῦντες ὑμᾶς καὶ παραμυθούμενοι, "exhorting you and encouraging." The two verbs are practically synonymous. The second is less common in Paul's writings than the first: when he uses it (or a cognate noun) it is regularly in association with παρακαλεῖν (or the noun παράκλησις), perhaps so as to emphasize the idea of encouragement (which is the predominant sense of παρακαλεῖν/παράκλησις in the NT). Lightfoot suggests that παρακαλεῖν may mean "exhort to a particular line of conduct" (cf. v 3, παράκλησις) and παραμυθεῖσθαι "encourage to continue in that course"; but it is doubtful if this fine distinction can be maintained. (Cf. 5:14; also Phil 2:1, παράκλησις . . . παραμύθιον.)

μαρτυρόμενοι, "charging (you)"; this verb has lost its original force of invoking witnesses (μάρτυρες). It has a more authoritative nuance than the two preceding verbs (cf. Gal 5:3; Eph 4:17).

εἰς τὸ περιπατεῖν ὑμᾶς, "that you should walk." (For the construction cf. 3:10; 4:9). This ethical sense of περιπατεῖν ("conduct oneself") is found in a number of NT writers (as well as in non-biblical writers) but is particularly common in Paul (cf. 4:1, 12; 2 Thess 3:6, 11). It may be compared with the use of ὁδός ("way") to denote a course of life, either absolutely (as when ἡ ὁδός is used of Christianity in Acts 9:2; 19:9, 23; 24:14, 22) or in a construction which makes its meaning plain (as in 1 Cor 4:17, where Paul speaks of τὰς ὁδούς μου τὰς ἐν Χριστῷ Ἰησοῦ, "my ways in Christ Jesus"). According to the context, περιπατεῖν may denote evil or good conduct (for the former cf. 2 Cor 4:2, περιπατοῦντες ἐν πανουργίᾳ, "walking in craftiness"; 10:2, κατὰ σάρκα περιπατοῦντας, "walking according to the flesh"). Here the context indicates clearly the character of the "walk": it is to be ἀξίως τοῦ θεοῦ, "in a manner worthy of God." Cf. Rom 16:2 (ἀξίως τῶν ἀγίων, "in a manner worthy of the saints"); Eph 4:1 (ἀξίως περιπατῆσαι τῆς κλήσεως, "walk worthily of the calling"); Phil 1:27 (ἀξίως τοῦ εὐαγγελίου τοῦ Χριστοῦ πολιτεύεσθε, "live worthily of the gospel of Christ"); Col. 1:10 (περιπατῆσαι ἀξίως τοῦ κυρίου, "walk worthily of the Lord").

τοῦ καλοῦντος ὑμᾶς, "the one who calls you." The act of calling is in the past (cf. ἐκάλεσεν ἡμᾶς ὁ θεός . . . ἐν ἁγιασμῷ, 4:7; similarly 2 Thess 2:14), but God is described as ὁ καλῶν ὑμᾶς, "your caller," in a timeless sense (cf. 5:24; Gal 5:8). For the aorist participle, read by some witnesses here, cf. Gal 1:6; 2 Tim 1:9.

εἰς τὴν ἑαυτοῦ βασιλείαν καὶ δόξαν, "into his own kingdom and glory." The kingdom of God, in the Pauline writings, is to be manifested with the inbreaking of the age to come, at the resurrection of the people of Christ (cf. 2 Thess 1:5). The interval between the resurrection of Christ and that of his people is the period of Christ's reign; when that period is completed, with the destruction of death, the last of the enemies referred to in Ps 110:1, Christ hands over the kingdom to God (1 Cor 15:23–28). The kingdom of God is held out as something which his children are to inherit—an inheritance from which evildoers are excluded (1 Cor 6:9, 10; Gal 5:21; Eph 5:5). The manifestation of the kingdom of God will coincide with the revelation of his glory, in which his children will share; cf. Rom 5:2, where they "rejoice in hope of the glory of God"; 8:18, where the sufferings of the present are insignificant in comparison with "the glory that is to be revealed to us"; 2 Cor 4:17, where the "slight momentary affliction" of the present is actually preparing for believers "an eternal weight of glory beyond all comparison."

In Col 1:12, 13, God is said not only to have qualified believers "to share in the inheritance of the saints in light" (which is tantamount to his calling them "into his own kingdom and glory") but also to have "delivered us from the dominion of darkness and transferred us to the kingdom of his beloved Son" (which is in keeping with Paul's teaching about Christ's present reign).

Paul does on occasion speak of "the kingdom of God" in a less explicitly future sense, to denote life in accordance with the gospel: "the kingdom

of God does not consist in talk but in power" (1 Cor 4:20; cf. 1 Thess
1:5); it means "righteousness and peace and joy in the Holy Spirit" (Rom
14:17; cf. 1 Thess 1:6). So here, those who are called by God "into his
own kingdom and glory" may already live in the good of that coming
heritage. They are enabled to do this, as other letters make plain, because
they have already received in the Spirit the firstfruits, the guarantee or
the seal of the glory yet to be revealed (Rom 8:23; 2 Cor 1:22; 5:5). This
distinctively Pauline presentation of the Spirit's present ministry does not
find expression in the Thessalonian correspondence, but it may be in some
degree implied.

Explanation

In their concern not to live at the expense of their converts, the missionaries worked with their hands to earn their own living. This was no doubt
inevitable when first they came to Thessalonica or any other pagan city;
there was no one there on whom they could depend for support. As Jews,
they might have sought the support and hospitality of members of the
Jewish community; but as their mission was the presentation of the law-
free gospel of Christ to Gentiles, Jewish support and hospitality could
not be counted upon, and in any case they preferred to be independent.
If voluntary hospitality was offered for the gospel's sake, that was another
matter. But this would not normally be forthcoming until their message
had been heard and accepted, as by Lydia in Philippi (Acts 16:14, 15)
and perhaps by Jason in Thessalonica (Acts 17:5–9). But even after they
had made converts, Paul and his co-workers took care to give no occasion
for saying that they lived at their converts' expense. Their situation was
different from that of the disciples whom Jesus sent out two by two during
his Galilean ministry. As Israelites announcing the fulfillment of God's
promises to his people they could expect to be provided with simple bed
and board by fellow Israelites, many of whom were themselves looking
for the kingdom of God.

Nor, in the earlier days of their stay in a previously unevangelized city,
could Paul, Silvanus and Timothy look for support to a home base. The
Jerusalem church, which was always in need of material support itself,
was in no position to send supplies to Silvanus, and even while Antioch
was Paul's base, there is no hint that the church there undertook to make
provision for his temporal needs. In any case, it is doubtful if Paul's relations
with the Antiochene church remained the same after his breach with Barnabas. His friends in Philippi sent him voluntary gifts while he was in Thessalonica, but these were occasional and probably insufficient to maintain him
for long.

The somewhat self-conscious way in which Paul repeatedly refers to
his earning his own living, sometimes emphasizing his working with his
"own hands," suggests that, even if he had been taught a trade, his outlook
was that of the "professional" class, not that of a manual laborer. But

the fact that, unlike so many of his own class or profession, he did earn his livelihood by manual labor was bound to make an impression on his converts and made it easier for them to pay heed to his exhortation that they too should work with their own hands and earn their own living (cf. 4:11; 2 Thess 3:10).

The Christian minister is expected to give practical instruction to his fellow Christians, but not by way of dictation. Since he cannot rule by decree if he is to be true to the spirit of Christ, he must guide by example. And people are more ready to be moved by the example of those who can honestly say, "our boast is this, the testimony of our conscience that we have behaved in the world, and still more toward you, with holiness and godly sincerity, not by earthly wisdom but by the grace of God" (2 Cor 1:12).

The highest of all incentives is set before the Thessalonians when they are charged "to lead a life worthy of God." One section of the Pentateuch is called "the law of holiness" because of its recurring refrain: "You shall be holy; for I the LORD your God am holy" (Lev 19:2). In the NT as in the OT the people of God are called upon to display his character. By faith the Thessalonian Christians were already heirs of God's kingdom and glory: let them lead lives worthy of that heritage and of the God who had called them to share in it.

Further Thanksgiving (1 Thess 2:13–16)

Bibliography

Ackroyd, P. R. "חצנ—εἰς τέλος." *Exp Tim* 80 (1968–69) 126. Bacon, B. W. "Wrath 'unto the uttermost'." *Expositor*, series 8, 24 (1922) 356–376. Bammel, E. "Judenverfolgung und Naherwartung. Zur Eschatologie des ersten Thessalonicherbriefs." *ZTK* 56 (1959) 294–315. Baur, F. C. *Paul: his Life and Works.* Tr. A. Menzies. II. London: Williams and Norgate, 1875, 85–97. Boers, H. "The Form-Critical Study of Paul's Letters: 1 Thessalonians as a Case Study." *NTS* 22 (1975–76) 140–158. Bornkamm, G. *Early Christian Experience.* Tr. P. L. Hammer. London: SCM Press, 1969, 1–13 ("God's Word and Man's Word in the New Testament"). Cerfaux, L. *The Christian in the Theology of St. Paul.* Tr. L. Soiron. London: Geoffrey Chapman, 1967. Cerfaux, L. *The Church in the Theology of St. Paul.* Tr. G. Webb and A. Walker. Edinburgh/London/New York: Nelson, 1959. Collins, R. F. "The Theology of Paul's First Letter to the Thessalonians." *Louv. Stud.* 6 (1977) 315–337. Coppens, J. "Miscellanées bibliques, LXXX. Une diatribe antijuive dans 1 Thess II, 13–16." *ETL* 51 (1975) 90–95. Davies, W. D. "Paul and the People of Israel." *NTS* 24 (1977–78) 4–39. Davies, W. D. *The Setting of the Sermon on the Mount.* Cambridge: Cambridge University Press, 1964. Eckart, K.-G. "Der zweite echte Brief des Apostels Paulus an die Thessalonicher." *ZTK* 58 (1961) 30–44. Ellison, H. L. *The Mystery of Israel: An Exposition of Romans 9–11.* Exeter: Paternoster Press, 1966. Gerhardsson, B. *Memory and Manuscript. Oral Tradition and Written Transmission in Rabbinic Judaism and Early Christianity.* Tr. E. J. Sharpe. Acta Seminarii Neotestamentici Upsaliensis, 22. Lund: Gleerup/Copenhagen: Munksgaard, [2]1964. Giblin, C. H. *In Hope of God's Glory.* New York: Herder, 1970. Goguel, M. *The Birth of Christianity.* Tr. H. C. Snape. London: Allen and Unwin, 1953. Jewett, R. "The Agitators and the Galatian Congregation." *NTS* 17 (1970–71) 198–212. Lake, K. *The Earlier Epistles of St. Paul.* London: Rivingtons, [2]1914. Michel, O. "Fragen zu 1 Thessalonicher 2, 14–16: Antijüdische Polemik bei Paulus." In W. Eckert *et al.* (ed.), *Antijudaismus im Neuen Testament? Exegetische und systematische Beiträge.* Abhandlungen zum christlich—jüdischen Dialog, 1. München: Kaiser, 1967, 50–59. Munck, J. *Christ and Israel.* Tr. I. Nixon. Philadelphia: Fortress, 1964. O'Brien, P. T. *Introductory Thanksgivings in the Letters of Paul.* NovTSup 49. Leiden: Brill, 1977. Okeke, G. E. "1 Thess. ii.13–16: The Fate of the Unbelieving Jews." *NTS* 27 (1980–81) 127–136. Orchard, J. B. "Thessalonians and the Synoptic Gospels." *Bib* 19 (1938) 19–42. Pearson, B. A. "1 Thessalonians 2:13–16: A Deutero-Pauline Interpolation." *HTR* 64 (1971) 79–94. Richardson, P. *Israel in the Apostolic Church.* SNTSMS 10. Cambridge: Cambridge University Press, 1969. Sanders, J. T. "The Transition from Opening Epistolary Thanksgiving to Body in the Letters of the Pauline Corpus." *JBL* 81 (1962) 348–362. Schermann, T. (ed.) *Prophetarum Vitae Fabulosae.* Leipzig: Teubner, 1907. Schippers, R. "The Pre-Synoptic Tradition in 1 Thessalonians II 13–16." *NovT* 8 (1966) 223–234. Schmithals, W. *Paul and the Gnostics.* Tr. J. E. Steely. Nashville/New York: Abingdon, 1972. Schoeps, H.-J. "Die jüdischen Prophetenmorde." In *Aus frühchristlicher Zeit.* Tübingen: Mohr, 1950, 126–143. Schubert, P. *Form and Function of the Pauline Thanksgivings.* BZNW 20. Berlin: Töpelmann, 1939. Torrey, C. C. (ed.) *The Lives of the Prophets.* JBLMS 1. Philadelphia: Society of Biblical Literature and Exegesis, 1946. **Wenham, D.** "Paul and the Synoptic Apocalypse." In *Gospel Perspectives* ii, ed. R. T. France and D. Wenham. Sheffield: JSOT Press (1981) 345–75. **White, J. L.** *Form and Function of the Body of the Greek Letter.* SBL Dissertation Series 2. Missoula, MT: Scholars Press, 1972. **Wilson, W. E.** "1 Thessalonians ii.16." *ExpTim* 35 (1923–24), 43–44.

Translation

¹³ *And* [a] *for this reason we also give thanks to God unceasingly, that when you received the word of God which you heard from us, you accepted it not as a merely human word, but as it truly is, the word of God, which works effectually in you believers.*

¹⁴ *For you, brothers, became imitators of the churches of God in Christ Jesus which are in Judea, in that you in your turn suffered the same things at the hands of your own fellow-countrymen as they for their part did at the hands of the Jews—* ¹⁵ *the very people who had killed the Lord Jesus and the* [b] *prophets and have driven us out, who do not please God and are opposed to all mankind,* ¹⁶ *who prevent us from speaking to the Gentiles with a view to their salvation. Their continuous aim has been to fill full the measure of their sins. But wrath* [c] *has overtaken* [d] *them for good and all.*

Notes

[a] καί is omitted by D F G byz lat syr^pesh.

[b] Between τούς and προφήτας D¹ Ψ byz syr insert ἰδίους ("their own prophets"); according to Tertullian (*Adv. Marc.* 5.15.1), the insertion is originally Marcion's.

[c] After ἡ ὀργή D F G 629 lat add τοῦ θεοῦ, "the wrath of God," which of course is implied (cf. Rom 1:18; Eph 5:6; Col 3:6; also John 3:36; Rev 19:15).

[d] For ἔφθασεν (aorist) ἔφθακεν (perfect) is read by B D* Ψ 104 *pc.* Whichever reading be adopted, it may reflect the OT prophetic perfect.

Form/Structure/Setting

Schmithals (*Paul and the Gnostics,* 176–181, 213) finds in 2:13 the beginning of a new letter, which continues to 4:1(2); this new letter has been adapted to its present position by the omission of the prescript and the amplification of an original εὐχαριστοῦμεν κτλ to καὶ διὰ τοῦτο καὶ ἡμεῖς εὐχαριστοῦμεν κτλ. This analysis of 1 Thessalonians has not commanded much agreement. But some critical questions are certainly raised by 2:13–16.

For example, do these four verses constitute a second thanksgiving, after the earlier and longer thanksgiving of 1:2–10 (so Sanders, "Transition," 356)? In favor of this it is pointed out that 2:12 ends with something in the nature of a doxology. Or should vv 13–16 be regarded as a continuation of the earlier thanksgiving, the intervening passage being a digression (so Schubert, *Form and Function,* 17, 18; according to him the thanksgiving continues from 1:2 to 3:13)? It is better to recognize 2:13 as introducing a further thanksgiving: the opening words καὶ διὰ τοῦτο καὶ ἡμεῖς εὐχαριστοῦμεν are too emphatic to be merely resumptive of εὐχαριστοῦμεν in 1:2, and the apologia of 2:1–12 is an integral part of the letter and no mere digression.

The four verses (13–16) have been considered as an interpolated paragraph. Pearson ("1 Thessalonians 2:13–16") finds a reference to the disaster of A.D. 70 in v 16c ("wrath has overtaken them for good and all"); he discerns in this clause and those immediately preceding an echo of 2 Chr 36:16 ("they kept mocking the messengers of God, despising his words, and scoffing at his prophets, till the wrath of the LORD rose against his people, till there was no remedy"). (The clause "preventing us from speaking to the Gentiles, with a view to their salvation" would be added to adapt the passage to the circumstances of the Pauline mission, as narrated in Acts.) But vv 15, 16 (it is argued) are too closely related to vv 13, 14 for the second half of the paragraph to be regarded as an interpolation and the first half as authentic; in any case, Pearson sees the thanksgiving of vv 13, 14 as "saying the same thing" as the opening part of the earlier thanksgiving of 1:2–10 (compare especially 1:6 with 2:14), so that "the conclusion . . . which form-critical analysis suggests is this: vv. 13–16 do not belong to Paul's original letter at all, but represent a later interpolation into the text" (91).

Boers ("Form Critical Study," 149–152) adds further form-critical arguments in support of Pearson's thesis: the elimination of vv 13–16 solves "most of the problems in connection with the form and function of the letter" and, in particular, reveals the intimate relation between the "apostolic apology" of 2:1–12 and the "apostolic Parousia" of 2:17–3:13 (see below, pp. 54, 65, 66).

In itself, "the structural argument is not certain" (Davies, "Paul and Israel," 6); the emphatic καὶ διὰ τοῦτο καὶ ἡμεῖς (v 13) may have special force in the circumstances of the missionaries' dialogue with the Thessalonian church (see comment below).

Attention has been drawn to similarities of theme and language between vv 15, 16 and passages in the synoptic Gospels, particularly Matt 23:29–36, with its emphasis on the killing (ἀποκτείνειν) of the prophets, the persecuting (διώκειν) of the messengers of God, the filling up (πληροῦν) of the measure of ancestral guilt, and the certainty of judgment on "this generation." While this series of parallels cannot be taken as evidence for the dependence of the present passage on Matthew (so Orchard, "Thessalonians and the Synoptic Gospels"), it certainly points to dependence on a common, "pre-synoptic" source (cf. Schippers, "The Pre-Synoptic Tradition," 230–234). An indication of the character of this source may be provided in Luke 11:49, where the warning of Matt 23:34–36 is introduced by the words: "Therefore also the Wisdom of God said . . ."—the source, that is to say, is a "wisdom" logion.

Comment

2:13. Καὶ διὰ τοῦτο καὶ ἡμεῖς εὐχαριστοῦμεν, "And for this reason we also give thanks." According to the context τοῦτο in διὰ τοῦτο may refer either backward or forward (the classical distinction between τοῦτο referring backward and τόδε referring forward was blurred in Hellenistic Greek). In Col 1:9 the similarly constructed διὰ τοῦτο καὶ ἡμεῖς . . . οὐ παυόμεθα . . . προσευχόμενοι refers backward to the news brought by Epaphras (vv 3–8); there is no reason for the apostle's prayers given in the words which follow, to which διὰ τοῦτο could refer forward. Here, however, the ὅτι clause which follows supplies the reason: "And for this reason we also give thanks . . .— namely, that . . ." The καί before διὰ τοῦτο is the simple copula; the καί after διὰ τοῦτο may emphasize either εὐχαριστοῦμεν, "and for this reason also we give thanks" (so BDF §442.12; O'Brien, *Introductory Thanksgivings* 154; also Boers, "Form-Critical Study," 150, citing von Dobschütz) or, as the word order might suggest, ἡμεῖς, "and for this reason we in our turn give thanks." The latter construction would be explained if Timothy brought back, whether by word of mouth or in writing, a message from the Thessalonians expressing their gratitude that the saving message had come to them: "We thank God that you brought us the gospel." To this the missionaries might well reply, "And we for our part thank God unceasingly that you accepted it." This thanksgiving does not merely continue or repeat that of 1:2–10; it amplifies it.

ἀδιαλείπτως, "without intermission," "unceasingly," as in 1:2, 3 (cf. 5:17; Rom 1:9).

ὅτι . . . ἐδέξασθε, "that (because) you accepted," catching up and explaining διὰ τοῦτο.

παραλαβόντες, "having received"; παραλαμβάνειν is the verb especially used of receiving a message or body of instruction handed down by tradition, to be delivered (παραδιδόναι) to others in turn. Cf. the noun παράδοσις ("tradition") in 2 Thess 2:15; 3:6 (also 1 Cor 11:2). The correlative verbs παραλαμβάνειν and παραδιδόναι are used together in 1 Cor 11:23; 15:3. Here, as in 1 Cor 15:3, the reference is to the gospel, delivered by the missionaries and received by the Thessalonians (cf. Davies, *Setting,* 354; B. Gerhardsson, *Memory and Manuscript* 265, 290, 295 f.).

λόγον ἀκοῆς παρ' ἡμῶν τοῦ θεοῦ, "(when you *received*) the word of God which you heard from us." So Davies translates (*Setting,* 354), taking λόγον closely with τοῦ θεοῦ and ἀκοῆς with παρ' ἡμῶν. Or the force may be: "you received the word of hearing (the word which you heard) from us, but really it was *God's* word" (τοῦ θεοῦ occupies an emphatic position after παρ' ἡμῶν and perhaps in contrast to it). For λόγος ἀκοῆς cf. Heb 4:2; also Rom 10:17, ἡ πίστις ἐξ ἀκοῆς, ἡ δὲ ἀκοὴ διὰ ῥήματος Χριστοῦ ("faith comes from what is heard, and what is heard comes by the preaching of Christ"); Gal 3:2, 5, ἐξ ἔργων νόμου ἢ ἐξ ἀκοῆς πίστεως ("by legal works or by hearing with faith"). The OT background for this use of λόγος ἀκοῆς or ἀκοὴ πίστεως in the sense of the gospel may be found in Isa 53:1, "Who has believed what he has heard from us?" (τίς ἐπίστευσεν τῇ ἀκοῇ ἡμῶν;), which is used in the NT as a *testimonium* of the gospel (cf. John 12:38; Rom 10:16). In παρ' ἡμῶν the preposition catches up the prefix of παραλαβόντες.

ἐδέξασθε οὐ λόγον ἀνθρώπων ἀλλὰ καθὼς ἐστιν ἀληθῶς λόγον θεοῦ, "you accepted it, not as a (merely) human word, but as it truly is, the word of God." While παραλαβόντες indicates that the message was delivered to them, ἐδέξασθε indicates their own initiative in eagerly embracing it.

Paul was accustomed to having his message dismissed by his enemies as man-made, something devised by himself; hence his solemn protest in Gal 1:11, 12: "the gospel which was preached by me . . . is not according to man; for I did not receive it (παρέλαβον) from man nor was I taught it (by man)." He therefore found it especially encouraging when it was sincerely and spontaneously welcomed as good news from God.

ὃς καὶ ἐνεργεῖται ἐν ὑμῖν τοῖς πιστεύουσιν, "which works effectively in you believers." The contrast between word and power is repeated from 1:5. The word of human beings, however wise in substance or eloquent in expression, cannot produce spiritual life: this is the prerogative of the word of God, which works effectually (ἐνεργεῖται) in believers. Like the Corinthians a few weeks later, the Thessalonians had proved that "the word of the cross . . . is the power of God" (1 Cor 1:18).

14. Ὑμεῖς γὰρ μιμηταὶ ἐγενήθητε, "for you became imitators." In 1:6 the Thessalonians are commended for imitating the missionaries, not least by becoming missionaries in their turn: this was a token of the genuineness of their faith. Now a further token of the genuineness of their faith is said to be their imitation of the Judean churches. But this was not a deliberate imitation—they knew of the Judean churches mostly by hearsay—rather, the experience of the Judean churches was reproduced in the Thessalonian church. This was no merely external resemblance. Persecution, according to the NT, is a natural concomitant of Christian faith, and for the believers in Thessalonica to undergo suffering for Christ's sake proves that they are fellow-members of the same body as the Judean churches.

τῶν ἐκκλησιῶν τοῦ θεοῦ τῶν οὐσῶν ἐν τῇ Ἰουδαίᾳ ἐν Χριστῷ Ἰησοῦ, "of the churches of God in Christ Jesus in Judea." Cf. the similar expression in Gal 1:22, ταῖς ἐκκλησίαις τῆς Ἰουδαίας ταῖς ἐν Χριστῷ, "the churches of Judea which are in Christ." These "churches of God" (cf. 2 Thess 1:4) comprised the original church of God in Jerusalem (cf. Gal 1:13; 1 Cor 15:9), now in dispersion (as a result of the persecution which broke out after Stephen's death), together with her daughter-churches. (In Acts 9:31 they are referred to comprehensively in the singular as "the church throughout all Judea and Galilee and Samaria.") The participle τῶν οὐσῶν is to be taken closely with ἐν τῇ Ἰουδαίᾳ. Cf. Acts 13:1, ἐν Ἀντιοχείᾳ κατὰ τὴν οὖσαν ἐκκλησίαν ("in Antioch, in the church that was there"), where (as also in Acts 11:22) the participle of εἶναι has practically the sense of "local" (we still speak of "the local church").

The phrase ἐν Χριστῷ Ἰησοῦ (cf. 1:1, ἐν θεῷ πατρὶ κτλ) denotes the fellowship which binds together Christian churches as surely as it does individual

Christians; their life is caught up into, and sustained from, the life of the risen Christ.

ὅτι τὰ αὐτὰ ἐπάθετε καὶ ὑμεῖς ὑπὸ τῶν ἰδίων συμφυλετῶν, "because you in your turn suffered the same things at the hands of your own fellow-countrymen." συμφυλέτης is a Hellenistic compound conveying the sense which in Attic Greek was conveyed by the simple φυλέτης, "member of the same φυλή (tribe)." According to Acts 17:5 the opposition to the missionaries in Thessalonica was fomented by members of the local Jewish community, but from the present reference it appears that the persecution of the converts was the work of their fellow-Thessalonians.

καθὼς καὶ αὐτοὶ ὑπὸ τῶν Ἰουδαίων, "as they for their part (suffered) at the hands of the Jews." καθὼς replaces ἅ, which might have been expected after the antecedent τὰ αὐτά. One could translate Ἰουδαῖοι here as "Judeans," since it was Jews of Judea who persecuted the Judean churches, and not "the Jews" in a more general sense—although it is "the Jews" in a more general sense who form the antecedent to the relative (participial) clauses of vv 15, 16.

The persecution of the Judean churches intended here might be the persecution following Stephen's death. But in that persecution Paul had played an active part; yet not the slightest hint of that is given here, in contrast to Gal 1:22, 23, where he is mentioned as the "former persecutor" of "the churches of Judea which are in Christ." One might think also (with Bacon) of the persecution of "some who belonged to the church" initiated between A.D. 41 and 44 by the elder Herod Agrippa (Acts 12:1). It appears, however, that the apostles, rather than the rank and file, were the targets of Herod Agrippa's attack. Probably we should think here of a more recent persecution associated with the increase of Zealot activity in Judea around the time of Ventidius Cumanus's arrival as procurator in A.D. 48 (cf. Josephus, *Antiq.* 20.105–136). Jewett finds good reason to believe that this activity was responsible for the circumcising campaign in the churches of Antioch and Galatia as well as for the pressure on Jewish Christians in Judea itself ("Agitators," 204–206).

15. τῶν καὶ τὸν κύριον ἀποκτεινάντων Ἰησοῦν, "who killed the Lord Jesus." Thus far one could agree with Giblin that Paul "does not intend to denounce any racial or national group, but to thank God for the apostolic effectiveness of the Thessalonians' conversion," and "to elaborate on the basic pattern of persecution which he sees verified in the life of the Church and, ultimately, in the life of Christ himself" (*In Hope*, 13). But why, then, are charges piled up against one national group in vv 15, 16, while nothing more is said of the other group mentioned—the readers' fellow-countrymen?

The first charge against the Ἰουδαῖοι (apart from their persecuting the churches of Judea) is that they "killed the Lord Jesus." This is the only place in the Pauline corpus where "the Jews" are made responsible for his death. Such language is more characteristic of the Fourth Gospel (where "the Jews" in this respect are the chief-priestly establishment); even in

Acts the responsibility is limited to the Jerusalemites and their rulers (Acts 2:23, 36; 3:13–17; 7:52; 13:27, 28). In the only other place in Paul's writings where the agents of Jesus' death are specified, they are "the rulers of this age" (1 Cor 2:8), by whom we are probably to understand the *kosmokratores* of the spiritual realm, who use human beings as their instruments (cf. Col 2:15).

καὶ τοὺς προφήτας, "and the prophets." Cf. Matt 23:37; Luke 11:47–51; 13:33, 34 (where Jerusalem is more particularly in view as the slayer of prophets); Acts 7:52 (where the killing of "the Righteous One" is the logical conclusion to the killing of those who foretold his coming). The deaths of the prophets are mostly undocumented in the OT, but at a later time they became the heroes of martyrologies which related, for example, how Isaiah was sawn in two under Manasseh (*Mart Isa* 5:1–14) and Jeremiah was stoned to death by his fellow-Jews who compelled him to go down to Egypt with them (cf. Tertullian, *Scorp.* 8; Jerome, *Adv. Jov.* 2.37). See Scherman (ed.), *Prophetarum Vitae Fabulosae;* Torrey (ed.), *Lives of the Prophets;* Schoeps, "Die jüdischen Prophetenmorde." On the other hand, Lake, with less probability, thinks that Christian prophets (such as Stephen and James the Zebedean) are in view here (*Epistles,* 87, n. 2).

καὶ ἡμᾶς ἐκδιωξάντων "and drove us out," perhaps with special reference to the recent expulsion of Paul and his friends from Thessalonica (Acts 17:5–10), followed by their forced departure from Beroea (Acts 17:13, 14).

καὶ θεῷ μὴ ἀρεσκόντων, "and do not please God." Cf. Rom 8:8, οἱ δὲ ἐν σαρκὶ ὄντες θεῷ ἀρέσαι οὐ δύνανται ("those who are 'in the flesh' cannot please God"), from which it is evident that in Paul's eyes the charge of displeasing God was one that could be leveled impartially against unbelieving Jews and Gentiles. By contrast, the Thessalonian Christians had been taught how they should please God (πῶς δεῖ ὑμᾶς . . . ἀρέσκειν θεῷ, 4:1). The impression that we have to do in vv 15, 16 with a piece of indiscriminate anti-Jewish polemic is strengthened by the following words: καὶ πᾶσιν ἀνθρώποις ἐναντίων, "and (are) contrary to all mankind." This sounds like an echo of slanders current in the Greco–Roman world. Tacitus, for example, says of the Jews, *aduersus omnes alios hostile odium,* "toward all others (i.e. not of their own race) they cherish hatred of a kind normally reserved for enemies" (*Hist.* 5.5.2). Earlier than Tacitus, and indeed contemporary with Paul, was the Egyptian Apion, who went so far as to say that the Jews swear by the Creator to show no good will to any alien, least of all to Greeks (Josephus, *C. Ap.* 2.121). (The same slander soon rubbed off on Christians who, according to Tacitus, *Ann.* 15.44.5, were accused of "hatred of the human race.") Such sentiments are incongruous on the lips of Paul (whose attitude to his fellow-Jews finds clear expression in Rom 9:1–5; 10:1–4; 11:25–32), nor can he be readily envisaged as subscribing to them even if they were expressed in this form by someone else.

16. κωλυόντων ἡμᾶς τοῖς ἔθνεσιν λαλῆσαι ἵνα σωθῶσιν, "preventing us from

speaking to the Gentiles with a view to their salvation." This conduct is repeatedly illustrated in Acts (e.g. 13:45–50; 14:2, 19, and, in Thessalonica itself, 17:5, ζηλώσαντες δὲ οἱ Ἰουδαῖοι). The ἵνα clause has its proper final force: the purpose of the missionaries' approach to the Gentiles was that they might come to salvation through believing the message; the purpose of the opposition was that the Gentiles might pay no heed to the message (and so, from the missionaries' point of view, be prevented from coming to salvation).

εἰς τὸ ἀναπληρῶσαι αὐτῶν τὰς ἁμαρτίας πάντοτε, "to fill up their sins continually"; cf. NEB: "All this time they have been making up the full measure of their guilt." In similar passages elsewhere in NT it is by their treatment of the Messiah that the heirs of those who killed the prophets complete the work that their fathers began; cf. Matt 23:32, καὶ ὑμεῖς πληρώσατε τὸ μέτρον τῶν πατέρων ὑμῶν ("do you, then, fill up the measure of your fathers"); also Acts 7:52 (cf. comment on καὶ τοὺς προφήτας, v 15). Here, however, the persecution of the Judean churches and the conduct reprobated in vv 15b–16a appear to be the "filling up" of the course of action initiated by the killing of "the Lord Jesus and the prophets."

The prefix ἀνα- in ἀναπληρῶσαι may be intensive: their cup of guilt was already well on the way to being filled, and their present conduct was filling it up to the brim (ἕως ἄνω, as in John 2:7). As for πάντοτε (a word of which pure Atticists disapproved), it emphasizes the continuousness of their persecution of the servants of God—of the prophets, then of Christ, and now of his messengers.

ἔφθασεν δὲ ἐπ' αὐτοὺς ἡ ὀργὴ εἰς τέλος, "but wrath has overtaken them for good and all." The "wrath" which is here said to have overtaken the Ἰουδαῖοι is an instance of the "coming wrath" (1:10) from which Jesus delivers his people. Without further delay it has come upon these Ἰουδαῖοι already. They have reached the point of no return in their opposition to the gospel and final, irremediable retribution is inevitable; indeed, it has come.

εἰς τέλος, "in full" (BDF § 207.3), "to the uttermost" (Lightfoot, 35). Ackroyd, "נצח," referring to D. W. Thomas, "The use of נצח as a superlative in Hebrew," JSS 1 (1956) 106–109, points out that εἰς τέλος, used in LXX to render נצח(ל), has in Hellenistic Greek the meaning "completely," "utterly" (as in John 13:1).

There is a remarkable parallel to this clause in T. Levi 6:11, ἔφθασεν δὲ ἡ ὀργὴ κυρίου ἐπ' αὐτοὺς εἰς τέλος, "but the wrath of the Lord came upon them (the people of Shechem) to the uttermost"; but it is not impossible that it has been influenced by the wording of our present passage.

Paul certainly did not believe in A.D. 57 that irrevocable retribution had overtaken the Jewish people; what had come on them, he said, was a partial and temporary "hardening" (πώρωσις) which was but the prelude, in the mysterious purpose of God, to the ultimate salvation of "all Israel" (Rom 11:25, 26). Unless he changed his mind radically on this subject in the interval of seven years between the writing of 1 Thessalonians and of Romans, it is difficult to make him responsible for the viewpoint expressed here.

It is uncertain what situation was interpreted as meaning that divine retribution had overtaken the Jews "for good and all" (NEB). Baur (*Paul* II, 88) thinks of the destruction of the temple and city of Jerusalem in A.D. 70. This agrees with Luke 21:20–24, where the desolation of Jerusalem is accompanied by the outpouring of "wrath (ὀργή) upon this people." Baur took this reference to the events of A.D. 70 (as he saw it to be) to be one of several proofs that 1 Thessalonians was a pseudepigraph; but if, on more general grounds, it be concluded that vv 15, 16 were added later to the text of 1 Thess 2, Baur's interpretation of v 16c could be maintained. True, the events of A.D. 70 did not have the disastrous effect on Jews of the dispersion that they had on those in Judea, but it is difficult to think of any other event or course of events in the first century to which the language of v 16c would be appropriate. Jewett ("Agitators," 205 n. 5) thinks of the massacre in the temple courts at the Passover of A.D. 49 (Josephus, *Bell.* 2.224–227; *Antiq.* 20.105–112); Bammel ("Judenverfolgung," 295, 306) thinks of the expulsion of Jews from Rome in that same year (Suetonius, *Claud.* 25.4). At the time when 1 Thessalonians was written, the coincidence of troubles for the Jews in so many parts of the world might have been thought to presage the end-time judgment, but the language of v 16c implies rather that the end-time judgment has come upon them ahead of time.

The question of the authenticity of vv 15 and 16, then, remains *sub judice.* Many scholars who, on balance, conclude that they are authentic are not completely satisfied with this conclusion. Even if "pre-synoptic" tradition is utilized in the wording of these verses, the writers must be supposed to have approved of it; otherwise they need not have used it. Few scholars could agree with Munck (*Christ and Israel,* 64) that v 16c "makes the same statement as Romans 11"—i.e. the wrath remains on the Jews until the end (εἰς τέλος) but then is lifted, the "end" coinciding with the coming of the Deliverer from Zion to turn away ungodliness from Jacob (Rom 11:25–27).

Davies ("Paul and Israel," 6–9) is conscious of the problem created by a comparison of our passage with the other Pauline letters, but "all this," he says, "warns against a too ready dismissal of 1 Thess ii. 13–16. On the whole, it is more justifiable to regard it as Pauline than otherwise." Nor, he argues, should we infer from this passage "that *all* Israel has been denied the election and the promise." The term here used is "Jews," not "Israelites" or "Hebrews": Paul "is thinking not of the Jewish people as a whole but of unbelieving Jews who have violently hindered the gospel." Similarly Marxsen, ad loc (49) insists that it is not "the Jews" as such who are denounced but those Jews who oppose the spread of the gospel and *thus* show themselves hostile to the best interests of mankind—to which it may be said that if this had been the meaning of the passage it might have been expressed more unambiguously.

Explanation

Paul and his friends could not refrain from overflowing in gratitude to God every time they thought of the Thessalonians' response to the gospel which they brought. They had no recourse to gimmicks to persuade people to accept their message; their preaching was not embellished with rhetorical devices. Paul's critics in Corinth may have been exaggerating when they said, "his bodily presence is weak, and his speech of no account" (2 Cor 10:10), but certainly there was nothing very attractive about his appearance or his delivery; and there is no reason to suppose that his companions made a better impression.

Yet the Thessalonian believers embraced the message promptly and wholeheartedly. This the missionaries found especially encouraging in the circumstances in which they came to Thessalonica, after the harsh treatment experienced in Philippi. It was to them a token that their message, presented in reliance upon the Spirit of God, was authenticated by the same Spirit in the hearers' hearts as the powerful and living Word of God. Bornkamm compares the response of the people of Sychar to the woman who told them about the amazing man she had met at the well: "It is no longer because of your words that we believe, for we have heard for ourselves, and we know that this is indeed the Savior of the world" (John 4:42).

Mention has been made already in the letter of the trouble which attended the bringing of the gospel to Thessalonica. Not only did the missionaries preach it "in the face of great opposition" (v 2); the believers in their turn "received the word in much affliction" (1:6). This affliction was rendered no lighter by the fact that they suffered it at the hands of their own people, their fellow-Thessalonians. They are now assured that there is nothing strange in this: the missionaries in fact might have quoted words which Jesus once spoke, echoing an OT prophet (Mic 7:6): "a man's foes will be those of his own household" (Matt 10:36). The earliest Christian churches, the church of Jerusalem and her daughter-churches, had experienced the same lot: their members were persecuted by *their* fellow-countrymen. Persecution for the sake of Christ is treated as evidence of the genuineness of the faith of those who suffer it. If people are persecuted for a form of belief or a course of action which they do not follow, they will protest; they may dissociate themselves from it in some practical and convincing way. But the Thessalonian Christians had no thought of disowning their new faith; they maintained it joyfully. They had been taught that persecution was a necessary part of Christian life. They had seen an example of this principle in the missionaries. Above all, Jesus himself had shown the way: he entered into glory through suffering, and so must his followers.

The Thessalonians' persecution lasted a long time, and so did their steadfastness. Some six years later Paul can still speak of the churches of Macedonia (not least, the church of Thessalonica) as enduring "a severe test of affliction" and continuing to give evidence of the reality of their faith in that "their abundance of joy and their extreme poverty have overflowed in a wealth of liberality" (2 Cor 8:1, 2). The "extreme poverty" might well have been the result of mob violence and looting; elsewhere in the NT members of another Christian group are reminded how, in the early days of their faith, they "joyfully accepted" the plundering of their property in addition to other forms of brutal maltreatment (Heb 10:32–34).

The difficulty of ascribing the denunciation of Jews in vv 15, 16 to Paul and his associates lies not in the fact that they themselves were also Jews. From the Song of Moses (Deut 32) onward, some of the most scathing denunciations of Jews in the Bible and out of it have been made by fellow-Jews, but they have been addressed to the people denounced. The words of vv 15, 16 are addressed to Gentiles and they have more in common with current Gentile disparagement of Jews than with the positive attitude of affection and hope which Paul elsewhere expresses with regard to his "kinsmen by race" (Rom 9:3).

Plans for a Second Visit (1 Thess 2:17–3:13)

(a) Out of Sight, Not Out of Mind (2:17–20)

Bibliography

Braumann, G., and **Brown, C.** "Present *(parousia)*." In *NIDNTT* 2.898–935. **Burkitt, F. C.** *Christian Beginnings.* London: University of London Press, 1924. **Deissmann, A.** *Light from the Ancient East.* Tr. L. R. M. Strachan. London: Hodder and Stoughton, [2] 1927. **Funk, R. W.** *Language, Hermeneutic, and Word of God.* New York: Harper, 1966. **Funk, R. W.** "The Apostolic *Parousia:* Form and Significance." In *Christian History and Interpretation: Studies Presented to John Knox,* ed. W. R. Farmer, C. F. D. Moule, R. R. Niebuhr. Cambridge: Cambridge University Press, 1967, 249–268. **Morris, L.** "Καὶ ἅπαξ καὶ δίς." *NovT* 1 (1956) 205–208. **Oepke, A.** "παρουσία, πάρειμι." *TDNT* 5.858–871. **Pearson, B. A.** "1 Thessalonians 2:13–16: A Deutero-Pauline Interpolation." *HTR* 64 (1971) 79–94. **Ramsay, W. M.** *St. Paul the Traveller and the Roman Citizen.* London: Hodder and Stoughton, [14] 1920. **Richardson, P.** *Israel in the Apostolic Church.* SNTSMS 10. Cambridge: Cambridge University Press, 1969. **Schmithals, W.** *Paul and the Gnostics.* Tr. J. E. Steely. Nashville/New York: Abingdon, 1972. **White, J. L.** *The Form and Function of the Body of the Greek Letter.* SBL Diss. Series 2. Missoula, MT: Scholars Press, 1972.

Translation

[17] *As for us, brothers, when we were bereft of you for the time being, in presence but not in heart, we bestirred ourselves the more abundantly, with great longing, to see you face to face again.* [18] *In fact we made up our minds to come to you—I Paul, for my part, more than once—but Satan hindered us.* [19] *For what is our hope, our joy, our crown of exultation,*[a] *in the presence of our Lord Jesus at his advent? Is it not indeed you?*[b] [20] *Yes, you are our glory and joy.*

Notes

[a] For καυχήσεως ("boasting") the synonym ἀγαλλιάσεως ("exultation") is read in A (cf. Tertullian, *De resurr. carn.* 24, *exultationis corona*).

[b] ἢ οὐχὶ καὶ ὑμεῖς; It seems preferable to accent the first word ἤ (synonymous with ἄρα), introducing a question not involving an alternative. If we accent ἤ (with the majority of editors, including Nestle-Aland[26]), it suggests that two questions have overlapped: (1) τίνες ἄλλοι ἢ ὑμεῖς; ("who other than you?") and (2) οὐχὶ καὶ ὑμεῖς; ("is it not indeed you?"). The interrogative clause of four words is parenthetical; the following phrase, "in the presence of our Lord Jesus at his advent," completes the question immediately preceding the parenthesis ("For what is our hope . . . ?").

Form/Structure/Setting

From 2:17 to 3:13 we have the section of the letter which White (*Form and Function*) calls the "body-closing." If the "body" of the letter imparts information, the "body-closing" is designed to maintain personal contact. A more acceptable designation for the section would indicate in some way the nature of its contents. Funk (*Language*, 274 n. 84; "The Apostolic *Parousia*") calls it "the apostolic *Parousia*," because in it the apostle's authority is made effective in the church addressed as though he were actually present (cf. 1 Cor 5:3–5). One important element in such a section he calls the "travelogue" (here, 3:1–8)—it embraces reasons for writing, the sending of a messenger and the intention to pay a personal visit, the writing of the letter and the sending of the letter being temporary substitutes for the personal visit. Funk (*Language*, 270) regards the whole section (2:17–3:8) as an integral part of the "body." Such matters of definition and classification vary from one student to the next.

The subsection 2:17–20 expresses the writers' fervent hope to revisit the Thessalonians and explains that hindrances, at present insuperable, have been put in their way.

Comment

2:17. ἡμεῖς δέ, "as for us." The writers resume the survey of their relations with the Thessalonian church, moving from the recollection of their manner of life while they were present with the church to an assurance of their longing to see their friends again.

ἀπορφανισθέντες ἀφ᾽ ὑμῶν, "bereft of you." They felt like parents who had lost their children, but happily (they hoped) only for the time being (πρὸς καιρὸν ὥρας) and only as regards bodily presence, not as regards abiding inward affection (προσώπῳ οὐ καρδίᾳ, with which cf. 1 Cor 5:3, ἀπὼν τῷ σώματι, παρὼν δὲ τῷ πνεύματι, "absent in body but present in spirit").

πρὸς καιρὸν ὥρας, "for the time being" combining πρὸς καιρόν (1 Cor 7:5) and πρὸς ὥραν (2 Cor 7:8; Gal 2:5; Phlm 15), both of which have the same sense of temporariness; the combination of the two intensifies this sense.

περισσοτέρως ἐσπουδάσαμεν . . . ἐν πολλῇ ἐπιθυμίᾳ. The piling up of words expressing eager longing emphasizes their ardent desire: "we bestirred ourselves the more abundantly, with great longing, to see you face to face again" (τὸ πρόσωπον ὑμῶν ἰδεῖν). There is nothing merely rhetorical about this language: Paul in particular, having no children of his own, found his unbounded capacity for paternal affection amply employed in his relationship with his converts. Cf. Gal 4:20, where he wishes he could be present right then with his Galatian converts (παρεῖναι πρὸς ὑμᾶς ἄρτι) and show them by his tone of voice the intensity of feeling which could not be adequately expressed in written words. On the other hand, when he knew that a personal encounter would be painful on both sides, he preferred to wait until the trouble had been set right, in written correspondence or through messengers, so that when in due course he met his converts, the occasion would be a joyful one for all of them (cf. 2 Cor 1:23–2:3; 13:10).

18. διότι "because"—"you can take this as true (the assurance of our longing to see you) *because* in fact we desired (and made an effort) to come to you . . ."

ἐγὼ μὲν Παῦλος, "I Paul." We may envisage Paul as interposing with these words, either orally while the letter was being dictated by a colleague or in writing when it was read over to him after completion (cf. Burkitt, *Christian Beginnings*, 132). Formally, μέν implies a following δέ, in the shape of some such phrase as οἱ δὲ ἄλλοι, "but as for the others (they may speak for themselves)." But only formally: all three spoke for themselves in confirming their desire to revisit Thessalonica (Timothy, in fact, was able to do so), but Paul has in mind special efforts that he himself had made.

καὶ ἅπαξ καὶ δίς, to be taken closely with ἐγὼ μὲν Παῦλος, probably, rather than with ἠθελήσαμεν ἐλθεῖν πρὸς ὑμᾶς, "we desired to come to you." For the phrase cf. Phil 4·16. Morris, after an examination of the phrase ἅπαξ καὶ δίς in LXX (cf. Deut 4:13; 1 Kgdms 17:39; Neh 13:20; 1 Macc 3:30), concludes that it means "more than once" and this is the sense here, the καί before ἅπαξ adding emphasis: "and that more than once."

καὶ ἐνέκοψεν ἡμᾶς ὁ σατανᾶς, "and (but) Satan hindered us." For ἐγκόπτειν in this sense cf. Rom 15:22, where Paul has been repeatedly hindered in his plans to visit Rome; Gal 5:7, where the Galatian Christians have been hindered in continuing the "race" they began so well.

σατανᾶς. The Aramaic emphatic state in −â supplied with the Greek masculine termination −ς is the invariable nominative form in NT (cf. Rom 16:20 for accusative σατανᾶν, 2 Thess 2:9 for gen. σατανᾶ, 1 Cor 5:5 for dative σατανᾷ). While שָׂטָן ("adversary," "prosecutor") is a common noun in the OT, Satan in the NT is the adversary *par excellence;* his main activity is putting obstacles in the path of the people of God, to prevent the will of God from being accomplished in and through them. Cf. 3:5, ὁ πειράζων, "the tempter."

Ramsay (*St. Paul*, 230–231) suggests that satanic agency was detected behind the politarchs' action in demanding security from Jason (Acts 17:9), binding him over to make sure that Paul, the alleged cause of the rioting, left Thessalonica and did not return. "This interpretation of the term 'Satan,' as denoting action taken by the governing power against the message from God, is in keeping with the figurative use of the word throughout the New Testament" (231).

In 2 Thess 2:9 the advent of the man of lawlessness is marked by the activity (ἐνέργεια) of Satan; this might indicate that satanic agency was discerned behind the lawless rioting of Acts 17:5 which forced the politarchs' hand. It is unlikely that, as Lightfoot tentatively suggests (cf. Pearson, "1 Thessalonians 2:13–16," 90 n. 94), there is any reference in the present passage to Paul's "splinter in the flesh" (2 Cor 12:7), even if it is called a "messenger (ἄγγελος) of Satan"—the effect of that visitation was not to hinder Paul but to discipline him and thus promote his usefulness in the gospel. Moreover, if this or some other illness is in view, it would not have hindered Silvanus, who is evidently included in "us" (Timothy was not hindered). Still less likely is the suggestion that the hindering was "prompted by Jews" (Richardson, *Israel,* 105 n. 3).

19. τίς γὰρ ἡμῶν ἐλπὶς ἢ χαρὰ ἢ στέφανος καυχήσεως; "For what is our hope, or joy, or crown of exultation?" The connective γάρ explains the writers' longing to see their Thessalonian friends. Those friends fill their hearts with hope and joy and exultation—hope that the divine work so well begun in them will increase to maturity, joy in the evident genuineness of their faith, exultation as they look forward to pointing to such converts as the fruit of their service before the tribunal of Christ. But nothing can disguise the pride and delight which they take in their converts themselves, who have become so dear to them (v 8). As parents rejoice in their children and cherish high hopes for them, so is it with the writers and their converts. Elsewhere Paul speaks of his converts as the "fruit" of his service (Rom 1:13), the "seal of his apostleship" (1 Cor 9:2) and, in words which echo what is said here, his "joy and crown" (Phil 4:1).

The "crown of exultation" alludes to the wreath which was awarded to the victor in an athletic contest: victory in such a contest afforded the victor and all associated with him ample ground for καύχησις ("boasting"). Paul repeatedly portrays the Christian life, and in particular his apostolic ministry, in athletic terms: in earthly races, he says, the contenders run "to receive a perishable wreath (στέφανος), but we an imperishable" (1 Cor 9:25). Here and now his converts are his prize, the token that he has not "run in vain" (Gal 2:2); but he looks forward to the occasion of final review and reward, when he will present his converts to the Lord who commissioned him, as evidence of the manner in which he has discharged his commission.

ἔμπροσθεν τοῦ κυρίου ἡμῶν Ἰησοῦ ἐν τῇ αὐτοῦ παρουσίᾳ, "in the presence of our Lord Jesus at his advent." This is the occasion of final review and reward. Paul, we know, was content to ignore assessments of his ministry made by others, and to abide the Lord's adjudication: "do not pronounce judgment before the time, before the Lord comes" (1 Cor 4:5), he said to his critics. When the time came, he was sure that the Lord's adjudication would depend on the quality of his converts. Therefore, for example, he urges the Philippian Christians to maintain a worthy life and witness "so that in the day of Christ I may be proud (εἰς καύχημα ἐμοί) that I did not run in vain or labor in vain" (Phil 2:16). What is called "the day of Christ" in Phil 2:16 is referred to here as Christ's Advent (παρουσία). This is the earliest occurrence in literature of παρουσία in its distinctive Christian sense of the advent of Christ in glory. (It appears in its non-theological sense of "presence" or "arrival" in 1 Cor 16:17; 2 Cor 7:6, 7; 10:10; Phil 1:26; 2:12.)

There were two contemporary uses of παρουσία which might have served as analogies for its distinctive Christian sense. One denoted the manifestation of a hidden divinity by some evidence of his power or in cultic action (this use is borrowed by Josephus to describe the coming of the God of Israel at various epochs in OT history; cf. *Antiq.* 3.80, 203; 9.55); the other denoted the official visit of a high-ranking personage to a province or city, when he was met on his approach by a deputation of leading citizens who escorted him formally for the remainder of his journey (for this meeting see comment on 4:17, εἰς ἀπάντησιν). In view of the near-divinization of some rulers, there can be no hard-and-fast distinction drawn between these two uses of παρουσία in the Hellenistic-Roman world. The παρουσία (Lat. *adventus*) of a very important person might inaugurate a new era, as happened with the visit of Hadrian to Athens and other Greek cities in A.D. 124—an inscription of A.D. 192/3 at Tegea is dated "in the year 69 of the first παρουσία of the god Hadrian in Greece" (cf. Deissmann, *Light from the Ancient East,* 372). Not long after 1 Thessalonians was written, coins bearing some such legend as *adventus Augusti* were struck at Corinth and Patras to commemorate an official visit of Nero. When Christians spoke of the παρουσία of their Lord, they probably thought of the pomp and circumstance attending those imperial visits as parodies of the true glory to be revealed on the day of Christ. (See *TDNT* 5.858–871; *NIDNTT* 2.898–935.)

This Christian sense of παρουσία occurs six times in the Thessalonian letters (here and in 3:13; 4:15; 5:23; 2 Thess 2:1, 8); elsewhere in Paul it is found only once (1 Cor 15:23). It appears four times in the Matthaean edition of the Olivet discourse (Matt 24:3, 27, 37, 39); also twice in James (5:7, 8), once in 1 John (2:28) and three times in 2 Peter (1:16; 3:4, 12, in the last of which places it is called "the παρουσία of the day of God"). See 2 Thess 2:9 for Antichrist's παρουσία.

That the Thessalonians had been taught to expect this great event is plain from 1:10; they had probably also been told that Christ at his Parousia would be accompanied by his "holy ones" (see 3:13), but there were certain associated details which they had still to learn (see 4:13–18).

20. ὑμεῖς γὰρ ἐστε ἡ δόξα ἡμῶν καὶ ἡ χαρά, "Yes; you are our glory and joy." The particle γάρ catches up the parenthetical question ἢ οὐχὶ καὶ ὑμεῖς; ("is it not indeed you?") of v 19 and gives it the affirmative answer which its form in any case implies: "Yes, it is you; *for* you are our glory and joy." For δόξα in the sense of "that in which one takes pride" cf. 1 Cor 11:7, where "the woman is the glory (δόξα) of the man" (or, perhaps, "a man's wife is his glory"), and possibly 2 Cor 8:23, where two messengers sent to Corinth with Titus are described as δόξα Χριστοῦ, "a credit to Christ" (or "men in whom Christ can take pride").

Explanation

It was not lack of interest or concern that prevented Paul and his companions from staying longer with their Thessalonian friends or going back to see them: it was circumstances over which they had no control and in which they discerned the malignant agency of Satan at work, aiming as usual to frustrate the work of God and to shake his people's faith. Paul in particular had made repeated efforts to return to Thessalonica, but these had come to nothing. He and the others assure the Thessalonians of their affectionate longing for them and their joyful confidence in them in view of the advent of Christ, when missionaries and converts together will appear before their Lord to receive (they trust) his commendation.

We may ask how it could be known when a check to apostolic planning was due to the overruling direction of the Holy Spirit (as in Acts 16:6, 7 where Paul and others were prevented from evangelizing proconsular Asia and Bithynia) and when it was due to satanic intervention (as on this occasion). It was probably evident—in retrospect, if not immediately—that the one check worked out for the advance of the gospel and the other for its hindrance.

The Thessalonian believers were the missionaries' hope and joy right there and then, and would continue to be so until the hope was realized and the joy consummated in the presence of their Lord. Then the believers would be to those who had brought the gospel to them a wreath of victory in which they could glory. When Paul, who is especially prone to use language of this kind, expresses himself thus we are not to suppose that, in his eyes, his converts were but the means to enhance his prestige. Rather, he and they were so completely bound in love together that their well-being was his great joy, as his, indeed, was theirs—so that, as he wrote later to the Corinthian church, "you may glory in us as we do in you on the day of the Lord Jesus" (2 Cor 1:14).

And how did glorying in his converts relate to Paul's resolve not "to glory except in the cross of our Lord Jesus Christ" (Gal 6:14)? His glorying in his converts, as he saw the grace of God manifested in them, was but a phase of his paramount glorying in the cross. They were the fruit of the preaching of the cross: Christ crucified was demonstrated afresh by their faith to be the power and wisdom of God.

It was, then, the writers' longing to revisit Thessalonica and their inability to do so that moved them to send this letter. Like most of the Pauline letters, this letter is a substitute for the personal presence and the word spoken face to face.

(b) *Mission of Timothy (3:1-5)*

Bibliography

Askwith, E. H. " 'I' and 'We' in the Thessalonian Epistles." *Expositor,* series 8, 1 (1911) 149–159. Chadwick, H. "1 Thess. 3 ³, σαίνεσθαι." *JTS,* n.s. 1 (1950) 156–158. Eckart, K.-G. "Der zweite echte Brief des Apostels Paulus an die Thessalonicher." *ZTK* 58 (1961) 30–44. Jewett, R. "Form and function of the apostolic benediction." *ATR* 52 (1969) 18–34. Kümmel, W. G. "Das literarische und geschichtliche Problem des ersten Thessalonicherbriefes." In *Neotestamentica et Patris-*

tica. Eine Freundesgabe O. Cullmann zu seinem 60. Geburtstag überreicht, ed. W. C. van Unnik. NovTSup 6. Leiden: Brill, 1962, 213–227. **Lake, K.** *The Earlier Epistles of St. Paul.* London: Rivingtons, ²1914. **Nestle, E.** "1 Thess. iii.3." *ExpTim* 18 (1906–7) 479. **Perdelwitz, R.** "Zu σαίνεσθαι ἐν ταῖς θλίψεσιν ταύταις, 1 Th 3, 3." *TSK* 86 (1913) 613–615.

Translation

¹ *For this reason, because we could hold out no longer* [a], *we resolved* [b] *to be left behind alone in Athens,* ² *and sent Timothy, our brother and fellow worker with God* [c] *in the gospel of Christ, to establish you firmly and encourage you* [d] *for the sake of* [e] *your faith,* ³ *so that no one should be perturbed* [f] *in the midst of these afflictions. You know yourselves that we are appointed* [g] *for this.* ⁴ *Indeed, when we were with you, we warned you that we are bound to suffer affliction, even as it has turned out, as you know.* ⁵ *Therefore, because I for my part could hold out no longer, I sent to learn about your faith, lest the tempter should have (successfully) tempted you and our labor should be in vain.*

Notes

[a] It is doubtful if the use of μηκέτι rather than οὐκέτι before στέγοντες is to be explained otherwise than as an instance of the encroachment of μή on οὐ in Hellenistic Greek, especially with a participle. Lightfoot tries to maintain the subjective force of μηκέτι by rendering the phrase "as being no longer able to contain, we thought fit . . ." (39). Cf. B. L. Gildersleeve, "The encroachments of μή on οὐ in later Greek," *AJP* 1 (1880), 45–57.

[b] εὐδοκήσαμεν. The augmented spelling ηὐδοκήσαμεν is exhibited in a few MSS (א B P). (Cf. 2.8.)

[c] συνεργὸν τοῦ θεοῦ. Variant readings seem to be mainly designed to avoid the boldness of calling Timothy "God's fellow-worker." B omits τοῦ θεοῦ, while א A P Ψ 6 81 629* 1241 1739 *pc* lat cop read διάκονον τοῦ θεοῦ. There are various conflations, e.g. διάκονον τοῦ θεοῦ καὶ συνεργὸν ἡμῶν D² byz syr^(pesh hcl**). The strength of συνεργὸν τοῦ θεοῦ (read by D* 33 lat^b m* Ambst Pelag) is that it explains the rise of the other readings.

[d] ὑμᾶς appears after παρακαλέσαι (as well as after στηρίξαι) in D¹ byz syr^pesh.

[e] ὑπέρ, for which περί is read by D² byz.

[f] The difficulty of finding a suitable meaning for σαίνεσθαι (see comment below) has led to variants and conjectures. F G read σιαίνεσθαι ("to feel disgust"); so at least K. Lachmann arranged the jumble of letters which the scribes produced as they tried to copy a reading which they did not understand. H. Venema (followed by Lachmann) conjectured (μηδὲν) ἀσαίνεσθαι (a verb cited by Hesychius, meaning "to suffer violence or outrage"); T. Beza and R. Bentley conjectured σαλεύεσθαι, "to be shaken" (cf. 2 Thess 2:2); A. D. Knox conjectured παθαίνεσθαι, "to be filled with emotion," "to break down" ("Τὸ μηδένα σαίνεσθαι ἐν ταῖς θλίψεσιν ταύταις," *JTS* 25, 1924, 290–291).

For the construction (τὸ μή with the infinitive expressing purpose) cf. 4:6, τὸ μὴ ὑπερβαίνειν. We might have expected εἰς before τὸ μὴ σαίνεσθαι, but perhaps εἰς before τὸ στηρίξαι κτλ does duty for the missing εἰς here.

[g] κεῖσθαι serves as a quasi-passive of τιθέναι, as in Phil 1:16, "I am posted (κεῖμαι) for the defense of the gospel."

Form/Structure/Setting

If a division of the letter is to be distinguished as the "travelogue," then this paragraph (3:1–5) comprises most of it. There are three main elements in this account of the sending of a messenger:

1. the introductory statement about his being sent (3:2a),
2. a statement of his credentials (3:2b),
3. a statement of the purpose in sending him (3:2c, 3a).

The first and third of these elements are repeated in v 5 in the first person singular, with special reference to Paul. We find these elements in accounts of the sending of the same messenger (Timothy) in 1 Cor 4:17; Phil 2:19–23, and with regard to other messengers in Phil 2:25–30; Col 4:7–9; Eph 6:21, 22.

Eckart ("Der zweite echte Brief . . .") propounded the view that 3:5 marks the beginning of a new letter (our 1 Thessalonians being a combination of two genuine Pauline letters to the Thessalonians, with a few non-Pauline additions); his arguments are refuted by Kümmel ("Das literarische und geschichtliche Problem . . .").

Comment

3:1. Διό, "For this reason," i.e. because of the eager longing to see the Thessalonian Christians again (2:17, 18).

μηκέτι στέγοντες, "because we could hold out no longer"; στέγειν, originally of keeping out or keeping in water or another fluid (e.g. of a watertight house or of a vessel that does not leak), comes from the latter sense to mean generally "to contain" and then "to endure," as in 1 Cor 9:12, πάντα στέγομεν ("we endure everything"); 13:7, (ἡ ἀγάπη) πάντα στέγει ("love endures everything").

εὐδοκήσαμεν καταλειφθῆναι ἐν Ἀθήναις μόνοι, "we resolved to be left behind in Athens alone." It is plain that Athens was but a temporary halting-stage on the way from Thessalonica to Corinth, and the same impression is given by Luke's narrative, although he makes Paul's short stay in Athens the setting for his speech on the knowledge of God to the court of the Areopagus (Acts 17:22–31).

Does the plural (εὐδοκήσαμεν . . . μόνοι) imply that Silvanus was with Paul in Athens? Probably it does. Lightfoot (followed in essence by Lake, *Epistles,* 74) suggested that, after Paul was escorted to Athens from Beroea (Acts 17:13–15), both Silvanus and Timothy followed him there; Paul (cf. v 5), with the concurrence of Silvanus (cf. v 2), then sent Timothy back to Thessalonica to see how the young church was faring, and Silvanus went back on some other errand to Macedonia. It was, according to Luke, while he was waiting for Silvanus (Silas) and Timothy to rejoin him in Athens, after his first arrival there, that Paul had the encounters described in Acts 17:16–34. Shortly after Timothy, and then Silvanus, left him, he went on from Athens to Corinth, where he was rejoined by Silvanus and Timothy on their return from their respective Macedonian errands (Acts 18:5). Soon after their return this letter was sent.

Opinions differ about the appropriateness of using the narrative of Acts as well as the data of 1 Thessalonians to reconstruct the missionaries' movements: much depends on varying estimates of the historical value of Acts. It is accepted in this commentary (on the basis of independent study) that the historical value of Acts is high. Yet this phase of the Acts narrative (including the missions in Thessalonica and Corinth and the visit to Athens) does not belong to the "we-narrative" (i.e. the narrator of Acts was not present at the events recorded), and Paul and Silvanus naturally had more detailed knowledge than was available to Luke. If Luke gives the impression that, despite Paul's instructions to Silvanus and Timothy to rejoin him in Athens, he left Athens before they arrived and was first rejoined by them in Corinth, that may be due to the incompleteness of his information; such an impression cannot stand before the plain statement of this verse. Despite the plural μόνοι (which is not unparalleled in the Pauline writings, though admittedly nowhere else with the impression of solitariness given by its collocation with καταλειφθῆναι, for which cf. Rom 11:3, ὑπελείφθην μόνος, "I alone am left"), it is difficult to regard the plural in this verse as epistolary when elsewhere in the letter it appears to be a real plural.

2. καὶ ἐπέμψαμεν Τιμόθεον, "and we sent Timothy." If we compare 1 Cor 4:17 (ἔπεμψα ὑμῖν Τιμόθεον) and Phil 2:19 (ἐλπίζω . . . Τιμόθεον ταχέως πέμψαι ὑμῖν), where Paul speaks in the first person singular of sending Timothy to Corinth and Philippi respectively, the natural inference from the plural ἐπέμψαμεν here is that Paul and Silvanus were jointly involved in sending Timothy back to Thessalonica (cf. Bengel: "ego et Silvanus"). In v 5, indeed, Paul takes personal responsibility for sending him (ἔπεμψα). This was fitting, since Timothy was Paul's aide-de-camp: the initiative was presumably Paul's and Silvanus agreed that Timothy should go.

τὸν ἀδελφὸν ἡμῶν καὶ συνεργὸν τοῦ θεοῦ, "our brother and fellow worker with God." The latter expression might conceivably mean "fellow worker with us in the work of God" but more probably means "God's fellow worker"—"fellow worker with God (in God's work)." Cf. 1 Cor 3:9, where Paul says, with more particular reference to Apollos and himself, θεοῦ γάρ ἐσμεν συνεργοί, "for we are God's fellow workers" meaning probably that they are fellow workers with God in his work rather than fellow workers one with another in God's work (although Bengel prefers the latter sense: "sumus *operarii* Dei, et *cooperarii* invicem"). When Paul refers to one or more persons as "my (our) fellow worker(s)" (Rom 16:3, 9, 21; Phil 2:25; Phlm 1, 24), he means "fellow worker(s) with me (us)"; analogously, when the qualifying genitive with συνεργός (-οί) is not μου or ἡμῶν but (τοῦ) θεοῦ, he means "fellow worker(s) with God," however hesitant some scribes or editors were about such a bold designation (see note c above). In Rom 16:21 Paul calls Timothy "my fellow worker" (ὁ συνεργός μου); in 1 Cor 4:17 he describes him as "my beloved and faithful child in the Lord," while in Phil 2:22 he says of him, "as a son with a father he has served (ἐδούλευσεν) with me in the gospel."

ἐν τῷ εὐαγγελίῳ τοῦ Χριστοῦ. Thus far in this letter the gospel has been called repeatedly "the gospel of God" (2:2, 5, 9) and once "our gospel"

(1:5); now it is called "the gospel of Christ" (cf. Rom 15:19; 1 Cor 9:12; 2 Cor 2:12; 9:13; 10:14; Gal 1:7; Phil 1:27; also 2 Thess 1:8, "the gospel of our Lord Jesus")—not only because Christ is its subject (it is, as Paul puts it in Rom 1:1–3, "the gospel of God . . . concerning his Son"), but also because he is its embodiment.

εἰς τὸ στηρίξαι ὑμᾶς καί παρακαλέσαι, "to establish you firmly and encourage you"—an antidote to the possibility of their being shaken or perturbed (σαίνεσθαι, v 3).

ὑπὲρ τῆς πίστεως ὑμῶν, "for the sake of your faith," i.e. to reinforce and strengthen it amid their afflictions. It has been asked why there should have been this concern about the faith of those whose life and witness were an example to believers elsewhere (cf. 1:7, 8). Schmithals argues (*Paul and the Gnostics*, 176–178) that in 2:13–4:1(2), which he takes to be a later letter than that which comprises the preceding and following material, joy is expressed at the dispelling of misgivings lest the Thessalonians should have been misled by gnostic teachers into concluding that *Paul's* afflictions deprived him of all credibility as an apostle of Christ. Rather, the good news referred to in 1:8 (see comment *ad loc.*) was received by the missionaries in Corinth, partly from Timothy on his return from Thessalonica and partly from others (such as Priscilla and Aquila).

3. τὸ μηδένα σαίνεσθαι, "that no one should be perturbed." The active σαίνειν is used of a dog's wagging its tail and then, with the accusative of the person, of its fawning on someone. Neither of these senses is relevant in this context. Chadwick mentions an occurrence of σαίνειν with the meaning "to perturb mentally" in a papyrus from Tura (discovered in 1941), edited by J. Scherer, *Entretien d'Origène avec Héraclide et les évêques ses collègues sur le Père, le Fils, et l'Âme* (Cairo: Publications de la Société Fouad I de Papyrologie, Textes et Documents IX, 1949), 140, line 5: τὰ μὲν περὶ πίστεως ὅσα ἔσηνεν ἡμᾶς συνεξετάσθη, "all matters concerning the faith which have perturbed us have been examined." This is the sense required here; there is therefore no need for emendations like those mentioned in note f above. The analogy of the papyrus extract just quoted might make one wonder if ὑπὲρ τῆς πίστεως ὑμῶν at the end of v 2 should not be taken closely with τὸ μηδένα σαίνεσθαι ("that no one should be perturbed with regard to your faith"), but the balance of the sentence rules this out.

ἐν ταῖς θλίψεσιν ταύταις, "in the midst of these afflictions" (cf. comment on 1:6). The Thessalonian Christians' sufferings at the hands of their fellow countrymen have been referred to in 2:14. The missionaries hoped that in spite of these sufferings their converts would stand firm—indeed, that these sufferings would serve to deepen their faith.

αὐτοὶ γὰρ οἴδατε, "for you yourselves know" as in 2:5. They knew without needing to be told now that believers in Christ are "appointed" (κείμεθα) to suffer for and with him, for the missionaries had told them this before they left Thessalonica (cf. v 4). If God has appointed (ἔθετο) his people to obtain salvation on the day of judgment (5:9), he has equally appointed them to endure affliction in their present mortal life. Thus, according to the consistent testimony of the NT, they follow the example of Christ (John 15:20) and indeed share his sufferings in the certain hope of sharing his glory hereafter: "if we suffer with him, that we may also be glorified with him" (εἴπερ συμπάσχομεν ἵνα καί συνδοξασθῶμεν, Rom 8:17). Such suffering is not only evidence for the reality of their faith; it is an earnest of the coming glory (cf. 2 Thess 1:4–10).

4. ὅτε πρὸς ὑμᾶς ἦμεν, "when we were with you." For this Hellenistic use of πρός with the accusative of persons in the sense of "with" (cf. Lat. *apud,* Fr. *chez*) cf. Mark 6:3, "are not his sisters here with us (πρὸς ἡμᾶς)?" The best known NT instance of this use of πρός is in John 1:1, 2, where the Word is said to have been in the beginning "with God" (πρὸς τὸν θεόν)—a statement fraught with theological significance, although there is no particular theological significance in the choice of πρός with the accusative rather than μετά with the genitive or σύν with the dative.

προελέγομεν ὑμῖν ὅτι μέλλομεν θλίβεσθαι, "we warned you that we are bound to suffer affliction"; cf. Acts 14:22, where Paul and Barnabas warn their South Galatian converts that "through many tribulations (διὰ πολλῶν θλίψεων) we must enter the kingdom of God" and strengthen and encourage them to persevere in faith and so be enabled to endure the afflictions.

5. διὰ τοῦτο κἀγώ . . . ἔπεμψα, "therefore I for my part . . . sent"; cf. καὶ διὰ τοῦτο καί in 2:13, with comment ad loc. Here, as there, διὰ τοῦτο points forward to the following clause: "*my* reason for sending . . . was to learn of your faith."

The opening words of v 5 (διὰ τοῦτο κτλ) are resumptive of v 1 (διὸ κτλ); κἀγώ (by crasis from καὶ ἐγώ) makes it plain that it was Paul who was chiefly impatient (μηκέτι στέγων) to find out what was happening to the Thessalonian believers and was chiefly responsible for sending Timothy (ἔπεμψα). For similar Pauline insertions cf. 2:18; 5:27.

μήπως ἐπείρασεν ὑμᾶς ὁ πειράζων, "lest perchance the tempter should have tempted you"—the aorist ἐπείρασεν here implies successful temptation, temptation which had succeeded in overthrowing their faith. The clause expresses apprehension over what might be discovered by Timothy on his arrival.

The tempter is identical with Satan of 2:18, bent on frustrating the work of God by putting hindrances in the missionaries' path or setting traps to bring about the converts' spiritual downfall. He is called ὁ πειράζων in Matthew's temptation narrative (Matt 4:3); cf. also 1 Cor 7:5, ἵνα μὴ πειράζῃ ὑμᾶς ὁ σατανᾶς διὰ τὴν ἀκρασίαν ὑμῶν, "lest Satan tempt you through your lack of self-control."

καὶ εἰς κενὸν γένηται ὁ κόπος ἡμῶν, "and our labor should be in vain," as it would be if the Thessalonians' faith collapsed. For the idea of labor in vain cf. 1 Cor 15:58; also Phil 2:16, where the Philippian Christians' perseverance will give Paul cause to rejoice on the day of Christ that he has neither run in vain nor labored in vain (οὐδὲ εἰς κενὸν ἐκοπίασα). In Isa 65:23 LXX God says, "My chosen ones will not labor in vain" (οὐ κοπιάσουσιν εἰς κενόν); contrast Isa 49:4, where the Servant complains that he has "labored in vain" (κενῶς ἐκοπίασα). In Gal 2:2 Paul lays his law-free gospel before the leaders of the Jerusalem church, "lest perchance I should prove to be running, or to have run, in vain" (εἰς κενόν); in 2 Cor 6:1 he warns the Corinthian Christians against receiving the grace of God in vain (εἰς κενόν). The sense of εἰς κενόν (κενῶς) is expressed also by εἰκῇ, as in Gal 4:11, "lest perchance I have labored over you in vain" (εἰκῇ κεκοπίακα), or (εἰς) μάτην, as in Ps 126 (MT 127):1, "the builders have labored in vain" (εἰς μάτην ἐκοπίασαν). (Cf. κενή, 2:1.)

Explanation

Since the setting of this paragraph belongs to the period following on the end of Paul's first visit to Thessalonica, there can be no reasonable doubt that the stay in Athens mentioned here is identical with that described in Acts 17:15–34. Indeed, the geographical sequence of Paul's ministry as recorded in Acts is confirmed point by point by the evidence of his letters.

It was Paul who took the initiative in sending Timothy back to Thessalonica; his reason for sending him was his concern lest the pressure of opposition should have proved too great for the Thessalonian Christians to resist and their faith might have collapsed. Then indeed the evangelizing energy of the weeks that he and his colleagues had spent in Thessalonica would have gone for nothing. But the confidence which he later expressed in 1 Cor 10:13 was illustrated by the experience of his Thessalonian friends: "God . . . will not let you be tempted beyond your strength, but with the temptation will also provide the way of escape, that you may be able to endure it."

How was it possible for Timothy to go back to Thessalonica, when the way was barred for Paul himself—and probably for Silvanus too? We can only speculate, but Timothy, as the junior partner in the missionary team, may not have been so much in the public eye as his two senior colleagues; moreover, Timothy, the son of a Greek father, perhaps looked like a Greek and therefore attracted no special attention in a Greek city, whereas Paul and Silvanus were full Jews and probably immediately recognizable as such—as they had been at Philippi (Acts 16:20).

How Paul and the others learned about the persecution which the church of Thessalonica had to endure after their departure we are not told, but it was not difficult for a message to be sent to them in Beroea or Athens with the news. Fortunately, they had warned their converts in Thessalonica, as elsewhere, that persecution and similar afflictions would be their inevitable lot. The suffering of the righteous had been felt as an acute problem in OT times; now it had come to be recognized as an essential feature of God's purpose for his people. Since their Lord had suffered, they knew that they could expect nothing else; they learned rather to "glory in tribulations" (Rom 5:3).

(c) *Joy and Thanksgiving at Timothy's Report (3:6–10)*

Bibliography

Funk, R. W. "The Apostolic *Parousia*: Form and Significance." In *Christian History and Interpretation: Studies Presented to John Knox*, ed. W. R. Farmer, C. F. D. Moule, R. R. Niebuhr. Cambridge: Cambridge University Press, 1967, 249–268. **Moule, C. F. D.** *The Origin of Christology*. Cambridge: Cambridge University Press, 1977. **O'Brien, P. T.** *Introductory Thanksgivings in the Letters of Paul*. NovTSup 49. Leiden: Brill, 1977. **O'Brien, P. T.** "Thanksgiving within the Structure of Pauline Theology." In *Pauline Studies: Essays Presented to F. F. Bruce*, ed. D. A. Hagner and M. J. Harris. Exeter: Paternoster Press/Grand Rapids, MI: Eerdmans, 1980, 50–66. **Spicq, C.** " Ἐπιποθεῖν. Désirer ou chérir?" *RB* 64 (1957) 184–195. **Wiles, G. P.** *Paul's Intercessory Prayers. The Significance of the Intercessory Prayer Passages in the Letters of St. Paul*. SNTSMS 24. Cambridge: Cambridge University Press, 1974.

Translation

⁶ *But now that Timothy has just come to us from you and brought us the good news of your faith and love, telling us that you always remember us kindly, and that you long to see us as we long to see you—* ⁷ *why then, brothers, we were reassured about you in all our distress and affliction,* ᵃ *through this faith of yours.* ⁸ *It is life to us, if* ᵇ *you stand fast* ᶜ *in the Lord.* ⁹ *What (adequate) thanksgiving can we render to God* ᵈ *for you at all the joy with which we rejoice on your account in the presence of our God* ᵉ*?* ¹⁰ *Night and day we pray with the utmost earnestness that we may see you face to face and make good the deficiencies in your faith.*

Notes

ᵃ καί is added before διὰ τῆς ὑμῶν πίστεως in A (D).

ᵇ ἐάν with the indicative is a colloquialism; the more classical ἐάν . . . στήκητε (subjunctive) is read by א* D E *pc*. For the indicative cf. Mark 11:25, ὅταν στήκετε.

ᶜ The Hellenistic present στήκειν (in NT more common in Paul than in other writers; cf. 2 Thess 2:15) is formed from the classical perfect ἔστηκα which continued to be used concurrently with στήκειν even by Paul (e.g. in 1 Cor 15:1, ἐν ᾧ καὶ ἑστήκατε).

ᵈ τῷ κυρίῳ ("to the Lord") is read for τῷ θεῷ ("to God") by א* D* F G latᵃ ᵇ ᵛᵉ·ᶜᵒᵈᵈ copᵇᵒ·ᶜᵒᵈᵈ.

ᵉ κυρίου is read for θεοῦ by א* 181 latᵃ ᵇ ᵐ ᵛᵉ·ᶜᵒᵈᵈ.

Form/Structure/Setting

The following elements distinguished by Funk in the "apostolic *Parousia*" ("The Apostolic *Parousia* . . . ," 252–260) are represented in this subsection:

1. Benefit from apostolic presence accruing to the writers—here in relation to Timothy's return and report (3:6–9)

2. Prayer-report with regard to apostolic presence (3:10a)
3. Benefit from apostolic presence accruing to the recipients (3:10b)

The sustained thanksgiving introduced in 1:2–10 and resumed in 2:13 is concluded in 3:9 with a rhetorical question, in which τίνα . . . εὐχαριστίαν δυνάμεθα . . . ἀνταποδοῦναι; ("what thanksgiving . . . can we render?") takes the place of the verb εὐχαριστοῦμεν, "we thank" (found in 1:2; 2:13).

O'Brien (*Introductory Thanksgivings*, 157) points out that issues of the past and present have been central from the beginning of the letter to 3:9, whereas v 10, with the "wish-prayer," exhortations and instructions that follow, "point forward to the future. Von Dobschütz and others are therefore correct when they observe that the movement from v. 9 to v. 10 marks a major turning-point in the whole letter."

The prayer-report of v 10 continues that of 1:2b–3 and incidentally indicates the main purpose of the letter—the letter is to serve as an interim communication until the prayer is answered and a reunion takes place. Then it will be practicable to fill in the remaining gaps in their faith more adequately; meanwhile, the more urgent matters have to be dealt with, as effectively as possible, by letter (cf. Wiles, 183–186).

Comment

3:6. Ἄρτι δὲ ἐλθόντος Τιμοθέου πρὸς ἡμᾶς ἀφ' ὑμῶν, "now that Timothy has just come to us from you": the letter was evidently written as soon as possible after Timothy's recent (ἄρτι) arrival.

καὶ εὐαγγελισαμένου ἡμῖν, "and has brought us the good news": this is an instance of the non-technical sense of εὐαγγελίζεσθαι (cf. Luke 1:19, where it is used of the good news brought by Gabriel, that Zechariah and Elizabeth are to have a son). The verb is normally used in the NT of preaching the gospel (the εὐαγγέλιον of 1:5, etc.).

τὴν πίστιν καὶ τὴν ἀγάπην ὑμῶν, "your faith and love." The faith and love which had begun to manifest themselves immediately after their conversion, while the missionaries were still with them (cf. 1:3), were still in evidence: their faith in God found active expression in their love for others and not least for the missionaries (cf. Gal 5:6, πίστις δι' ἀγάπης ἐνεργουμένη, "faith working through love").

καὶ ὅτι ἔχετε μνείαν ἡμῶν ἀγαθὴν πάντοτε, "and that you always have kind remembrances of us." The adjective means not merely that they remembered them well (in the sense of not having forgotten them) but that their memory of them was happy and friendly, whereas they might have recalled them with bitterness as visitors who brought them nothing but trouble.

ἐπιποθοῦντες ἡμᾶς ἰδεῖν καθάπερ καὶ ἡμεῖς ὑμᾶς, "longing to see us as we long to see you": for the writers' longing to see their Thessalonian friends see 2:17. The present language (especially ἐπιποθοῦντες, "eagerly longing, yearning") suggests the intensity of their ἀγάπη. Paul at various times uses ἐπιποθεῖν to express the intensity of his own feelings for his converts and other Christians (cf. Rom 1:11; Phil 1:8; also 2 Tim 1:4); it was a great encouragement to learn of the responsive intensity of affection on the part of the Thessalonians.

7. διὰ τοῦτο παρεκλήθημεν, "for this reason we were encouraged (reassured)." Here διὰ τοῦτο refers back to a reason already stated—Timothy's good news. Paul expresses himself similarly in 2 Cor 7:3–7, written in response to the good news brought to him by Titus about the spiritual health of the Corinthian Christians, after a long period of great anxiety.

ἐφ' ὑμῖν, "over you," "with regard to you."

ἐπὶ πάσῃ τῇ ἀνάγκῃ καὶ θλίψει ἡμῶν, "in all our distress and affliction." The preposition is best understood as having temporal force here; cf. 2 Cor 1:4 (ἐπὶ πάσῃ τῇ θλίψει); Phil 1:3 (ἐπὶ πάσῃ τῇ μνείᾳ ὑμῶν). We cannot make a fine distinction between the "distress" and "affliction" as though the former denoted physical privation and the latter sufferings inflicted by others (cf. Lightfoot). The distress and affliction at this time may have been more psychological than physical. For one thing, their anxiety over the Thessalonians had been hard to bear; for another thing, it is evident that the first phase of Paul's stay in Corinth was beset by "weakness and much fear and trembling" (1 Cor 2:3). And no wonder: having been expelled from one place after another in Macedonia, Paul and the others might well have wondered if, in spite of their confident interpretation of the call of God (Acts 16:10), they had been divinely guided to that province after all. They had no reason to expect more positive acceptance in Achaia, to which they had now perforce come. But Timothy's report on the state of the Thessalonian church dissipated their fears. The gospel had taken firm root in the capital city of Macedonia: the seed had been sown in fertile ground and the fruit was already beginning to appear. If the Thessalonians had not allowed their tribulations to destroy their Christian faith and love, Paul and Silvanus found in this good news a sovereign remedy for their own "distress and affliction." (It might be mentioned that a few commentators, such as von Dobschütz, take the θλίψεις of v 3a to be the missionaries' afflictions, not the Thessalonians'; but this is not the natural construction to put on the words—the first person plural of κείμεθα and μέλλομεν in vv 3b, 4 is inclusive, not exclusive.)

διὰ τῆς ὑμῶν πίστεως. It is "through your faith"—i.e. through the news that your faith holds firm—that we have been reassured. Cf. v 2, ὑπὲρ τῆς πίστεως ὑμῶν.

8. ὅτι νῦν ζῶμεν, ἐὰν ὑμεῖς στήκετε ἐν κυρίῳ, "because now we live, if you stand fast in the Lord," i.e. the news of your unwavering faith and love is the very breath of life to us. After their anxiety over the Thessalonians Paul and the others felt great relief; they could now breathe freely. Paul's concern for his converts and sense of oneness with them breathes through all his correspondence. When they were led astray, he was indignant; when they slipped back, he was distressed; when they showed evidence of living lives worthy of the gospel, he was overjoyed. The importance of standing steadfast in the faith is repeatedly emphasized in his letters; cf. 1 Cor

16:13 (στήκετε ἐν τῇ πίστει); Gal 5:1 (στήκετε οὖν); Phil 1:27 (ὅτι στήκετε ἐν ἑνὶ πνεύματι); 4:1 (οὕτως στήκετε ἐν κυρίῳ, the same idiom as here). As between ἐν κυρίῳ and ἐν Χριστῷ or ἐν Χριστῷ Ἰησοῦ (cf. 2:14), Moule (*Christology*, 58–62) discerns a tendency for the latter to be "associated with the *fait accompli* of God's saving *work*," the former "with its implementation and its working out in human conduct"; he acknowledges an indebtedness here to M. Bouttier, *En Christ* (Paris: Presses Universitaires de France, 1962), 55.

9. τίνα γὰρ εὐχαριστίαν δυνάμεθα . . . ἀνταποδοῦναι, "for what (kind of) thanksgiving can we . . . render?" This rhetorical question is reminiscent of Ps 116:12 (LXX 115:3), τί ἀνταποδώσω τῷ κυρίῳ περὶ πάντων ὧν ἀνταπέδωκέν μοι, "What shall I render to the LORD for all his bounty to me?" The conjunction γάρ explains their treating the news of the Thessalonians' steadfastness as the breath of life. "We live (we say), for this is our constant prayer for you, and to know that it is being answered is life itself to us; there is nothing for which we thank God more."

ἀνταποδοῦναι, "to give back as an equivalent," although there is not the emphasis on equivalence here that there is in 2 Thess 1:6.

τῷ θεῷ, "to God." As in 1:2; 2:13 and elsewhere, "the apostle's prayers of thanksgiving are directed to the God of the Psalmists . . . , who is known to Paul as the Father of Jesus Christ (cf. Col. 1:3), and they are offered 'always' (πάντοτε, 1 Cor. 1:4; Phil. 1:4; Col. 1:3; 1 Thess. 1:2; 2 Thess. 1:3; 2:13; Phlm. 4) or 'unceasingly' (ἀδιαλείπτως, 1 Thess. 1:2; 2:13), expressions which do not refer to continual prayer but to the apostle's remembrance of them in his regular times of prayer" (O'Brien, "Thanksgiving," 56).

ἐπὶ πάσῃ τῇ χαρᾷ ᾗ αἴρομεν δι' ὑμᾶς, "in all the joy with which we rejoice on your account." Here is a recompense indeed for "all our distress and affliction" of v 7. The anxiety which they had felt about their Thessalonian friends had intensified their general "distress and affliction"; the joy which they now felt over the Thessalonians made them forget it all.

ἔμπροσθεν τοῦ θεοῦ ἡμῶν, "in the presence of our God." This or a similar phrase (expressed with ἔμπροσθεν) is more common in 1 Thessalonians than in any other Pauline letter. In 2:19 and 3:13 it has an eschatological reference; here, as above in 1:3, it refers to the missionaries' present practice. As they constantly remember their friends in thanksgiving and prayer "in the presence of our God and Father" (1:3), so now they rejoice over them in God's presence. This consciousness of the divine presence "excludes any notion of personal success or fleshly satisfaction on Paul's part. Thus the apostle, with a deep sense of gratitude, turns consciously to God to render thanksgiving for that which makes him rejoice" (O'Brien, *Introductory Thanksgivings*, 157).

10. νυκτὸς καὶ ἡμέρας, "night and day" (cf. 2:9) is to be taken with δεόμενοι.

ὑπερεκπερισσοῦ, "exceedingly abundantly," as in 5:13; Eph 3:20. In Dan 3:22 (Theod.) Nebuchadnezzar's furnace is said to have been heated ἐκ περισσοῦ, "excessively," but here the prefix ὑπερ- adds a further degree to that. Paul is fond of compounds expressing superlativeness; cf.

ὑπερπερισσεύεσθαι of the superabundant grace of God in Rom 5:20, and of the superabundant joy with which Paul received reassuring news about the church of Corinth in 2 Cor 7:4 (which, like the present news from Thessalonica, more than compensated for all his "affliction," θλῖψις).

δεόμενοι, "praying," "requesting," even while they rejoiced at the report brought by Timothy. The thanksgiving of v 9 leads up to this prayer report, which in turn anticipates the "wish-prayer" of vv 11–13.

εἰς τὸ ἰδεῖν ὑμῶν τὸ πρόσωπον, echoing 2:17 (ἐσπουδάσαμεν τὸ πρόσωπον ὑμῶν ἰδεῖν). The simple infinitive is sufficient after a verb of praying; the construction εἰς τὸ ἰδεῖν (equivalent of ἵνα ἴδωμεν) expresses purpose (cf. 2:12; 4:9). To see the Thessalonians was both the content and the purpose of their prayer to God.

καὶ καταρτίσαι τὰ ὑστερήματα τῆς πίστεως ὑμῶν, "and to make good the deficiencies in your faith." In the light of the enthusiastic welcome given to Timothy's news about their faith and love in vv 6–8, it is unlikely that the quality of the Thessalonians' faith was felt to be defective; rather, there were important areas in which they required further instruction. What some of those areas were may be gathered from the subject matter of 4:1–5:22. Since it was not likely that in the near future there would be an opportunity to give the Thessalonians the necessary instruction face to face, it was given in the next part of the letter. As usual, the written word was a substitute for the spoken word.

Explanation

Timothy's brief visit to the Thessalonian church had brought him great satisfaction. The members were delighted to see him and have news of the movements and well-being of Paul and Silvanus since their summary expulsion from Thessalonica. As Timothy told them of Paul and Silvanus's affectionate longing to see them again, they replied, "Tell them that we remember them with great affection and are as eager to see them as they are to see us."

When Timothy rejoined his senior colleagues and brought them this news, telling them that the faith of the Thessalonian Christians had not wavered under stress, they were relieved and filled with joy: a burden was lifted from their minds and life seemed good. The Thessalonians' conversion was no momentary response to the gospel: it was a real turning to God which brought the grace and power of his Spirit into their lives and enabled them to stand firm in the face of opposition.

Their relief and joy overflowed in renewed thanksgiving to God; at the same time their longing to see their Thessalonian friends face to face once more was redoubled. While their faith was standing the test of persecution, it required to be fostered and encouraged so that it might grow to maturity; they stood in need of further instruction in Christian ethics and doctrine. Something could be done in a letter to impart this instruction, but a personal visit would be much better.

(d) *Prayer for the Thessalonian Christians (3:11–13)*

Bibliography

Collins, R. F. "The Theology of Paul's First Letter to the Thessalonians." *Louv. Stud.* 6 (1977) 315–337. **Hewett, J. A.** "1 Thessalonians 3:13." *ExpTim* 87 (1975–76) 54–55. **Glasson, T. F.** *The Second Advent: The Origin of the NT Doctrine.* London: Epworth Press, ²1947. **Jewett, R.** "Form and Function of the Apostolic Benediction." *ATR* 52 (1969) 18–34. **Lake, K.** *The Earlier Epistles of St. Paul.* London: Rivingtons, ²1914. **Mearns, C. L.** "Early Eschatological Development in Paul: the evidence of I and II Thessalonians." *NTS* 27 (1980–81) 137–157. **Montague, G. T.** *Growth in Christ.* Kirkwood, Mo: Maryhurst Press, 1961, 3–13. **O'Brien, P. T.** *Introductory Thanksgivings in the Letters of Paul.* NovTSup 49. Leiden: Brill, 1977. **Ross, J. M.** "1 Thessalonians 3:11." *BT* 26 (1975), 444. **Vanderhaegen, J.** "Le désir de l'Apôtre." *AsSeign* n.s. No. 5 (1969) 62–70. **Wiles, G. P.** *Paul's Intercessory Prayers.* SNTSMS 24. Cambridge: Cambridge University Press, 1974.

Translation

¹¹ *Now may our God and Father himself and our Lord Jesus direct* ᵃ *our way to you,* ¹² *and may the Lord enlarge* ᵇ *you and make you abound in love* ᶜ *to one another and to all, even as we (abound) to you,* ¹³ *so as to establish your hearts blameless in holiness* ᵈ *in the presence of our God and Father, at the advent of our Lord Jesus with all his holy ones. [Amen.]* ᵉ

Notes

ᵃ κατευθύναι, aorist optative. The optative mood expressing wish is the "proper optative"; E. D. Burton (*Syntax of the Moods and Tenses in NT Greek*, Edinburgh: T. & T. Clark, ³1898, 79) lists 35 occurrences of this in NT, of which 15 are accounted for by the idiomatic μὴ γένοιτο (14 times in Paul). Of the remaining 20 the Pauline corpus accounts for 14, and of these 1 and 2 Thessalonians account for five and four respectively (cf. v 12; 5:23; 2 Thess 2:17; 3:5, 16).

ᵇ πλεονάσαι, aorist optative of wish (with transitive force).

ᶜ περισσεύσαι τῇ ἀγάπῃ. περισσεύσαι, aorist optative of wish (with transitive force). The variant τῆς ἀγάπης (F G) for τῇ ἀγάπῃ (dative) exhibits the classical use of the genitive after a verb of filling.

ᵈ ἀμέμπτους ἐν ἁγιωσύνῃ. For the adjectival form ἀμέμπτους B L 33 81 *al* lat read the adverb ἀμέμπτως (cf. 2:10; 5:23); for ἁγιωσύνη ("holiness") A *pc* read δικαιοσύνη ("righteousness").

ᵉ ἀμήν is read by ℵ* ² A D* 81 629 *pc* latᵃ ᵐ ᵛᵍ copᵇᵒ; it is omitted by ℵ¹ B D² F G Ψ byz latᵛᵉᵗ syr copˢᵃ.

Form/Structure/Setting

This subsection is referred to by Wiles (*Prayers,* 52) as "the first of the two main wish-prayers in the epistle" (the second being 5:23). It is called a "wish-prayer" because it is expressed in the optative rather than in the imperative mood. The distinction between the direct prayer and the wish-prayer is largely stylistic; there is no more essential difference between the two forms than there is in OT between "Arise, O LORD . . ." in Num 10:35 and "Let God arise . . ." in Ps 68:1 (LXX 67:2, where indeed the third person aorist imperative ἀναστήτω is used by the translator and not the optative ἀνασταίη).

The emphatic αὐτός, found also at the beginning of the wish-prayer in 5:23, may echo the language of the synagogue liturgy, where the address would be in the second person, σὺ δέ (ואתה); this goes back in turn to the language of the Psalter, as (e.g.) in Ps 22:19 (LXX 21:20), σὺ δέ, κύριε (ואתה יהוה), "But thou, O LORD."

The wish-prayer has been anticipated in the prayer report of v 10; it is rounded off with an eschatological climax (cf. 1:10; 2:19, 20).

The subsection forms the conclusion to the section commencing at 2:17 (the "apostolic Parousia") and provides a transition to the paraenesis which follows (4:1–5:22).

Comment

3:11. Αὐτὸς δὲ ὁ θεὸς καὶ πατὴρ ἡμῶν καὶ ὁ κύριος ἡμῶν Ἰησοῦς κατευθύναι τὴν ὁδὸν ἡμῶν πρὸς ὑμᾶς, "Now may our God and Father himself and our Lord Jesus direct our way to you." This close association of Christ with God the Father (cf. 1:1)—here, in his sharing the divine prerogative of directing the ways of men and women (cf. Pss 32:8; 37:23; Prov 3:6b; 16:9)—is theologically significant. The singular verb κατευθύναι is probably not theologically significant: in such a construction with two subjects the verb commonly agrees with the nearer of the two. Cf. 2 Thess 2:16, 17, where "our Lord Jesus Christ" precedes "God our Father" in the composite subject (again, with a singular verb in the predicate).

The verb κατευθύνειν means "to make right" ("to correct") or "to make straight"; cf. Ps 37 (LXX 36):23, παρὰ κυρίου τὰ διαβήματα ἀνθρώπου κατευθύνεται ("by the Lord a man's steps are made straight"); 40:2 (LXX 39:3), καὶ κατηύθυνεν τὰ διαβήματά μου ("and he gave me a secure footing"); Prov 4:26, τὰς ὁδούς σου κατεύθυνε ("make your ways straight"). It occurs in two other NT passages: 2 Thess 3:5 and Luke 1:79, τοῦ κατευθῦναι τοὺς πόδας ἡμῶν εἰς ὁδὸν εἰρήνης ("to direct our feet into the way of peace"). If the writers' way is made straight to the Thessalonians, they will come to them the sooner, without detours or deviations.

12. ὑμᾶς δὲ ὁ κύριος πλεονάσαι καὶ περισσεύσαι τῇ ἀγάπῃ, "and may the Lord enlarge you and make you abound in love." The wish-prayer is continued with two further optatives. By ὁ κύριος we are probably to understand Jesus: he is the one κύριος as the Father is the one θεός (1 Cor 8:6). The enlargement prayed for may be spiritual (cf. the sense of πλατύνειν in 2 Cor 6:11, 13) rather than numerical. Cf. 2 Thess 1:3 (πλεονάζει ἡ ἀγάπη), where the active verb has intransitive force, unlike the transitive force of

πλεονάσαι here. For Paul's desire to see his converts abounding in love cf. Phil 1:9 (ἵνα ἡ ἀγάπη ὑμῶν ἔτι μᾶλλον καὶ μᾶλλον περισσεύῃ, "that your love may abound yet more and more," where also the active verb (unlike περισσεύσαι here) has intransitive force.

εἰς ἀλλήλους καὶ εἰς πάντας, "to one another and to all." The same expression recurs in 5:15. It is doubtful if, for all its emphasis, it should be related to Harnack's hypothesis that there were two distinct groups in the Thessalonian church—a Jewish Christian and a Gentile Christian (as suggested by Lake, *Epistles*, 89–90). Certainly it conveys the writers' concern for the unity of all the believers in Thessalonica, but εἰς πάντας does not mean merely "all the brethren" (5:26, 27) but all mankind. The love of God poured into the believers' hearts by the Holy Spirit could not be reserved for members of their own fellowship; it must overflow to others without restriction.

καθάπερ καὶ ἡμεῖς εἰς ὑμᾶς (sc. περισσεύομεν τῇ ἀγάπῃ), "just as we (abound in love) towards you." Cf. the καθάπερ clause (similarly with verb to be supplied from the preceding clause) at the end of v 6.

13. εἰς τὸ στηρίξαι ὑμῶν τὰς καρδίας, "so as to establish your hearts firmly" (cf. v 2, εἰς τὸ στηρίξαι ὑμᾶς). As in 2:4, the heart is not only the seat of understanding and will, but the place where the hidden motives of life and conduct take shape. If the readers receive this ethical stability within, they need have no fear of the outcome on the day when the Lord "will bring to light the things now hidden in darkness and will disclose the purposes of the heart" (1 Cor 4:5).

ἀμέμπτους ἐν ἁγιωσύνῃ, "blameless in holiness" (cf. 5:23, ἁγιάσαι . . . ἀμέμπτως). The writers have already pointed out that they themselves behaved blamelessly (ἀμέμπτως) toward the Thessalonians (2:10); true blamelessness in word and action must be the fruit of inner sanctification. Cf. Phil 2:15, where the Christians of Philippi are urged to live among their pagan neighbors as the "blameless (ἄμωμα) children of God." How sanctification is to be manifested in specific areas of conduct appears further in 4:3.

ἔμπροσθεν τοῦ θεοῦ καὶ πατρὸς ἡμῶν, "in the presence of our God and Father." To be blameless in God's sight is more important than being blameless by worldly standards. Their appearance before God at the Parousia will consummate their sanctification: here and in 5:23 the (proleptic) reference is to the completion of the process which is otherwise (cf. 2:12) designated their being "glorified" (cf. Rom 8:17, 30, τούτους καὶ ἐδόξασεν, "those he also glorified"). Whereas in 2:19 the missionaries speak of their converts as their "crown of exultation in the presence of our Lord Jesus at his Parousia," here they speak of their appearance then "in the presence of our God and Father." Similarly the tribunal (βῆμα) before which they are to stand is variously called "the tribunal of Christ" (2 Cor 5:10) and "the tribunal of God" (Rom 14:10)—so completely are the functions of the Father shared with the Son.

ἐν τῇ παρουσίᾳ τοῦ κυρίου ἡμῶν Ἰησοῦ, "at the advent of our Lord Jesus."

The Parousia is not only the event at the end of time which brings the sanctification of believers: it should provide the Thessalonians, as it provided Paul himself, with an incentive to holy living and faithful service.

In this phrase Mearns ("Early Eschatological Development," 144) discerns a *double entendre:* the words in themselves "could well have been understood in the sense of the realized eschatology of the royal presence now of the risen Lord in his Kingdom," but they are here used in a context which makes them the vehicle of a futurist eschatology, now imparted by Paul as a "new interpretation": his apprehensiveness about its reception "is probably reflected in the somewhat clumsy way he adds the last phrase to the sentence." But the idea that Paul's eschatological outlook underwent a change between his preaching in Thessalonica and the writing of this letter lacks solid foundation.

μετὰ πάντων τῶν ἁγίων αὐτοῦ, "with all his holy ones." Cf. the description of the day of Yahweh in Zech 14:5 (LXX), καὶ ἥξει κύριος ὁ θεός μου καὶ πάντες οἱ ἅγιοι μετ᾽ αὐτοῦ ("and the Lord my God will come, and all the holy ones with him"). This description is based on that of earlier theophanies in the OT: when God reveals himself, for deliverance or for judgment, he is regularly attended by his angels. At the giving of the law he shone forth "with myriads of holy ones" (Deut 33:2); at the battle celebrated in Ps 68 (LXX 67) he ensured his people's victory when he appeared "with mighty chariotry, twice ten thousand, thousands upon thousands" (v 17). When, in Daniel's vision of the Day of Judgment, the Ancient of Days takes his seat, "a thousand thousands served him, and ten thousand times ten thousand stood before him" (Dan 7:10). This language is echoed in *1 Enoch* 1:6, 7 (quoted in Jude 14, 15), where the Lord is seen coming to execute judgment "with his holy myriads."

Glasson (*The Second Advent*, 172–176) suggests, from a study of early Christian writers from Paul to Augustine, that there was a Testimony collection of OT texts interpreted with reference to the Parousia of Christ (he cites Pss 50:3; 68:1–7; 80:1; 82:8; 107:20; Isa 26:19; 42:13; 63:9; 64:1; 66:18; Hab 2:3; Zeph 1:15; Mal 4:1). He points out how the tradition survives in that stanza of Charles Wesley's "Lo, he comes with clouds descending" which ends with the coda:

> Jah, Jehovah,
> Everlasting God, come down!

"All the essential details" of NT portrayals of the Parousia "are found in the O.T. description of the coming theophany. Broadly speaking, the Christians took over the O.T. doctrine of the Advent of the Lord, making the single adjustment that the Lord was the Lord Jesus" (176).

In the Markan tradition of the sayings of Jesus, the Son of Man "comes in the glory of the Father with the holy angels" (Mark 8:38). These may be the angels whom, at his coming, he will send out to "gather his elect from the four winds" (Mark 13:27). In John's Apocalypse the rider on the white horse whose name is "The Word of God" is attended when he comes to judge the nations by "the armies of heaven" (Rev 19:14), presumably to be recognized as angelic hosts. On the other hand, when the Lamb is seen standing on Mount Zion he is accompanied by "the hundred and forty-four thousand who had been redeemed from the earth" (Rev 14:1–5), the foundation members of the new humanity.

There is an antecedent probability that the "holy ones" of our present passage are angels. But in Pauline usage they may also include believing men and women; in 2 Thess 1:10, for example (see comment ad loc.), the "holy ones" in whom the Lord Jesus is to be glorified at his revelation from heaven (cf. "the angels of his power" in 2 Thess 1:7) stand in parallelism with "all the believers" in whom he is to be marveled at. That occasion is described in Rom 8:19 as "the revealing of the sons of God" because they will be seen associated with their Lord and invested with his glory.

For other theophanic features incidental to the Parousia of Christ cf. 4:16, 17 ("trumpet of God," "clouds"); 2 Thess 1:7 ("flaming fire"); 2:8 ("breath of his mouth"), with comments ad loc.

[ἀμήν]. If the "Amen" is part of the original text (see note e above), it illustrates the primitive Christian response to the mention of the Advent of Christ (more fully in Rev 22:20, ἀμήν, ἔρχου κύριε Ἰησοῦ, "Amen, come, Lord Jesus").

Explanation

Paul and his friends bring the first half of their letter to an end by praying for a speedy reunion with the Thessalonian Christians and for their growth in love and holiness in view of the Advent of Christ.

The prayer is presented jointly to "our God and Father" and to "our Lord Jesus." They are not addressed in the vocative case, to be sure: the prayer is expressed in the third person and not in the second. But there is no difference in principle between saying, "O God our Father and our Lord Jesus, direct our way . . ." and saying "May God our Father and our Lord Jesus direct our way . . ." The second part of the prayer, indeed, is presented to Jesus alone, for he is certainly "the Lord" who is asked to "enlarge" the Thessalonians and make them "abound in love" to one another and to all others.

Again, to appear before the Lord Jesus at his Advent involves appearing at the same time "before our God and Father." It is noteworthy, too, that the Advent of Jesus is described in terms used in the OT on those occasions when the God of Israel reveals himself in glory, attended by his heavenly hosts. The unobtrusive spontaneity with which such language is applied to Jesus by more NT writers than one is more eloquent than any formal creedal statement could be. We cannot miss the startling implications of the use of such language by one with Paul's Pharisaic upbringing. His reassessment of Christ, by contrast with his former estimate of him before the Damascus road confrontation, had been revolutionary indeed.

The holiness which the writers desire to see in their readers' lives is, in practice, likeness to Christ—a likeness to be produced increasingly within them by the Spirit whom they have received. The reference in this context to "the Advent of our Lord Jesus with all his holy ones" is especially apposite because their entering into his manifested glory then will consummate their present growth in holiness. How relevant to their daily life in a pagan city this present growth in holiness is appears in the exhortation which now follows.

Exhortation   (1 Thess 4:1–5:24)

(a) On Keeping the Traditions (4:1, 2)

Bibliography

Bjerkelund, C. J. *Parakalô: Form, Funktion und Sinn der Parakalô-Sätze in den paulinischen Briefen.* Bibliotheca Theologica Norvegica 1. Oslo: Universitetsforlaget, 1967. **Cullmann, O.** "*Kyrios* as Designation for the Oral Tradition concerning Jesus." *SJT* 3 (1950) 180–197. **Cullmann, O.** "The Tradition." In *The Early Church.* Ed. and tr. A. J. B. Higgins. London: SCM Press, 1956, 55–99. **Dunn, J. D. G.** *Jesus and the Spirit.* London: SCM Press, 1975. **Hanson, R. P. C.** *Tradition in the Early Church.* London: SCM Press, 1962. **Moule, C. F. D.** *The Origin of Christology.* Cambridge: Cambridge University Press, 1977. **Nieder, L.** *Die Motive der religiös-sittlichen Paranese in den paulinischen Gemeindebriefen.* München: Zink, 1956.

Translation

¹ *For the rest, then* ᵃ, *brothers, we request and appeal to you in the Lord Jesus that* ᵇ, *as you have received from us the way to conduct yourselves so as to please God, even as you do conduct yourselves* ᶜ, *you may abound more and more (in this kind of conduct).* ² *For you know what charges we gave you through the Lord Jesus.*

Notes

ᵃ οὖν is omitted by B* 33 629 1739* lat^{vg. codd} syr^{pesh} cop^{bo}.
ᵇ ἵνα is omitted by ℵ A D² Ψ byz syr^{hcl}.
ᶜ The clause καθὼς καὶ περιπατεῖτε is omitted by D² Ψ byz syr^{pesh}.

Form/Structure/Setting

The paraenetic division of the letter now begins.

In several Pauline letters the paraenetic division follows, and is logically dependent on, a preceding doctrinal division; it is therefore appropriately introduced with οὖν, "therefore" (cf. Rom 12:1; Eph 4:1; Col 3:5). This paraenetic division does not follow on an exposition of doctrine; its introductory οὖν accordingly has no strong inferential force and simply serves the purpose of a connective particle.

These two verses (4:1, 2) provide the introduction to the paraenetic division. The paraenesis which follows repeats, and in some respects amplifies, the instruction already delivered to the Thessalonians by word of mouth. With the καθὼς . . . ἵνα construction of v 1 may be compared Col 2:6, "As then you have received (ὡς οὖν παρελάβετε) Christ Jesus the

Lord, walk (περιπατεῖτε) in him," where the injunction is similarly to work out in practical life the "tradition" received in words.

Schmithals (*Paul and the Gnostics*, 212, 213) has argued that "Thessalonians B," editorially interrupted after 2:12 by the insertion of "Thessalonians D," is resumed at 4:2.

Comment

4:1 Λοιπὸν οὖν, "For the rest, then." λοιπόν exemplifies the accusative of respect; cf. 1 Cor 1:16; 2 Tim 4:8; also 2 Thess 3:1; Phil 3:1; 4:8, where τὸ λοιπόν is used. When the genitive τοῦ λοιποῦ occurs in a similar sense (e.g. Gal 6:17; Eph 6:10) it should probably be treated as genitive of time within which (with χρόνου understood).

ἐρωτῶμεν, "we request" (cf. 5:12). ἐρωτᾶν, used in classical Greek only of asking a question, has the additional sense of making a request in Hellenistic Greek. (With the doublet ἐρωτῶμεν . . . καὶ παρακαλοῦμεν cf. Latin *oramus atque obsecramus.*)

παρακαλοῦμεν (cf. v 10; 5:14; 2 Thess 3:12) is somewhat more emphatic or formal than ἐρωτῶμεν, "we make our appeal." Paul tends to use παρακαλῶ at turning points in his argument, especially when he is launching into a paraenetic phase in his correspondence (e.g. Rom 12:1; 1 Cor 1:10; 2 Cor 6:1; 10:1; Eph 4:1). C. J. Bjerkelund (*Parakalô*, 125–140) finds a recurrent epistolary formula in Hellenistic Greek, where παρακαλῶ or παρακαλοῦμεν is followed by a vocative (like ἀδελφοί here), a prepositional phrase (here, ἐν κυρίῳ 'Ιησοῦ), a request or command expressed in the infinitive (like περισσεύειν κτλ in vv 10, 11) or by means of ἵνα with the subjunctive (as here).

ἐν κυρίῳ 'Ιησοῦ, implying not only his authority (which is indicated by διά in v 2) but "a sense that Christ is thoroughly involved in the situation or action in question—*a consciousness of Christ*" (Dunn, *Jesus and the Spirit*, 324, his italics; cf. Moule, *Christology*, 54–63). The writers, being themselves "in the Lord Jesus," are counseling fellow-members of Christ. Cf. 2 Thess 3:12.

ἵνα, left hanging for the time being, but repeated and completed at the end of the sentence (ἵνα . . . περισσεύητε μᾶλλον, "that you may abound more and more").

καθὼς παρελάβετε, a further reference (cf. 2:13) to the "tradition" which the missionaries had delivered to the Thessalonian believers. In 2:13 it was the saving message that they received; here the reference is to ethical teaching.

The tradition (παράδοσις) of Christ in the apostolic writings has three main components: (1) a summary of the gospel story, whether it takes the form of preaching (κήρυγμα) or confession of faith; (2) a rehearsal of deeds and words of Christ; (3) ethical and procedural guidelines for Christians. These guidelines are derived from the teaching and example of

Christ, who is indeed the embodiment of the tradition: "as you received (παρελάβετε) Christ Jesus the Lord, so live in him, rooted and built up in him, just as you were taught . . ." (Col 2:6, 7). The tradition was apparently delivered in the form of a catechesis, grouped under such captions as "Put off (old vices)," "put on (new virtues)," "be subject (to those in authority and one to another)," "watch and pray" (cf. Col 3:5–4:6). Paul can safely assume that the Roman Christians, who were not his own converts, have learned such a catechesis (Rom 6:17): "you have become obedient from the heart to the form of teaching to which you were committed" (εἰς ὃν παρεδόθητε, meaning perhaps "which you had delivered to you"). Paul and his colleagues made it their aim so to imitate Christ that they in turn became embodiments of the ethical tradition; cf. Phil 4:9, "what you have learned and received (παρελάβετε) and heard and seen in me, do." See also 2 Thess 2:15; 3:6–10, with comments.

τὸ πῶς δεῖ ὑμᾶς περιπατεῖν, "how you ought to walk." The τό introduces a noun clause (more precisely, an indirect question; cf. Acts 4:21, τὸ πῶς κολάσωνται αὐτούς); its presence or absence makes no difference to the sense. For the ethical use of περιπατεῖν cf. 2:12, with comment. For non-Pauline instances in NT cf. Acts 21:21 (τοῖς ἔθεσιν περιπατεῖν, "to observe the customs"); 1 John 2:6 (ὁ λέγων ἐν αὐτῷ μένειν ὀφείλει καθὼς ἐκεῖνος περιεπάτησεν καὶ αὐτὸς [οὕτως] περιπατεῖν, "he who says he abides in him ought to walk in the same way in which he walked").

περιπατεῖν καὶ ἀρέσκειν θεῷ, a hendiadys: "to walk and to please God" means "to walk so as to please God" (for pleasing God cf. 2:4, 15, with comments).

καθὼς καὶ περιπατεῖτε ("even as you do walk"), parenthetic. For the writers' assurance that the Thessalonians are already fulfilling their prayers or exhortations cf. v 10; 5:11.

ἵνα περισσεύητε μᾶλλον, repeating the earlier ἵνα and completing the ἵνα clause: "that you may abound the more (in the kind of conduct that pleases God)."

2. οἴδατε γάρ, "for you know." Once again (cf. 1:5; 2:1, 2, 5, 11; 3:3, 4) it is plain that the readers' memories are being refreshed; they are not being told something for the first time but reminded of what they know already.

τίνας παραγγελίας ἐδώκαμεν ὑμῖν, "what charges (instructions) we gave you" (cf. the verb παραγγέλλειν in v 11). There is an authoritative note about the word παραγγελία. The apostolic tradition is not to be treated indifferently; it is to be accepted because it is the tradition of Christ, by whose authority the apostles deliver it. This is indicated by the following phrase, διὰ τοῦ κυρίου Ἰησοῦ, "through the Lord Jesus" (for similar Pauline expressions with διά, especially strengthening παρακαλῶ, cf. Rom 12:1; 15:30; 1 Cor 1:10; 2 Cor 10:1). The apostolic tradition does not derive from the apostles themselves; it is "the commandment (ἐντολή) of the Lord" (1 Cor 14:37) and to be obeyed as such.

Explanation

The urgency with which the apostles and their associates set the ethical standards of the gospel before their converts suggests that there may have been a tendency to resist the inculcation of such standards or to think them unimportant. Was Christ not his people's liberator? Had he not set them free from codes and taboos which held them in bondage? Why then were they expected to submit to what some of them regarded as a new set of rules?

The answer was that Christ their liberator had brought them new life, and this new life had a positive ethical content. It was new life in Christ, and was to be recognized by those features which belonged to the character of Christ. Christ led a life that brought pleasure to God, and taught his followers how to live so as to please God. The apostles imposed no arbitrary controls on their converts to prevent them from realizing their Christian freedom; they taught them Christ's way of freedom in which they would find deliverance from the fetters of old sinful habits. The "charges" which they gave them in the name of Christ were not external regulations to which they must painstakingly conform; they were part of the outworking of the new life maintained within them by the Holy Spirit.

(b) *On Sexual Purity (4:3–8)*

Bibliography

Adinolfi, M. "La santità del matrimonio in 1 Tess 4, 1–8." *RivB* 24 (1976) 165–184. **Adinolfi, M.** "Le frodi di 1 Tess 4, 6a e l'epiclerato." *BibOr* 18 (1976) 29–38. **Adinolfi, M.** "Etica 'commerciale' e motivi parenetici in 1 Tess 4, 1–8." *BibOr* 19 (1977) 9–20. **Baltensweiler, H.** *Die Ehe im Neuen Testament.* Stuttgart: Zwingli, 1967. **Baltensweiler, H.** "Erwägungen zu 1 Thess 4, 3–8." *TZ* 19 (1963) 1–13. **Beauvery, R.** "Πλεονεκτεῖν in I Thess 4, 6a." *VD* 33 (1955) 273–286. **Brillet, G.** "Dieu veut nous sanctifier dans le Christ (1 Th 4, 1–7)." *AsSeign* n.s. No. 28 (1963) 16–26. **Giblin, C. H.** *In Hope of God's Glory.* New York: Herder, 1970. **Gill, S. M.** "In das Gewerbe seines Nächsten eingreifen (1 Thess 4, 6)." *BZ* 11 (1967) 118. **Linder, J. R.** "Exegetische Bemerkungen zu einigen Stellen des Neuen Testaments. 1 Thess 4, 3–5." *TSK* 40 (1867) 516–521. **Maurer, C.** σκεῦος. *TDNT* vii, 361–362, 365–367. **Ogara, F.** "Haec est . . . voluntas Dei, sanctificatio vestra (1 Thes 4, 1–7)." *VD* 18 (1938) 65–72. **Rickards, R. R.** "1 Thessalonians 4:4–6." *BT* 29 (1978) 245–247. **Schmithals, W.** *Paul and the Gnostics.* Tr. J. E. Steely. Nashville/ New York: Abingdon, 1972. **Vogel, W.** "Εἰδέναι τὸ ἑαυτοῦ σκεῦος κτᾶσθαι. Zur Deutung von 1 Thess 4, 3 ff in Zusammenhang der paulinischen Eheanfassung." *TBl* 13 (1934) 83–85. **Wiederkehr, D.** *Die Theologie der Berufung in den Paulusbriefen.* Freiburg: Universitätsverlag, 1963.

Translation

> [3] *For this is God's will—your sanctification:*
> *that you should abstain from* [a] *fornication,*

⁴ *that each of you should learn to gain control over his "vessel"*
in sanctification and honor.
⁵ *not in lustful passion,*
like the Gentiles who have no knowledge ᵇ *of God.*
⁶ *None of you should trespass* ᶜ
or behave covetously against his brother in the matter, ᵈ
because the Lord is an avenger in all these things,
as indeed we warned you insistently.
⁷ *For God has not called us for impurity but in sanctification.*
⁸ *Therefore any one who disregards (this charge)*
does not disregard man
but God,
who indeed ᵉ *gives* ᶠ *you* ᵍ *his Holy Spirit.*

Notes

ᵃ πάσης ("all") is inserted before πορνείας ("fornication") by ℵ ² Ψ *pc;* πάσης τῆς by F Gᶜ.
ᵇ τὰ μὴ εἰδότα. In Hellenistic Greek μή is the negative regularly used with the participle (cf. 2:15, τῶν . . . θεῷ μὴ ἀρεσκόντων), although even in classical Greek it might be expected here; it is a characteristic of Gentiles that they do not know (the living and true) God.
ᶜ τὸ μὴ ὑπερβαίνειν, the same construction as in 3:3, τὸ μηδένα σαίνεσθαι (see p. 59, note f): "in order not to trespass."
ᵈ KJV "in *any* matter" may presuppose the non-accentuation of τῷ in ἐν τῷ πράγματι as τῳ, the equivalent of τινι (cf. the conjecture of H. Grotius, ἔν τινι πράγματι).
ᵉ καί ("indeed") between the article and διδόντα is omitted by A B D ¹ I 33 614 1739 * *al* latᵇ syrᵖᵉˢʰ copᵇᵒ Ambst Spec.
ᶠ For διδόντα (present participle) δόντα (aorist participle) is read by ℵ ² A Ψ byz syr cop Clem. Al.
ᵍ For ὑμᾶς ("you") ἡμᾶς ("us") is read by A 6 365 1739 1881 *pc* latᵃ ᶠ ᵐ ᵗ ᵛᵍ·ᶜˡ syrʰᶜˡ.

Form/Structure/Setting

This exhortation to holiness is concluded with the τοιγαροῦν clause of v 8. The exhortation itself, as is pointed out by Giblin (*In Hope*, 18), is constructed on an *inclusio* pattern, exhibited in the translation above. The *inclusio* is based on the repeated ἁγιασμός (vv 3a, 4b, 7), caught up by τὸ πνεῦμα . . . τὸ ἅγιον (v 8).

Comment

4:3. Τοῦτο γάρ ἐστιν θέλημα τοῦ θεοῦ, "for this is God's will." To please God (v 1) is to do his will. For the omission of the article before θέλημα cf. 1 Cor 16:12 (οὐκ ἦν θέλημα); 1 Macc 3:60 (ὡς δ' ἂν ᾖ θέλημα ἐν οὐρανῷ); but here the noun is explicitly defined by τοῦ θεοῦ. Lightfoot suggests that the article is omitted because the will of God is wider than "your sanctification"; he quotes J. A. Bengel ad loc.: "multae sunt *voluntates*" (Bengel appeals to the plural θελήματα in Acts 13:22). But the will of God for his people is not wider than their sanctification; his will is precisely that they should be holy, as he himself is holy (Lev 11:44, 45, etc.; 1 Pet 1:15,

16). The anarthrous θέλημα is better explained if it be taken as the predicate: "This—namely, your sanctification (as more closely defined in the words that follow)—is God's will (for you)." Cf. 5:18, with comment.

ὁ ἁγιασμὸς ὑμῶν, "your sanctification"; if ἁγιωσύνη (3:13) is the state of being holy, ἁγιασμός is the process of making holy. This is the earliest Christian occurrence of ἁγιασμός (for ἁγιάζειν, the verb from which it is derived, cf. 5:23); in earlier Greek it is used of consecration to some religious purpose, but not even in LXX does it bear the strong ethical sense which it has here and in later Christian literature. In the present context its antithesis is ἀκαθαρσία (v 7).

ἀπέχεσθαι ὑμᾶς ἀπὸ τῆς πορνείας, "that you abstain from fornication." The language is similar to that of the Jerusalem decree, ἀπέχεσθαι . . . (τῆς) πορνείας (Acts 15:20, 29); it might not be irrelevant to recall that Silvanus (Silas) was one of the two commissioners appointed by the leaders of the Jerusalem church to carry the letter embodying the decree to the church of Antioch and her daughter-churches (Acts 15:22, 27).

Chastity is not the whole of sanctification, but it is an important element in it, and one which had to be specially stressed in the Greco-Roman world of that day. While πορνεία means primarily traffic with harlots (πόρναι), like Heb. זנות (traffic with זונות), it may denote any form of illicit sexual relationship. But "immorality" (RSV) is too vague a rendering. In some NT passages πορνεία appears to have a more technical sense of sexual union within forbidden degress of consanguinity or affinity (as in 1 Cor 5:1, in the exceptive clauses of Matt 5:32; 19:9, and in the Jerusalem decree, Acts 15:20, 29; 21:25); but here it has its more general sense. Christianity from the outset has sanctified sexual union within marriage (as in Judaism); outside marriage it was forbidden. This was a strange notion in the pagan society to which the gospel was first brought; there various forms of extra-marital sexual union were tolerated and some were even encouraged. A man might have a mistress (ἑταίρα) who could provide him also with intellectual companionship; the institution of slavery made it easy for him to have a concubine (παλλακή), while casual gratification was readily available from a harlot (πόρνη). The function of his wife was to manage his household and be the mother of his legitimate children and heirs. There was no body of public opinion to discourage πορνεία, although someone who indulged in it to excess might be satirized on the same level as a notorious glutton or drunkard. Certain forms of public religion, indeed, involved ritual πορνεία. In Thessalonica it was sanctioned by the cult of the Cabiri of Samothrace, although it is doubtful if, as J. B. Lightfoot suggests, "we may suppose that St. Paul alluded" to the Cabiric rites "when he deprecated any connexion between his gospel and uncleanness" (*Biblical Essays*, London: Macmillan, 1893, 257, 258). When the gospel was introduced into pagan society, therefore, it was necessary to emphasize the complete breach with accepted mores in this area which was demanded by the new way of life in Christ. Cf. 1 Cor 6:12–20, with its peremptory φεύγετε τὴν πορνείαν, "shun fornication!" (v 18).

4. εἰδέναι ἕκαστον ὑμῶν, "that each of you learn."

τὸ ἑαυτοῦ σκεῦος κτᾶσθαι. Translators and commentators are divided on the question whether this means "to gain mastery over his body" (NEB) or "to take a wife for himself" (RSV). The latter interpretation, which can claim the support of Theodore of Mopsuestia (ad loc.) and Augustine (De nuptiis 1.9), has in its favor the normal use of κτᾶσθαι ("acquire"); the principal argument against it is the unnatural sense which it requires for σκεῦος ("vessel"). In classical usage it is the perfect of κτᾶσθαι that means "possess"; if, however, the present infinitive be translated here "gain control over," its proper force is retained and a more natural sense is preserved for σκεῦος.

The idea that σκεῦος may mean "wife" cannot be defended by an appeal to 1 Pet 3:7; there both man and woman are σκεύη as creatures of God, the woman being the ἀσθενέστερον σκεῦος of the two. She is certainly not her husband's σκεῦος—indeed, although she herself is called a σκεῦος, the expression "weaker vessel" refers more particularly to her body (as the "vessel" in our present text is the man's body). There is no NT parallel for calling a man's wife his σκεῦος, which implies (as Lightfoot says) a "low sensual view of the marriage relation" and a "depreciatory estimate of the woman's position," as though her raison d'être were to provide a means by which her husband might satisfy his sexual appetite without infringing the divine law. It is impermissible to adduce 1 Cor 7:2 as a parallel, for there fornication is avoided by each man's having his own wife and each woman's having her own husband; the relationship is mutual and neither is the σκεῦος of the other, both being persons in their own right.

The sense of "body" for σκεῦος is suggested by other metaphorical occurrences of the word in the Pauline writings, especially 2 Cor 4:7, "we have this treasure in earthen vessels" (ἐν ὀστρακίνοις σκεύεσιν); cf. Rom 9:22, 23, where the σκεύη of wrath or mercy are human beings created by God to serve his purpose. In Acts 9:15 Paul himself is called the Lord's "chosen instrument" (σκεῦος ἐκλογῆς) for the propagation of the gospel.

The LXX phrase κτᾶσθαι γυναῖκα (Ruth 4:10; Sir 36:24) does not support the rendering "acquire a wife" here, for there the object of κτᾶσθαι is explicitly γυναῖκα. There is one OT precedent for the use of "vessel" in the present kind of context (with special reference to the genitalia): in 1 Sam (LXX 1 Kgdms) 21:5, when the priest of Nob tells David that he and his companions may eat the holy bread "if only the young men have kept themselves from women," David replies, "the young men's vessels (כלי) are holy" (the sense is obscured in LXX, but כלי is rendered σκεύη). This is the force of σκεῦος here: "that each of you learn to gain control over his own 'vessel.' "

ἐν ἁγιασμῷ καὶ τιμῇ, "in sanctification and honor." The body belongs to the Lord and must be consecrated to him; the preservation of bodily honor (cf. 1 Cor 6:20, δοξάσατε δὴ τὸν θεὸν ἐν τῷ σώματι ὑμῶν, "So glorify God in your body") is contrasted with the sexual excesses which involve ἀτιμάζεσθαι τὰ σώματα αὐτῶν ἐν αὐτοῖς, "the dishonoring of their bodies among themselves" (Rom 1:24).

5. μὴ ἐν πάθει ἐπιθυμίας, "not in lustful passion." The body must be treated as the Lord's property and not used as a means of wanton self-indulgence. The neutral sense of πάθος ("experience," "emotion") is not found in NT, where it is invariably used *in malam partem;* cf. Rom 1:26, "God gave them over to dishonorable passions" (πάθη ἀτιμίας); Col 3:5, where the word figures in a list of vices: "fornication, uncleanness, passion (πάθος), evil desire (ἐπιθυμία κακή) and covetousness" (πλεονεξία, with which cf. v 6 below, πλεονεκτεῖν). Similarly ἐπιθυμία is most often used *in malam partem*, of evil desires, in NT (for exceptions see 2:17 above; Luke 22:15; Phil 1:23); cf. Rom 1:24, "God gave them over in the lusts of their hearts" (ἐν ταῖς ἐπιθυμίαις τῶν καρδιῶν αὐτῶν); Gal 5:24, "Those who belong to Christ Jesus have crucified the flesh with its passions and desires" (σὺν τοῖς παθήμασιν καὶ ταῖς ἐπιθυμίαις).

καθάπερ καὶ τὰ ἔθνη τὰ μὴ εἰδότα τὸν θεόν, "like the Gentiles who do not know God." Behavior of the kind reprobated here is put down to deliberate ignorance, or indeed ignoring, of God in Rom 1:28 (οὐκ ἐδοκίμασαν τὸν θεὸν ἔχειν ἐν ἐπιγνώσει, "they did not see fit to acknowledge God"); cf. Eph 4:17. The wording echoes that of Ps 79 (LXX 78):6, ἔθνη τὰ μὴ γινώσκοντά σε, "the nations that do not know thee." Cf. 2 Thess 1:8.

6. τὸ μὴ ὑπερβαίνειν. For the construction cf. note c above. The force of ὑπερβαίνειν (here only in NT) is of crossing a boundary—here of crossing a forbidden boundary, and hence trespassing (sexually) on territory which is not one's own. Jerome (on Eph 5:3) has a phrase which aptly expresses the sense: *"transgredi concessos fines nuptiarum"* ("to transgress the permitted bounds of marriage").

It is not universally agreed that the theme of v 6 is still sexual purity: some (e.g. Beauvery, "Πλεονεκτεῖν") argue that what is now forbidden is overreaching someone (especially a fellow Christian) in the field of commerce, and support this interpretation by an appeal to the further definition of ὑπερβαίνειν as πλεονεκτεῖν ("coveting"), which implies greed for property, rather than inordinate sexual appetite. But πλεονεκτεῖν is the desire to possess more than one should in any area of life, and the nouns πλεονέκτης ("covetous person") and πλεονεξία ("covetousness," found in a more general sense in 2:5) repeatedly occur in close association with words denoting fornication or impurity (cf. 1 Cor 5:10, 11; Eph 4:19; 5:3, 5). It is the general context that must determine the precise force of πλεονεκτεῖν here. Schmithals (apart from his view that the influence of gnostic libertinism is under attack in this paragraph) expresses the thought reasonably well: "no one is to 'enrich' himself in this matter at his brother's expense, by taking his wife away from him" (*Paul and the Gnostics,* 157)—although the woman in question might be another member of the brother's household, not necessarily his wife (Schmithals has in mind the promiscuity allegedly practiced at meetings of certain heretical sects, but this is irrelevant here).

ἐν τῷ πράγματι, "in the matter (under discussion)," i.e. sexual relations, not a business deal (so Beauvery) nor yet a legal process. This last suggestion is made by Baltensweiler ("Erwägungen"), who sees a reference here to the law in Athens and some other Greek city-states affecting the position of an heiress (ἐπίκληρος). When an heiress inherited an estate, in the absence of any direct male heir, the next of kin could claim her in marriage in order to keep the property in the family, even if her existing marriage had to be annulled on this account. The situation frequently involved lawsuits; it gave ample scope for the display of πλεονεξία and (where the resultant marriage was between two people so closely akin that their union was forbidden by biblical law) it led to a state of technical πορνεία. Baltensweiler thinks that a case of this kind had cropped up in the Thessalonian church and that an apostolic ruling had been sought on it. But there is no indication of this, nor yet is there any indication that this specific form of πλεονεξία or πορνεία is in view. It may well be that Timothy had brought back a report on sexual laxity among the Christians of Thessalonica, possibly with reference to a particular irregularity involving a member of the church and the family of another member.

τὸν ἀδελφὸν αὐτοῦ, "his brother," meaning probably a fellow Christian (although the action would be equally reprobated if the victim of the "trespass" were a pagan).

διότι ἔκδικος κύριος περὶ πάντων τούτων, "because the Lord is an avenger in all these matters." The κύριος is Jesus; this is in line with general Pauline usage and is required by the change of subject to ὁ θεός in v 7. The only other NT instance of ἔκδικος uses the word of the civil magistrate (Rom 13:4). In 2 Thess 1:8 it is "the Lord Jesus" who will mete out ἐκδίκησις ("retribution") on the ungodly; in 1 Cor 4:5 it is "the Lord" who at his coming "will bring to light the things now hidden in darkness and will disclose the purposes of the heart." In Eph 5:6 and Col 3:5, 6 "the wrath (ὀργή) of God" falls on those guilty of fornication, impurity, covetousness and associated vices. For the construction with περί cf. 1 Macc 13:6, ἐκδικήσω περὶ τοῦ ἔθνους μου ("I will take vengeance for my nation").

καθὼς καὶ προείπαμεν ὑμῖν, "as we told you before," "as we warned you." Ethical guidance in this field of conduct had formed part of the oral instruction given to the Thessalonian church before the missionaries' departure; it was a necessary part of the charge "to lead a life worthy of God" (2:11, 12). It was probably Timothy's report that indicated that further admonition was necessary on this subject. Cf. 2 Cor 12:20 13:2 for similar necessity at Corinth.

διεμαρτυράμεθα, "we insisted" (cf. μαρτυρόμενοι, 2:12).

7. οὐ γὰρ ἐκάλεσεν ἡμᾶς ὁ θεὸς ἐπ᾽ ἀκαθαρσίᾳ: "for God did not call us for impurity" (cf. 2:3). The mention of ἀκαθαρσία confirms that the subject of v 6 is sexual rather than commercial behavior. The use of ἐπί with the dative to express purpose is classical; cf. (in NT) Gal 5:13 (ἐπ᾽ ἐλευθερίᾳ ἐκλήθητε, "you were called to freedom"); Eph 2:10 (ἐπὶ ἔργοις ἀγαθοῖς, "for good works"); 2 Tim 2:14 (ἐπὶ καταστροφῇ, "for destruction").

ἀλλ᾽ ἐν ἁγιασμῷ, "but in sanctification"; the change of preposition from ἐπί to ἐν implies that sanctification is part of the Christian calling; by calling his people God sanctifies them in the sense of setting them apart for himself; they are already κλητοὶ ἅγιοι, "saints by calling" (Rom 1:7; 1 Cor 1:2), and must manifest their sanctification in the ways of daily life. Cf. 2 Thess 2:13, 14; 2 Tim 1:9; 1 Pet 1:2, 15. The climax of sanctification appears in 3:13; 5:23, 24.

For καλεῖν ἐν cf. 1 Cor 7:15, ἐν δὲ εἰρήνῃ κέκληκεν ὑμᾶς ὁ θεός ("God has called you in peace").

8. τοιγαροῦν, "therefore," a compound particle as emphatic in Hellenistic Greek as it was in classical Greek. Its only other NT occurrence is Heb 12:1.

ὁ ἀθετῶν, "he who disregards" perhaps with τὴν παραγγελίαν, "the charge" (cf. v 2) implied as object, although the personal objects to ἀθετεῖ in the following part of the sentence suggest that the implied object to ὁ ἀθετῶν is also personal. The verb ἀθετεῖν is used in a formal or legal sense of "annulling" a will (Gal 3:15) or similar document; in the present nontechnical contextitmeans"disregard"or"reject."

οὐκ ἄνθρωπον ἀθετεῖ ἀλλὰ τὸν θεόν, "does not disregard man, but God." There is no article with ἄνθρωπον as there is with θεόν, perhaps because no particular human being is in mind, but there is only one God. Schmithals, however, thinks that Paul is the ἄνθρωπος in question; since he and his colleagues left Thessalonica, the church, he argues, had been visited by gnostic libertines who urged the Christians to forget Paul's restrictive teaching on sexual ethics, assuring them that a more permissive policy would mean indeed a rejection of Paul's ruling but not of the law of God (*Paul and the Gnostics*, 157, 158). Paul retorts that the charge the Thessalonians had received on this matter was not his, but God's. In this and other sections of the letter, the difficulty about Schmithals's view is that, if such troublemakers had visited the Thessalonian church, more explicit reference to them might have been expected.

τὸν [καὶ] διδόντα τὸ πνεῦμα αὐτοῦ τὸ ἅγιον εἰς ὑμᾶς, "who indeed gives his Holy Spirit to you" (or ". . . sets his Holy Spirit within you"). The gift of the *Holy* Spirit (his holiness is emphasized by the position of τὸ ἅγιον) demands practical holiness in the lives of those whom he indwells. Cf. 1 Cor 6:19, where fornication is a sin committed against the believer's body which is a "sanctuary (ναός) of the Holy Spirit."

Explanation

The injunction to holiness concentrates on the matter of sexual morality. This is not the whole of holiness, but it is an important aspect of it, and one which needed to be especially stressed when converts from Greek paganism were being instructed in the Christian way. The practice of fornication, which the Thessalonian Christians are urged to avoid, meant in the strict sense commerce with prostitutes, but covered many forms of extramarital sexual intercourse. The idea of confining sexual intercourse within marriage was foreign to Greek conventional morality of the period. The general attitude is frequently illustrated by a quotation from Demosthenes's oration *Against Neaera:* "We keep mistresses for pleasure, concubines for our day-to-day bodily needs, but we have wives to produce legitimate children and serve as trustworthy guardians of our homes." That was the outlook of a reputable citizen of Athens in the fourth century B.C. Over two centuries earlier Solon, the great legislator of Athens, is said to have legalized prostitution and proclaimed that the profits from state brothels should be used for the building of temples. No official religious sanction could be expected against the practice of prostitution. Here we are concerned only with heterosexual union, since that is what is under discussion in the present context.

The double standard for the two sexes was taken for granted. Married men were allowed a freedom which was out of the question for married women. The state of affairs which had lately obtained in the highest quarters in Rome, where the empress herself was charged with practicing prostitution, was scandalous by any standards. Moderation in sexual activity, as in other forms of indulgence, was proper to a civilized man. And a number of people might band themselves together in a cult group or similar association pledged to a stricter chastity than was current in their environment.

It may be that Timothy, on his return from Thessalonica, reported an undesirable laxity in sexual relations in the church there. There is no evidence of any attempt at Thessalonica (as there was later at Corinth) to justify this laxity on the ground that, for men of the Spirit, bodily functions were religiously irrelevant (sex being as indifferent as food) or by an appeal to Paul's own teaching about Christian freedom. Neither is it implied in this paragraph that the Thessalonian Christians took the initiative in raising the question.

In general, the teaching of this paragraph was on the same lines as proselytes to Judaism would have received (including the reference to the Holy Spirit), although it is Christianized by its context. The high standard of Jewish sexual ethics was known and respected in the lands of the dispersion. Monogamy was now the norm among Jews, even if the ancient law of Israel countenanced a plurality of wives. The schools of legal interpretation among the Jews differed on the question of valid grounds for divorce. Jesus radicalized this aspect of Jewish ethics (among others) by forbidding divorce among his followers, because it was contrary, he said, to the Creator's purpose in instituting marriage (Mark 10:2–12). According to Matthew (19:10), his disciples were so disconcerted by this ruling that their immediate conclusion was that it was best for a man not to marry at all. (They viewed his ruling as an encroachment on male privilege, whereas Jesus probably intended it as a protection for disadvantaged women.) Jesus' ruling, nevertheless, was taken over by the early church, and Paul applies it as something not to be questioned (1 Cor 7:10, 11).

Here, however, specific questions about marriage are not raised. It is taken for granted that married life is the norm for Christians (this was not affected by the fact that a few Christians knew themselves to be expressly called to a celibate life). But sexual relations are to be practiced exclusively within marriage, and any form of sexual aggression against the family life of others is condemned. The Spirit whom Christians have received is the Spirit of *holiness,* and nothing unholy can be tolerated in one whom he indwells: self-control is part of the fruit which his presence yields in a believer's life (Gal 5:22, 23).

This exhortation to sexual purity, then, is probably to be recognized as the first instance of the writers' resolve to make good the deficiencies in the faith of their Thessalonian friends, since it was not practicable at present to make them good by a personal visit and face-to-face conversation.

(c) On Brotherly Love (4:9–12)

Bibliography

Faw, C. E. "On the writing of First Thessalonians." *JBL* 71 (1952) 217–232. Foerster, W. "Εὐσέβεια in den Pastoralbriefen." *NTS* 5 (1958–59) 213–218. Harris, J. R. "A Study in Letter-Writing." *Expositor,* series 5, 8 (1898) 161–180. Schmithals, W. *Paul and the Gnostics.* Tr. J. E. Steely. Nashville/New York: Abingdon, 1972. Spicq, C. "La charité fraternelle selon 1 Th 4, 9." In *Mélanges bibliques rédigés en honneur de André Robert.* Paris: Bloud et Gay, 1957, 507–511. Tambyah, T. I. "Θεοδίδακτοι: A Suggestion of an Implication of the Deity of Christ." *ExpTim* 44 (1932–33) 527–528.

Translation

9 *With regard to brotherly love you have no need (for us) to write to you* [a], *for you yourselves are divinely taught to love* [b] *one another—* 10 *indeed, you do it* [c] *to all the brothers* [d] *in the whole of Macedonia. But we appeal to you, brothers, abound (in this) more and more;* 11 *make it your aim to lead a quiet life, to attend to your own affairs and to work with your own* [e] *hands, as we charged you,* 12 *so that you may conduct yourselves becomingly toward those who are outside (your ranks), and may have need of nothing.*

Notes

[a] ἔχομεν ("we have") is read for ἔχετε ("you have") by ℵ² D* F G Ψ 1739 1881 *pc* lat syr^{hel}; εἴχομεν ("we had") is read by B I lat^{vg.codd}. "We have no need to write to you" gives excellent sense and construction; it is possible that the reading "you have" is due to the influence of 5:1, as is the reading γράφεσθαι (H 81 *pc* Aug) for γράφειν ("you have no need to be written to").

[b] εἰς τὸ ἀγαπᾶν, where εἰς τό is best seen as "acting for the epexegetic inf" (MHT i, 219).

[c] καί ("even") is inserted by B before εἰς πάντας τοὺς ἀδελφούς.

[d] τούς (emphasizing the attributive relationship of the following ἐν ὅλῃ τῇ Μακεδονίᾳ to τοὺς ἀδελφούς) is read in ℵ² B D¹ H Ψ byz lat^{vg.cod}; it is omitted by ℵ* A D* F G 629 lat.

[e] ἰδίαις ("own") is read in ℵ* A D¹ byz; it is omitted by ℵ² B D* F G Ψ 1739 1881 *pc* syr^{hel}.

Form/Structure/Setting

The opening words of this paragraph (Περὶ δέ "now concerning," "with respect to") raise the possibility that at this stage in the letter, the writers are replying to questions raised in a letter sent to them by the Thessalonian church (comparable to the letter from the Corinthian church to which Paul begins his reply in 1 Cor 7:1).

The sending of a letter from Thessalonica was defended by Harris ("A Study in Letter-Writing"), B. W. Bacon (*INT,* 73), D. Smith (*Life and Letters,* 152–166), A. E. Barnett (*The NT: Making and Meaning,* 37) and in the commentaries of G. Milligan (126), J. E. Frame (140) and E. J. Bicknell (xvii, 40). More recently Faw ("On the Writing . . .") has laid special stress on the occurrence here and below (4:13; 5:1) of περὶ δέ (or an equivalent expression), which is "(1) a formula of reply to specific questions or problems, especially where there is a series of such; (2) in series of replies it is properly used to introduce those from the second point onward; (3) in Pauline usage it is confined to answering of specific questions or problems brought up in letters from the churches to which he is writing" (221).

It is indeed conceivable that the writers had received a letter from the Thessalonian church, whether it was brought back by Timothy or dispatched independently. But if Timothy had conveyed their questions and problems by word of mouth, they would have been dealt with in exactly the same way as if they had been formulated in a letter. Questions and problems the Thessalonians certainly had, especially as regards things to come. But it is unlikely that, whether orally or in writing, they would have used such general phraseology as: "What should we do about brotherly love (φιλαδελφία)?" It is more likely that the writers knew that, for all their practice of this grace, the conduct of some of the church members conflicted with its requirements, and they proceeded to give some spontaneous admonition on this point.

Comment

4:9. Περὶ δὲ τῆς φιλαδελφίας, "But concerning brotherly love." It is unlikely that περὶ δέ refers to a question sent to the missionaries by the Thessalonian Christians; it is not the kind of specific subject on which ruling would be sought, and the writers indicate that it is not something on which the Thessalonians require instruction (apart, as appears from v 11, from one matter which affects brotherly love). φιλαδελφία is more restricted than ἀγάπη, which is to be extended "to all" (3:12). The noun appears only in one other place in the Pauline corpus (Rom 12:10); cf. also Heb 13:1; 1 Pet 1:22; 2 Pet 1:7 *bis* (the adjective φιλάδελφος occurs in 1 Pet 3:8). It is not found before the Hellenistic period; in LXX it is confined to a later book which was not translated from Hebrew (4 Macc 13:23, 26; 14:1). It is derived from φιλάδελφος, "loving one's brother," which appears occasionally in Attic Greek (cf. Soph. *Ant.* 527; Xen. *Mem.* 2.3.17). Quite apart from the use of this compound, love within the fellowship of brothers and sisters in Christ is inculcated throughout the NT.

οὐ χρείαν ἔχετε γράφειν ὑμῖν, "you have no need (for us) to write to you," because they had already been made aware of their duty to practice brotherly love and were indeed actively practicing it. Cf. 5:1.

αὐτοί γὰρ ὑμεῖς θεοδίδακτοί ἐστε εἰς τὸ ἀγαπᾶν ἀλλήλους, "for you yourselves are divinely taught to love one another." This is the only occurrence of θεοδίδακτος in the NT and its earliest extant occurrence in Greek literature. In the new age, according to Isa 54:13, all the children of Zion will be "taught of the Lord" (LXX διδακτοὺς θεοῦ, quoted in John 6:45); cf. 1 John 2:20 for the sense. Love of one's neighbor was enjoined in the OT law (cf. Lev 19:18) and reaffirmed in the teaching of Jesus (Mark 12:31; cf. John 13:34, ἵνα ἀγαπᾶτε ἀλλήλους, where Jesus' love for his followers is the model for their love one for another). In Paul's teaching such love belongs to the fruit of the Spirit (Gal 5:22); it is the effect of the Spirit's pouring out the love of God into the hearts of believers (Rom 5:5).

When it is said that they are divinely taught to love one another, the reference may be both to the teaching of Jesus and to the inward action of the Spirit. Milligan refers to B. F. Westcott's comment on John 6:45 that "the phrase [διδακτοὶ θεοῦ] describes not only one divine communication, but a divine relationship" (*The Gospel according to St. John*, London: John Murray, 1880, 105), adding that "it is as those who have been born of God, and whose hearts are in consequence filled with God's spirit, that the Thessalonians on their part (αὐτοὶ . . . ὑμεῖς, "you yourselves") can no longer help loving" (ad loc.). Tambyah ("Θεοδίδακτοι . . .") sees in the compound adjective an implication of the deity of Christ. It may be gathered, moreover, that the formulation of brotherly love in the injunction ἀγαπᾶτε ἀλλήλους is not confined to the Johannine tradition of the sayings of Jesus.

10. καὶ γὰρ ποιεῖτε αὐτό, "for indeed you are doing it." For this confidence that they are already doing what their Christian commitment requires them to do cf. v 1 (καθὼς καὶ περιπατεῖτε); 5:11 (καθὼς καὶ ποιεῖτε).

εἰς πάντας τοὺς ἀδελφοὺς [τοὺς] ἐν ὅλη τῇ Μακεδονίᾳ, "to all the brothers in the whole of Macedonia." The Thessalonian Christians had evidently made good use of the lines of communication which linked their city with other places in the province (cf. 1:7, 8).

Παρακαλοῦμεν δὲ ὑμᾶς, "but we appeal to you." Cf. v 1, with comment.

περισσεύειν μᾶλλον, "that (you) abound more and more" identical with ἵνα περισσεύητε μᾶλλον in v 1, except that the ἵνα clause has been replaced by the synonymous infinitive. There the injunction was more generally to lead lives pleasing to God; here it has specific reference to brotherly love.

11. καὶ φιλοτιμεῖσθαι ἡσυχάζειν, "and to be ambitious to be quiet" (i.e. to lead quiet lives and not to be agitators). It is something of an oxymoron for φιλοτιμεῖσθαι to be associated with ἡσυχάζειν. Ambition usually involves more energetic action. Schmithals (*Paul and the Gnostics*, 158–160) thinks

that the kind of agitation which is discouraged here was motivated by gnostic enthusiasm. This, he thinks, was the result of a gnostic invasion of the Thessalonian church since the missionaries had left; he compares 2 Thess 3:6–13 and various passages in the Pastoral Letters (1 Tim 5:13–15; 2 Tim 3:1–9; Tit 1:10, 11). Cf. Foerster ("Εὐσέβεια . . . ," 216): in those places in the Pastoral Letters "we have to do with an enthusiastic gnosticizing movement, as is evident already in both the Thessalonian letters, in both of which the idea of 'quietness' appears in this connection." It is more commonly supposed that undue eschatological excitement had induced a restless tendency in some of the Thessalonian Christians and made them disinclined to attend to their ordinary business. The frequency with which this sort of thing has happened over the centuries makes it quite probable that it could happen in Thessalonica around A.D. 50. Cf. 2 Thess 2:2.

The various forms of φιλοτιμία inculcated here are closely related to φιλαδελφία. The conduct of one member of the community affects the welfare of the whole community; the reputation of the community suffers if a few members gain notoriety as idle busybodies, instead of minding their own affairs, πράσσειν τὰ ἴδια (cf. 2 Thess 3:11, with comment).

καὶ ἐργάζεσθαι ταῖς [ἰδίαις] χερσὶν ὑμῶν, "and to work with your own hands." The missionaries themselves had set a good example in the matter of working with their own hands and earning their own living (cf. 2:9). Brotherly love demanded sober and industrious habits; they had been told this by word of mouth (καθὼς ὑμῖν παρηγγείλαμεν) and are now reminded of it in writing (cf. 2 Thess 3:7–10).

12. ἵνα περιπατῆτε εὐσχημόνως πρὸς τοὺς ἔξω, "that you conduct yourselves becomingly toward outsiders." Cf. Col 4:5; "conduct yourselves wisely (ἐν σοφίᾳ) toward outsiders (πρὸς τοὺς ἔξω)"; also 1 Cor 5:12, 13, where οἱ ἔξω, the unbelievers, are contrasted with οἱ ἔσω, the members of the church. In the Pastoral Letters, elders in particular are required to have a good reputation among outsiders (ἀπὸ τῶν ἔξωθεν, 1 Tim 3:7).

καὶ μηδενὸς χρείαν ἔχητε, "and have need of nothing." If all the able-bodied members worked with their hands they would be able to support themselves and their dependents, and not fall into destitution and become a charge on the generosity of others. It was taken for granted that those who were destitute through no choice of their own would be supported by the church (cf. Eph 4:28; 1 Tim 5:3–8); this was a natural function of φιλαδελφία.

Explanation

In the OT the commandment to love God with all one's being and the commandment to love one's neighbor as oneself are the two great commandments; all the others are corollaries of these. In the NT they are reaffirmed by Jesus, one of whose followers sums up Christian duty in the statement "that he who loves God should love his brother also" (1 John 4:21).

The Thessalonian Christians had learned, almost by the instinct of the new life imparted to them, to love one another. The commandment of God, reaffirmed by Jesus, was being translated into real experience by the Spirit who now dwelt within them. Brotherly love was not a subject on which they had great need of apostolic instruction. And yet they had to understand that some forms of conduct were incompatible with brotherly love. One of these was the sexual invasion of another's person and household against which they were warned in the previous paragraph. Another was the tendency to put less into the common stock than they took out, to neglect their ordinary day-by-day tasks in such a way as to become a financial burden on others. The missionaries had not only impressed on them their obligation to do their own work and earn their own living; they had shown them a practical example in this regard. Yet some members of the church were ignoring both the admonition and the example. Timothy had probably brought a report to this effect on his recent return from Thessalonica.

Those who were behaving in this way were not only being burdensome to their fellow Christians; they were incurring a bad reputation among non-Christians, not only for themselves but for the Christian faith. "If this is Christianity," non-Christians might say as they saw those idlers, "we do not think much of it." The idlers, indeed, were not only neglecting the things they ought to be doing; they were actively engaged in things they ought not to be doing, by officious interference in other people's business. There is a great difference between the Christian duty of putting the interests of others before one's own (Phil 2:4) and the busybody's compulsive itch to put other people right. Here, then, was another area in which deficiencies had to be made good.

But what was responsible for this spirit of restlessness? One suggestion is that gnosticizing visitors had filled the minds of some Thessalonian Christians with an unsettling enthusiasm, such as is attested for one or two other churches in the Pauline mission field. But there is no clear evidence for influences of this kind in the Thessalonian church at this stage. Another suggestion is that the minds of some of the Christians were unsettled because of the expectation that the Parousia of Christ, with the new order which it would inaugurate, would take place very soon. The Thessalonian letters present ample evidence of such eschatological interest and, indeed, excitement. This may have had an effect on some members of the church like the effect produced in Pontus about the beginning of the third century by a bishop who, according to Hippolytus of Rome (*Commentary on Daniel,* 4.19), announced that the Parousia would come by the end of a particular year: many of his flock sold their property and so became destitute. Or, quite apart from eschatological excitement, some members of the church may have taken advantage of the brotherly love of their fellow Christians and been content to live at their expense.

Non-Christians must be given no pretext for thinking that Christians were unprofitable members of society. The church could not discharge its ministry of witness and reconciliation in the world unless its members adorned the gospel with their lives as well as proclaiming it with their lips. It was necessary, therefore, for Paul and his associates to issue an admonition in line with the dominical injunction: "Let your loins be girded and your lamps burning, and be like men who are waiting for their master" (Luke 12:35, 36).

(d) *On the Faithful Departed (4:13–18)*

Bibliography

Askwith, E. H. "The Eschatological Section of 1 Thessalonians." *Expositor,* series 8, 1 (1911) 59 67. **Büttner, F.** "Über die Entrückung der Gläubigen (I Thess 4, 17)." *NKZ* 9 (1898) 707–721. **Cerfaux, L.** *Christ in the Theology of St. Paul.* Tr. G. Webb and A. Walker. New York: Herder, 1959, 31–68. **Colunga, A.** "No os aflijáis como los que carecen de esperanza." In *En torno al problema de la escatología individual del Antiguo Testamento: Otros Estudios.* Madrid: Librería Científica Medinaceli, 1955, 285–300. **Dahl, M. E.** *The Resurrection of the Body.* SBT 36. London: SCM, 1962. **Delorme, J.** "Sur un texte de S. Paul (1 Thess IV, 13–17). L'avènement du Seigneur et la présence de fidèles." *Ami du Clergé* 65 (1955) 247–251. **Ellingworth, P.** "Which way are we going? A verb of movement, especially in 1 Thess 4:14b." *BT* 25 (1974) 426–431. **Giblin, C. H.** *In Hope of God's Glory.* New York: Herder, 1970. **Grass, H.** *Ostergeschehen und Osterberichte.* Göttingen: Vandenhoeck & Ruprecht, ⁴1970. **Green, E. M. B.** "A Note on 1 Thessalonians iv. 15–17." *ExpTim* 69 (1957–58) 285–286. **Haack, E.** "Eine exegetisch-dogmatische Studie zur Eschatologie über 1 Thessalonicher 4, 13–18." *ZST* 15 (1938) 544–569. **Harnisch, W.** *Eschatologische Existenz. Ein exegetischer Beitrag zum Sachanliegen von 1 Thessalonicher 4, 15–5, 11.* Göttingen: Vandenhoeck und Ruprecht, 1973. **Harris, J. R.** "A Study in Letter-Writing." *Expositor,* series 5, 8 (1898) 161–180. **Hartman, L.** *Prophecy Interpreted. The Formation of Some Jewish Apocalyptic Texts and of the Eschatological Discourse Mark 13 par.* ConB: NT Series, 1. Lund: Gleerup, 1966, 181–190. **Hayes, D. A.** "A Study of Pauline Apocalypse." *BW* 37 (1911) 163–175. **Hoffmann, P.** *Die Toten in Christus. Eine religionsgeschichtliche und exegetische Untersuchung zur paulinischen Eschatologie.* Münster: Aschendorff, 1966. **Jeremias, J.** *Unknown Saying of Jesus.* Tr. R. H. Fuller. London: SPCK, ²1964. **Kaye, B. N.** "Eschatology and Ethics in 1 and 2 Thessalonians." *NovT* 17 (1975) 47–57. **Kennedy, H. A. A.** *St. Paul's Conceptions of the Last Things.* London: Hodder and Stoughton, 1904. **Lake, K.** *The Earlier Epistles of St. Paul.* London: Rivingtons, ²1914. **Langevin, P.-É.** "Nous serons pour toujours avec le Seigneur." *AsSeign* n.s. No. 63 (1971) 13–19. **Marxsen, W.** "Auslegung von 1 Th 4, 13–18." *ZTK* 66 (1969) 22–37. **Mearns, C. L.** "Early Eschatological Development in Paul: the evidence of I and II Thessalonians." *NTS* 27 (1980–81) 137–157. **Moore, A. L.** *The Parousia in the New Testament.* NovTSup 13. Leiden: Brill, 1966. **Mounce, R. H.** "Pauline Eschatology and the Apocalypse." *EvQ* 46 (1974) 164–166. **Nepper-Christensen, P.** "Das verborgene Herrnwort. Eine Untersuchung über 1 Thes 4, 13–18." *ST* 19 (1965) 136–165. **Romeo, A.** "Nos qui vivimus qui residui sumus (1 Thess 4, 13–18)." *VD* 9 (1939) 307–312, 339–347,

360–364. **Rossano, P.** "A che punto siamo con 1 Thess 4, 13–17?" *RivB* 4 (1956) 72–80. **Schmithals, W.** *Paul and the Gnostics.* Tr. J. E. Steely. Nashville/New York: Abingdon, 1972. **Tannehill, R. C.** *Dying and Rising with Christ.* BZNW 32. Berlin: Töpelmann, 1967, 130–134. **Uprichard, R. H. E.** "Exposition of 1 Thessalonians 4. 13–18." *IrBibSt* 1 (1979) 150–156. **Veldhuizen, A. van** "1 Thessal. 4, 15–17." *ThSt* 29 (1911) 101–106. **Vos, G.** *The Pauline Eschatology.* Grand Rapids: Eerdmans, 1952. **Waterman, G. H.** "The Sources of Paul's Teaching on the Second Coming of Christ in 1 and 2 Thessalonians." *JETS* 18 (1975) 105–113. **Wenham, D.** "Paul and the Synoptic Apocalypse." In *Gospel Perspectives,* ed. R. T. France and D. Wenham, ii. Sheffield: JSOT Press (1981) 345–75. **Wilcke, H.-A.** *Das Problem eines messianischen Zwischenreiches bei Paulus.* ATANT 51. Zürich: Zwingli Verlag, 1967, 109–147. **Wimmer, A.** "Trostworte des Apostels Paulus an Hinterbliebene in Thessalonich (1 Th 4, 13–17)." *Bib* 36 (1955) 273–286.

Translation

[13] *Now, brothers, we do not wish* [a] *you to be ignorant with regard to those who are asleep,* [b] *in order that you may not grieve like the others who have no hope.* [c] [14] *For if we believe that Jesus died and rose, so also God* [d] *will bring (back) with him those who have fallen asleep through Jesus.*

[15] *For we tell you this by the word of the Lord:* [e] *we who are alive, who survive to the advent of the Lord,* [f] *shall have no precedence* [g] *over those who have fallen asleep,* [16] *because the Lord himself will descend from heaven with a shout of command, with an archangel's voice and with the trumpet of God. The dead in Christ* [h] *will rise first;* [i] [17] *then we who are alive, who survive,* [j] *shall be caught away in clouds together with them to meet* [k] *the Lord in the air. Thus we shall be forever with* [l] *the Lord.* [18] *So, comfort one another with these words.* [m]

Notes

[a] For οὐ θέλομεν ("we do not wish") οὐ θέλω ("I do not wish") is read by 104 614 630 pc lat[vg.codd] syr (under the influence of Rom 1:13, etc.).

[b] κοιμωμένων, for which the perfect κεκοιμημένων ("have fallen asleep") is read by D (F G which exhibit the corrupt form κεκοιμήνων) Ψ byz.

[c] οἱ μὴ ἔχοντες ἐλπίδα (οἱ is omitted by F G). For μή with the participle cf. 2:15; 4:5. Apart from Hellenistic usage, μή could be explained here as generic; it is characteristic of pagans that they have no hope in face of death.

[d] καὶ ὁ θεός, for which B 1739 pc read ὁ θεὸς καί.

[e] ἐν λόγῳ κυρίου. Since both nouns are anarthrous, "the word of the Lord" (rather than "a word . . .") is probably the appropriate rendering.

[f] For κυρίου B reads Ἰησοῦ.

[g] οὐ μὴ φθάσωμεν (οὐ μή with the aorist subjunctive is the most definite form of negative statement regarding the future).

[h] οἱ νεκροὶ ἐν Χριστῷ, for which F G* have the more classical construction οἱ νεκροὶ οἱ ἐν Χριστῷ.

[i] For πρῶτον (adverb) πρῶτοι (in agreement with νεκροί) is read by D* F G lat.

[j] οἱ περιλειπόμενοι, omitted by F G lat[a b] Tert Ambst Spec.

[k] εἰς ἀπάντησιν, for which D* F G read εἰς ὑπάντησιν (cf. Matt 25:1).

[l] For σύν ("with") B reads ἐν ("in").

[m] τοῦ πνεύματος ("of the Spirit") is added in 1739c pc.

Form/Structure/Setting

Although this subsection is not introduced by περὶ δέ, like those immediately preceding and following (4:9; 5:1), its contents make it highly probable that it provides an answer to a question asked (whether orally or by letter) by the Thessalonian church. Harris, indeed, who argued that the writers gave a series of replies to questions raised in a letter from Thessalonica, ventured to reconstruct that letter, which (he suggested) included the words: "But we desire to know concerning them that are fallen asleep . . ." ("A Study in Letter-Writing . . . ," 173).

The writers' reply to the question about the lot of the faithful departed seems to draw on a primitive Christian tradition of eschatological teaching which can be discerned also in the Olivet discourse of the synoptic Gospels, especially in its Matthaean form. This tradition speaks of the coming of the Lord as his Parousia (cf. Matt 24:3, 27, 37, 39; 1 Thess 2:19; 3:13; 5.23, 2 Thess 2:1, 8) and represents it as taking place from or in heaven (cf. 1:10; 2 Thess 1:7; Matt 24:30 par.), with clouds (cf. Matt 24:30 par.; Rev 1:7), accompanied by angels (cf. 3:13; 2 Thess 1:7; Matt 24:31 par.) and announced by a trumpet blast (cf. Matt 24:31; 1 Cor 15:52). For other features, such as the manifestation of power and glory and the execution of judgment on the ungodly, see 5:3; 2 Thess 1:7–10; 2:8. The Thessalonian Christians had presumably been taught much of this tradition, but were not sure how their departed friends figured in the program.

Comment

4:13 Οὐ θέλομεν δὲ ὑμᾶς ἀγνοεῖν, ἀδελφοί, "But we do not wish you to be ignorant, brothers"—a common Pauline locution, an emphatic way of saying "we wish you to know" (cf. Col 2:1), whether with reference to apostolic experiences (2 Cor 1:8) and travel plans (Rom 1:13) or with reference to disclosures of the divine purpose (Rom 11:25) and principles of personal conduct (1 Cor 10:1) and church practice (1 Cor 12:1). Whatever the subject matter in question, it is evidently considered important that the readers should be aware of it.

The subject to be dealt with here—the lot of the faithful departed at the Parousia—is apparently one on which the Thessalonian Christians had not been adequately informed. We need not suppose, with W. Schmithals, that they had recently been misled by gnosticizing visitors who denied the resurrection hope (*Paul and the Gnostics*, 160–162); still less need we suppose, with Mearns, that Paul was now concerned to correct "an exaltation theology of present glory" which he himself had originally taught at Thessalonica ("Early Eschatological Development," 141).

περὶ τῶν κοιμωμένων, "with regard to those who are asleep." The use of "sleep" as a euphemism for "death" was commonplace in antiquity; cf. the OT idiom "to sleep with one's fathers" (e.g. of David, 1 Kgs [LXX 3 Kgdms] 2:10, ἐκοιμήθη μετὰ τῶν πατέρων). In Greek it is attested from Homer onward, even of death in battle (κοιμήσατο χάλκεον ὕπνον, "he slept the sleep of bronze," *Iliad* 11.241). Not only κοιμᾶσθαι but εὕδειν and its compound καθεύδειν are found in this sense (cf. 5:10). Christians took it up as a congenial mode of expression, death being viewed by them as a sleep from which one would awake to resurrection life. In contemporary paganism it was too often viewed as a sleep from which there would be no awaking; cf. Catullus (5.4–6):

soles occidere et redire possunt:
nobis, cum semel occidit breuis lux,
nox est perpetua una dormienda.

The sun can set and rise again
But once our brief light sets
There is one unending night to be slept through.

(It is probably from the "optimistic" nuance of κοιμᾶσθαι that the Jewish and Christian term κοιμητήριον, "cemetery," was derived.)

The κοιμώμενοι here are deceased Christians, presumably members of the Thessalonian church. Questions had been raised about their lot and prospects; to these questions, probably conveyed by Timothy (whether orally or in writing), an answer is now given.

ἵνα μὴ λυπῆσθε καθὼς καὶ οἱ λοιποί, "that you should not sorrow as do the others." For καί in this position cf. v 5, καθάπερ καὶ τὰ ἔθνη. For οἱ λοιποί of the pagan world cf. Eph 2:3, "we were by nature children of wrath, like the rest of mankind" (ὡς καὶ οἱ λοιποί); it is used of the nonelect of Israel in Rom 11:7. These "others" here are "the Gentiles who do not know God" (v 5); to be without God is to be without hope (cf. Eph 2:12, ἐλπίδα μὴ ἔχοντες καὶ ἄθεοι ἐν τῷ κόσμῳ). The hopelessness of much of the pagan world of that day in the face of death is well illustrated by contemporary literary and epigraphic material. According to Theocritus (*Idyll* 4.42), "hopes are for the living; the dead are without hope" (ἐλπίδες ἐν ζώοισιν, ἀνέλπιστοι δὲ θανόντες), and the lines of Catullus have been quoted already. A letter of condolence from the second century A.D. (P. Oxy. 115), addressed to a couple who had lost a son by a friend of theirs who had suffered a similar bereavement herself, says, "I sorrowed and wept over your dear departed one as I wept over Didymas, . . . but really, there is nothing one can do in the face of such things. So, please comfort each other."

The hope which believing Jews and Christians had in face of death was the hope of resurrection; for Christians this hope was grounded in the resurrection of Christ.

14. εἰ γὰρ πιστεύομεν, "for if we believe." Christian faith may be expressed either as faith *in* . . . or (as here) as faith *that* . . . (cf. Rom 6:8; 10:9). Faith *that* . . . is equivalent to faith *in* God who has given an assurance regarding the past (by raising Jesus from the dead) and a promise regarding the future (that he will also raise believers in Jesus).

ὅτι Ἰησοῦς ἀπέθανεν καὶ ἀνέστη, "that Jesus died and rose"—the irreducible basis of the gospel (cf. 1 Cor 15:3, 4: ὅτι Χριστὸς ἀπέθανεν . . . καὶ ὅτι ἠγέρθη . . .). That a pre-Pauline creedal formula is being quoted is suggested by (1) the use of Ἰησοῦς rather than Χριστός (which is commoner in Paul) and (2) the use of ἀνέστη rather than ἠγέρθη (ἐγείρειν is the verb regularly used in the Pauline letters for resurrection, whether of Christ or of his people, ἀνιστάναι being found only here and in v 16, and in Eph 5:14).

While Paul prefers to use κοιμᾶσθαι for the death of believers, neither he nor any other NT writer uses it for the death of Christ himself. In 1 Cor 15:20 Christ, being raised from the dead, is "the first fruits of those who have fallen asleep" (τῶν κεκοιμημένων), but he is nowhere said to have "fallen asleep" in this sense himself. This is not because the figure would have been thought inappropriate for death by crucifixion; it was no more inappropriate for death by crucifixion than for death by stoning, yet it is used of Stephen (Acts 7:60, ἐκοιμήθη). Chrysostom (Hom. 7, ad loc.) says that, whereas departed believers are called "those who are asleep," it is said of Christ that "he died," because the mention of resurrection immediately follows. But the use of the straightforward verb ἀποθνῄσκειν (to die) of Christ is probably intended to stress the reality of his death, as something not to be alleviated by any euphemism. The reality of his death points to the divine miracle accomplished in his resurrection. His people's resurrection is a corollary of his, and therefore their death can be described as "falling asleep" in the new Christian sense of that figure, but there was no precedent for his resurrection. "If we believe that Jesus died and rose again," the fullness of Christian hope follows. The continuing life of his people depends on, and is indeed an extension of, his own risen life (cf. Rom 8:11; also John 14:19, "because I live, you will live also").

οὕτως καὶ ὁ θεὸς τοὺς κοιμηθέντας διὰ τοῦ Ἰησοῦ ἄξει σὺν αὐτῷ, "so also God will bring (back) with him those who have fallen asleep through Jesus." For the general statement cf. 1 Cor 6:14, "God raised the Lord and will also raise us up by his power," and 2 Cor 4:14, "he who raised the Lord Jesus will raise us also with Jesus" (σὺν Ἰησοῦ, which has the same force as σὺν αὐτῷ here). Although later in time, the resurrection of the people of Christ is their participation in his resurrection; they are to be raised from the dead "with him" (the similar language of Rom 6:3–8 includes a reference to the baptismal anticipation of the coming resurrection). Since σὺν αὐτῷ is clearly attached to ἄξει, "will bring" (sc. back from death; although cf. Ellingworth, "Which way . . . ?" for the view that it means "take up," sc. to himself), it is best to construe διὰ τοῦ Ἰησοῦ with τοὺς κοιμηθέντας ("those who have fallen asleep . . . through Jesus"). This seems to be required by the balance of the sentence; otherwise, ἄξει would be overweighted with a prepositional phrase both before and after, and it would be difficult to see any essential difference between the two phrases. (RSV, with several other versions and commentaries, takes both phrases

with the verb "will bring": "even so, through Jesus, God will bring with
him those who have fallen asleep.") If "through Jesus" be construed with
"those who have fallen asleep," then it balances "with him" naturally construed with "will bring." Death "through Jesus" is but the prelude to resurrection "with Jesus." The phrase διὰ τοῦ Ἰησοῦ "points to Jesus as the mediat-
ing link between His people's sleep and their resurrection at the hands
of God" (Milligan, 57). Askwith ("Eschatological Section," 62, 63) takes
the preposition to be the διά of attendant circumstances: "they were in a
certain relationship with the risen and living Jesus when they died." NEB
renders simply "those who died as Christians"; cf. 1 Cor 15:18, οἱ
κοιμηθέντες ἐν Χριστῷ, which it renders "those who have died within Christ's
fellowship."

Lake (*Epistles*, 88) ventilates the possibility that τοὺς κοιμηθέντας διὰ τοῦ
Ἰησοῦ implies martyrdom for Jesus' sake, though he finds the prepositional
phrase difficult—"in what sense διά?" (The best answer to that question
is probably provided by Askwith; see above.) But the references in both
1 and 2 Thessalonians to the "afflictions" endured by the Christians of
Thessalonica scarcely give the impression that positive martyrdom was
involved.

The aorist κοιμηθέντας relates to the moment of their falling asleep (dying), whereas the present κοιμωμένων in v 13 relates to their consequent
state of sleep (death). (In the NT the present tense of κοιμᾶσθαι in the
sense of death appears only in v 13 and in 1 Cor 11:30.)

15. Τοῦτο γὰρ ὑμῖν λέγομεν ἐν λόγῳ κυρίου, "for we tell you this by the
word of the Lord," The demonstrative τοῦτο refers to the immediately
following statement, introduced by ὅτι. "The word of the Lord" (or "*a*
word of the Lord") might refer to an utterance of the historical Jesus
handed down by tradition in the church or to a prophetic utterance in
Jesus' name. Giblin (*In Hope* . . . , 21) would render "on the authority
of the Lord (rather than on any quoted word of the Lord)"—but how
was the Lord's authority on such an issue conveyed if not in word? Rigaux
(ad loc. 538, 539) holds that the reference is to the general tenor of
Jesus' apocalyptic teaching—but does even its general tenor say anything
on the particular issue of the precedence of the believing dead over the
living at the Parousia/Resurrection?

"The tradition of the Jerusalem Church is at least in substance behind
the 'word of the Lord' on the parousia and resurrection in 1 Thess. 4:15–
17, though it is not certain whether Paul is here quoting a traditionally
transmitted saying or whether he is appealing to a revelation accorded
to him by the exalted Lord" (Bultmann, *Theology of NT*, i, 188, 189). If
we think of the utterance as a *verbum Christi*, then it has not been preserved
in the synoptic or Johannine traditions. Jesus indeed confirmed the belief
that there would be a "resurrection of the just" (Luke 14:14) as well as
of the unjust (cf. John 5:28, 29). He told how the Son of Man at his Advent
would, by the agency of his angels, "gather his elect from the four winds"
(Mark 13:27 par. Matt 24:31), but in that context he appears to have said

nothing about resurrection. The substance of the communication made by the writers in our present passage is that, at the Parousia, the believing dead will be raised up before the translation of living believers, and on this point no *verbum Christi* has survived.

On the other hand, the writers may be communicating something which was uttered by a prophet in the name of the risen Lord. In OT times the λόγος κυρίου was regularly conveyed through the lips of prophets (cf. Hos 1:1, etc.). Paul and Silvanus were themselves acknowledged to be prophets (cf. Acts 13:1; 15:32). For a prophetic "word of the Lord" bearing on his Advent cf. Rev 16:15 (which indeed is based on a saying of his preserved in the gospel tradition; see 5:2 below with comment).

Less probable is the suggestion by Dibelius that the communication "is possibly derived from an apocalypse" (*Die Formgeschichte des Evangeliums*, Tübingen: Mohr, ³1959, 242)or that of Bornkamm that it is "an apocryphal word of the Lord which certainly came into being only in the post-Easter church" (*Paul*, 221). Even if it was a post-Easter utterance, it may properly be regarded as an authentic "word of the Lord" through a prophet and in no sense "apocryphal." If it was conveyed by prophecy, it is comparable to the further revelation on the same subject disclosed by Paul as a "mystery" in 1 Cor 15:51. But the exact nature and origin of this λόγος κυρίου has still to be left *sub judice* as it was by Bultmann (quoted above).

ἡμεῖς οἱ ζῶντες οἱ περιλειπόμενοι εἰς τὴν παρουσίαν τοῦ κυρίου, "we who are alive, who survive until the Lord's advent." The writers rank themselves with those who will live to see the Parousia, referring to them in the first person plural, whereas "those who have fallen asleep" are referred to in the third person. Cf. 1 Cor 15:52, where Paul says that at the last trump "the dead will be raised incorruptible and we (καὶ ἡμεῖς, i.e. the living) shall be changed." In 1 Cor 6:14 ("God . . . will raise us also") those who are to be raised are spoken of in the first person plural, but no distinction is drawn there between those who have died and those who will still be alive: "us" means "us Christians" generally. By the time 2 Cor was written, however, Paul explicitly associated himself with those who would die before the Parousia and would have to be raised from the dead: cf. 2 Cor 4:14, "he who raised the Lord Jesus will raise us also with Jesus and present us (who have been raised) with you (who will still be alive)."

οὐ μὴ φθάσωμεν τοὺς κοιμηθέντας, "shall by no means have any precedence over those who have fallen asleep" (for τοὺς κοιμηθέντας cf. v 14). The verb φθάνειν (cf. 2:16) means to anticipate someone in doing something. Presumably the Thessalonian Christians had wondered if those of their number who had died would suffer any disadvantage through not being alive to witness the Parousia and participate in its attendant glory. Since they had learned about Jesus' being raised from the dead (1:10), they had probably learned something about the eventual Resurrection of his people; but they were not sure what relation the Resurrection bore to the Parousia. If it took place after the Parousia, then the dead would miss something which the living would enjoy, even if they were eventually to be brought back to resurrection life. Hence the readers are assured that their departed friends will suffer no disadvantage when the Lord comes.

16. ὅτι αὐτὸς ὁ κύριος . . . καταβήσεται ἀπ᾽ οὐρανοῦ, "because the Lord himself . . . will descend from heaven"—the Lord himself and no deputy: "αὐτός Ipse, grandis sermo" (J.A. Bengel, ad loc.). For the emphasis cf. Acts 1:11 (οὗτος ὁ Ἰησοῦς . . . ἐλεύσεται, "this Jesus . . . will come"): also (more generally) Isa 63:9, LXX (οὐ πρέσβυς οὐδὲ ἄγγελος, ἀλλ᾽ αὐτὸς κύριος ἔσωσεν αὐτούς, "no ambassador nor messenger, but the Lord himself saved them"). Cf. also the divine assertion quoted in the Passover Haggadah: אני הוא ולא אחר, "I myself and no other (will act to deliver Israel from Egypt)."

If we are dealing here with a *verbum Christi* preserved in the tradition, our present wording may be an interpretative substitute for an original "The Son of Man will descend . . ." (cf. Mark 13:26; Luke 17:24), as Jeremias suggests (*Unknown Sayings*, 81). If, on the other hand, we are dealing with a prophetic utterance, our present wording might replace an original "I" (as in Rev 16:15; 22:12, etc.).

ἀπ᾽ οὐρανοῦ, "from heaven," as in 2 Thess 1:7; cf. also 1:10 above, ἐκ τῶν οὐρανῶν.

ἐν κελεύσματι: "with a word of command." This military noun occurs once in LXX: Prov 30:27, "the locust marches at one word of command" (ἀφ᾽ ἑνὸς κελεύσματος). In Aeschylus *Pers.* 397 the earlier form κέλευμα is used of the encouragement of oarsmen by the boatswain (κελευστής) at the battle of Salamis (ἐκ κελεύματος); in Thucydides *Hist.* 2.92 κέλευσμα is used of the cheer with which the Athenian fighters encouraged one another at the battle of Naupactus (ἀπὸ ἑνὸς κελεύσματος). Philo (*De praem. et poen.* 117) speaks of God as gathering people together from the ends of the earth with one shout of command (ἑνὶ κελεύσματι). Here it is the Lord himself who shouts the quickening word, which commands a ready and obedient response (cf. John 5:25, "the dead shall hear the voice of the Son of God, and those who hear shall live").

ἐν φωνῇ ἀρχαγγέλου, "with an archangel's voice." It is doubtful if we should think of one individual archangel here, whether Michael or another. The only other place in the Greek Bible where ἀρχάγγελος occurs is Jude 9 (Μιχαὴλ ὁ ἀρχάγγελος). Jewish tradition knew of seven archangels, "the seven holy angels who present the prayers of the saints and stand before the presence of the glory of the Holy One" (Tob 12:15; cf. Rev 8:2). In *1 Enoch* 20:1–7 (Greek) they are called ἀρχάγγελοι and their names are listed as Uriel, Raphael, Raguel, Michael, Sariel, Gabriel and Remiel. (The archangel Jeremiel in 4 Ezra 4:36 is probably to be identified with Remiel.)

ἐν σάλπιγγι θεοῦ, "with the trumpet of God," harking back perhaps to Isa 27:13 (σαλπιοῦσιν τῇ σάλπιγγι τῇ μεγάλῃ, "sound the great trumpet"), where the "great trumpet" summons the Jewish exiles home from Assyria and Egypt (the words are echoed to this day in synagogue worship in the tenth of the Eighteen Benedictions: "Sound the great trumpet for our liberation; lift up the ensign to gather our exiles . . ."). Cf. also Joel 2:1,

15; Zech 9:14. NT parallels are the "last trumpet" of 1 Cor 15:52 (similarly summoning the dead to rise); Matt 24:31 (where the Son of Man at his coming "will send out his angels with a loud trumpet call" to "gather his elect"); Rev 11:15 (where the seventh of the angels "who stand before God" blows his trumpet as a signal that secular world dominion has been superseded by the eternal "kingdom of our Lord and of his Christ" and that the time has come "for the dead to be judged"). From the close association of angels with the trumpet blast in the last two passages it is probable that the "archangel's voice" and "trumpet of God" here are two ways of expressing one and the same summons. C. F. D. Moule (*The Origin of Christology*, Cambridge: Cambridge University Press, 1977, 42) compares the description of the opposite movement in Ps 47 (LXX 46): 6: ἀνέβη ὁ θεὸς ἐν ἀλαλαγμῷ, κύριος ἐν φωνῇ σάλπιγγος, "God has gone up with a shout, the Lord with the sound of a trumpet."

καὶ οἱ νεκροὶ ἐν Χριστῷ ἀναστήσονται πρῶτον, "and the dead in Christ will rise first." The use of ἀναστήσονται instead of the Pauline ἐγερθήσονται suggests that a pre-Pauline confession is being quoted (see comment on ἀνέστη, v 14). (Even so, the qualification of the dead as being ἐν Χριστῷ is probably Pauline.) But if a pre-Pauline confession is being quoted, the readers are presumably being reminded of something they had already been taught—that the dead would rise. They still needed to be told, however, how this resurrection hope (which relieved them of sorrowing like those who did not share it) was related to the hope of the Parousia of Christ.

With οἱ νεκροὶ ἐν Χριστῷ cf. 1 Cor 15:18 (οἱ κοιμηθέντες ἐν Χριστῷ, "those who have fallen asleep in Christ"); Rev 14:13 (οἱ νεκροὶ οἱ ἐν κυρίῳ ἀποθνῆσκοντες, "the dead who die in the Lord"). Those who have existed ἐν Χριστῷ in mortal life remain ἐν Χριστῷ after death. It is importing an element extraneous to the context to construe ἀναστήσονται πρῶτον as though it denoted the "first resurrection" (ἡ ἀνάστασις ἡ πρώτη) of Rev 20:5 (so Giblin, *In Hope* . . . 23). That the dead would rise was known already; what was now divulged was that the dead in Christ would rise *first:* the added adverb πρῶτον being caught up by the immediately following ἔπειτα so as to indicate that, far from suffering any disadvantage at the Parousia, the faithful departed would actually have precedence over those still alive. *Their* resurrection would be the first result of the coming of the Lord; only after that would those still alive enter into their heritage. Temporal sequence is certainly expressed by πρῶτον . . . ἔπειτα, despite the argument of Grass that what is meant is the priority which the dead have "in the Lord's love" (*Ostergeschehen*, 151). Questions of sequence and precedence in the resurrection were discussed in some Jewish circles, as appears later in the first century in 4 Ezra 5:42, where the Lord assures Ezra that "just as for those who are last there is no delay, so for those who are first there is no haste."

17. ἔπειτα, "then," "next in order." Cf. 1 Cor 15:23, where the Resurrection sequence (τάγμα) is said to be: "Christ the first fruits (ἀπαρχή),

then (ἔπειτα) those who belong to Christ at his parousia." Here, however, ἔπειτα relates to the survivors, who yield in precedence to "the dead in Christ" at his Parousia.

ἡμεῖς οἱ ζῶντες οἱ περιλειπόμενοι, repeated from v 15. "After the dead in Christ have been raised, we . . . shall be snatched away together with them" (ἅμα σὺν αὐτοῖς ἁρπαγησόμεθα). The force of the preposition σύν is strengthened by the preceding ἅμα. From the Latin equivalent of ἁρπάζειν (rapere) this incident in the Parousia is sometimes called the "Rapture" (snatching away) of believers. The verb ἁρπάζειν implies violent action, sometimes indeed to the benefit of its object, as when the Roman soldiers snatched Paul from the rioters in the Jerusalem council-chamber (Acts 23:10) or when the male child in the apocalyptic vision was caught up to God to preserve him from the great red dragon (Rev 12:5). It is used in Acts 8:39 for the Spirit's snatching Philip away after his interview with the Ethiopian chamberlain and (more germanely to the present passage) of Paul's being caught up to the third heaven or paradise (2 Cor 12:2, 3).

Nothing is said here of the transformation of οἱ ζῶντες οἱ περιλειπόμενοι to fit them for the conditions of their new existence; Paul deals with this question later, in 1 Cor 15:50–52.

ἐν νεφέλαις, "in clouds"—not simply because clouds suggested themselves as convenient vehicles for transportation through space but because clouds are a regular feature of biblical theophanies; the divine glory is veiled in clouds, shines forth from them and retreats into them. Cf. the thick cloud on Sinai when Yahweh came down to impart the law to his people (Exod 19:16) and when Moses went up to receive the revelation (Exod 24:15–18), or the cloud that enveloped the divine presence in the wilderness tabernacle (Exod 40:34) and in Solomon's temple (1 Kings 8:10, 11; cf. Ps 97:2). Specially relevant to the NT background are the "clouds of heaven" with which "one like a son of man" came to be presented before the Ancient of Days in Dan 7:13 (cf. Mark 13:26 par.; 14:62 par.; Rev 1:7). Similar theophanic imagery appears in the narratives of the transfiguration (Mark 9:7 par.) and ascension (Acts 1:9): the "cloud" which received Jesus out of the disciples' sight on the latter occasion has a bearing on the angelic assurance that he would come "in the same way" as they had seen him go (Acts 1:11).

εἰς ἀπάντησιν τοῦ κυρίου, "to meet the Lord." When a dignitary paid an official visit (παρουσία) to a city in Hellenistic times, the action of the leading citizens in going out to meet him and escort him back on the final stage of his journey was called the ἀπάντησις. So Cicero, describing Julius Caesar's progress through Italy in 49 B.C., says, "Just imagine what ἀπαντήσεις he is receiving from the towns, what honors are paid to him!" (Ad Att. 8.16.2), and five years later he says much the same about Caesar's adopted son Octavian: "The municipalities are showing the boy remarkable favor. . . . Wonderful ἀπαντήσεις and encouragement!" (Ad Att. 16.11.6). Cf. Matt 25:6, where the bridal party is summoned to go out and meet the bridegroom (εἰς ἀπάντησιν αὐτοῦ), so as to escort him with a torchlight procession to the banqueting hall, and Acts 28:15, where Christians from Rome walk south along the Appian Way to meet Paul and his company (εἰς ἀπάντησιν ἡμῖν) and escort them on the remainder of their journey to Rome.

These analogies (especially in association with the term παρουσία) suggest the possibility that the Lord is pictured here as escorted on the remainder of his journey to earth by his people—both those newly raised from the dead and those who have remained alive. But there is nothing in the word ἀπάντησις or in this context which *demands* this interpretation; it cannot be determined from what is said here whether the Lord (with his people) continues his journey to earth or returns to heaven. Similarly it is not certain whether the Son of Man, coming "in clouds" (Mark 13:26 par.; 14:62 par.), is on his way to earth or (as in Dan 7:13) to the throne of God.

εἰς ἀέρα, "into the air." We should not overpress the classical distinction between the lower air (ἀήρ) and the upper air (αἰθήρ, not found in the NT), although the mention of clouds would in any case suggest the lower air.

καὶ οὕτως πάντοτε σὺν κυρίῳ ἐσόμεθα, "and (having) thus (joined him) we shall be continually with the Lord"—the climax of blessedness. Cf. Phil 1:23, where Paul expresses his desire "to depart (ἀναλῦσαι) and be with Christ (σὺν Χριστῷ), for that is far better." There, however, Paul refers not to the Resurrection at the Parousia, but to his mode of existence immediately after death, as in 2 Cor 5:8, where to be away from the body is to be "at home with the Lord" (ἐνδημῆσαι πρὸς τὸν κύριον).

18. Ὥστε παρακαλεῖτε ἀλλήλους, "so, encourage one another." The same expression occurs of general Christian duty in 5:11 below, but in the present context the sense of "comfort" is uppermost. P.Oxy. 115 (the letter of condolence mentioned in the comment on v 13 above) ends with the admonition to the bereaved parents παρηγορεῖτε οὖν ἀλλήλους ("So, comfort each other"); but the Thessalonian Christians are given solid grounds for comfort and hope.

ἐν τοῖς λόγοις τούτοις, "with these words" (instrumental ἐν), especially as they are communicated with the authority of the Lord himself (ἐν λόγῳ κυρίου, v 15).

Explanation

A third area in which deficiencies in the Thessalonian Christians' understanding of the faith required to be made good had to do with the Advent of Christ and attendant events. They were by no means completely ignorant about these matters. They knew not only that Jesus was risen and alive but that he would return: they had been taught to expect his coming from heaven. They had been taught, too, that his coming would be sudden, like the coming of a thief by night (5:2). Again, when they had learned about the resurrection of Christ, it is most probable that they had been told that his resurrection was the prelude to his people's resurrection—

to the resurrection, at least, of those who died before his Advent. But some uncertainty remained in their minds.

The nature of this uncertainty can only be inferred from the writers' reference to it here. Some of their number had died recently, it appears, and they wondered if those departed friends might not miss something to which survivors until the Lord's Advent could look forward—some participation in the glory of the occasion perhaps. If they knew in some form the saying of Jesus about some of his followers who "will not taste death before they see the Kingdom of God come with power" (Mark 9:1), they may have wondered what would happen to those who did "taste death" before that event. There is no positive evidence that gnosticizing visitors to Thessalonica or independent thinkers within their own circle called the Resurrection hope in question. But the death of their friends filled their hearts with sorrow and they needed a message of reassurance, based on a more precise statement of the Christian hope.

Hope was one of the chief emphases of the gospel; it was a feature of Christian existence. Believers in Christ are contrasted with "others who have no hope." The Jews, or most of them, maintained the hope of resurrection, and in the pagan world there were those whose initiation into one or another of the mystery cults guaranteed them the hope of immortality (although it is not difficult to divine what the apostles would have thought of the stability of such a hope). But there is ample evidence that among pagans generally there was a sad sense of hopelessness in the face of death. Indeed, even in a Christian environment this sense of hopelessness finds expression where the hope of the gospel is not cherished as a lively inward conviction; in a Derbyshire church, for example, a late eighteenth-century monument in memory of a young girl has an inscription concluding with the words: "The unfortunate parents ventured their all on this frail bark, and the wreck was total."

The hope of resurrection is based, as it is later in 1 Corinthians 15, on the assurance that Jesus died and rose. Nothing is said here, as it is in later Pauline writings, of the hope of resurrection and glory as guaranteed by the indwelling Spirit (Rom 8:11) or the indwelling Christ (Col 1:27). On the subject of resurrection, as on other subjects treated in the Thessalonian letters, the teaching is that common to the early Gentile mission (to which of course Paul subscribed) rather than distinctively Pauline.

The anxiety which some of the readers feel about their departed friends is set at rest by the affirmation, made on the authority of the Lord himself, that at his Advent "the dead in Christ" will be raised first; only then will believers who have not died be gathered together with them to join their Lord and be forever with him. Thus every blessing which the survivors are to experience then will be fully shared by their departed friends; these will suffer no disadvantage at all through having died before the Advent. "Tidings of comfort and joy," indeed!

The Advent of the Lord is described in terms associated with manifestations of the divine glory in the OT. If an OT prophet could cry to the

God of Israel, "O that thou wouldst rend the heavens and come down" (Isa 64:1), the answer to such a prayer is promised in Christ's descent from heaven. The archangelic voice and the trumpet-call add emphasis to the shout of command which summons the dead back to life; the clouds in which Christ gathers his people to himself are the clouds which, in OT and NT imagery alike, envelop the radiance of the divine presence. There is no need to be overly concerned because the imagery is that of the tri-level universe. Anyone leaving the earth and its atmosphere must appear to be going up, and anyone reentering it must appear to be coming down. More importantly, "up" and "down" terminology is traditionally used to express transcendence and condescension. The imagery, which is especially characteristic of apocalyptic literature, becomes progressively less prominent in later Pauline letters, but the teaching which it conveys is maintained.

Nothing is said here—or, for that matter, anywhere else in the Pauline corpus of the resurrection of those who are not in Christ. In Acts 24:15 Paul tells Felix that he shares the Pharisaic hope "that there will be a resurrection of both the just and the unjust." In John 5:28, 29, it is apparently one and the same voice of the Son of God which calls all who are in the tombs to come forth, "those who have done good, to the resurrection of life, and those who have done evil, to the resurrection of judgment." On Paul's principles, any resurrection of unbelievers would be different in character from the resurrection of believers: the resurrection of believers was their participation in Christ's resurrection, and this could not be said of the resurrection of unbelievers. It is precarious to draw inferences from Paul's silence about his views on the nature and timing of the resurrection of those not in Christ.

Because the resurrection hope, for Paul, was grounded in the saving work of Christ, the question *when* it would be realized was of secondary importance. He nowhere claims to know the time of the expected Advent of Christ, so he could not know whether he would be alive or not when it took place. If, in his earlier letters, he associates himself with those who will survive to the great event and, in his later letters, with those who will then be raised from the dead, this was a natural shift in perspective arising from advancing years and changing circumstances. The shift in perspective involved no change in eschatological faith and no diminution of hope. The so-called "delay of the parousia" was no problem for Paul.

(e) *On Times and Seasons (5:1–11)*

Bibliography

Aalen, S. *Die Begriffe "Licht" und "Finsternis" im Alten Testament, im Spätjudentum und im Rabbinismus.* Oslo: Det Norske Videnskapsakademi, 1951. **Barr, J.** *Biblical Words for Time.* SBT 33. London: SCM Press, 1962. **Bovon, F.** "Une formule prépaulinienne dans l'épître aux Galates (Ga 1, 4–5)." In *Paganisme, Judaïsme, Christianisme,*

Mélanges offerts à M. Simon, ed. A Benoit, M. Philonenko, C. Vogel. Paris: Boccard, 1978, 91–107. **Edgar, T. R.** "The Meaning of 'Sleep' in 1 Thessalonians 5:10." *JETS* 22 (1979) 345–349. **Förster, G.** "1 Thessalonicher 5, 1–10." *ZNW* 17 (1916) 169–177. **Friedrich, G.** "1. Thessalonicher 5, 1–11, der apologetische Einschub eines Späteren." *ZTK* 70 (1973) 288–315. **Fuchs, E.** *Glaube und Erfahrung. Zum christologischen Problem im Neuen Testament.* Tübingen: Mohr, 1965, 334–363 ("Die Zukunft des Glaubens nach 1. Thess 5, 1–11"). **Glasson, T. F.** *The Second Advent.* London: Epworth Press, ²1947. **Harnisch, W.** *Eschatologische Existenz. Ein exegetischer Beitrag zum Sachanliegen von 1 Thessalonicher 4:15–5:11.* Göttingen: Vandenhoeck & Ruprecht, 1973. **Harris, J. R.** "A Study in Letter-Writing." *Expositor* series 5, 8 (1898) 161–180. **Hartman, L.** *Prophecy Interpreted.* ConB: NT Series, 1. Lund: Gleerup, 1966. **Hooker, M. D.** "Interchange in Christ." *JTS* n.s. 22 (1971), 349–361. **Hooker, M. D.** "Interchange and Atonement." *BJRL* 60 (1977–78), 462–481. **Kaye, B. N.** "Eschatology and Ethics in 1 and 2 Thessalonians." *NovT* 17 (1975), 47–57. **Langevin, P.-É.** *Jésus Seigneur et l'eschatologie. Exégèse de textes prépauliniens.* Bruges/Paris: Desclée et Brouwer, 1967, 124–153 (" 'Jour de Yahvé' et seigneurie de Jésus en 1 Th 5, 2"). **Laub, F.** *Eschatologische Verkündigung und Lebensgestaltung nach Paulus.* Biblische Untersuchungen, 10. Regensburg: Pustet, 1973. **Laughton, E.** "Subconscious Repetition and Textual Criticism." *Classical Philology* 45 (1950), 73–83. **Lövestam, E.** *Spiritual Wakefulness in the New Testament.* Lunds Universitets Årsskrift, N.F., Avd. 1, Bd. 55, No. 3. Lund: Gleerup, 1963. **Mattern, L.** *Das Verständnis des Gerichtes bei Paulus.* ATANT 47. Zürich: Zwingli Verlag, 1966. **Moore, A. L.** *The Parousia in the New Testament.* NovTSup 13. Leiden: Brill. 1966. **Müller, U. B.** *Prophetie und Predigt im Neuen Testament.* Gütersloh: Mohn, 1975. **Newman, J. H.** "Waiting for Christ." In *Parochial and Plain Sermons,* vi. London: Longmans, 1896, 234–254. **Nieder, L.** *Die Motive der religiös-sittlichen Paränese in den paulinischen Gemeindebriefen.* München: Zink, 1956. **Orchard, J. B.** "Thessalonians and the Synoptic Gospels." *Bib* 19 (1938) 19–42. **Plevnik, J.** "1 Thess 5, 1–11: Its Authenticity, Intention and Method." *Bib* 60 (1979) 71–90. **Rigaux, B.** "Tradition et rédaction dans 1 Th. v. 1–10." *NTS* 21 (1974–75) 318–340. **Robinson, J. A. T.** *Jesus and His Coming.* London: SCM Press, 1957, 104–117 ("The Challenge of Thessalonians"). **Sáenz Galache, M.** " 'Dios no nos ha destinado a la colera' (1 Tes 5, 9). Angustia existencial del hombre y premio escatológico de Dios." *Ciudad de Dios* 187 (1974) 107–134. **Scott, C. A. A.** *Christianity According to St Paul.* Cambridge: Cambridge University Press, 1927. **Semmelroth, O.** "Erbauet einer den anderen (1 Thess 5, 11)." *Geist und Leben* 30 (1957) 262–271. **Stachowiak, L. R.** "Die Antithese Licht-Finsternis. Ein Thema der paulinischen Paränese." *TQ* 143 (1963) 385–421. **Vanderhaegen, J.** "Espérer le jour du Seigneur (1 Th 5, 1–6)." *AsSeign* n.s. No. 64 (1969) 10–17. **Waterman, G. H.** "The Sources of Paul's Teaching on the Second Coming of Christ in 1 and 2 Thessalonians." *JETS* 18 (1975) 105–113. **Wenham, D.** "Paul and the Synoptic Apocalypse." In *Gospel Perspectives,* ed. R. T. France and D. Wenham, ii. Sheffield: JSOT Press (1981) 345–75.

Translation

¹ *But with regard to the times and seasons, brothers, you have no need to be written to:* ² *you yourselves know perfectly well that the day of the Lord* [a] *is coming like a thief by night.* ³ *When* [b] *they are saying, "Peace and security," it is then that sudden destruction comes on* [c] *them, like birth-pangs* [d] *on a woman with child, and they will not escape.* [e] ⁴ *But you are not in darkness, brothers, for that*

day to overtake you [f] *like a thief.* [g] [5] *You are all sons of light, sons of day; we do not belong* [h] *to night or darkness.* [6] *So then, let us not sleep as* [i] *the others do; let us keep awake* [j] *and be sober.* [7] *For those who sleep sleep by night and those who get drunk* [k] *are drunk by night;* [8] *but let us who belong to daylight keep sober, putting on the breastplate of faith and love, and the hope of salvation for a helmet,* [9] *because God has not appointed* [l] *us for wrath, but for the obtaining of salvation through our Lord Jesus Christ,* [m] [10] *who died for* [n] *us, so that, whether we are awake or asleep,* [o] *we might live* [p] *together with him.* [11] *Therefore, encourage one another and build one another up,* [q] *as indeed you are doing.*

Notes

[a] ἡμέρα κυρίου, both nouns anarthrous, but ἡ is placed before ἡμέρα by A Ψ 0226 byz. In LXX and NT either both nouns are anarthrous or (as in 2 Thess 2:2) both have the article; no difference in meaning is discernible between the two constructions.

[b] ὅταν, to which δέ is added by א² B D 0226 1739 1881 *pc* syr[hcl] and γάρ by Ψ byz lat[a] [vg].

[c] For αὐτοῖς ἐφίσταται B reads ἐπίσταται αὐτοῖς, while some western witnesses (F G lat[b] d Aug[pt]) read αὐτοῖς φανήσεται ("will be manifested to them").

[d] ὠδίν, Hellenistic nominative for classical ὠδίς, more commonly used in the plural.

[e] For οὐ μή with the aorist subjunctive see p. 94 above, note g (on 4:15). D* F G read the future indicative ἐκφεύξονται.

[f] ἵνα . . . καταλάβῃ, here expressing result, not (as in classical usage) purpose; cf. BDF § 391 (5).

[g] For ὡς κλέπτης ("as a thief") ὡς κλέπτας ("as thieves"), referring to those overtaken, not to the Day of the Lord, is read by A B cop[bo (pt)]. Lightfoot was disposed to accept κλέπτας, mainly because it was more likely to be changed to κλέπτης (in the light of v 2) than *vice versa.*

[h] οὐκ ἐσμέν, for which οὐκ ἐστέ ("you are not," "you do not belong") is read by D* F G lat[vet vg.codd] syr[Pesh] cop[sa] Ambst. For oscillation between 1st and 2nd plural cf. Gal 3:23–27; Col 2:13.

[i] Between ὡς and οἱ λοιποί א² D F G byz *al* insert καί (by assimilation to 4:13).

[j] The late present γρηγορέω is a back-formation from ἐγρήγορα, the classical perfect (intransitive) of ἐγείρω ("waken"); cf. στήκω from ἕστηκα (see p. 65, note c, on 3:8).

[k] μεθυσκόμενοι, for which B Clem Al[pt] A read μεθύοντες. While μεθύσκεσθαι originally means "get drunk" and μεθύειν "be drunk" the distinction is difficult to maintain here.

[l] ἔθετο, aorist middle. The use of the middle voice of τιθέναι in a sense hardly distinguishable from the active has classical antecedents; cf. BDF § 316 (1).

[m] Χριστοῦ is omitted by P[30 (vid)] B lat[b] m* cop[sa].

[n] For ὑπέρ א* B 33 read περί.

[o] εἴτε γρηγορῶμεν εἴτε καθεύδωμεν (cf. Phil 1:27). The construction εἴτε . . . εἴτε followed by the subjunctive without ἄν is not Attic but is found in Ionic (epic and Herodotus).

[p] For ζήσωμεν the future indicative ζήσομεν is read by A *pc*.

[q] εἰς τὸν ἕνα in the sense of ἀλλήλους, perhaps to be explained as a Semitism; cf., however, Theocritus, *Id.* 22.65, εἰς ἐνὶ χεῖρας ἄειρον ("they raised their hands one to another").

Form/Structure/Setting

The authenticity of 5:1–11 is denied by Friedrich ("1. Thessalonicher 5, 1–11 . . ."), who finds here a post-Pauline alteration of the perspective of 4:13–18; there the purpose is to remove anxiety, here to warn against false security arising out of the apparent delay of the Parousia. No delay, however, is envisaged here: the Parousia may be expected in the lifetime of the readers, who are urged to be alert and ready for it when it comes.

A valuable analysis of this subsection is given by Rigaux ("Tradition et rédaction . . ."): it is seen to deal progressively with *(1)* the Day of the Lord (vv 1–3), *(2)* the call for watchfulness (vv 4–8a), *(3)* Christian existence (vv 8b–10), with v 11 forming a general conclusion to 4:13–5:10.

The dependence of the treatment of the Day of the Lord and the call for watchfulness on various strands of the synoptic tradition has been generally observed. Robinson (*Jesus and His Coming*, 116, 117) recognizes that the passage "preserves genuine echoes of the words of Jesus," but adds that the more apocalyptic the material is, "the less claim it has to represent primitive tradition, and *vice versa.*" (This last judgment depends on a negative estimate of the apocalyptic element in Jesus' authentic teaching.) But no one strand of synoptic tradition is preferred to another. Sometimes (over and above parallels with Mark and Q respectively) affinities are closer with Matthew's special material (this is particularly so in 4:16, 17) and sometimes with Luke's special material (as in 5:8–11). It was argued in 1938 by Orchard ("Thessalonians and the Synoptic Gospels") that Paul in Thessalonians draws on Matthew and that Luke in turn draws on Paul. Most estimates of the date of Matthew rule out its being available in A.D. 50, and the balance of internal probability is against the likelihood,of Luke's acquaintance with Paul's letters. The evidence of 1 Thess 4:13–5:11 (and of 2:13–16) suggests access rather to various strands of gospel tradition in what may be called a presynoptic stage. Moreover, if these strands included some material which we recognize as special to Matthew and Luke respectively, then certain elements in that material which, on the basis of the study of the Gospels alone, might be set down as redactional were themselves based on tradition.

A similar drawing on presynoptic tradition is probable for Rom 13:10–13, where the same motifs are present as are found here.

A chiastic construction is to be observed in v 5: φωτός-ἡμέρας/νυκτός-σκότους ("light-day/night-darkness").

Comment

5:1. Περὶ δὲ τῶν χρόνων καὶ τῶν καιρῶν, "But with regard to the times and seasons" (NEB "About dates and times"). This subsection opens in much the same way as the subsection about brotherly love (4:9; see comment). The collocation of χρόνοι and καιροί appears also in Acts 1:7; the phrase may have been a conventional doublet, like our own "times and seasons," with no particular emphasis on a difference between the two nouns. Such a difference was pointed out by Augustine (*Ep.* 197.2), who distinguishes καιροί in the sense of opportune moments from χρόνοι in the sense of stretches of time—a distinction taken over by Lightfoot and other commentators. The distinction holds good generally in classical Greek but had become largely otiose by Hellenistic times, and it is probable that here, "as in other cases of paronomasia, the combination had become stereotyped and the original distinction between the words was forgotten" (K. Lake and H. J. Cadbury, *The Acts of the Apostles* = *BC* 4, London: Macmillan, 1933, 8).

οὐ χρείαν ἔχετε ὑμῖν γράφεσθαι, "you have no need to be written to" (cf. 4:9, where the active γράφειν is used). Whereas in 4:9 there was no need to write to them about φιλαδελφία because a divinely implanted instinct taught them to love one another, here there is no need to write to them about χρόνοι καὶ καιροί because the missionaries have already taught them the outline of events attending the Day of the Lord (cf. 2 Thess 2:5). On one particular matter—the relation of the Parousia to the resurrection of the dead in Christ—they required the specific instruction given in 4:13–18, but they were credited with a clear understanding of the signs of the times and the approaching end of the age.

2. αὐτοὶ γὰρ ἀκριβῶς οἴδατε, "for you yourselves know (cf. 1:5; 2:1, with comments) perfectly well"—"you are rightly informed" (Harris, "A Study . . . ," 173 n. 1). Paul and his companions had evidently taught them about things to come while they were in Thessalonica, basing their teaching on transmitted words of Jesus.

ὅτι ἡμέρα κυρίου ὡς κλέπτης ἐν νυκτὶ οὕτως ἔρχεται, "that the day of the Lord comes like a thief by night." The figure of the thief by night occurs in Jesus' teaching about the coming of the Son of Man (Matt 24:43 par. Luke 12:39, a Q logion) and in prophetic utterances made in his name in the Apocalypse (Rev. 3:3; 16:15); cf. 2 Pet 1:10. A similar figure occurs in Luke 21:34–36 and general teaching to the same effect in Luke 17:24–32. The point of the comparison is the call for vigilance: "if the householder had known at what hour the thief was coming, he would have been awake and would not have left his house to be broken into" (Luke 12:39). Similarly, the Day of the Lord will come unexpectedly; it is important therefore to be on the alert and not be taken by surprise.

The Day of the Lord (יום יהוה) is an OT concept: it was the day when Yahweh would vindicate his righteous cause and execute impartial judgment (cf. Amos 5:18; Joel 2:31; Mal 4:5). In early Christian usage, with the acknowledgment of Jesus as Lord, Jesus was viewed as the κύριος whose day it was; hence, in addition to being called the Day of the Lord (cf. 2 Thess 2:2; 1 Cor 5:5; 2 Pet 3:10), it is called "the day of Christ" (Phil 1:10; 2:16), "the day of Jesus Christ" (Phil 1:6), "the day of our Lord Jesus" (2 Cor 1:14), "the day of our Lord Jesus Christ" (1 Cor 1:8). Where the context is sufficient, it is sometimes referred to simply as "the day" (v 4; Rom 13:12; 1 Cor 3:13; Heb 10:25) or "that day" (2 Thess 1:10). It is, in other words, the day of Christ's revelation in glory, when he comes to vindicate his people and judge the world in righteousness (cf. Acts 17:31). His day is contrasted in 1 Cor 4:3 with ἀνθρωπίνη ἡμέρα, the day of merely human judgment.

3. ὅταν λέγωσιν· εἰρήνη καὶ ἀσφάλεια, τότε αἰφνίδιος αὐτοῖς ἐφίσταται ὄλεθρος, "when they are saying, 'Peace and security,' then sudden destruction comes

on them." In Jesus' warning about the coming of the Son of Man, he reminds his hearers how the people of Noah's day and, later, the inhabitants of Sodom and the neighboring cities were engaged in the ordinary pursuits of peace, without any suspicion of danger, when sudden disaster overtook them. With the αἰφνίδιος ὄλεθρος here may be compared the ὄλεθρος αἰώνιος of 2 Thess 1:9, except that the "eternal destruction" there is specifically said to be penal, which is not necessarily so with the "sudden destruction" here. A closer parallel to the present warning is provided by the dominical admonition of Luke 21:34–36, where "that day" will come suddenly (ἐπιστῇ . . . αἰφνίδιος) on all the inhabitants of the whole earth, including unwatchful disciples. (That is the only other NT occurrence of the classical adjective αἰφνίδιος. In LXX it is found, as is the adverb αἰφνιδίως, only in books not translated from a Hebrew original.)

The wording εἰρήνη καὶ ἀσφάλεια may have been prompted by some OT prophets' denunciation of those who say "Peace" when there is no peace (cf. Jer 6:14; Ezek 13:10).

ὡς ἡ ὠδὶν τῇ ἐν γαστρὶ ἐχούσῃ, "like birth pangs on a woman with child." It is unlikely that there is any allusion here to the messianic birth pangs, חבלו של משיח (cf. Mark 13:8, ἀρχὴ ὠδίνων ταῦτα); the point of comparison is the sudden onset of labor pains with their inescapable outcome. The figure is common enough in the OT prophets, where it usually denotes anguish and dismay, without the present emphasis on suddenness (cf. Isa 13:8; 21:3; 37:3; Jer 6:24, etc.).

καὶ οὐ μὴ ἐκφύγωσιν, "and they will by no means escape." By contrast, in Luke 21:36 those who are watchful may pray confidently to "have strength to escape (ἐκφυγεῖν) all these things that will take place, and to stand before the Son of Man."

4. ὑμεῖς δέ, ἀδελφοί, οὐκ ἐστε ἐν σκότει, "but you, brothers, are not in darkness." Cf. Rom 13:12, where Christians are exhorted to "cast off the works of darkness."

ἵνα ἡ ἡμέρα ὑμᾶς ὡς κλέπτης καταλάβῃ, "so that the day should surprise you like a thief." The "day" is the Day of the Lord, but the antithesis with σκότος imparts to the word something of the sense of daylight (cf. Rom 13:12, "the night is far gone, the day is at hand"). The simile ὡς κλέπτης harks back to v 2; for the figure in general Lightfoot compares Euripides, *Iph. in Taur.* 1025–26:

Ιφ. ὡς δὴ σκότος λαβόντες ἐκσωθεῖμεν ἄν;
ΟΡ. κλεπτῶν γὰρ ἡ νύξ, τῆς δ' ἀληθείας τὸ φῶς

("Could we escape by seizing the opportunity of darkness?/Yes, for night is the time for thieves, daylight is the time for truth").

According to 2 Thess 2:5, the readers had been told of the coming of the "lawless one" which would precede the Day of the Lord, but it would be precarious to suppose that it was this knowledge that taught them when to expect the Day of the Lord, so that it would not take them by surprise. Rather, they are urged to remain alert so as to be ready for the great day, no matter when it comes.

5. πάντες γὰρ ὑμεῖς υἱοὶ φωτός ἐστε, "for you are all sons of light." Cf. Luke 16:8, "the sons of this age (οἱ υἱοὶ τοῦ αἰῶνος τούτου) are wiser in their own generation than the sons of light (ὑπὲρ τοὺς υἱοὺς τοῦ φωτός)"; John 12:36, "while you have the light, walk in the light, that you may become sons of light (υἱοὶ φωτός)"; Eph 5:8, "once you were darkness, but now you are light in the Lord; walk as children of light (ὡς τέκνα φωτός)." The phrase (Heb. בני אור) is current in the Qumran texts for the elect community and its supporters, as "sons of darkness" (בני חשך) denotes the nonelect and godless (notably in the *Rule of War*). While the actual expression "sons of light" does not occur in 1 John, the antithesis of light and darkness (in an ethical sense) is particularly prominent there. Since God is light, his children's lives are characterized by light: no one can have fellowship with him and "walk in darkness" (1 John 1:5, 6).

υἱοὶ ἡμέρας, "sons of day" (a synonym of υἱοὶ φωτός). The day had not yet arrived, but believers in Christ were children of day already, by a form of "realized eschatology." The day, in fact, had cast its radiance ahead with the life and ministry of the historical Jesus and the accomplishment of his saving work; when it arrived in its full splendor, they would enter into their inheritance of glory and be manifested as children of day. Those, on the other hand, who have not come to the light but still live in darkness will be caught off guard by the day when it comes.

Οὐκ ἐσμὲν νυκτὸς οὐδὲ σκότους, "we do not belong to night or darkness." The genitives νυκτός and σκότους might be explained as dependent on υἱοί, understood from the preceding clause, but are more probably to be taken simply as descriptive genitives; cf. v 8 (ἡμεῖς δὲ ἡμέρας ὄντες); Heb 10:39 (οὐκ ἐσμὲν ὑποστολῆς . . . ἀλλὰ πίστεως, where, however, Vg renders "non sumus subtractionis *filii* . . . sed fidei")

6. ἄρα οὖν, "so therefore," a common collocation in Paul, introducing a further stage in an argument or a summing up. Here it marks the transition to direct exhortation: our status is that of "sons of light," so therefore let us be watchful. Cf. 2 Thess 2:15.

μὴ καθεύδωμεν, "let us not sleep," the injunction implicit in the *verba Christi* about the thief by night: if the householder had known when the thief would come, he would not have slept but would have stayed awake (Matt 24:43 par. Luke 12:39). Cf. Mark 13:35, 36, where the servants left in charge by their master are warned to stay awake, "lest he come suddenly and find you asleep (καθεύδοντας)."

ὡς οἱ λοιποί, "like the others." Cf. 4:13 (καθὼς καὶ οἱ λοιποί); also 4:5: "like the Gentiles who do not know God." Here οἱ λοιποί are the rest of humankind.

γρηγορῶμεν, "let us keep awake." Cf. Mark 13:35, 37 par. (γρηγορεῖτε). In Rev 16:15 the dominical announcement "Behold, I come as a thief" is followed immediately by the beatitude μακάριος ὁ γρηγορῶν, "blessed is the one who keeps awake."

καὶ νήφωμεν, "and let us be sober." Sleep and drunkenness are associated with night (v 7); watchfulness and sobriety are appropriate for "sons of day." Cf. the combination of νήφειν and γρηγορεῖν in 1 Pet 5:8, "Be sober, be watchful."

7. Οἱ γὰρ καθεύδοντες νυκτὸς καθεύδουσιν καὶ οἱ μεθυσκόμενοι νυκτὸς μεθύουσιν, "For those who sleep sleep by night and those who get drunk are drunk by night." The language here is not figurative but factual: night is the time when people sleep; night is the time when people get drunk (and therefore reckless). In association with Jesus' words about the thief by night come warnings against getting drunk and therefore being unprepared (Matt 24:48–51 par. Luke 12:45, 46).

8. ἡμεῖς δὲ ἡμέρας ὄντες νήφωμεν, "but let us who belong to daylight be sober." For ἡμέρας ὄντες cf. v 5 with comment; for νήφωμεν cf. v 6. The paraenesis of vv 8–11 is closely parallel to that of Luke 21:34–36.

ἐνδυσάμενοι θώρακα πίστεως καὶ ἀγάπης καὶ περικεφαλαίαν ἐλπίδα σωτηρίας, "having put on the breastplate of faith and love and, as a helmet, the hope of salvation." With ἐνδυσάμενοι cf. Rom 13:12, ἐνδυσώμεθα δὲ τὰ ὅπλα τοῦ φωτός. It might be said that our present passage gives us an inventory of the "armor of light."

For the triad of Christian graces cf. 1:3 with comment. For the closer collocation of faith and love cf. Gal 5:6, πίστις δι᾽ ἀγάπης ἐνεργουμένη, "faith which works through love." A more elaborate presentation of "the panoply of God" comes in Eph 6:11–18, where the breastplate is righteousness and the helmet salvation. The armor metaphor may go back to Isa 59:17, where Yahweh himself puts on righteousness as a breastplate (LXX θώραξ) and wears the helmet (περικεφαλαία) of salvation on his head (cf. Wis 5:17–20, where the Lord arms himself to do battle against the ungodly).

ἐλπίδα σωτηρίας, the hope of the coming day when salvation will be consummated—the salvation for which God has appointed his children (v 9). Cf. Gal 5:5, "through the Spirit, by faith, we wait for the hope of righteousness (ἐλπίδα δικαιοσύνης)." In this hope, with faith and love, the believer is equipped with all necessary protection against the judgment to be unleashed on the Day of the Lord.

9. ὅτι οὐκ ἔθετο ἡμᾶς ὁ θεὸς εἰς ὀργήν, "because God has not appointed us for wrath." As in 1:10, the ὀργή is the judgment of the end-time, from which Jesus delivers his people. So here, it is "through our Lord Jesus Christ" (διὰ τοῦ κυρίου ἡμῶν Ἰησοῦ Χριστοῦ) that God has appointed them "for the obtaining of salvation" (εἰς περιποίησιν σωτηρίας). The phrase "through our Lord Jesus Christ" is amplified by the clause "who died for us" in v 10: that is to say, it is through his death that his people receive salvation. Whether salvation or life be spoken of, the two terms are practically synonymous in NT usage. In the Syriac NT the noun ḥayye ("life") does duty for both; it renders σωτηρία here. The salvation in view here includes salvation from eschatological "wrath" (cf. Rom 5:9, quoted in comment on 1:10) but positively it involves being raised to life with

Christ. It is that definitive and consummated salvation which, as Paul says in another epistle, "is nearer to us now than when we first believed" (Rom 13:11, in a context where the same call for vigilance is sounded). Cf. 2 Thess 2:13, 14; also Heb 10:39, where the περιποίησις ψυχῆς ("gaining of one's soul") through faith is set in contrast with ἀπώλεια ("perdition") through falling back.

An alternative rendering of εἰς περιποίησιν σωτηρίας advocated by Lightfoot, "for the adoption of salvation"—i.e. "for our adoption (by God), which consists in our salvation"—is strained.

The term σωτηρία, occurring in vv 8 and 9 (and in 2 Thess 2:13), seems to be used by Paul to include all the blessings of the gospel—present life in Christ and future life with Christ, the indwelling Spirit maintaining the former and guaranteeing the latter; redemption from the mastery of sin, justification by faith, adoption into God's family, progressive conformity to the character of Christ, preservation from the end-time "wrath" and the hope of glory. "The conception of Salvation provides both a centre and a framework for all the religious and ethical ideas which have real importance in Christianity as St Paul understood it" (C. A. A. Scott, *Christianity according to St Paul*, vii).

10. τοῦ ἀποθανόντος ὑπὲρ ἡμῶν, ἵνα . . . ἅμα σὺν αὐτῷ ζήσωμεν, "who died for us, in order that . . . we might live together with him." The closing words echo those at the end of 4:17, "and thus we shall be forever with the Lord."

The form of this sentence, where the statement of the death or self-giving of Christ is followed by a clause expressing its purpose, is a recurring one in the letters of Paul. It is Christ "who gave himself for our sins, that (ὅπως) he might deliver us from the present evil age" (Gal. 1:4); "to this end Christ died and lived again, that (ἵνα) he might be Lord both of the dead and of the living" (Rom 14:9); "he died for all, that (ἵνα) those who live might live no longer for themselves but for him who for their sake died and was raised" (2 Cor 5:15); God "for our sake made him to be sin who knew no sin, so that (ἵνα) in him we might become the righteousness of God" (2 Cor 5:21). A pre-Pauline formula has been discerned in the first of these quotations (Bovon, "Une formule prépaulinienne"), and the fact that our present passage is similarly introduced by the article-plus-participle construction (equivalent to a relative clause) might suggest that we are dealing with such a formula here too; of this, however, it is impossible to be sure. Like 2 Cor 5:15, 21, the present passage strikes the note of interchange: Christ died that his people might live. Hooker, who finds in these and other passages illustrations of Irenaeus's dictum that "Christ became what we are, in order that we might become what he is" (*Adv. Haer.* 5, preface), concludes that "the idea of interchange of experience in Christ is a vital clue to Paul's understanding of atonement" ("Interchange and Atonement," 481). Here the aorist ζήσωμεν implies that the life which the people of Christ receive through his surrender of his own life is the resurrection life to be entered into at his Parousia: like the "salvation" of v 9, the "life" of v 10 is eschatologically definitive. Even those who survive until the Parousia enter into a new order of life then (cf. 1 Cor 15:50–54).

The preposition most commonly used to express the saving efficacy of Christ's death *for* his people is ὑπέρ, "on behalf of." In the "interchange" texts quoted above, it appears in Gal 1:4 (ὑπὲρ τῶν ἁμαρτιῶν ἡμῶν, cf. 1 Cor 15:3); 2 Cor 5:15 (ὑπὲρ πάντων), 21 (ὑπὲρ ἡμῶν); also Rom 5:6, 8; 8:32; 14:15, etc. Paul never uses ἀντί in this soteriological sense; its one such occurrence (and a highly important one) in the NT is Mark 10:45 par., λύτρον ἀντὶ πολλῶν. (See also 1 Tim 2:6, ἀντίλυτρον ὑπὲρ πάντων, with E. K. Simpson's comment ad loc. in *The Pastoral Epistles,* London: Tyndale Press, 1954, 43, 44, and his "Note on the Meaning of ΥΠΕΡ in Certain Contexts," 110–112.)

This statement, then, that "Christ died for us, in order that we might live with him," is the most explicit statement in the Thessalonian letters of the saving purpose of the death of Christ. It is mentioned as something known to the readers; it had doubtless been emphasized as the gospel was first preached to them (cf. the insistence on Christ crucified in 1 Cor 2:2 and Gal 3:1).

εἴτε γρηγορῶμεν εἴτε καθεύδωμεν, "whether we are awake or asleep," i.e. whether we are alive or dead at the Parousia. The readers are given "a definite assurance that life and death, 'waking' and 'sleeping' . . . , constitute no unbridgeable gulf: both alike, those still alive and those fallen asleep, will soon be forever united with the Lord" (Bornkamm, *Paul,* 222).

The verbs γρηγορεῖν and καθεύδειν are those used in v 6 for moral watchfulness and carelessness respectively, but that is not their sense here. It is ludicrous to suppose that the writers mean, "Whether you live like sons of light or like sons of darkness, it will make little difference: you will be all right in the end." As W. Kelly puts it (ad loc.), "the necessary inference . . . would be that, whether we be spiritually watchful or slothful, we shall alike enjoy the portion of everlasting blessedness together with Christ. Does not this sound uncommonly like moral indifferentism?"

If it be asked if it is likely that the same verbs would be used in two different senses within such a brief space, it must be said in reply that there is nothing unusual or improbable in this. It is a well attested feature of less formal literature, both ancient and modern, that "a single word or phrase persists in the writer's mind by its own force, independently of any sense-recurrence" (Laughton, "Subconscious Repetition," 75).

While καθεύδειν may not be so frequently attested as κοιμᾶσθαι in the sense of death, it occurs in that sense often enough to establish that (like the uncompounded εὕδειν) it was indeed so used. In the NT Jesus' words about Jairus's daughter, οὐκ ἀπέθανεν ἀλλὰ καθεύδει, "she is not dead but sleeping" (Mark 5:39 par.), while capable of more than one interpretation, probably have the same sense as his words about Lazarus: ὁ φίλος ἡμῶν κεκοίμηται, "our friend has fallen asleep" (John 11:11). In Eph 5:14 the parallel commands ἔγειρε ὁ καθεύδων ("awake, O sleeper") and ἀνάστα ἐκ τῶν νεκρῶν ("arise from the dead") are synonymous. In Dan 12:2 (LXX and Theodotion) καθεύδειν is used of those "who *sleep* in the dust of the earth," and in Ps 88:5 (LXX 87:6) of those who "*lie* in the grave." For εὕδειν in the same sense cf. Homer, *Il.* 14.482, Πρόμαχος δεδμημένος εὕδει/ ἔγχει ἐμῷ ("Promachus sleeps, having been mastered by my spear"); Sophocles *Oed. Col.* 621, οὑμὸς εὕδων καὶ κεκρυμμένος νέκυς/ψυχρός ("my cold corpse, asleep and concealed").

11. Διὸ παρακαλεῖτε ἀλλήλους, as in 4:18, although here the more general sense of "encourage one another" rather than the specific sense of "comfort one another" is indicated by the context.

καὶ οἰκοδομεῖτε εἷς τὸν ἕνα, "and build one another up," i.e. help one another to grow spiritually. This metaphorical sense of οἰκοδομεῖν is particularly common in 1 Corinthians; it is preeminently by love that Christians, and the church as a whole, are built up (1 Cor 8:1). The noun οἰκοδομή is similarly used, but not in 1 or 2 Thessalonians.

The eschatological hope, then, is not an excuse for idling but an incentive for action, and especially for mutual aid. Every church member has a duty to help in "building up" the community, so that it may attain spiritual maturity.

καθὼς καὶ ποιεῖτε, "as indeed you are doing." Cf. 4:1, 10. It can be irritating to be told to do what one is already doing; this note of commendation would guard against such a possibility. Some of the Thessalonians might have yielded to the temptation to grow slack, but they were only a few; the conduct of the majority calls forth approval.

Explanation

Although the Thessalonians needed to be reassured about the lot of their departed friends at the expected Advent of Christ, they appear to have had otherwise a fairly clear understanding of the character of that advent and its attendant circumstances.

It is plain that the Christian Advent hope had been enriched with elements from the OT expectation of the Day of the Lord: indeed, that very expression had been taken over into the Christian vocabulary, the "Lord" being now understood as Jesus. In the gospel tradition we similarly find the language and imagery earlier used of the Day of the Lord reappearing in Jesus' teaching about the coming of the Son of Man. The Day of the Lord would bring judgment on the unrighteous: to them it would be "darkness, and not light" (Amos 5:20). So in the Gospels the Son of Man comes at a time when he is least expected and to those who are morally unprepared for him his coming will mean retribution: it will be "that day of wrath, that dreadful day." But the children of light—those whose lives are lived in the sight of God and in conformity with his will—are always in a state of preparedness for the great day: they do not know when it will come, but it will not take them at a disadvantage.

It is sad when people live in a dream world of false security, like the inhabitants of Laish, "quiet and unsuspecting," who were caught unawares by the Danite invaders (Judg 18:7, 27). They are bound to have a rude awakening.

There are other crises than the final Day of the Lord, which share something of its character. They too may come without warning. To be ready for them it is necessary to be constantly alert and sober. This is as true in personal life as it is in national and international affairs. That is the point of the parable of the ten virgins: "Keep awake therefore, for you know neither the day nor the hour" (Matt 25:13).

The call for vigilance is voiced in terms of keeping awake and having one's wits about one, rather than being overcome by drowsiness and intoxication; it is voiced also in military terms. Spiritual armor is a necessary defense against spiritual assaults. The figure of clothing oneself is common in the NT epistles when the cultivation of Christian virtues is the subject; here the cultivation of Christian virtues—faith, love and hope—is likewise the subject, but now they are the defensive armor, the breastplate and helmet, to be put on by the children of light. (Nothing is said in this context about weapons of attack.)

William Neil observes that "the real point of this whole paragraph, whose motto, Watch and pray, should be graven on the shield of every Christian warrior, is the paradox so difficult to us, but much less difficult to minds schooled in the prophets, of stressing the imminence of the Parousia while denying its immediacy." Perhaps it was not a question of denying its immediacy but rather of not asserting its immediacy. If its immediacy were asserted, then its timing would presumably be known: it would take place without any intervening event or course of events. The Parousia may have been expected within that generation, but in circumstances of stress and persecution even a short time could suffice to make hope wane and expectation grow dim. The writers endeavor to encourage their converts to maintain their faith and fervor, to cultivate and practice the Christian graces, and thus to be ready for the Advent of their Lord and the enjoyment of eternal bliss with him. Death before his Advent would make no difference to this sure prospect: "If we live, we live to the Lord, and if we die, we die to the Lord; so then, whether we live or whether we die, we are the Lord's" (Rom 14:8).

Plainly the Advent hope is treated as an incentive to Christian life and conduct here and now. The motive power for Christian life and conduct is supplied by the indwelling Spirit (cf. 4:8); it is his indwelling presence, indeed, as other letters of Paul make plain, that insures that the Advent hope is no vain hope but one which, because it is so well founded, is ethically fruitful in the present mortal existence.

But is the relative nearness, not to say imminence, of the expected Advent essential to its providing an incentive to holy living? Clearly the perspective of believers living in the first Christian generation must differ from that of their successors today; the possibility that Christ might return within that generation ceased around A.D. 70. But it helps to realize that it is not so much an event as a person who is near: "the Lord is at hand" and it is he himself who is his people's hope. This realization is plainly shared with his friends by Paul himself, and it is expressed by other NT writers. When the full manifestation is granted and the beatific vision at last enjoyed, then, says John, "we shall be like him, for we shall see him as he is; and every one who thus hopes in him [in the person, not the event] purifies himself he as is pure" (1 John 3:2, 3). Here is ground enough for the mutual encouragement and strengthening which, at the end of this subsection, the readers of the letter (today, as in A.D. 50) are enjoined to practice.

In a sermon preached in the 1830s John Henry Newman had these wise words to say:

> Though time intervene between Christ's first and second coming, it is not *recognized* (as I may say) in the gospel scheme, but is, as it were, an accident. For so it was, that up to Christ's coming in the flesh, the course of things ran straight towards that end, nearing it by every step, but now, under the Gospel, that course has (if I may so speak) altered its direction, as regards His second coming, and runs, not towards the end, but along it, and on the brink of it; and is at all times equally near that great event, which, did it run towards it, it would at once run into. Christ, then, is ever at our doors.

(f) *On Recognition of Leaders (5:12, 13)*

Bibliography

Banks, R. *Paul's Idea of Community. The Early House Churches in their Historical Setting.* Exeter. Paternoster Press. 1980. **Bjerkelund, C. J.** *Parakalô.* Oslo: Universitetsforlaget, 1967. **Fung, R. Y. K.** "Charismatic versus Organized Ministry? An Examination of an Alleged Antithesis." *EvQ* 52 (1980) 195–214. **Holmberg, B.** *Paul and Power. The Structure of Authority in the Primitive Church as Reflected in the Pauline Epistles.* Con B: NT Series 11. Lund: Gleerup, 1978. **Hort, F. J. A.** *The Christian Ecclesia.* London: Macmillan, 1897. **Käsemann, E.** "Ministry and Community in the New Testament." In *Essays on New Testament Themes.* Tr. W. J. Montague. SBT 41. London: SCM Press, 1964, 63–94. **Lightfoot, J. B.** "The Christian Ministry." In *Saint Paul's Epistle to the Philippians.* London: Macmillan, ⁶1881, 181–269, reprinted in *Dissertations on the Apostolic Age.* London: Macmillan, 1892, 137–246. **Lindsay, T. M.** *The Church and the Ministry in the Early Centuries.* London: Hodder and Stoughton, 1902. **Manson, T. W.** *The Church's Ministry.* London: Hodder and Stoughton, 1948. **Schweizer, E.** *Church Order in the New Testament.* Tr. F. Clarke. SBT 32. London: SCM Press, 1961. **Tragan, P.-R.** "Un texte ancien sur l'organisation de l'Église: 1 Thessaloniciens 5, 12–13." In *Ministères et célébration de l'eucharistie.* Sacramentum I = Studia Anselmiana 61. Roma: Editrice Anselmiana, 1973, 149–180.

Translation

[12] *Now we ask you, brothers, to know those who work hard among you and care for* [a] *you in the Lord and instruct you,* [13] *and to esteem* [b] *them very highly* [c] *in love because of their work. Be at peace among yourselves.* [d]

Notes

ᵃ For προϊσταμένους the Hellenistic προϊστανομένους is read by P³⁰(vid) ℵ A.

ᵇ For the infinitive ἡγεῖσθαι the imperative ἡγεῖσθε is read by B Ψ 6 81 1739 *al.*

ᶜ For ὑπερεκπερισσοῦ B D* F G *pc* read ὑπερεκπερισσῶς, while P ³⁰(vid) reads ἐκ περισσοῦ.

ᵈ The original classical plural of the reflexive ἑαυτόν is σφᾶς αὐτούς, but from an early date the form ἑαυτούς occurs; in addition, this third-personal form encroached on the province of the first and second persons: here ἐν ἑαυτοῖς means "among yourselves." For ἑαυτοῖς many witnesses (including P³⁰ ℵ D* F G P Ψ 81 1881*; cf. Vg *cum eis*) read αυτοις, which could be understood either as αὐτοῖς ("be at peace with them," i.e. with the προϊστάμενοι) or as αὐτοῖς (equivalent to ἑαυτοῖς).

Form/Structure/Setting

The construction with ἐρωτῶμεν is completely comparable to that with παρακαλοῦμεν, which Bjerkelund has investigated (see 4:1, ἐρωτῶμεν . . . καὶ παρακαλοῦμεν . . . , with comment). But the ἐρωτῶμεν construction here, like the παρακαλοῦμεν construction in v 14, lacks the customary prepositional phrase (as found in 4:1, ἐν κυρίῳ Ἰησοῦ), and is concerned with relations between the community addressed and specific groups or individuals (cf. Bjerkelund, *Parakalô*, 128)—a form found repeatedly in concluding requests or appeals (cf. Rom 16:17–20; 1 Cor 16:15–18; Phil 4:2, 3).

The last clause of this subsection, εἰρηνεύετε ἐν ἑαυτοῖς, expressing a common Christian exhortation, probably goes back to Jesus' admonition to his disciples, εἰρηνεύετε ἐν ἀλλήλοις, "be at peace among one another" (preserved in Mark 9:50), which in turn has no lack of OT antecedents; cf. Ps 34:14 (LXX 33:15), ζήτησον εἰρήνην καὶ δίωξον αὐτήν, "seek peace and pursue it."

Comment

5:12. Ἐρωτῶμεν δὲ ὑμᾶς, ἀδελφοί, "Now we ask you, brothers": for ἐρωτᾶν in the postclassical sense of making a request cf. 4:1.

εἰδέναι τοὺς κοπιῶντας ἐν ὑμῖν καὶ προϊσταμένους ὑμῶν ἐν κυρίῳ καὶ νουθετοῦντας ὑμᾶς, "to know those who work hard among you and care for you in the Lord and instruct you." Since the three present participles are governed by a single definite article, the reference is to one group of people who perform the three specified services in the church. From its position as the second in a series of three participles, of which the first and third are not official designations, προϊσταμένους is plainly not an official designation. In Rom 12:8 ὁ προϊστάμενος comes fourth in a series of five distinct categories of minister: ὁ διδάσκων, the teacher; ὁ παρακαλῶν, the exhorter; ὁ μεταδιδούς, the one who shares his goods with others, . . . ὁ ἐλεῶν, the one who performs acts of mercy or charity (the singular definite article being generic in each instance); here too ὁ προϊστάμενος cannot be regarded as an official designation. If the corresponding noun προστάτης were used, it might be regarded as a title; as it is, προστάτης does not occur in the NT. The feminine προστάτις is used of Phoebe in Rom 16:2

(προστάτις πολλῶν, "a helper or patron of many"), but even there it is not her official title: in so far as she has an official title, it is "διάκονος (minister, servant, deacon) of the church in Cenchreae." (It is noteworthy that the only person named in the NT as διάκονος of a local church is a woman.)

The verb προΐστασθαι combines the ideas of leading, protecting and caring for (cf. Reicke, 700). Apart from the two occurrences mentioned, it is found in the NT only in the Pastoral Letters: three times of looking after one's own household (1 Tim 3:4, 5, 12), twice of caring for (promoting) good works (Tit. 3:8, 14), once of elders in the church (1 Tim 5:17, where elders who rule well, οἱ καλῶς προεστῶτες πρεσβύτεροι, are to be held worthy of double honor or honorarium; with this phrase cf. Herm. *Vis.* 2.4.3, οἱ πρεσβύτεροι οἱ προϊστάμενοι τῆς ἐκκλησίας, "the elders who are in charge of the [Roman] church"). For ἐν κυρίῳ see comments on 3:8; 4:1.

These persons care for the church by working hard (κοπιᾶν) on its behalf; one form of their care is the instruction (νουθετεῖν) of their fellow Christians. Their hard work was a "labor of love" (1:3), not something undertaken for their own advantage or prestige, although the analogy of other churches (cf. Gal 6:6) suggests that in Thessalonica too the church's responsibility for the material needs of the προϊστάμενοι was not to be overlooked. In such selfless κόπος the missionaries themselves had set an example (2:9; 3:5). As for νουθετεῖν, this might be general instruction or, where wrong tendencies had to be corrected, admonition and warning (as in v 14; 2 Thess 3:15).

A parallel to the Thessalonian προϊστάμενοι is provided by the household of Stephanas at Corinth: its members had "devoted themselves to the service (διακονία) of the saints" and therefore, with others who did similar work, were to be given their due position in the church (1 Cor 16:15, 16). The ἡγούμενοι ("leaders") of Heb 13:17 may be compared: they likewise were to receive obedience and submission, "for they are keeping watch over your souls, as men who will have to give account." The same kind of recognition and appreciation is to be given by the Thessalonian church to its προϊστάμενοι.

13. καὶ ἡγεῖσθαι αὐτοὺς ὑπερεκπερισσοῦ ἐν ἀγάπῃ διὰ τὸ ἔργον αὐτῶν, "and to hold them in very high esteem and love because of their work." For ὑπερεκπερισσοῦ cf. 3:10. The highest possible regard is due to such people, not because of their status but because of their work. In Christian ministry generally status depends on function and not *vice versa.* It was not important that those who served the church in various ways should be given distinctive titles, and even when they were given titles (like the ἐπίσκοποι and διάκονοι of Phil 1:1), these might differ from one place to another. What was important was that the service should be rendered, and that those who rendered it should receive affectionate recognition and gratitude, in the spirit of Jesus' teaching that, in his kingdom, the lowliest service carried with it the highest honor (Mark 10:42–45 par.; Luke 22:24–27).

εἰρηνεύετε ἐν ἑαυτοῖς, "be at peace among yourselves." It may be asked why this injunction should come here, immediately after the call to recognize those who cared for the church. It may be that the recognition of such people and deference to their judgment would check any tendency to anarchy, with consequent strife, that might manifest itself among them. The call for peace (cf. 1:1) is common in the Pauline and other epistles of the NT, as in Rom 12:18; 14:19; 2 Cor 13:11; Eph 4:3; Col 3:15; 2 Tim 2:22; Heb 12:14, and echoes the dominical injunction mentioned above.

Explanation

It will make for the effective life and witness of the church and for peaceful relations among its members if its leaders are recognized and honored and their directions followed. The corollary of this is that the leaders should be the kind of people who deserve to be recognized and honored by their fellow Christians.

No fixed pattern of rule appears to have been imposed on the Pauline churches. The precedent of the church of Jerusalem, which by this time was governed by a body of elders under the chairmanship of James the Just, was not followed as a matter of course. The policy of Paul and his colleagues seems to have been to wait until qualities of spiritual leadership displayed themselves in certain members of a church and then to urge the others to acknowledge and respect those as leaders. One of the most obvious qualities of leadership was a readiness to serve the church and care for its needs. Such leaders did not do the appropriate work because they had been appointed as leaders; they were recognized as leaders because they were seen to be doing the work.

Some men and women were in an especially suitable position to care for the church—those, for example, whose homes served as meeting places, like Gaius at Corinth (Rom 16:23) or Nympha in the Lycus valley (Col 4:15). Ernst von Dobschütz lists this service as first in a series of ten ways in which provision was made for the church by those capable of making it. The others were: seeing to the good order of church meetings, leading in prayer, leading in scripture reading, leading in song, undertaking the maintenance of itinerant fellow Christians, supporting the poor, going bail where necessary (as Jason did in Thessalonica), representing brothers and sisters who had to appear in court on charges arising out of their faith, journeying on the church's behalf. As procedure became increasingly regularized, most of these services became the responsibility of the president or bishop, but in the early stages of church life they were undertaken voluntarily. When persecution broke out, it was the people who rendered such services who were most in the public eye and were therefore the first targets for attack.

There is no hint that the church members who took a lead in such ways had any special charismatic gifts. There was a place for charismatic ministry in the church of Thessalonica, as the references to prophecy in the following context indicate, but administrative ability was valued as an endowment of the Spirit alongside prophetic utterance and similar gifts. At this early date there was no antithesis between the two types of ministry.

(g) *On Various Christian Duties (5:14–22)*

Bibliography

Best, E. "Prophets and Preachers." *SJT* 12 (1959) 129–150. **Cullmann, O.** *Des sources de l'Evangile à la formation de la théologie chrétienne.* Neuchâtel: Delachaux et Niestlé, 1969, 176–180 ("Méditation sur I Th. 5.19–21"). **Frame, J. E.** "Οἱ ἄτακτοι (1 Thess. 5:14)." In *Essays in Modern Theology . . . a Testimonial to C. A. Briggs.* New York: Scribners, 1911, 191–206. **Hansel, F. M. A.** "Über die richtige Auffassung der Worte Pauli 1 Thess 5, 21 f." *TSK* 9 (1836) 170–184. **Hill, D.** *New Testament Prophecy.* London: Marshall, Morgan & Scott, 1979. **Langevin, P.-É.** "Conseils et prière." *AsSeign* n.s. No. 7 (1969) 34–39. **Martin, R. P.** *Worship in the Early Church.* London: Marshall, Morgan & Scott, 1964. **Rinaldi, G.** "Il Targum palestinese del Pentateuco." *BibOr* 17 (1975) 75–77. **Spicq, C.** "Les Thessaloniciens 'inquiets' étaient-ils des paresseux?" *ST* 10 (1957) 1–13. **Unnik, W. C. van** "Den Geist löschet nicht aus." *NovT* 10 (1968) 255–269.

Translation

14 *Now we appeal to you, brothers:*
admonish the disorderly,
comfort the fainthearted,
help the weak,
be patient toward all.
15 *See to it* [a] *that no one renders evil for evil to any one, but at all times pursue what is good, both* [b] *for one another and for all.*
16 *Rejoice at all times,*
17 *pray constantly,*
18 *give thanks in everything,*
for this is God's will for you in Christ Jesus.
19 *Do not quench the Spirit,*
20 *do not despise prophesyings,*
21 *but* [c] *test everything,*
hold fast what is good,
22 *abstain from every kind of evil.*

Notes

[a] ὁρᾶτε μή τις . . . ἀποδῷ (*v.l.* ἀποδοῖ): μή with subjunctive would be sufficient to express the prohibition (cf. 2 Thess 2:3, μή τις ὑμᾶς ἐξαπατήσῃ, "let no one deceive you"); the preceding ὁρᾶτε ("see to it") adds emphasis (cf. Matt 9:30, ὁρᾶτε μηδεὶς γινωσκέτω, "see to it: let no one get to know"). See BDF §§ 364 (3), 370 (4), 461 (1).
[b] καί before εἰς ἀλλήλους is read by P[30] ℵ[2] B Ψ byz lat[vg.st] syr[hcl]; it is omitted by ℵ* A D F G 1739 1881 *pc* lat[vet vg.cl] syr[pesh] Ambst Spec.
[c] δέ after πάντα is omitted by ℵ* A 81 614 *pm* lat[f*] syr[pesh] Tert Did.

Form/Structure/Setting

The outstanding feature of this subsection is the triple series of short cola (each colon comprising a verb in the imperative with an object or an adverbial amplification). Colon 1 (v 14) consists of four pastoral injunctions; colon 2 (vv 16–18a) of three directions for manifesting the will of God in one's spiritual life; colon 3 (vv 19–22) of five exhortations relating to the prophetic ministry.

Similar series of short cola are found elsewhere in the OT and NT; cf. Isa 1:16, 17; Matt 10:8; Luke 6:27, 28; Rom 12:9–16; 1 Pet 2:17.

Possibly instruction was given in this form to serve as an easily memorized catechesis. On the two series of cola in vv 16–22 a further suggestion is made by Martin (*Worship*, 135, 136), who acknowledges his indebtedness to some thoughts expressed by J. M. Robinson. He notes that in each colon the verb stands last, and that there is a preponderance of words beginning with π. "When the passage is set down in lines," he observes, "it reads as though it contained the 'headings' of a Church service"— emphasis being laid on the introductory note of "glad adoration," with prayer and thanksgiving, on the liberty of the Spirit and on the avoidance of anything unseemly. He compares the fuller counsels on the church's public worship in 1 Corinthians 14.

Comment

5:14. Παρακαλοῦμεν δὲ ὑμᾶς, ἀδελφοί, "And we appeal to you, brothers." Cf. vv 12–13 (p. 118); 4:1, 10. It might be argued, with Chrysostom and other Greek commentators, that these words are addressed to the προϊστάμενοι, whose responsibility it was to administer admonishment where necessary and exercise care for those who needed it. In that case ὑμᾶς would be emphatic ("you for your part"). But there is nothing in the text to indicate this. It could be indicated in speech by a change of intonation, by a significant look or gesture. In a written letter, however, the change of address and emphasis would have to be indicated verbally, and Greek is not lacking in means to give expression to such a change. As it is, παρακαλοῦμεν δὲ ὑμᾶς, ἀδελφοί, here is exactly parallel to ἐρωτῶμεν δὲ ὑμᾶς, ἀδελφοί, at the beginning of v 12, and it is natural to suppose that the same ἀδελφοί are addressed in both places. The various forms of service enjoined in the words that follow are certainly a special responsibility of leaders, but not their exclusive responsibility: they are ways in which all the members of the community can fulfill the direction of v 11 to encourage and strengthen one another.

νουθετεῖτε τοὺς ἀτάκτους, "admonish the disorderly." The ἄτακτοι are those who are undisciplined, not maintaining proper order (τάξις) but playing truant; more particularly in this context they are the "loafers" (Moffatt) who neglect their daily duty and live in idleness, at the expense of others, ignoring the injunction of 4:11 and the example of 2:9. Cf. 2 Thess 3:6–

12. The instruction (νουθετεῖν) which such persons required included a note of disapproval of their present conduct; they had to be told to mend their ways. And the community as a whole had an interest in setting them right; if they lived in idleness it was the community that had to support them, and it was the community's reputation that was endangered by their irregular way of life. It must not be thought that the leaders were hypercritical in their attitude to such people; the whole community should dissociate itself in a practical manner from the discreditable course they were pursuing. (There is little to be said for Frame's idea that tension had resulted from the leaders' severity toward the idlers; hence the call for peace in v 13.)

παραμυθεῖσθε τοὺς ὀλιγοψύχους, "comfort the fainthearted." For παραμυθεῖσθαι cf. 2:12. The ὀλιγόψυχος (here only in NT) stands at the opposite pole to the μεγαλόψυχος, the high-souled person (exactly equivalent to Sanskrit mahātmā, from maha-ātmā), Aristotle's ideal man, "who claims much and deserves much" (Eth. Nic. 4. 3.3, 1123b). Whereas the μεγαλόψυχος (not found in the NT) is self-sufficient and self-confident, the ὀλιγόψυχος is inadequate and diffident. Aristotle calls him the μικρόψυχος and does not regard him as an exemplary character: the most μικρόψυχος of all is he "who claims less than he deserves when his deserts are great" (Eth. Nic. 4.3.7). How would he have rated Paul, not to speak of Jesus? In the Christian community the ὀλιγόψυχος, for all his conscious inadequacy and diffidence, is to be encouraged and made to feel someone who counts: his gifts may not be great but, with encouragement, they can be developed and make a valuable contribution to communal well-being. (In LXX ὀλιγόψυχος, ὀλιγοψυχία and ὀλιγοψυχεῖν occur several times, rendering a variety of Hebrew words and phrases, e.g. קצר רוח "short of temper" in Prov. 14:29; נכאה רוח "a broken spirit," in Prov 18:14.)

ἀντέχεσθε τῶν ἀσθενῶν, "help the weak"—especially the "weak in faith" (cf. Rom 14:1). In its other NT occurrences (Matt 6:24 par. Luke 16:13; Tit 1:9) ἀντέχεσθαι means "hold fast to"; here it implies holding in the sense of holding up, supporting. Cf. Rom 15:1, "we who are strong ought to bear (βαστάζειν) the infirmities of the weak (τὰ ἀσθενήματα τῶν ἀδυνάτων)."

μακροθυμεῖτε πρὸς πάντας, "be patient toward all." In Gal 5:22 μακροθυμία is included in the ninefold fruit of the Spirit. It is a quality of God, who is "patient and full of mercy," μακρόθυμος καὶ πολυέλεος (Exod 34:6; Ps 103 [LXX 102]:8), and is to be reproduced in human beings who bear the image of God. In T. Jos. 2:7 Joseph relates how he was steadfast (ἐμακροθύμησα) in all his temptations, adding that μακροθυμία "is a great medicine and endurance (ὑπομονή) yields many good things." "Love is patient," says Paul (ἡ ἀγάπη μακροθυμεῖ, 1 Cor 13:4), and he urges his Christian friends to display μακροθυμία to one another and to all (cf. Eph 4:2; Col 1:11; 3:12). Its exercise is especially necessary in leaders, but in this as in other respects they show an example which their brothers and sisters are to follow.

15. ὁρᾶτε μή τις κακὸν ἀντὶ κακοῦ τινι ἀποδῷ, "See to it that no one renders to any one evil for evil." The same injunction to nonretaliation appears in almost identical terms in Rom 12:17a (μηδένι κακὸν ἀντὶ κακοῦ ἀποδιδόντες). This is basic Christian teaching; it goes back to the words of Jesus (Matt 5:44–48 par. Luke 6:27–36), which in turn have OT antecedents (cf. Prov 25:21). The paraenesis now becomes more general.

ἀλλὰ πάντοτε τὸ ἀγαθὸν διώκετε, "but constantly pursue what is good"; cf. Rom 12:17b (προνοούμενοι καλὰ ἐνώπιον πάντων ἀνθρώπων, "taking thought for what is good in the sight of all"). Lightfoot suggests that τὸ ἀγαθόν is what is beneficial, whereas τὸ καλόν in v 21 is that which is morally good; but it is doubtful if the distinction can be pressed. Here it is not τὸ ἀγαθόν in the abstract that is meant, but that which is good and helpful to others, even to enemies (as opposed to κακόν in the preceding clause); cf. Luke 6:27, καλῶς ποιεῖτε τοῖς μισοῦσιν ὑμᾶς, "do good to those who hate you."

[καὶ] εἰς ἀλλήλους καὶ εἰς πάντας, "both to one another and to all," as in 3:12, where love is to be shown within the brotherhood as well as to all the human family; see comment ad loc. For διώκειν in an ethical sense cf. 1 Cor 14:1, where the object is love, 1 Tim 6:11 and 2 Tim 2:22, where it is righteousness, and Heb 12:14, where it is peace (to be pursued μετὰ πάντων) and holiness.

16. Πάντοτε χαίρετε, "rejoice at all times"; cf. Phil 4:4, χαίρετε ἐν κυρίῳ πάντοτε, "rejoice in the Lord at all times." The rejoicing enjoined here is likewise ἐν κυρίῳ, although this is not explicitly said. Cf. also Rom 14:17, where χαρὰ ἐν πνεύματι ἁγίῳ ("joy in the Holy Spirit") is part of what the kingdom of God means. Joy is a fruit of the Spirit (Gal 5:22); cf. Phil 2:17, 18, for the mutual and shared joy of apostle and converts.

17. ἀδιαλείπτως προσεύχεσθε, "pray incessantly"; cf. the fuller wording of Eph 6:18, διὰ πάσης προσευχῆς καὶ δεήσεως προσευχόμενοι ἐν παντὶ καιρῷ ἐν πνεύματι ("praying with all prayer and supplication at all times in the Spirit"). For the adverb ἀδιαλείπτως cf. 1:2/3 (in reference to recollection, as in Rom 1:9); 2:13 (in reference to thanksgiving). According to Jesus, people "ought always to pray and never lose heart" (Luke 18:1). Cf. Rom 12:12, τῇ προσευχῇ προσκαρτεροῦντες ("persevering in prayer"), which probably conveys the sense of the present passage.

18. ἐν παντὶ εὐχαριστεῖτε, "give thanks in everything"—i.e. in every situation, in all circumstances. Thanksgiving is closely associated with prayer (as in 1:2); cf. Phil 4:6, "in everything (ἐν παντί) in prayer and supplication with thanksgiving (μετὰ εὐχαριστίας) let your requests be made known to God." Ingratitude is one of the features of pagan depravity in Rom 1:21; the children of God are expected to "abound in thanksgiving" (Col 2:7; cf. Col 3:15, 17; 4:2; Eph 5:4, 20).

τοῦτο γὰρ θέλημα θεοῦ ἐν Χριστῷ Ἰησοῦ εἰς ὑμᾶς, "for this is God's will in Christ Jesus for you." See 4:3 with comment ad loc. for the anarthrous θέλημα. There God's will is his people's sanctification, which is all-comprehending in its scope (in 4:3–8 one particular application is dealt with); no part of life is excluded from its operation (v 23). Here the sanctifying work of the Spirit within finds expression in rejoicing, prayer and thanksgiving, for vv 16–18 are closely bound together and τοῦτο γὰρ θέλημα θεοῦ is a coda to all three. "God's will in Christ Jesus" may be paraphrased as "God's will for you as members of the Christian fellowship." It is in this fellowship, too, that they can carry out God's will effectively.

19. τὸ πνεῦμα μὴ σβέννυτε, "do not quench the Spirit." It is doubtful if we should press the use of the present imperative with μή here and in v 20 to mean that the recipients are being told to stop doing something they have already begun to do. Like the positive imperatives in vv 16–18 and 21–22, the negative imperatives in vv 19 and 20 indicate what they must habitually do (or refrain from doing).

The verb "quench" is related to the figure of fire used in various places (e.g. Matt 3:11 par. Luke 3:16; Luke 12:49; Acts 2:3; Rom 12:11) to denote the Holy Spirit or his activity. As the context goes on to make plain, the activity chiefly in view here is prophecy. In this respect the Spirit may be quenched when the prophet refuses to utter the message he has been given, or when others try to prevent him from uttering it. A good example of the former is Jeremiah's attempt to speak no more in Yahweh's name, when the word held back became, as he said, "a burning fire shut up in my bones" (Jer 20:9), which could not be quenched or controlled. An example of the latter is found in Amos 2:12, where the people of Israel are condemned because they "commanded the prophets, saying, 'You shall not prophesy.' " Cf. Mic 2:6; also *Tg. Neof.* Num 11:28, where Joshua says to Moses regarding Eldad and Medad, "Take the Holy Spirit from them," מנע מנהון רוח קודשה (cf. G. Rinaldi, "Il Targum . . .").

20. προφητείας μὴ ἐξουθενεῖτε, "do not despise prophesyings." When the prophetic gift is exercised in church, the utterance must be received seriously and not be ignored. The prophet in the church, like John in the Apocalypse, was the spokesman of the risen Christ. "The prophetic charisma, spread abroad through the Church by the Spirit . . . , goes back ultimately to Christ, the revelation of the Father" (Hill, *NT Prophecy*, 150, 151). A specially high authority thus attached to this gift. There may have been a tendency at Thessalonica, as later at Corinth, to value more spectacular gifts above prophecy; hence the warning that prophecy must not be depreciated but heard with the respect due to the Spirit whose voice is communicated through the prophet. Cf. 1 Cor 14:1, "earnestly desire the spiritual gifts (τὰ πνευματικά), but preferably that you may prophesy" (also 14:39, ζηλοῦτε τὸ προφητεύειν). The gift of administrative ability (cf. v 12 above) is distinguished in 1 Cor 12:28 from the gift of prophesying, but both play a helpful part in the upbuilding of the church.

21. πάντα δὲ δοκιμάζετε, "but test everything" (neuter plural rather than accusative singular, "every person"). The gift of prophecy lent itself to imitation, and it was important that counterfeit prophets should be de-

tected. No criteria are suggested here for distinguishing genuine prophecy from false; consistency with revelation already received would be one obvious test. The prophet's testimony to Christ was crucial: as Paul says in 1 Cor 12:3, the confession κύριος Ἰησοῦς, "Jesus is Lord," is an infallible token of the Spirit's voice, whereas ἀνάθεμα Ἰησοῦς, "Jesus be cursed," would self-evidently proceed from a very different source. It is desirable that all who are exposed to prophetic utterances should be able to recognize the truth when they hear it; cf. the direction in 1 Cor 14:29, "let two or three prophets speak, and let the others weigh what is said" (διακρινέτωσαν). It is specially necessary that those in positions of responsibility should be able to exercise this kind of discernment. In 1 Cor 12:10 "the ability to distinguish between spirits" (διακρίσεις πνευμάτων) is a gift given to some, but nothing is implied about a special gift of discernment here. It would be part of the ministry of the προϊστάμενοι to encourage genuine spiritual exercises and to suppress what was not genuine.

τὸ καλὸν κατέχετε, "hold fast what is good." The reference may primarily be to prophetic utterances: those which were recognized as divinely inspired should receive careful attention and be translated into appropriate action. It is possible, however, that this clause goes more closely with the following one than with the preceding one.

22. ἀπὸ παντὸς εἴδους πονηροῦ ἀπέχεσθε, "abstain from every kind of evil." The sense of "species" or "kind" for εἶδος is quite classical (cf. Thucydides *Hist.* 2.50, τὸ εἶδος τῆς νόσου, "the nature of the disease") and is attested far beyond the classical period (cf. Eusebius *HE* 5.1.6, πᾶν εἶδος ὀνειδισμοῦ, "every kind of abuse"). The present injunction could also refer to prophetic utterances; indeed, it is possible to treat πονηροῦ as attributive to εἴδους (rather than as a genitive dependent on it) and translate "abstain from every evil kind (of utterance)." An utterance which is "evil" would be one running contrary to gospel faith and practice; such an utterance is to be rejected. But when this clause and the preceding one are taken together, we have the two sides of a principle which is of general application; cf. Isa 1:16, 17, "Cease to do evil, learn to do good" (LXX παύσασθε ἀπὸ τῶν πονηριῶν ὑμῶν, μάθετε καλὸν ποιεῖν). One kind of evil from which it is necessary to abstain has been mentioned in 4:3 (ἀπέχεσθαι ὑμᾶς ἀπὸ τῆς πορνείας).

Explanation

The Christian community is to be a little welfare state, a society practicing mutual aid among its members in spiritual and material respects alike. Within its fellowship those who need help should be given the help they need. A special responsibility in this regard rests on the leaders of the community, but it is a ministry in which all can have some share. The timid must be encouraged, the weak must be strengthened, those who stray must be led back to the right path, and all must be treated with patience—especially those who make the greatest demands on the patience of their fellow Christians.

Christian life is to be lived in an atmosphere of continuous joy, prayer and thanksgiving. In the eyes of their neighbors some early Christians had little enough ground for joy, especially when they were exposed to harassment and social ostracism because of their faith. But they had inner resources which enabled them to rejoice not merely in spite of those afflictions but because of them, like the Jerusalem apostles who, after a judicial flogging, left the council chamber "rejoicing that they were counted worthy to suffer dishonor for the name" (Acts 5:41). To "pray without ceasing" does not mean that every other activity must be dropped for the sake of prayer but that every activity must be carried on in a spirit of prayer which is the spontaneous outcome of a sense of God's presence. As for thanksgiving, that is the natural response of a heart conscious of the greatness of God's grace. "In the New Testament," said Thomas Erskine of Linlathen, "religion is grace, and ethics is gratitude."

Members of such a fellowship will not be content to care for one another only; as the God whom they call Father is good to all, irrespective of their deserts, so must they be.

The gift of prophecy—the declaration of the mind of God in the power of the Spirit—made an indispensable contribution to the church of NT days. The prophets in the local congregations may not have risen to the heights of the great OT prophets, but what they said was to be accepted as the will of God. This did not mean that all who called themselves prophets were to be acknowledged as such. The prophets and their prophecies were to be tested. That was so in OT times; for example, a prophet whose predictions did not come true was to receive no credence (Deut 18:21, 22) and even if his words did come true, if their tendency was to turn the hearers away from their allegiance to the living God, then he was to receive the penalty due to a false prophet (Deut 13:1–5). The main criterion by which NT prophets were to be tested was their effective confession of Jesus as Lord (1 Cor 12:3). At a later stage this test was made more specific: to confess Jesus as Lord is (among other things) to confess his incarnation; therefore, "every spirit which confesses that Jesus Christ has come in the flesh is of God" (1 John 4:2), whereas a prophet who denies this (especially by denying the identity of Jesus of Nazareth with the eternal Son of God) is shown thereby to be inspired by "the spirit of antichrist" (1 John 4:3)

The use of God's gift of reason is a corrective to unrestrained enthusiasm. There is a saying widely ascribed to Jesus by writers in the early Christian centuries: "Become approved moneychangers." This was sometimes explained in terms of 1 Thess 5:21, 22. For example, Clement of Alexandria quotes it in the form: "Become approved moneychangers, who reject much, but retain the good." The distinguishing of genuine from counterfeit coinage is a good figure of speech for the distinguishing of true from false prophecy—or any other kind of religious teaching.

(h) *Second Wish-Prayer for the Thessalonian Christians (5:23, 24)*

Bibliography

Festugière, A.-M. "La trichotomie de 1 Thess v, 23 et la philosophie grecque."
RSR 20 (1930) 385–415. **Johnson, A. R.** *The Vitality of the Individual in the Thought
of Ancient Israel.* Cardiff: University of Wales Press, 1949. **McCaig, A.** "Thoughts
on the Tripartite Theory of Human Nature." *EvQ* 3 (1931) 121–138. **Marshall,
W.** *The Gospel Mystery of Sanctification.* [1692] Edinburgh: James Taylor, 1887. **Martin,
R. P.** *Worship in the Early Church.* London: Marshall, Morgan & Scott, 1964.
Montague, G. T. *Growth in Christ.* Kirkwood, MO: Maryhurst Press, 1961. **Neill,
S. C.** *Christian Holiness.* London: Lutterworth Press, 1960. **Robinson, H. W.** *The
Christian Doctrine of Man.* Edinburgh: T. & T. Clark, ³1926. **Schweizer, E.** "Zur
Trichotomie von 1 Thess 5, 23 und der Unterscheidung des πνευματικόν vom ψυχικόν
in 1 Kor 2, 14; 15, 44; Jak 3, 15; Jud 19." *TZ* 9 (1953) 76–77. **Stacey, W. D.** *The
Pauline View of Man.* London: Macmillan, 1956. **Stempvoort, P. A. van** "Eine stilis-
tische Lösung einer alten Schwierigkeit in I Thess. v. 23." *NTS* 7 (1960–61) 262–
265. **Unnik, W. C. van** "Aramaeismen bij Paulus." *Vox Theologica* 14 (1942) 122–
123. **Veloso, M.** "Contenido antropológico de 1 Tesalonicenses 5, 23." *Revista
Bíblica* 41 (1979) 129–140. **Wiederkehr, D.** *Die Theologie der Berufung in den Paulusbriefen.* Freiburg: Universitätsverlag, 1963. **Wiles, G. P.** *Paul's Intercessory Prayers.*
SNTSMS 24. Cambridge: Cambridge University Press, 1974.

Translation

²³ *Now may the God of peace himself sanctify you completely, and may your
spirit and soul and body be preserved* ᵃ *in entirety, free from blame, at the advent
of our Lord* ᵇ *Jesus Christ.* ²⁴ *He who calls you is faithful; he will do it.*

Notes

ᵃ For τηρηθείη D* reads τηρηθείην, plainly a scribal slip (hardly, as van Stempvoort suggests,
for τηρηθείεν).

ᵇ Marcion read καὶ σωτῆρος between κυρίου and ἡμῶν ("our Lord and Savior Jesus Christ").

Form/Structure/Setting

As the earlier wish-prayer of 3:11–13 concludes the "apostolic parousia"
of 2:17–3:10, this wish-prayer concludes the paraenesis of 4:1–5:22. Both
are expressed by means of aorist optatives, both begin with the emphatic
(and possibly liturgical) αὐτός and both end on an eschatological note.
(Cf. Wiles, *Prayers*, 63–68.)

Martin (*Worship*, 136), having observed that the short clauses of vv 16–
22 read like the "headings" of a church service, points out the appropriateness of their being concluded with "a comprehensive prayer for the entire
fellowship (verse 23), expressed in the confidence that God will hear and
bless (verse 24)."

V 23 contains a chiasmus: ἁγιάσαι . . . ὁλοτελεῖς being followed by ὁλόκληρον . . . τηρηθείη. Van Stempvoort, however, sees this chiasmus incorporated in a more comprehensive one, as he attaches καὶ ὁλόκληρον ὑμῶν τὸ πνεῦμα to the preceding words so as to form part of the first clause of the prayer; the second clause then begins καὶ ἡ ψυχὴ καὶ τὸ σῶμα, forming a chiastic counterpart to ὑμῶν τὸ πνεῦμα at the end of the first clause ("Eine stilistische Lösung . . ."). But this is an unnatural way to divide the sentence.

Comment

5:23. Αὐτὸς δὲ ὁ θεός, as at the beginning of the first wish-prayer (3:11).

ὁ θεὸς τῆς εἰρήνης, "the God of peace," as in Rom 15:33; 16:20; Phil 4:9 (also Heb 13:20). Cf. 2 Cor 13:11 (ὁ θεὸς τῆς ἀγάπης καὶ εἰρήνης, "the God of love and peace"); 2 Thess 3:16 (ὁ κύριος τῆς εἰρήνης, "the Lord of peace"). A similar wish-prayer in Rom 15:13 is introduced by ὁ . . . θεὸς τῆς ἐλπίδος ("the God of hope"). The sum total of gospel blessings can be expressed by εἰρήνη (cf. 1:1), the designation ὁ θεὸς τῆς εἰρήνης pointing to God as the source of them all. If there was any tendency to conflict in the Thessalonian church (cf. v 13, εἰρηνεύετε ἐν ἑαυτοῖς), the God of peace could be relied upon to heal it with his reconciling grace. "God is not the God of disorder (ἀκαταστασία) but of peace" (1 Cor 14:33a). Even if the general, all-embracing sense of εἰρήνη is intended, the more particular sense need not be excluded.

ἁγιάσαι ὑμᾶς ὁλοτελεῖς; "may (he) sanctify you completely." This wish-prayer is in essence a repetition in different words of that in 3:11–13, the climax of which is the prayer that the Thessalonians' hearts may be established "unblamable in holiness" at the Parousia. Here, as there, the optatives are in the aorist tense. The "complexive" aorist is regularly used in prayers (BDF § 337 [4]). In direct prayers the aorist imperative is used; in a wish-prayer the imperative is replaced by the optative, but the aorist remains. That is sufficient explanation of the aorist ἁγιάσαι but it is clear from the context that, if ἁγιάζειν is a process, it is the completion of the process that is in view here, as in 3:13. The importance of sanctification (ἁγιασμός) in the practical area of sexual life has been emphasized in 4:3, 4, 7, where it is implied that sanctification (in all areas of life) is the work of the indwelling Holy Spirit (4:8).

This is the only place in the NT where ὁλοτελής occurs. Its earliest attestation is in Aristotle (*Plant.* 1.2.20.817b). Vettius Valens uses it (*Anth.* 247.8), but an instance closer in date to ours comes in an inscription recording Nero's announcement of "complete exemption from taxation" (ἀνεισφορίαν . . . ὁλοτελῆ) to all Greeks at the Isthmian Games of A.D. 67 (*SIG*³ 814.45; *IG* 7.2713.45).

καὶ ὁλόκληρον ὑμῶν τὸ πνεῦμα καὶ ἡ ψυχὴ καὶ τὸ σῶμα ἀμέμπτως . . . τηρηθείη, "and may your spirit and soul and body be preserved in entirety, free from blame." This is another way of expressing the desire for their complete sanctification. The adjective ὁλόκληρον qualifies all three of the nouns which follow (its relation to them being predicative); it agrees in number and gender with the nearest of the three. For the classical ὁλόκληρος (a synonym of ὁλοτελής) cf. Jas 1:4, ἵνα ἦτε τέλειοι καὶ ὁλόκληροι, "that you may be perfect and complete" (also Acts 3:16 for the ὁλοκληρία, "perfect health," of the man who had been cured of his congenital lameness). For ἀμέμπτως cf. the adjective ἀμέμπτους in the wish-prayer of 3:13 (with comment ad loc.).

It is precarious to try to construct a tripartite doctrine of human nature on the juxtaposition of the three nouns, πνεῦμα, ψυχή and σῶμα. The three together give further emphasis to the completeness of sanctification for which the writers pray, but the three together add but little to the sense of ὑμῶν τὰς καρδίας ("your hearts") in 3:13. The distinction between the bodily and spiritual aspects of human nature is easily made, but to make a comparable distinction between "spirit" and "soul" is forced. Few would care to distinguish sharply among the four elements "heart" (καρδία), "soul" (ψυχή), "mind" (διάνοια) and "strength" (ἰσχύς) of Mark 12:30 (amplifying the threefold "heart, . . . soul, and . . . might" of Deut 6:5). The distinction made by Paul between ψυχή and πνεῦμα in 1 Cor 15:45 has no bearing on the present passage: there the distinction lies between the "living person" (ψυχὴ ζῶσα) which the first Adam became at his creation (Gen 2:7) and the "life-giving spirit" (πνεῦμα ζῳοποιοῦν) which the second Adam has become in resurrection. It is the contrast between the two nouns in that sense that constitutes the contrast between the adjectives ψυχικός and πνευματικός in 1 Cor 15:44, 46 (ψυχικός means χοϊκός as πνευματικός means ἐπουράνιος). The contrast between ψυχικός and πνευματικός in 1 Cor 2:14, 15 depends on the contrast between the soul of man and the Spirit of God; the understanding of the ψυχικὸς ἄνθρωπος is confined to the capacity of "the spirit of man (τὸ πνεῦμα τοῦ ἀνθρώπου) within him" (1 Cor 2:11), and without the indwelling Spirit of God he cannot appreciate the πνευματικά, the "things of God" (1 Cor 2:11). In that context πνεῦμα is practically synonymous with νοῦς (cf. 1 Cor 2:16).

Plato speaks of the mind as being in the soul, and the soul in the body (νοῦν μὲν ἐν ψυχῇ, ψυχὴν δὲ ἐν σώματι, Tim. 30B), but for him the νοῦς was part of the ψυχή. Marcus Aurelius distinguishes σῶμα, ψυχή, νοῦς by saying that sensations belong to the body, impulses to the soul and opinions to the mind (σώματος αἰσθήσεις, ψυχῆς ὁρμαί, νοῦ δόγματα, Med. 3.16). MM (s.v. ὁλόκληρος) quote from the third-century magic P Lond 121, line 590, διαφύλασσέ μου τὸ σῶμα τὴν ψυχὴν ὁλόκληρον, "keep my body [and] my soul in sound health." These are partial parallels to the present terminology, but throw little light on its details: what the writers mean is, "May every part of you be kept entirely without fault." On the "complexive" aorist optative τηρηθείη cf. what is said on ἁγιάσαι earlier in the verse.

ἐν τῇ παρουσίᾳ τοῦ κυρίου ἡμῶν Ἰησοῦ Χριστοῦ, "at the advent of our Lord Jesus Christ," as in the parallel wish-prayer in 3:13 (except that Χριστοῦ is missing there and "with all his holy ones" is not added here). In both places the construction is compendious; the writers' prayer is that their converts may be preserved entirely without fault *until* the Parousia and be so found *at* the Parousia, when they will be perfected in holiness.

24. πιστὸς ὁ καλῶν ὑμᾶς, "he who calls you is faithful." Cf. 2:12; 4:7. It is God who calls his people to sanctification (cf. 1 Pet 1:15) and he supplies the grace without which his call cannot be realized. " 'I think there is meaning in that present participle,' Bishop Westcott once remarked to a friend" (Neill, *Christian Holiness*, 25). Much the same affirmation (including πιστὸς ὁ θεός) is made in 1 Cor 1:8, 9. Cf. Rom 8:30, "whom he called . . . , them he also glorified," where conformity to the image of Christ is the goal and climax of sanctification.

ὃς καὶ ποιήσει, "who indeed will do it." He who initiates the work of sanctification in his people's lives can be relied upon to complete the work. Cf. Phil 1:6, "he who began a good work in you will bring it to completion at (ἄχρι) the day of Jesus Christ."

Explanation

The series of exhortations which began in 4:1 is rounded off with a prayer for the readers' entire and final sanctification and preservation. It has been indicated already (4:8) that the Spirit of God, who is himself holy, is the sanctifier of those in whose lives he dwells. This sanctifying work, as is stated explicitly elsewhere in Paul's letters, results in their being increasingly transformed into the likeness of Christ, "from one degree of glory to another," until they are perfectly glorified with him at his advent (2 Cor 3:18; Col 3:4). This attainment of perfect glory is the completion of their sanctification, which is prayed for here; it marks the climax of God's purpose for his people, and he can be counted upon to accomplish his own purpose.

Perhaps the most important point to observe in the much debated reference to "spirit and soul and body" is the inclusion of the body in God's saving and sanctifying purpose. This may have been difficult for Greeks to accept, in view of the depreciation of the body in several of their philosophical schools of thought, but Paul insists on it. Earlier in this letter the Thessalonians have been taught to gain control over their bodies "in sanctification and honor" (4:4). So the Corinthians are told that "the body is for the Lord," it will be raised up by his power to a new order of existence, and here and now it is "a temple of the Holy Spirit"; so, says Paul, "glorify God in your body" (1 Cor 6:13–20).

Letter Closing   (1 Thess 5:25–28)

Bibliography

Askwith, E. H. " 'I' and 'We' in the Thessalonian Epistles." *Expositor,* series 8, 1 (1911) 149–159. **Banks, R.** *Paul's Idea of Community. The Early House Churches in their Historical Setting.* Exeter: Paternoster Press. Grand Rapids, MI. Eerdmans. 1980. **Boers, H.** "The Form-Critical Study of Paul's Letters: I Thessalonians as a Case Study." *NTS* 22 (1975–76) 140–158. **Champion, L. G.** *Benedictions and Doxologies in the Epistles of Paul.* Oxford: published privately, 1934. **Dix, G.** *The Shape of the Liturgy.* Westminster: Dacre Press, 1945. **Ellis, E. E.** "Paul and his Co-Workers." *NTS* 17 (1970–71) 437–452. **Harnack, A. von** "Das Problem des zweiten Thessalonicherbriefs." *SAB* 31 (1910) 560–578. **Hofmann, K. M.** *Philema Hagion. BFCT* 2.38. Gütersloh: Bertelsmann, 1938. **Marshall, I. H.** *Last Supper and Lord's Supper.* Exeter: Paternoster Press, 1980. **Martin, R. P.** *Worship in the Early Church.* London: Marshall, Morgan & Scott, 1964.

Translation

[25] Pray also [a] for us, brothers.
[26] Greet all the brothers with a holy kiss.
[27] I adjure [b] you by the Lord that this letter be read to all the [c] brothers.
[28] The grace of our Lord Jesus Christ be with you. [d]

Notes

[a] καί ("also") before περὶ ἡμῶν is omitted by א A D[2] F G Ψ byz lat syr[pesh] cop[bo].
[b] For ἐνορκίζω א D[a] F G Ψ byz read ὁρκίζω.
[c] ἁγίοις ("holy") is inserted before ἀδελφοῖς by P[46(vid)] א[2] A Ψ byz lat[a vs] syr cop[bo].
[d] ἀμήν is added by א A D[2] Ψ byz lat[a m vs] syr cop[bo]. It was the congregational response made when the letter closing was read in church services.

Form/Structure/Setting

"The Pauline letter closing has three items—doxology, greetings (usually with a request for prayers), benediction" (Boers, "The Form Critical Study . . . ," 140). There is no formal doxology in the letter closing of 1 Thessalonians, although the affirmation of God's trustworthiness in v 24 might to some extent be regarded as serving the purpose of a doxology. The other items are here: the request for prayer (v 25), the greetings (v 26) and the benediction (v 28). In addition, there is the solemn adjuration inserted between the greetings and the benediction, insisting that the letter be read to "all the brothers" (v 27).

The direction regarding the "holy kiss" in v 26 suggests a eucharistic setting. The exchange of the kiss in such a setting is attested by Justin

Martyr (c. A.D. 150): it came after the prayers and before the bringing in of the bread and wine (*I Apol* 65.2). The omission of the kiss of greeting even at an ordinary social meal was an occasion for remark (Luke 7:45); it was the more appropriate that it should feature in the meal where those in the fellowship of the reconciled celebrated the one whose reconciling sacrifice had united them.

It may well be that the writers envisage the letter being read at a eucharistic assembly of the church—after the prayers, perhaps, and just before the normal moment for the exchanged kiss. This would not be an isolated instance among the Pauline letters: at the end of 1 Cor (16:20–22) the direction to "greet one another with a holy kiss" is followed by the quotation of some words from the eucharistic service. "If we may regard the closing verses of 1 Corinthians as a lead-in to the Lord's Supper, we can draw the conclusion that the Supper was introduced by the kiss of peace as a sign of loving fellowship among the members. This was accompanied both by the pronouncement of a curse upon any who did not truly love the Lord and by the pronouncement of a blessing upon the Lord's people" (Marshall, *Last Supper and Lord's Supper*, 145). (In the light of this, a comparison of *Marana-tha* in 1 Cor 16:22 with ἔρχου κύριε Ἰησοῦ, "Come, Lord Jesus" in Rev 22:20 may suggest that the Apocalypse similarly was read at eucharistic assemblies of the churches of Asia to which it was sent.)

Comment

5:25. Ἀδελφοί, προσεύχεσθε [καὶ] περὶ ἡμῶν, "Pray also for us, brothers." As the writers have voiced their prayer for the Thessalonian Christians, they invite the Thessalonians in their turn (καί) to pray for them. Such requests for prayer appear in a number of Pauline letters; cf. Rom 15:30–32; 2 Cor 1:11; Eph 6:19, 20; Phil 1:19; Col 4:3, 18; Phlm 22.

26. Ἀσπάσασθε τοὺς ἀδελφοὺς πάντας ἐν φιλήματι ἁγίῳ, "Greet all the brothers with a holy kiss"—a *holy* kiss, signifying the bond that unites them in a holy fellowship. Practically the same injunction appears in Rom 16:16; 1 Cor 16:20; 2 Cor 13:12. In 1 Pet 5:14 the same kiss is called the "kiss of love" (φίλημα ἀγάπης); later it was generally called the "kiss of peace" (cf. Hippolytus, *Ap. Trad.* 4.1; 18.3; 22.6). The *Apostolic Constitutions* (early 4th century) lay it down that at the Eucharist "the men are to give one another the kiss in the Lord (τὸ ἐν κυρίῳ φίλημα) and the women likewise to one another" (2.57.17). (See above.)

The direction that "all the brothers" (and sisters) should share in this greeting may be intentionally emphatic (more emphatic than the ἀλλήλους of Rom 16:16; 1 Cor 16:20; 2 Cor 13:12); if there were tensions within the church—tensions (say) between the Gentile and Jewish members—these might be resolved by the "holy kiss," from which none was to be excluded. There is no implication that the direction is addressed to the προϊστάμενοι, who were to kiss the rank and file as a token that the peace called for in v 13 was now restored, any more than it is addressed to the rank and file who were to include even the προϊστάμενοι in their greeting as a token of the unity between leaders and led.

27. Ἐνορκίζω ὑμᾶς τὸν κύριον ἀναγνωσθῆναι τὴν ἐπιστολὴν πᾶσιν τοῖς ἀδελφοῖς, "I adjure you by the Lord that the letter be read to all the brothers." The sudden switch from the plural to the singular of the first person is significant; the most probable explanation is that Paul took over the pen at this point and added the adjuration and the concluding benediction with his own hand (cf. Askwith, " 'I' and 'we' . . ."). Earlier instances of Paul's interposing something on his own account have come at 2:18 and 3:5 (see also 2 Thess 2:5 and especially 3:17, with comment).

The compound ἐνορκίζειν, otherwise known only from a few inscriptions and from Josephus (*Antiq.* 8.404), is a strengthened form of ὁρκίζειν (cf. Mark 5:7; Acts 19:13), bearing the same formal relation to it as the adjective ἔνορκος ("under oath") bears to ὅρκος ("oath"); cf. also ἐξορκίζειν (Matt 26:63). The accusative τὸν κύριον is common for the person or thing invoked in the oath (cf. τὸν θεόν, Mark 5:7, τὸν Ἰησοῦν, Acts 19:13; contrast κατὰ τοῦ θεοῦ τοῦ ζῶντος, Matt 26:63).

Paul's use of the adjuration need not imply that he was unaware of Jesus' ban on the use of oaths by his followers (μὴ ὀμόσαι ὅλως, Matt 5:34); this is not a strengthening of a statement of his own by the invocation of the divine name (for which cf. 2:5; Gal 1:20; Rom 9:1; Phil 1:8) but an appeal to those addressed to act in this matter as responsible to the Lord himself. But why should he insist so solemnly that "the letter" (i.e. the letter now being concluded) should be read to "all the brothers"? It sounds very much as though he feared that some Thessalonian Christians might not have it communicated to them.

It is difficult to accept Harnack's theory that the Gentile and Jewish Christians of Thessalonica met separately and that, while the letter was sent to the Gentile group, Paul wished to make sure that the Jewish group should read it too (see Introduction, p. xli). Ellis ("Paul and his Co-Workers," 451 n. 1) suggests that the "brothers" here may be Paul's co-workers, "especially those evangelizing a neighbouring area," who "might not hear a letter sent to the congregation and yet might have need of its teachings for their own work." It is more likely that such "co-workers" would be the first to receive the letter and that it would be their responsibility to make sure that it was read to "all the brothers" (cf. Masson, ad loc., for the view that the primary recipients were the προϊστάμενοι). It is best, on the whole, to conclude that Paul wished to make sure that the ἄτακτοι heard the letter. There was much in it that would be especially beneficial for them, but if their ἀταξία included a tendency to absent themselves from meetings of the church (cf. Heb 10:25), they might not be present when the letter was read; the responsible leaders of the church should therefore see to it that they were made acquainted with its contents. For a direction about the reading of other Pauline letters cf. Col 4:16. The "reading" implied is public reading at a meeting of the whole church.

28. Ἡ χάρις τοῦ κυρίου ἡμῶν Ἰησοῦ Χριστοῦ μεθ' ὑμῶν, "The grace of

our Lord Jesus Christ be with you." The "grace" of the opening salutation (1:1) is caught up and repeated in this closing benediction. This is the basic epistolary benediction in the Pauline corpus; it is variously expanded in one letter and another (in Col 4:18 it is abridged to ἡ χάρις μεθ' ὑμῶν, "grace be with you"). Cf. 2 Thess 3:18 (where πάντων is added before ὑμῶν).

Explanation

As the writers have prayed for their readers' supreme and final blessing, so they request their readers, on their part, to pray for them. The apostle and his companions were exposed to special dangers and trials and realized their constant need of prayer support.

They invite their readers to kiss one another in token of their unity and love in Christ, taking care that no one be omitted. They urge them also to take care that no one be missed when their letter is read: all must hear its contents, not least those who are disposed to play truant. The letter would fail to achieve its purpose if such people did not get the message especially meant for them. Then, with a final benediction, the letter closes.

The Second Letter
to the Thessalonians

STRUCTURE

1. PRESCRIPT (1:1–2)

2. THANKSGIVING, ENCOURAGEMENT AND PRAYER (1:3–12)
   (a) *Thanksgiving* (1:3–4)
   (b) *Encouragement* (1:5–10)
   (c) *Prayer Report* (1:11–12)

3. THE RISE AND FALL OF THE MAN OF LAWLESSNESS (2:1–12)

4. FURTHER THANKSGIVING, ENCOURAGEMENT AND PRAYER (2:13–17)
   (a) *Thanksgiving* (2:13–14)
   (b) *Encouragement* (2:15)
   (c) *First Wish-Prayer* (2:16–17)

5. FURTHER PRAYER (3:1–5)
   (a) *Prayer Request* (3:1–2)
   (b) *Expression of Confidence* (3:3–4)
   (c) *Second Wish-Prayer* (3:5)

6. EXHORTATION (3:6–16)
   (a) *On Idleness* (3:6–13)
   (b) *On Discipline* (3:14–15)
   (c) *Third Wish-Prayer* (3:16)

7. LETTER CLOSING (3:17–18)

Prescript (2 Thess 1:1-2)

Bibliography

Harnack, A. von, "Das Problem des zweiten Thessalonicherbriefs." *SAB* 31 (1910) 560–578. **Lohmeyer, E.** "Probleme paulinischer Theologie. I. Briefliche Grussüberschriften." *ZNW* 26 (1927) 158–173. **Roller, O.** *Das Formular der paulinischen Briefe: Ein Beitrag zur Lehre vom antiken Briefe.* Stuttgart: W. Kohlhammer, 1933. **White, J. L.** *The Form and Function of the Body of the Greek Letter.* SBL Dissertation Series 2. Missoula, Montana: Scholars Press, 1972.

Translation

[1] *Paul, Silvanus and Timothy to the church of the Thessalonians* [a] *in God our Father and the Lord Jesus Christ:* [2] *grace to you and peace from God our* [b] *Father and the Lord Jesus Christ.*

Notes

[a] After τῇ ἐκκλησίᾳ Θεσσαλονικέων Harnack tentatively conjectured (on no textual evidence) that τῶν ἐκ τῆς περιτομῆς ("who are of the circumcision") had fallen out (in line with his theory of the destination of 2 Thess; see p. xli).

[b] ἡμῶν is omitted after ἀπὸ θεοῦ πατρός by B D P 0111ᵛⁱᵈ 33 1739 1881 *pc.* It is exhibited by the great majority of witnesses. It could have been added by assimilation to the other Pauline prescripts where the phrase occurs; but its omission might be accounted for by the wish not to repeat it after ἐν θεῷ πατρὶ ἡμῶν in v 1.

Form/Structure/Setting

See on 1 Thess 1:1. The prescript of 2 Thess differs from that of 1 Thess by the addition of ἡμῶν after ἐν θεῷ πατρί and the addition of ἀπὸ θεοῦ πατρὸς [ἡμῶν] καὶ κυρίου Ἰησοῦ Χριστοῦ after χάρις ὑμῖν καὶ εἰρήνη. The latter addition brings the prescript into line with that of most other Pauline letters.

Comment

1. Παῦλος καὶ Σιλουανὸς καὶ Τιμόθεος. Precisely as in 1 Thess 1:1 (see comment ad loc.).

τῇ ἐκκλησίᾳ Θεσσαλονικέων ἐν θεῷ πατρὶ ἡμῶν καὶ κυρίῳ Ἰησοῦ Χριστῷ, as in 1 Thess 1:1 (see comment ad loc.), except that ἡμῶν, "our," after πατρί, "Father," present here, is lacking there.

2. χάρις ὑμῖν καὶ εἰρήνη, as in 1 Thess 1:1 (see comment ad loc.). The

fuller χάρις ἔλεος εἰρήνη, "grace, mercy, peace" appears in 1 Tim 1:2; 2 Tim 1:2.

ἀπὸ θεοῦ πατρὸς [ἡμῶν] καὶ κυρίου Ἰησοῦ Χριστοῦ, "from God [our] Father and the Lord Jesus Christ." These words, habitually appended to χάρις ὑμῖν καὶ εἰρήνη in the Pauline letters (cf. Rom 1:7; 1 Cor 1:3; 2 Cor 1:2; Gal 1:3; Eph 1:2; Phil 1:2; Col 1:2, with the omission of καὶ κυρίου Ἰησοῦ Χριστοῦ; Phlm 3; also, with minor variations, 1 Tim 1:2; 2 Tim 1:2; Tit 1:4), are missing from 1 Thess 1:1 (for a possible stylistic reason see comment ad loc.).

Explanation

Paul, Silvanus (Silas) and Timothy, the three missionaries who had first brought the gospel to Thessalonica and planted the church in that city, address the church a second time, in terms not unlike those in which they had greeted it at the beginning of their earlier letter.

Thanksgiving, Encouragement and Prayer (2 Thess 1:3–12)

(a) Thanksgiving (1:3–4)

Bibliography

Aus, R. D. "The Liturgical Background of the Necessity and Propriety of Giving Thanks according to 2 Thess 1:3." *JBL* 92 (1973) 432–438. **Cerfaux, L.** *The Church in the Theology of St. Paul.* Tr. G. Webb and A. Walker. Edinburgh/London/New York: Nelson/Herder and Herder 1959. **O'Brien, P. T.** *Introductory Thanksgivings in the Letters of Paul.* NovTSup 49. Leiden: Brill, 1977. **Schubert, P.** *Form and Function of the Pauline Thanksgivings.* BZNW 20. Berlin: Töpelmann, 1939.

Translation

³ We are bound to give thanks to God for you always, brothers, as is fitting, because your faith grows abundantly and the mutual love of each one of you all multiplies, ⁴ so that we ourselves boast ᵃ *of you in the churches of God for your patience and faith in all your persecutions and the afflictions which* ᵇ *you endure.* ᶜ

Notes

ᵃ For the compound ἐγκαυχᾶσθαι the simple καυχᾶσθαι is read by D Ψ byz, καυχήσασθαι by FG.

ᵇ αἷς is an instance of Attic attraction; it is attracted from the accusative ἅς (object of ἀνέχεσθε) into the dative case of its antecedent θλίψεσιν.

ᶜ For ἀνέχεσθε B reads ἐνέχεσθε ("you are involved").

Form/Structure/Setting

This introductory thanksgiving is generally similar to that of 1 Thess 1:2, 3, though it has distinctive features, such as εὐχαριστεῖν ὀφείλομεν, "we are bound to give thanks," instead of εὐχαριστοῦμεν, "we give thanks," and the added clause καθὼς ἄξιόν ἐστιν, "as it is fitting." According to R. D. Aus ("Liturgical Background"), both the ὀφείλομεν construction and the καθώς clause are liturgical expressions for the necessity and propriety of thanking God (cf. the words in the Anglican communion service: "It is very meet, right, and our bounden duty, that we should at all times, and in all places, give thanks unto thee, O Lord . . ."). If this is recognized, it rebuts the imputation of relative coolness sometimes made against this thanksgiving report over against that of 1 Thess 1:2, 3; in any case the suggestion of coolness is sufficiently removed by the affectionate vocative ἀδελφοί. The ground of the thanksgiving is indicated by the causal ὅτι clause. The ὥστε clause of v 4 points to the consequence of the apostles' thankful joy; they boast about the Thessalonians' faith and endurance under tribulation to all the churches with which they are currently in contact.

The thanksgiving report is recalled in very similar words in 2:13.

Comment

1:3. Εὐχαριστεῖν ὀφείλομεν τῷ θεῷ πάντοτε περὶ ὑμῶν, ἀδελφοί, καθὼς ἄξιόν ἐστιν, "it is our duty to thank God for you at all times, brothers, as is fitting." A certain formality has been detected in this language, by contrast with the warmth of 1 Thess 1:2 (εὐχαριστοῦμεν τῷ θεῷ πάντοτε περὶ πάντων ὑμῶν, "we give thanks to God always for all of you"), and used as an argument against the authenticity of 2 Thessalonians. But if the Thessalonian Christians had protested against what they regarded as the excessive commendation expressed in the earlier letter, the writers might well have replied, "It is only fitting that we should thank God for you; it is indeed our bounden duty"—and that is the force of the present wording (much of which is repeated in 2:13). The Thessalonians deserve all the thanksgiving with which the writers' hearts are filled on their account, because of the encouragement brought by the news of their ever-increasing faith and love.

ὅτι ὑπεραυξάνει ἡ πίστις ὑμῶν καὶ πλεονάζει ἡ ἀγάπη ἑνὸς ἑκάστου πάντων ὑμῶν εἰς ἀλλήλους, "because your faith grows abundantly and the mutual love of each one of you all multiplies." Two of the three graces mentioned in the introductory thanksgiving of 1 Thess 1:3 find renewed mention here (cf. 1 Thess 3:6). As for the companion grace of hope, while the actual word ἐλπίς occurs in this letter only in 2:16, the ground of their hope—their vindication at the Advent of Christ—is dealt with at length from v 5 onward (see also comment on τῆς ὑπομονῆς ὑμῶν, v 4).

If time had elapsed since the sending of 1 Thessalonians to allow further news to reach the writers about the recipients' spiritual health, this could account for the superlative language used here. The earlier report was encouraging; the latest news was even more encouraging. Then, their faith had been evident in action but suffered from certain deficiencies which required to be made good (1 Thess 1:3; 3:10); now, it was growing more and more. Then, the writers prayed that the Thessalonians' love one to another might "increase and abound" (1 Thess 3:12); now, they thank God that this prayer has been answered. It is certainly more satisfactory to suppose that the same readers are being addressed as in 1 Thessalonians; there is nothing in the wording to suggest that the writers, concerned not to give Jewish Christians in Thessalonica the impression that the high commendation expressed in 1 Thessalonians about the faith and love of the Gentile Christians implied that their own cultivation of these graces was overlooked, now turn to them and say, "We thank God for you too, because you have (if anything) surpassed the others in these qualities."

The classical compound ὑπεραυξάνειν, "flow abundantly" is not found elsewhere in the NT, but Paul is fond of compounds with ὑπερ- (cf. ὑπερεκπερισσοῦ, "superabundantly," 1 Thess 3:10; 5:13; ὑπερπερισσεύειν, "superabound," Rom 5:20; 2 Cor 7:4). For εἰς ἀλλήλους, "to one another" cf. 1 Thess 3:15; 5:15 (καὶ εἰς πάντας "and to all men" is not added here). The emphatic ἑνὸς ἑκάστου πάντων ὑμῶν, "each one of you all" (more emphatic than ἕνα ἕκαστον ὑμῶν, "each one of you," 1 Thess 2:11) makes one wonder about the τινας . . . ἐν ὑμῖν, "some . . . among you" of 3:11 who were not conspicuous for Christian faith and love; it can probably be assumed that these formed an uncharacteristic minority, whose waywardness, though regrettable, did not detract from the satisfaction with which the community as a whole was viewed.

4. ὥστε αὐτοὺς ἡμᾶς ἐν ὑμῖν ἐγκαυχᾶσθαι, "so that we ourselves boast about you." This is the only NT instance of the late compound ἐγκαυχᾶσθαι (found four times in LXX), but the simple καυχᾶσθαι (the ground of boasting being indicated by ἐν, ὑπέρ or ἐπί) is common in the Pauline letters, not least where the apostle boasts to others about his converts (cf. 2 Cor 7:14; 9:2). What is said here is consistent with 1 Thess 1:8 (there is no need to say anything about the Thessalonians' faith and witness, because the facts speak for themselves); there might indeed be no *need* for the writers to say anything, but they said it nonetheless. They could not keep silence about men and women who were their "glory and joy" (1 Thess 2:20). For a later instance of Paul's boasting about the Macedonian churches (certainly including Thessalonica) to another church (the Corinthian) cf. 2 Cor 8:1–5. Why the writers should insist that "we ourselves boast about you" is uncertain. Others—the αὐτοί ("they themselves") of 1 Thess 1:9— had spoken of the Thessalonians' initial obedience to the gospel, and perhaps had gone on to speak of their progress in Christian life. If others had done so, why should not their own parents in the faith boast about them? They had the greatest right to do so; they knew them best.

ἐν ταῖς ἐκκλησίαις τοῦ θεοῦ, "in the churches of God," especially here those in Achaia. Reference has been made already to "the churches of God" (1 Thess 2:14), but those were the Judean churches, comprising the mother church of Jerusalem and her daughter churches, formed either by evangelization or by dispersion. It is primarily the Jerusalem church that is meant by "the church of God" which Paul in his earlier days persecuted (Gal 1:13; 1 Cor 15:9; cf. Phil 3:6). But now, with the advance of the gospel, other "churches of God" have come into being—especially, from Paul's point of view, what he calls "the churches of the Gentiles" (Rom 16:4). The believers in Corinth, for example, constitute "the church of God which is at Corinth" (1 Cor 1:2; 2 Cor 1:1; cf. 1 Cor 10:32; 11:22). The sum total of such local churches makes up "the churches of God" in the sense intended here (cf. 1 Cor 11:16); they are also called "the churches of Christ" (Rom 16:16) or "the churches of the saints" (1 Cor 14:33). Mention is made of the church (singular) of a specified city (like Thessalonica) or the churches (plural) of a specified province (like Macedonia, 2 Cor 8:1). While the Christian use of ἐκκλησία was taken over from its LXX application to the religious community of Israel (see comment on 1 Thess 1:1), and was first current among the Jewish disciples in Jerusalem, it quickly became naturalized in the Gentile mission field, like most of the designations given to the OT people of God (see comment on v 10 below, ἐν τοῖς ἁγίοις αὐτοῦ).

ὑπὲρ τῆς ὑπομονῆς ὑμῶν καὶ πίστεως, "for your patience and faith." Whereas the "faith" of v 3 is general, here the reference is more particularly to the faith which enables them to remain steadfast under persecution and other forms of trial (cf. 1 Thess 3:7). The ὑπομονή is the "patience of hope" or "patient hope" mentioned in 1 Thess 1:3; indeed, it might be said that the present mention of ὑπομονή compensates for the lack of reference to hope alongside the faith and love of v 3. Lake (*Epistles*, 89) follows Harnack's thesis in saying that Paul here "repeats—perhaps one may say, is careful to repeat—the commendation given to the Gentile Christians for their steadfastness; the Jewish Christians were not their inferiors in this respect." But again, there is nothing in the immediate context to suggest this particular understanding of the words.

ἐν πᾶσιν τοῖς διωγμοῖς ὑμῶν καὶ ταῖς θλίψεσιν αἷς ἀνέχεσθε, "in all your persecutions and the trials which you endure." Cf. 1 Thess 1:6 (ἐν θλίψει πολλῇ, "in much affliction"); 2:14 (τὰ αὐτὰ ἐπάθετε, "you suffered the same things"); 3:3–5, 7. Despite the aorist ἐπάθετε in 1 Thess 2:14, it is not clear that the afflictions of 1 Thessalonians belong to the (recent) past in contrast to the present afflictions of 2 Thessalonians—a point sometimes made in favor of dating 2 Thessalonians before 1 Thessalonians (see p. xli above). Still less is it clear that the persecutions of 2 Thessalonians were endured by Jewish Christians in contrast to the persecution of Gentile Christians referred to in 1 Thessalonians (cf. Lake, *Epistles*, 88, 89). The persecution of the Thessalonian Christians may have been less severe at some times than at others, but it was still going on at the time of Timothy's visit (1 Thess 3:3) and had not ceased when 2 Thessalonians was written.

Explanation

As in the previous epistle, so now in this Paul and his colleagues pour out joyful thanks to God for the continued growth of the Thessalonian Christians' faith, love and patient endurance. Although news of all this has spread abroad, not least among their fellow Christians in other places, the writers cannot refrain from adding their testimony; indeed, they boast to other churches about the progress of the Thessalonian church. Such boasting does not conflict with the principle of boasting only "in the Lord" (1 Cor 1:31; 2 Cor 10:17). Where boasting only in the Lord is insisted upon, it is as a corrective to boasting in one's own endowments or achievements, but the missionaries do not boast in what they have achieved, but in what God has achieved, at Thessalonica. Like Paul at a rather later date, they desire to magnify "the grace of God which has been shown in the churches of Macedonia" (2 Cor 8:1)—this is one form of boasting in the Lord.

(b) *Encouragement* (1:5–10)

Bibliography

Aus, R. D. "The Relevance of Isaiah 66:7 to Revelation 12 and 2 Thessalonians 1." *ZNW* 67 (1976) 252–268. **Cerfaux, L.** "Les 'Saints' de Jérusalem." *ETL* 2 (1925) 510–529 = *Recueil Lucien Cerfaux*, ii. Gembloux: J. Duculot, 1954, 389–414. **Glasson, T. F.** *The Second Advent*. London: Epworth Press, ²1947. **Katz, P.** "Ἐν πυρὶ φλογός." *ZNW* 46 (1953) 133–138. **Kennedy, H. A. A.** *St. Paul's Conceptions of the Last Things*. London: Hodder & Stoughton, 1904. **Linder, J. R.** "Exegetische Bemerkungen zu einigen Stellen des Neuen Testaments: 2 Thess. 1, 5–6." *TSK* 40 (1867) 522–524. **Mattern, L.** *Das Verständnis des Gerichtes bei Paulus*. ATANT 47. Zürich: Zwingli, 1966. **Vos, G.** *The Pauline Eschatology*. Grand Rapids, MI: Eerdmans, 1952. **Weizsäcker, C. von** *The Apostolic Age of the Christian Church*, i–ii. Tr. J. Millar. London: Williams & Norgate, ³1907–1912.

Translation

⁵ *This is a* ᵃ *sure token of God's righteous judgment, so that you may be counted worthy* ᵇ *of the kingdom of God, for which indeed you are suffering;* ⁶ *since it is a righteous thing in God's sight to repay*
affliction to those who afflict you
⁷ *and to you who are afflicted relief with us,*
at the revelation of the Lord Jesus from heaven
with his mighty angels, ᶜ
in flaming fire, ᵈ
⁸ *meting out* ᵉ *vengeance to those*
who do not know God,
and who disobey ᶠ *the gospel of our Lord Jesus.*
⁹ *They will pay the penalty of eternal destruction* ᵍ
from the presence of the Lord
and from the glory of his power,
¹⁰ *when he comes*
to be glorified in his holy ones
and to be marveled at in all who have believed ʰ
(because our testimony to you was believed), ⁱ
on that day.

Notes

ᵃ One may understand ὅ ἐστιν before ἔνδειγμα (ὅ having as its antecedent the preceding clause αἷς ἀνέχεσθε or even τῆς ὑπομονῆς ὑμῶν καὶ πίστεως), or take ἔνδειγμα as standing in apposition to αἷς ἀνέχεσθε (or even to τῆς ὑπομονῆς ὑμῶν καὶ πίστεως). Cf. Rom 12:1, where τὴν λογικὴν λατρείαν, "your spiritual worship" stands in apposition to παραστῆσαι . . . τῷ θεῷ, "to present your bodies . . . to God" (see BDF § 480 [6]).

ᵇ εἰς τὸ καταξιωθῆναι ὑμᾶς, "so that you may be counted worthy"; for the construction cf. 1 Thess 2:16, εἰς τὸ ἀναπληρῶσαι, "so as to fill up" (similarly expressing consequence).

ᶜ After μετ᾽ ἀγγέλων δυνάμεως αὐτοῦ (qualifying genitive) καί is added by F G latᵇ ᵈ Irenˡᵃᵗ Tert.

d ἐν πυρὶ φλογός ℵ A 0111 byz lat^d m syr^{hcl.ms} Ambst; ἐν φλογὶ πυρός is read by B D F G Ψ 2464 pc lat^a vg syr cop Iren^{lat} Tert.

e For διδόντος the nominative διδούς is read by D* F G Ψ pc lat^b vg.cod.

f For ὑπακούουσιν the aorist ὑπακούσασιν is read by 1908 lat^d vg.codd cop^{bo}.

g For ὄλεθρον the adjective ὀλέθριον (agreeing with δίκην) is read by A 33 pc Mcion. K. Lachmann preferred this reading which, says Lightfoot, "if better supported by external authority, would deserve some consideration." The genitive ὀλέθρου is read by lat^{b d} Iren^{lat} ("poenas . . . interitus aeternas").

h πιστεύσασιν, for which the present πιστεύουσιν is read by Ψ 33 630 2464 pc lat^t syr^{pesh} cop^{sa bo.pt} Iren^{lat.pt}.

i For ἐπιστεύθη 104 pc read ἐπιστώθη ("was entrusted").

Form/Structure/Setting

The encouragement in this subsection is based on the prospect of vindication on the Day of the Lord. The Day is described in language largely derived from the LXX, much of the *parallelismus membrorum* or couplet form, characteristic of OT oracles, being preserved (as has been indicated in the arrangement of the translation; see above). In one place, at least, the device of parallelism has been taken over by the Christian composer: in v 8 the OT locution "those who do not know God" has received a Christian gloss in the parallel clause, "who disobey the gospel of our Lord Jesus."

There are some indications that the writers have drawn upon an early Christian description of the Day of the Lord, in which special emphasis was laid on the judgment then to be executed. W. Bornemann in his commentary (1894) suggested that vv 7b–10a represent an early Christian psalm. It is scarcely likely that such a composition was meant for Christians to sing; the spirit which breathes in (say) Psalm 149 is not well attested for the primitive church. We might suppose it to be part of an early confession of faith (the part dealing with the last things), but it is much more satisfactory to think of it as belonging to an early "testimony" collection. Von Weizsäcker (*Apostolic Age*, i, 132, 133) argued that Paul compiled his own "testimony" book: this he found established by the repeated phenomenon in the Pauline letters of "the collection of a number of texts, drawn from very different books [of the OT], to support one principle," together with the "much more advanced procedure" in which texts are carefully drawn from various contexts so as to furnish thesis, antithesis and solution for extended arguments. But in 2 Thess 1:5–10 we are not dealing with distinctively Pauline doctrine; the eschatological teaching here is, so far as can be judged, that generally held throughout the early church, and the testimony collection by means of which it is set forth originated in pre-Pauline Christianity and continued to be developed as a growing tradition which is abundantly attested in Justin Martyr and especially in Cyprian's *Testimonia aduersus Iudaeos*. In the section of that work entitled "Quod ipse iudex uenturus sit" (2.28), we find texts from the Psalter, Isaiah and Malachi brought together to provide details of what will take place when Christ comes to judge the earth, "the Lord" of the OT passages being interpreted as Jesus, as in this subsection. (See also Glasson, *The Second Advent*, 172–176, quoted on p. 73 above.)

Comment

1:5. ἔνδειγμα ("sure token") stands in apposition not to any single word in v 4 but to the general sense of ἐν πᾶσιν . . . αἷς ἀνέχεσθε. The fact that they are enduring persecution and affliction for Christ's sake is a sure token of God's righteous judgment, which will be vindicated in them and in their persecutors at the Advent of Christ. This is the only NT occurrence of ἔνδειγμα, but cf. the related ἔνδειξις, used by Paul in Rom 3:25, 26; 2 Cor 8:24, and especially in the similar context of Phil 1:28, where the Philippian Christians' refusal to be intimidated by their opponents is an ἔνδειξις to the latter "of their destruction (ἀπώλεια), but of your [the Christians'] salvation, and that from God." With τῆς δικαίας κρίσεως cf. the compound δικαιοκρισία ("righteous judgment") in Rom 2:5.

As in 1 Thess 2:14; 3:3, 4, the Thessalonians' suffering tribulation is said to be a proof of the genuineness of their faith; their steadfastness under it marks them out as worthy of the divine kingdom. In both places in the Thessalonian correspondence where the coming kingdom of God is mentioned, the idea of worthiness finds a place (cf. 1 Thess 2:12).

εἰς τὸ καταξιωθῆναι ὑμᾶς τῆς βασιλείας τοῦ θεοῦ, "that you may be counted worthy of the kingdom of God"; cf. Luke 20:35, "those who are counted worthy (καταξιωθέντες) to attain to that age and to the resurrection from the dead." The kingdom of God here, as in 1 Thess 2:12 (see comment ad loc.), is identical with "that age," in which the children of God will enjoy resurrection life.

ὑπὲρ ἧς καὶ πάσχετε, "for which indeed you are suffering." This is hardly tantamount to saying that they are suffering in order to inherit the kingdom of God; rather, their suffering for the sake of the kingdom of God is their suffering for the sake of Christ, the αὐτοβασιλεία (as Origen put it, *Comm. in Matt.* 14.7); cf. Phil 1:29, τὸ ὑπὲρ αὐτοῦ πάσχειν ("to suffer for his sake"). The kingdom of God is entered through tribulation (Acts 14:22), but the kingdom cannot be said to be the purpose of the tribulation on the part of those who inflict it or even on the part of those who endure it.

6. εἴπερ here in the Attic sense "if (as is the fact)," "since." There is no implication of doubt where the righteousness of God is involved. "Your endurance of tribulation is a sure token of God's righteous judgment, since (εἴπερ) it is a righteous thing in God's sight (δίκαιον παρὰ θεῷ) to give you relief from your afflictions and to mete out affliction to those who afflict you" (ἀνταποδοῦναι τοῖς θλίβουσιν ὑμᾶς θλῖψιν). For a different sort of ἀνταποδοῦναι cf. 1 Thess 3:9. When the ἀνταποδοῦναι is predicated of God it may denote either blessing or judgment: blessing, as of the reward to be bestowed (ἀνταποδοθήσεται . . . σοι) at the resurrection of the righteous (Luke 14:14); judgment, as in the targumic quotation of Deut 32:35, "Vengeance (ἐκδίκησις, as in v 8 below) is mine; I will repay

(ἀνταποδώσω)" in Rom 12:19; Heb 10:30. Both forms of requital are in view here. In the light of other echoes of Isaiah 66 in this subsection, Isa 66:6 LXX may be relevant: ἀνταποδιδόντος ἀνταπόδοσιν τοῖς ἀντικειμένοις, "(the voice of the Lord) rendering recompense to his enemies." But there is no lack of similar OT texts, e.g. Ps 137 (LXX 136):8, μακάριος ὃς ἀνταποδώσει σοι τὸ ἀνταπόδομά σου, ὃ ἀνταπέδωκας ἡμῖν ("Blessed is he who recompenses you with the recompense with which you requited us").

7. καὶ ὑμῖν τοῖς θλιβομένοις ἄνεσιν μεθ' ἡμῶν, "and (it is a righteous thing in God's sight to recompense) you who are being afflicted with relief together with us." Relief (ἄνεσις) is in itself simply the lifting of the pressure caused by their persecution, but it is accompanied by the positive blessing of participation in God's "own kingdom and glory" (1 Thess 2:12). "With us" is apposite because the missionaries had their own share of sufferings to bear (cf. 1 Cor 4:9–13) and a corresponding meed of glory to look forward to (cf. 2 Cor 4:17, 18). The Parousia, then, will be the occasion for equitable retribution and reward. For the reversal of roles in the life to come cf. Luke 16:25; but the reversal is not arbitrary but ethically appropriate.

ἐν τῇ ἀποκαλύψει τοῦ κυρίου Ἰησοῦ ἀπ' οὐρανοῦ, "at the revelation of the Lord Jesus from heaven" (for ἀπ' οὐρανοῦ cf. 1 Thess 4:16; also ἐκ τῶν οὐρανῶν, 1 Thess 1:10). From this point to v 10a the language is largely a cento of theophanic phrases from OT, what is said of "the LORD" (Yahweh) in them being applied to "the Lord Jesus" here. The Parousia of Christ is called his ἀποκάλυψις in 1 Cor 1:7 (also in 1 Pet 1:7, 13; 4:13, "the revelation of his glory"); cf. ἐπιφάνεια in 2:8 below. It is the occasion when "the glory is to be revealed" (ἀποκαλυφθῆναι) to those who suffer with Christ at present (Rom 8:18); it is accordingly called the "revealing (ἀποκάλυψις) of the sons of God"—i.e. their being revealed as the sons of God, invested with his glory (Rom 8:19). The OT promise that "the glory of the LORD shall be revealed" (Isa 40:5) takes on fuller significance in the light of the work of Christ.

μετ' ἀγγέλων δυνάμεως αὐτοῦ, "with angels of his power," a Hebraism for "his mighty angels"; his angels, according to Ps 103 (LXX 102):20, are "mighty in strength" (δυνατοὶ ἰσχύι). For angelic attendance at theophanies see comment on 1 Thess 3:13. The same attendance marks the Advent of the Son of Man, when he "comes in his glory, and all the angels with him" (Matt 25:31).

There are variations in the division between vv 7 and 8: in RSV v 7 ends with "in flaming fire"; in Nestle-Aland [26] v 8 begins with ἐν πυρὶ φλογός.

8. ἐν πυρὶ φλογός, "in fire of flame," i.e. "in flaming fire." The variant ἐν φλογὶ πυρός (see note d above) appears (with the variant ἐν πυρὶ φλογός) in Exod 3:2, in the account of the theophany at the burning bush; cf. Acts 7:30, "an angel appeared to him [Moses] in a flame of fire (ἐν φλογὶ πυρός, v. l. ἐν πυρὶ φλογός) in a bush." (See Justin, I Apol. 62, 63; Dial. 60.4, for the argument that it was Christ before his incarnation who ap-

peared to Moses ἐν πυρὶ φλογός from the bush.) Yahweh descended on Mount Sinai "in fire" at the giving of the law (Exod 19:18); cf. the presence of fire in the theophanies of Deut 33:2; Ps 18:8; Ezek 1:13, 27; Hab 3:4. Fire figures especially in depictions of divine judgment; in Dan 7:9, 10, where the Ancient of Days takes his seat, "his throne was fiery flames (φλὸξ πυρός), its wheels were burning fire (πῦρ φλέγον, Theod.); a stream of fire (ποταμὸς πυρός) issued and came forth from before him." Cf. Isa 66:15, 16, where Yahweh comes "in fire (ἐν πυρί) to execute vengeance (ἐκδίκησις) . . . in flames of fire (ἐν φλογὶ πυρός)"—perhaps the OT text which more than any other underlies the present wording.

διδόντος ἐκδίκησιν, "giving (executing) vengeance"; cf. Isa 66:15 quoted in preceding comment. (Cf. 1 Thess 4:6, ἔκδικος κύριος.) The future exercise of judgment by Christ in the NT is derived in part at least from Dan 7:13, 14, where the Ancient of Days bestows authority on the "one like a son of man." Cf. John 5:27, where the Father gives the Son authority to execute judgment "because he is Son of Man" (ὅτι υἱὸς ἀνθρώπου ἐστίν); also Mark 8:38; Acts 10:42; 17:31.

τοῖς μὴ εἰδόσιν θεόν. In OT parlance "those who do not know God" are the Gentiles; cf. Ps 79 (LXX 78):6, "Pour out thy anger on the nations that do not know thee (ἐπὶ ἔθνη τὰ μὴ γινώσκοντά σε)." Similarly in Ps 9:17 (LXX 9:18) "the wicked" (οἱ ἁμαρτωλοί) who depart to Sheol are equated with "all the nations that forget God (πάντα τὰ ἔθνη τὰ ἐπιλανθανόμενα τοῦ θεοῦ)." It is not inadvertent ignorance that is meant but that inexcusable refusal to know God for which the pagan world is condemned in Rom 1.19–28. "they did not see fit to acknowledge God (οὐκ ἐδοκίμασαν τὸν θεὸν ἔχειν ἐν ἐπιγνώσει)." If eternal life consists in knowing (ἵνα γινώσκωσιν) the only true God (John 17:3), not to know him implies exclusion from that life. This knowledge of God is not simply the inferring of his existence and power from the works of creation; it is that ethically fruitful knowledge of God (ἐπίγνωσις θεοῦ) which is more desirable than burnt offerings (Hos 6:6), and for lack of which the people of God themselves were perishing in Hosea's day (Hos 4:1, 6). (Cf. 1 Thess 4:5 with comment ad loc.)

τοῖς μὴ ὑπακούουσιν τῷ εὐαγγελίῳ κτλ. Those who do not know God are more precisely defined as "those who disobey the gospel." Lightfoot indeed argues that the repetition of the article before μὴ ὑπακούουσιν indicates that "two distinct classes are here meant." If we were dealing with a regular Greek construction, this would be a weighty (but not conclusive) argument, as it is, we are dealing with a passage which follows the parallelistic style of OT prophecy and poetry, so that τοῖς μὴ ὑπακούουσιν τῷ εὐαγγελίῳ κτλ stands in synonymous parallelism to τοῖς μὴ εἰδόσιν θεόν (cf. Ps 36:10 [LXX 35:11], where τοῖς γινώσκουσίν σε and τοῖς εὐθέσι τῇ καρδίᾳ are similarly synonymous). For ὑπακούειν τῷ εὐαγγελίῳ cf. Rom 10:16, οὐ πάντες ὑπήκουσαν τῷ εὐαγγελίῳ, "all have not believed the gospel," stated as a fulfillment of the question in Isa 53:1 ("who has believed our message?") in those Israelites of the apostolic age who, having heard the gospel, did not believe it. The identification of "those who do not know God" as "those who do not obey the gospel of our Lord Jesus" shows that the present reference is not to Gentiles only but to Jews and Gentiles indiscriminately (cf. Rom 2:9). Among those to whom ἐκδίκησις will be meted out, the persecutors of the Thessalonian believers are more immediately in the writers' minds.

9. οἵτινες δίκην τίσουσιν, "who will pay the penalty." It is difficult to make a distinction in sense here between οἵτινες and οἱ. In fact, for Paul the compound forms are regularly used instead of the simple in the nominative plural of the relative pronoun (cf. H. J. Cadbury, "The Relative Pronouns in Acts and Elsewhere," *JBL* 42, 1923, 150–157).

ὄλεθρον αἰώνιον, "eternal destruction," accusative in apposition to δίκην. "Eternal destruction" is the alternative to God's gift to believers—"eternal life" (ζωὴ αἰώνιος) (cf. Rom 2:7; 5:21; 6:22, 23; Gal 6:8). If eternal life is the life of the age (αἰών) to come, the resurrection age, "eternal destruction" is the destruction of the age to some, with a strong implication of finality. Cf. 1 Thess 5:3, αἰφνίδιος . . . ὄλεθρος.

ἀπὸ προσώπου τοῦ κυρίου καὶ ἀπὸ τῆς δόξης τῆς ἰσχύος αὐτοῦ, a phrase markedly similar to one which recurs in Isa 2:10, 19, 21, ἀπὸ τοῦ προσώπου τοῦ φόβου κυρίου καὶ ἀπὸ τῆς δόξης τῆς ἰσχύος αὐτοῦ ("from before the terror of the LORD and from the glory of his power"), in reference to the judgment to be executed on the Day of Yahweh "when he rises to terrify the earth." Here the "eternal destruction" consists in exclusion from the presence of him with whom is "the fountain of life" (Ps 36:9 [LXX 35:10]). The κύριος here is Jesus (cf. 1 Thess 5:2), as the following clause makes plain. In the judgment scene of Matt 25:41, 46 (cf. Luke 13:27) the Son of Man's "Depart from me," addressed to those on his left hand, involves their departure "into eternal punishment (εἰς κόλασιν αἰώνιον)."

10. ὅταν ἔλθῃ, "when he comes"; cf. Ps 96 (LXX 95):13, ὅτι ἔρχεται κρῖναι τὴν γῆν ("for he comes to judge the earth"); again, OT theophanic language is used of Jesus.

ἐνδοξασθῆναι ἐν τοῖς ἁγίοις αὐτοῦ, "to be glorified in his holy ones." For the attendance of the ἅγιοι at the Parousia of Christ cf. 1 Thess 3:13, with comment ad loc. While the ἅγιοι here might be the angels of v 7, the parallelism between this ἐνδοξασθῆναι clause and the following θαυμασθῆναι clause strongly suggests the identity of the ἅγιοι and the πιστεύσαντες. Believers in Christ are described by Paul as κλητοὶ ἅγιοι, "holy ones by calling" (Rom 1:7; 1 Cor 1:2), because God has called them ἐν ἁγιασμῷ (1 Thess 4:7). The use of ἅγιοι for disciples of Jesus may have originated in the Jerusalem church; Paul can refer to its members as οἱ ἅγιοι without qualification (1 Cor 16:1; 2 Cor 9:1; cf. Rom 15:25, 31; Acts 9:13, etc.). In Eph 2:19 Gentile believers are said to have become συμπολῖται τῶν ἁγίων, as those who have been naturalized among the people of God (or, in the figure of Rom 11:16–24, those who have been grafted into the good olive tree); hence members of the Pauline churches are freely referred to as the ἅγιοι (cf. also 2 Cor 1:1; Phil 1:1; Col 1:2, 4; Phlm 5, 7).

It is probably in his people, then, that Christ at his coming is to be glorified. With ἐνδοξασθῆναι (in the NT only here and in v 12) cf. συνδοξασθῆναι in Rom 8:17. Christ at his coming is glorified in them; they are glorified with him. The coupling of suffering with glory in Rom 8:17 (εἴπερ συμπάσχομεν ἵνα καὶ συνδοξασθῶμεν) is relevant to the present context, where the coming investment with glory is associated with the ἄνεσις from tribulation held out to the persecuted Thessalonian Christians (v 7). Cf. Col 3:4, "when Christ, our life, is manifested, then you also will be manifested with him in glory (ἐν δόξῃ)." An OT precedent for the wording here is Ps 89:7 (LXX 88:8), ὁ θεὸς ἐνδοξαζόμενος ἐν βουλῇ ἁγίων, but there the ἅγιοι are the heavenly members of Yahweh's council, as also in Ps 68:35 (LXX 67:36), θαυμαστὸς ὁ θεὸς ἐν τοῖς ἁγίοις αὐτοῦ, where the verbal adjective θαυμαστός provides an OT precedent for the phrase immediately following in our present passage, καὶ θαυμασθῆναι ἐν πᾶσιν τοῖς πιστεύσασιν, "and to be marveled at in all those who have believed." Those who have believed the gospel have taken the opposite decision to those who disobey it (v 8). For this use of the aorist participle of πιστεύειν cf. Acts 4:32; 11:17. The community of believers is God's masterpiece (his ποίημα, Eph 2:10); the wisdom and skill of the artist are displayed in the quality of his masterpiece, which wins him the admiration of those who appreciate it (cf. Eph 3:10).

ὅτι ἐπιστεύθη τὸ μαρτύριον ἡμῶν ἐφ᾽ ὑμᾶς, "because our testimony to you was believed," almost a parenthesis, explaining and amplifying τοῖς πιστεύσασιν. Lightfoot treats the clause as elliptical: according to him, the full sense is ". . . in all those who have believed, *and therefore in you*, for our testimony was believed by you." In this he is right, but his rendering "our testimony was believed by you" reflects his judgment that ἐφ᾽ ὑμᾶς is to be taken not with μαρτύριον but with ἐπιστεύθη as though the force of the construction were "belief in our testimony directed itself to reach you" (which is too awkward to be acceptable). Bengel takes ἐφ᾽ ὑμᾶς to mean "as far as you, in the west" (cf. 2 Cor 10:13, ἄχρι καὶ ὑμῶν); this overloads the sense.

With τὸ μαρτύριον ἡμῶν cf. τὸ εὐαγγέλιον ἡμῶν (2:14; 1 Thess 1:5; 2 Cor 4:3); τὸ κήρυγμα ἡμῶν (1 Cor 15:14). It is their testimony because they are the witnesses; it is Christ's testimony (1 Cor 1:6) because it is to him that the witness is borne.

ἐν τῇ ἡμέρᾳ ἐκείνῃ, after the near-parenthetical ὅτι clause, goes closely in sense with ἐνδοξασθῆναι and θαυμασθῆναι. "That day" is the Day of the Lord (cf. 2:2; 1 Thess 5:2); cf. ἐν τῇ ἡμέρᾳ ἐκείνῃ, Isa 2:11, 17 (from a context echoed in v 9 above).

Explanation

The fact that they were being persecuted for their Christian confession, and were enduring the persecution with fortitude and faith, provided firm evidence not only of the genuineness of the Thessalonians' commitment to the gospel but also of the certainty of their inheritance in the coming kingdom of God. Jesus encouraged his disciples to rejoice when they were persecuted for his sake because, he said, "your reward is great in heaven" (Matt 5:11, 12 par. Luke 6:22, 23). This note recurs again and again throughout the NT. The trials which believers have to suffer at present, says Peter, are sent "so that the genuineness of your faith, more precious than gold which though perishable is tested by fire, may redound to praise and glory and honor at the revelation of Jesus Christ" (1 Pet 1:7). Paul speaks repeatedly to the same effect. He tells the Philippian Christians that it is a special honor not only to believe in Christ but to suffer for his sake as well, and that their suffering for Christ's sake is as certain a token of their final salvation as it is an omen of destruction to their opponents, who cause them to suffer (Phil 1:28, 29). So the Thessalonians are told that their roles and those of their persecutors will be reversed at the Advent of Christ; their persecutors will receive the judgment which their conduct deserves, while they themselves will enjoy relief and reward.

You will enjoy "relief with us," say the writers, who had themselves endured persecution in one place after another. But one of the writers had himself been an outstanding persecutor, until he was conscripted into the service of the risen Christ on the Damascus road. The outlook for persecutors, then, is not entirely hopeless; for them as for other sinners the way of repentance is wide open. Paul's conversion indeed did not bring him exemption from tribulation; as he had made others suffer for Christ's sake, so, said the Lord, "I will show him how much he must suffer for the sake of my name" (Acts 9:16). But suffering for Christ's sake was something which Paul gladly welcomed; in fact, he was eager to absorb as much as possible of this suffering in his own person so that there might be less of it for his fellow Christians to endure.

The Advent of Christ is here (as in 1 Pet 1:7, quoted above) called his "revelation." The idea conveyed is of his coming out into public view from a place of concealment. Jesus similarly speaks of "the day when the Son of Man is revealed" (Luke 17:30), and makes it plain that his being revealed will be an occasion of sudden judgment. The judgment which in the OT is the prerogative of God is exercised in the NT by Jesus, the Son of Man. The "flaming fire" in which he is revealed is a symbol of judgment: the Day of the LORD is described by an OT prophet as "the day . . . burning like an oven, when all the arrogant and all evildoers will be stubble" (Mal 4:1). Even believers are given the salutary reminder in Heb 12:29 that "our God is a consuming fire."

But for his persecuted followers "the revelation of the Lord Jesus from heaven" will be an occasion of vindication and honor. When he appears in glory he will be glorified in them; they will share and reflect his glory, so that his revelation will be at the same time, as Paul puts it in Rom 8:19, "the revelation of the *sons* of God." Nothing can so much redound to his honor as the presentation of sinful men and women redeemed and glorified through his sacrifice on the cross. They will be glorified with him; he will be glorified in them.

A hope so great, and so divine,
May trials well endure.

(c) *Prayer Report* (1:11–12)

Bibliography

Artola, A.-M. "Le Christ se manifeste dans la communauté chrétienne (2 Th 1:11–2:2)." *AsSeign* n.s. No. 62 (1970) 75–80. **O'Brien, P. T.** *Introductory Thanksgivings in the Letters of Paul.* NovTSup 49. Leiden: Brill, 1977. **Wiederkehr, D.** *Die Theologie der Berufung in den Paulusbriefen.* Freiburg: Universitätsverlag, 1963. **Wiles, G. P.** *Paul's Intercessory Prayers.* SNTSMS 24. Cambridge: Cambridge University Press, 1974. **Williams, N. P.** *The Grace of God.* London/New York/Toronto: Longmans Green & Co., 1930.

Translation

[11] *With this end in view we pray for you constantly, that our God may count you worthy of his calling and fulfill [a] every desire of goodness and work of faith in power,* [12] *so that [b] the name of our Lord Jesus [c] may be glorified in you, and you in him, according to the grace of our God and the Lord Jesus Christ.*

Notes

[a] For the aorist subjunctive πληρώσῃ the future indicative πληρώσει is read by A K P Ψ 6 2464 *al.*

[b] ὅπως with the subjunctive, expressing purpose, is perhaps used for the sake of variation after the preceding ἵνα clause; cf. 1 Cor 1:29; 2 Cor 8:14. See BDF § 369 (4).

[c] Χριστοῦ is inserted after Ἰησοῦ by A F G P Ψ 33 81 1739 1881 *pm* lat syr cop[bo.pt] Ambst.

Form/Structure/Setting

This prayer report (so called because it is not a direct prayer in the imperative or a wish-prayer in the optative but a statement that prayer is being offered for a particular object or with a particular purpose) performs the same kind of function as the wish-prayer of 1 Thess 3:11–13 in closing a section of the letter. Two petitions are indicated by the subjunctives ἀξιώσῃ "make you worthy," and πληρώσῃ "may fulfill," after ἵνα and the purpose of the petitions is indicated by the further subjunctive ἐνδοξασθῇ after ὅπως.

Comment

1:11. Εἰς ὅ, "with this end in view." The apostolic writers in 1 Thess 2:19, 20, express their confidence that the Thessalonian Christians will give them cause for boasting and rejoicing "in the presence of our Lord Jesus at his advent." Here they assure them afresh of their constant prayers to the same effect. The consummation of glory on the Day of the Lord is closely related to holy living here and now. For holiness now and glory hereafter God has called them (cf. 1 Thess 2:12; 4:7; 5:24); the prayer is therefore voiced that they may be counted worthy of this calling (cf. v 5). Only God can pronounce them worthy of it, and he will do so (cf. 1 Thess 5:24, ὃς καὶ ποιήσει) if they conduct themselves in a manner worthy of it cf. Eph 4:1, ἀξίως περιπατῆσαι τῆς κλήσεως ἧς ἐκλήθητε; ". . . lead a life worthy of the calling to which you have been called." The prayer looks forward to the recompense to be received at the Parousia, that the Thessalonians may on that day be adjudged to have acquitted themselves worthily; but this involves a prayer for their present spiritual progress (cf. Phil 3:14, where Paul's aiming at the "prize of God's upward call in Christ Jesus" involves his present unremitting persistence in the race set before him).

καὶ πληρώσῃ πᾶσαν εὐδοκίαν ἀγαθωσύνης "and (that) he may fulfill every desire of goodness." Is the desire of goodness God's (cf. Phil 2:13, θεὸς γάρ ἐστιν ὁ ἐνεργῶν ἐν ὑμῖν καὶ τὸ θέλειν καὶ τὸ ἐνεργεῖν ὑπὲρ τῆς εὐδοκίας, "for God is at work in you, both to will and to work for his good pleasure") or theirs (in contrast to οἱ . . . εὐδοκήσαντες τῇ ἀδικίᾳ, "who . . . took pleasure in unrighteousness," 2:12 below)? If it is theirs (as is probable), God alone can bring it to fulfillment: every "desire of goodness," like every "work of faith" (ἔργον πίστεως), is wrought in them effectively (ἐν δυνάμει) by the Holy Spirit (cf. Gal 5:22, 23). For ἔργον πίστεως cf. 1 Thess 1:3.

12. ὅπως ἐνδοξασθῇ τὸ ὄνομα τοῦ κυρίου ἡμῶν Ἰησοῦ ἐν ὑμῖν, "that the name of our Lord Jesus may be glorified in you." It has been stated in v 10 that Christ at his coming will be glorified in his people. But there is no difference in principle between his being glorified in them then and his being glorified in them now. His "name"—i.e. his reputation—is "glorified" when those who bear that name bring credit to it by their lives, like the messengers of the churches in 2 Cor 8:23 who are "a credit to Christ" (δόξα Χριστοῦ). This ethical sense of ἐνδοξασθῆναι is found in LXX: God, for example, will be "glorified" by his Servant's obedience (ἐν σοὶ ἐνδοξασθήσομαι, "in you I will be glorified," Isa 49:3). For similar sense expressed in related words cf. Isa 24:15 (τὸ ὄνομα κυρίου ἔνδοξον ἔσται , "give glory . . . to the name of the LORD"); Mal 1:11 (τὸ ὄνομά μου δεδόξασται ἐν τοῖς ἔθνεσιν, "my name is great among the nations").

καὶ ὑμεῖς ἐν αὐτῷ. For this reciprocity in glorifying cf. John 13:31, "Now has the Son of Man been glorified (ἐδοξάσθη) and God has been glorified (ἐδοξάσθη) in him," where the Son of Man's δοξασθῆναι is his being "lifted up" (ὑψωθῆναι, see John 12:23, 32), and God is glorified in his obedience (cf. John 10:18), as he is in the Servant's obedience in Isa 49:3.

κατὰ τὴν χάριν τοῦ θεοῦ ἡμῶν καὶ κυρίου Ἰησοῦ Χριστοῦ, "according to the grace of our God and the Lord Jesus Christ." The fact that θεοῦ and κυρίου are under the regimen of the one article might suggest the rendering "the grace of Jesus Christ our God and Lord"; but this would be an un-Pauline locution and in any case the anarthrous κύριος in reference to Jesus (whether followed or not by Ἰησοῦς or Ἰησοῦς Χριστός) is not unparalleled (cf. 3:4, 12; 1 Thess 4:1, etc.). Moreover, "that one article in the singular rightly in Greek designates even distinct persons, if the object be to express their union in a common category (as here in 'grace'), ought to be known not only to scholars in general, but familiarly to all students of the later body of revelation in its original tongue" (Kelly, 99–100).

The use of "grace" in this clause goes far to substantiate Williams's thesis of the "frank equation of 'grace' with the Person of the Holy Spirit" (*Grace,* 110).

Explanation

The prayer reported in this subsection emphasizes again the ethical implications of the eschatological prospect held out to the Thessalonian Christians in the words immediately preceding. This prospect is not only an incentive to the patient endurance of affliction for Christ's sake; it is also an incentive to a life of positive action in keeping with the purpose for which God has called them. The God who calls his people "into his own kingdom and glory" (1 Thess 2:12) requires in them conduct worthy of that call, and he provides the necessary motive power for such conduct by his Spirit who indwells them. If their Lord is to be glorified in them at his Advent, he must be glorified in their present way of life. Yahweh spoke in earlier days of "the people whom I formed for myself that they might declare my praise" (Isa 43:21)—declare it with their lives as well as with their lips—and these words are adapted and applied by another NT writer to the community of Christ's disciples: "God's own people, that you may declare the wonderful deeds (excellences) of him who called you out of darkness into his marvelous light" (1 Pet 2:9). Those who bear the name of Christ must glorify God in that name (cf. 1 Pet 4:16), and they can do so only by living in such a way as to reflect credit on the name. The missionaries' prayer has the Advent in view, but it will be fulfilled then only as their converts are progressively transformed by the Spirit here and now into the image of Christ, "from one degree of glory to another" (2 Cor 3:18). The hope of glory depends on the revelation and supply of grace, and the grace revealed and supplied is inseparable from the Spirit of God.

The Rise and Fall of the Man of Lawlessness (2 Thess 2:1-12)

Bibliography

Alers, G. A. "τὸ κατέχον en ὁ κατέχων." *Th.St.* 6 (1888) 154–176. **Artola, A.-M.** "Le Christ se manifeste dans la communauté chrétienne (2 Th 1:11–2:2)." *AsSeign* (n.s.) No. 62 (1970) 75–80. **Askwith, E. H.** " 'I' and 'We' in the Thessalonian Epistles." *Expositor*, series 8, 1 (1911) 149–159. **Aus, R. D.** "God's Plan and God's Power: Isaiah 66 and the Restraining Factors of 2 Thess 2:6–7." *JBL* 96 (1977) 537–553. **Aus, R. D.** "The Relevance of Isaiah 66:7 to Revelation 12 and 2 Thessalonians 1." *ZNW* 67 (1976) 252–268. **Barnouin, M.** "Les problèmes de traduction concernant II Thess. ii.6–7." *NTS* 23 (1976–77) 482–498. **Beasley-Murray, G. R.** *Jesus and the Future*. London: Macmillan, 1954. **Betz, O.** "Der Katechon." *NTS* 9 (1962–63) 276–291. **Bousset, W.** *The Antichrist Legend*. Tr. A. H. Keane. London: Hutchinson, 1896. **Bruce, F. F.** "Eschatology in the Apostolic Fathers." In *The Heritage of the Early Church: Essays in Honor of G. V. Florovsky*, ed. D. Neiman and M. Schatkin. Orientalia Christiana Analecta 195. Rome: Pontificium Institutum Studiorum Orientalium, 1973, 77–89. **Bruce, F. F.** "Josephus and Daniel." *ASTI* 4 (1965) 148–162. **Brunec, M.** "De 'Homine Peccati' in 2 Th 2, 1–12." *VD* 35 (1957) 72–73. **Cerfaux, L.** *Christ in the Theology of St. Paul*. Tr. G. Webb and A. Walker. Edinburgh/London/New York: Nelson; Herder and Herder, 1959, 31–68 ("The Second Coming"). **Coppens, J.** "Les deux obstacles au retour glorieux du Sauveur." *ETL* 46 (1970) 383–389. **Cothenet, E.** "La deuxième épître aux Thessaloniciens et l'apocalypse synoptique." *RSR* 42 (1954) 5–39. **Cowles, H.** "On 'The Man of Sin' 2 Thess 2:3–9." *BS* 29 (1872) 623–640. **Cullmann, O.** "Le caractère eschatologique du devoir missionnaire et de la conscience apostolique de saint Paul. Étude sur le κατέχον (-ων) de 2 Thess. 2:6–7." *RHPR* 16 (1936) 210–245. **Darby, J. N.** "Notes on the Epistles to the Thessalonians." In *Collected Writings*, ed. W. Kelly. London: Morrish, 1867–1900, xxvii, 437–455. **Davies, W. D.** "Paul and the People of Israel." *NTS* 24 (1977–78) 4–39. **Deeleman, C. F. M.** "2 Thess 2, 1–12." *Th.St.* 23 (1905) 252–276. **Denis, A.-M.** "L'apôtre Paul, prophète messianique des Gentils." *ETL* 33 (1957) 245–318. **English, E. S.** *Re-Thinking the Rapture*. Travelers Rest, S.C.: Southern Bible Book House, 1954. **Ernst, J.** *Die eschatologischen Gegenspieler in den Schriften des Neuen Testaments*. BU 3. Regensburg: Pustet, 1967. **Ford, D.** *The Abomination of Desolation in Biblical Eschatology*. Washington, D.C.: University Press of America, 1979. **Freese, F.** "τὸ κατέχον und ὁ κατέχων (2 Thess. 2, 6 u. 7)." *TSK* 93 (1920–21) 73–77. **Fulford, H. W.** "ἕως ἐκ μέσου γένηται (2 Thess 2 7)." *ExpTim* 23 (1911–12) 40–41. **Furfey, P. H.** "The Mystery of Lawlessness." *CBQ* 8 (1946) 179–191. **Giblin, C. H.** *In Hope of God's Glory*. New York: Herder, 1970. **Giblin, C. H.** *The Threat to Faith: An exegetical and theological re-examination of 2 Thessalonians 2*. AnBib 31. Rome: Pontifical Biblical Institute, 1967. **Glasson, T. F.** *The Second Advent*. London: Epworth, ²1947. **Glasson, T. F.** *His Appearing and His Kingdom*. London: Epworth, 1953. **Gonzalez Ruiz, J. M.** "La incredulidad de Israel y los impedimentos del Anticristo, segun 2 Tes. 2,6–7." *EstBib* (n.s.) 10 (1951) 189–203. **Griffiths, J. G.** "2 Thessalonians 2:4." *ExpTim* 52 (1940–41) 38. **Gundry, R. H.** *The Church and the Tribulation*. Grand Rapids, MI: Zondervan, 1973. **Hamann, H.** "Brief Exegesis of 2 Thess. 2:1–12 with Guidelines for the Application of the

Prophecy Contained Therein." *CTM* 24 (1953) 418–433. **Hartl, V.** "ὁ κατέχων ἄρτι (2 Thess 2, 7)." *ZTK* 45 (1921) 455–475. **Hartman, L.** *Prophecy Interpreted. The Formation of Some Jewish Apocalyptic Texts and of the Eschatological Discourse Mark 13 par.* ConB, NT series 1. Lund: Gleerup, 1966, 195–205. **Hort, F. J. A.** *Life and Letters,* ed. A. F. Hort. London: Macmillan, 1896. **James, M. R.** "Man of Sin and Antichrist." *HDB* iii, 226–228. **Kaye, B. N.** "Eschatology and Ethics in 1 and 2 Thessalonians." *NovT* 17 (1975) 47–57. **Kelly, W.** *The Rapture of the Saints: Who suggested it, or rather, On what Scripture?* London: T. Weston, 1903. **Kennedy, H. A. A.** *St. Paul's Conceptions of the Last Things.* London: Hodder & Stoughton, 1904. **Knox, J.** " A Note on II Thessalonians 2:2." *ATR* 18 (1936) 72–73. **Lake, K.** *The Earlier Epistles of St. Paul.* London: Rivingtons, ²1914. **Lindemann, A.** "Zum Abfassungszweck des Zweiten Thessalonicherbriefes." *ZNW* 68 (1977) 35–47. **Lofstrom, E. E.** "Lawlessness and the Restrainer: A New Translation of 2 Thessalonians 2:6–8." *ExpTim* 28 (1916–17) 379–380. **Mackintosh, R.** "The Antichrist of 2 Thessalonians." *Expositor,* series 7, 2 (1906) 427–432. **McNamara, M.** *The New Testament and the Palestinian Targum to the Pentateuch.* AnBib 27. Rome: Pontifical Biblical Institute, 1966, 246–252 ("The Revelation of the Messiah in the Targums and the Epiphaneia of Christ in St. Paul"). **Marín, F.** "Pequena apocalipsis de 2 Tes 2, 3–12." *EstEcl* 51 (1976) 29–56. **Mauro, P.** *The Seventy Weeks and the Great Tribulation.* Boston, MA: Hamilton Bros., 1923. **Mearns, C. L.** "Early Eschatological Development in Paul: The Evidence of I and II Thessalonians." *NTS* 27 (1980–81) 137–157. **Miguens, M.** "L'apocalisse 'secondo Paolo'." *BibOr* 2 (1960) 142–148. **Moore, A. L.** *The Parousia in the New Testament.* NovTSup 13. Leiden: Brill, 1966. **Moran, J. W.** "Is Antichrist a Man?" *AER* 92 (1935) 578–585. **Morgenstern, J.** "The Chanukkah Festival and the Calendar of Ancient Israel." *HUCA* 20 (1947) 1–136. **Morgenstern, J.** "The King-God among the Western Semites and the Meaning of Epiphanes." *VT* 10 (1960) 156–165. **Mounce, R. H.** "Pauline Eschatology and the Apocalypse." *EvQ* 46 (1974) 164–166. **Munck, J.** *Paul and the Salvation of Mankind.* Tr. F. Clarke. London: SCM Press. 1959. **Nestle, E.** "2 Th 2 ³." *ExpTim* 16 (1904–5) 472–473. **Nestle, E.** "Zu Daniel, 2. Der Greuel der Verwüstung." *ZAW* 4 (1884) 248. **Newton, B. W.** *Prospects of the Ten Kingdoms of the Roman Empire.* London: Houlston, ²1873, 272–293 ("On 2 Thessalonians ii"). **Orchard, J. B.** "Thessalonians and the Synoptic Gospels." *Bib* 19 (1938) 19–42. **Orchard, J. B.** "Ellipsis and Parenthesis in Ga 2:1–10 and 2 Th 2:1–12." In *Paul de Tarse: Apôtre de notre temps,* ed. L. De Lorenzi. Série monographique de "Benedictina": Section paulinienne 1. Rome: Abbey of St. Paul Without the Walls, 1979, 249–258. **Pax, E.** *Epiphaneia. Ein religionsgeschichtlicher Beitrag zur biblischen Theologie.* Münchener Theologische Studien. München: Zink, 1955, 221–228 ("2 Thess 2, 13–15"). **Reeves, M.** *Joachim of Fiore and the Prophetic Future.* London: SPCK, 1976. **Reimpell, J. C.** "Das κατέχειν im 2. Thessalonicherbrief." *TSK* 60 (1887) 713–736. **Renan, E.** *Antichrist.* Tr. W. G. Hutchinson. London: W. Scott, 1899. **Rigaux, B.** "L'Antéchrist." *AsSeign* No. 6 (1965) 28–39. **Rigaux, B.** *L'antéchrist et l'opposition au royaume messianique dans l'Ancien et le Nouveau Testament.* Gembloux: Duculot/Paris: Gabalda. 1932. **Robinson, D. W. B.** "II Thess. 2:6: 'That which restrains' or 'That which holds sway'?" *SE* 4 = TU 87 (1964) 635–638. **Schippers, R.** *Mythologie en Eschatologie in 2 Thessalonicenzen 2, 1–17.* Assen: Van Gorcum, 1961. **Schmid, J.** "Der Antichrist und die hemmende Macht." *TQ* 129 (1949) 323–343. **Schmithals, W.** *Paul and the Gnostics.* Tr. J. E. Steely. Nashville/New York: Abingdon, 1972. **Sirard, L.** "La parousie de l'Antéchrist, 2 Thess 2, 3–9." in *Studiorum Paulinorum Congressus 1961.* AnBib 17–18. Rome: Pontifical Biblical Institute, 1963, ii, 89–100. **Solovyev, V.** "Short Narrative about the Antichrist." In *War and Christianity*, ed. S. Graham. Tr. W. J. Barnes and H. H. Haynes. London: Constable, 1915, 144–188. **Stauffer, E.** *Christ and the Caesars.* Tr. K. and R. G. Smith. London: SCM Press, 1955. **Stephenson, A. M. G.** "On the Meaning of ἐνέστηκεν ἡ ἡμέρα τοῦ κυρίου in 2 Thessalonians 2.2." *SE* 4 = TU 102 (1968) 442–451. **Strobel, A.** *Untersuchungen zum eschatologischen Verzögerungsproblem.* NovTSup 2. Leiden: Brill, 1961. **Stürmer, K.** *Auferstehung und Erwählung: Die doppelte Ausrichtung der paulinischen Verkündigung.* BFCT 2.53. Gütersloh: Bertelsmann, 1953. **Tregelles, S. P.** *The Man of Sin* (1840). London/Aylesbury: Hunt, Barnard & Co., reprint 1930. **Ubbink, J. T.** "ὡς δι' ἡμῶν (2 Th. 2:2), een exegetisch-isagogische puzzle?" *NedTTs* 7 (1952–53) 269–295. **Vos, G.** *The Pauline Eschatology.* Grand Rapids, MI: Eerdmans, 1952. **Walvoord, J. F.** *The Blessed Hope and the Tribulation.* Grand Rapids, MI: Zondervan. 1976. **Warfield, B. B.** "The Prophecies of St. Paul" (1886). In *Biblical and Theological Studies*, ed. S. G. Craig. Philadelphia: Presbyterian and Reformed Pub. Co., 1952, 463–502. **Waterman, G. H.** "The Sources of Paul's Teaching on the Second Coming of Christ in 1 and 2 Thessalonians." *JETS* 18 (1975) 105–113. **Wenham, D.** "Paul and the Synoptic Apocalypse." In *Gospel Perspectives*, ed. R. T. France and D. Wenham, ii. Sheffield: JSOT Press, 1981, 345–375.

Translation

[1] *Now, brothers, with regard to the advent of our* [a] *Lord Jesus Christ and our assembling to him,* [2] *we beg you not to be quickly shaken out of your wits or* [b] *disturbed, neither by a spirit-inspired utterance nor by a spoken word nor by a letter purporting to be (written) by us, to the effect that* [c] *the day of the Lord* [d] *is present.*

[3] *See that no one deceives you by any means. (That day will not arrive) unless*
    the rebellion comes first
    and the man of lawlessness [e] *is revealed,*
    the son of perdition,
[4] *who opposes and exalts himself*
    over every so-called god or object of worship,
    so that he takes his seat [f] *in the sanctuary of God,*
    proclaiming himself to be God.

[5] *Do you not remember that I told you this while I was* [g] *still with you?* [6] *And now you know what is holding him back, so that he may be revealed at his* [h] *proper time.* [7] *For the mystery of lawlessness is already active; only there is one who is holding it back until he is removed.* [8] *And then*
    the lawless one will be revealed,
    he whom the Lord Jesus [i] *will destroy* [j]
       with the breath of his mouth,
    and bring to an end
       with the dawning of his Advent.
[9] *His advent, according to the activity of Satan,*
    is attended by all power and fraudulent signs and wonders,
[10] *and by all deceit of unrighteousness* [k]
    for those who are on the way to perdition, [l]

because they did not accept the love of the truth,[m]
so as to find salvation.
[11] *And therefore God sends*[n] *them a working of delusion,*
so that they should believe the lie,
[12] *that all*[o] *should be judged who did not believe the truth,*
but took pleasure in unrighteousness.[p]

Notes

[a] ἡμῶν ("our") is omitted in B Ψ 33 *pc* lat^(vg.cod) syr^(hcl).

[b] μηδέ, in place of which μήτε is read by D² byz and μήποτε ("lest perchance") by 33 *pc.*

[c] ὡς ὅτι, an unclassical combination, found also in 2 Cor 5:19; 11:21. Here and in 2 Cor 11:21 Vg renders ὡς ὅτι by *quasi* ("as though").

[d] For κυρίου D² byz read Χριστοῦ (cf. AV "the day of Christ").

[e] For ἀνομίας ("lawlessness") A D F G Ψ byz lat syr Iren^(lat) Euseb read ἁμαρτίας (cf. AV "the man of sin").

[f] Before καθίσαι D² byz syr^(pesh hcl**) insert ὡς θεόν (cf. AV "so that he as God sitteth in the temple of God"); FG* insert ἵνα θεόν.

[g] For ταῦτα ἔλεγον ("I told these things") lat^b [d] Ambst read ταῦτα ἐλέγετο ("these things were told"), a construction which requires the replacement of nominative ὤν ("being") by genitive absolute ἐμοῦ ὄντος (so D* Ambst); lat^b reads *cum essemus,* "when we were (with you)."

[h] For ἑαυτοῦ ("his own") ℵ* A I K P 33 81 *al* read αυτου, which might be taken as αὑτοῦ ("his own") or αὐτοῦ ("his").

[i] Ἰησοῦς is omitted in B D² byz cop^(bo.cod).

[j] For ἀνελεῖ ("will destroy") ℵ D* ^(vid) F G 33 1739 *pc* read the aorist optative ἀνέλοι ("may he destroy"); D² Ψ byz cop read ἀναλώσει ("will consume"; cf. AV).

[k] ἀδικίας, to which τῆς is prefaced by ℵ² D Ψ byz.

[l] τοῖς ἀπολλυμένοις, to which ἐν is prefaced by ℵ² D¹ Ψ byz syr.

[m] For τῆς ἀληθείας Iren^(lat) (in one place: *Adv. Haer.* 5.28.2) reads τοῦ θεοῦ *(dei);* D* reads τῆς ἀληθείας Χριστοῦ.

[n] For πέμπει (present), πέμψει (future) is read by ℵ² D² Ψ byz lat^(vet vg.cl) cop^(sa.codd) bo Ambst Iren^(lat).

[o] For πάντες ℵ A F G 33 81 104 1739 *pc* read ἅπαντες.

[p] τῇ ἀδικίᾳ, to which ἐν is prefaced by ℵ² A D¹ Ψ byz.

Form/Structure/Setting

If any section can claim to be described as the "body" of this letter, it is 2:1–12. This is not only the most distinctive feature of 2 Thessalonians; it probably represents the purpose of the letter: what precedes leads up to it and what follows leads on from it.

Giblin (*The Threat to Faith,* 36, 37) arranges the section (and indeed the whole chapter) in an elaborate schema, characterized by multiple *inclusio.* Analyzing it less elaborately, we may recognize in much of it, especially in vv 3b–4 and 8–12, the same reproduction of OT phraseology and OT parallelism as was found in the similar eschatological passage in 1:6–10. An attempt is made in the translation (above) to indicate the parallel structure.

Between the two passages thus characterized comes a more prosaic passage (vv 5–7), dealing with the present restraint imposed on the emergence of the lawless power, which is probably Paul's personal contribution to the account of the rise and fall of Antichrist (part of the common stock of primitive Christian eschatology). (The phrases τὸ κατέχον of v 6 and ὁ κατέχων of v 7 scarcely stand in poetic parallelism to one another.)

Comment

2:1 Ἐρωτῶμεν δὲ ὑμᾶς, ἀδελφοί, "we beg you, brothers" as in 1 Thess 5:12, is a variant form of the παρακαλοῦμεν construction (see 1 Thess 4:1 with comment), followed not only by the vocative ἀδελφοί but also by a prepositional phrase (ὑπὲρ τῆς παρουσίας κτλ) and a request expressed by εἰς τό with the infinitive (v 2).

ὑπὲρ τῆς παρουσίας, "concerning the advent." The occasional use of ὑπέρ in the sense of περί (cf. John 1:30; 2 Cor 12:8) is found in Attic and Hellenistic Greek (BDF § 231); the reverse use of περί in the sense of ὑπέρ is also attested (BDF § 229 [1]).

καὶ ἡμῶν ἐπισυναγωγῆς ἐπ᾽ αὐτόν, "and our gathering together to him"; this is evidently a reference to the event described in 1 Thess 4:17, when the people of Christ (whether resurrected or surviving to the Parousia) will be transported to meet him and to be eternally with him. (The only other NT instance of ἐπισυναγωγή is in Heb 10:25, in reference to a local gathering of Christians. In 2 Macc 2:7 it is used of the regathering of Israel after the Babylonian exile.)

With this understanding of ἐπισυναγωγή and with the occurrence of παρουσία (as in 1 Thess 4:15) it is difficult to suppose that the "day of the Lord" in this section (v 2) belongs to a different time from that in view in 1 Thess 4:13–18, as is held by the Darbyite school of dispensationalism. It is remarkable, nevertheless, that (according to Kelly, *Rapture*, 5–8) J. N. Darby recorded that it was 2 Thess 2:1, 2 which, about 1830, "made me understand the rapture of the saints before—perhaps a considerable time before—the day of the Lord (that is, before the judgment of the living)."

2. εἰς τὸ μὴ ταχέως σαλευθῆναι ὑμᾶς ἀπὸ τοῦ νοός, "(we ask you) not to be quickly shaken out of your wits." For εἰς τό with the infinitive in such a construction cf. 1 Thess. 2:12; 3:10; 4:9 (BDF § 402 [2]). For ἀπό strengthening the separative force of the genitive cf. Rom 7:6; 2 Cor 11:3; Gal 5:4 (BDF § 211).

μηδὲ θροεῖσθαι, "nor to be disturbed." The verb is used in a similar eschatological context in the Olivet discourse (Mark 13:7 par. Matt 24:6).

μήτε διὰ πνεύματος, "neither by spirit," i.e. by a prophetic utterance made in the power of the Spirit of God or of another spirit. The prophecy might be a false prophecy or it might be a genuine prophecy misunderstood. For πνεῦμα in relation to prophecy in the church cf. 1 Cor 14:12, 32; 1 John 4:1–3. Prophecy was encouraged in the Thessalonian church (1 Thess 5:19, 20) and no doubt things to come figured largely in such prophecy:

possibly the "word of the Lord" of 1 Thess 4:15 was communicated in this form. But discrimination was necessary (1 Thess 5:21, 22) and nowhere more so than with prophecies relating to future events.

μήτε διὰ λόγου, "nor by spoken word." Here λόγος is distinguished from prophecy, which might be communicated (as most often) by spoken word or (as occasionally) by written word (cf. ὁ ἀναγινώσκων νοείτω, "let the reader take note," Mark 13:14; also Rev 1:3, 11, etc.); it is also distinguished from the written word of an epistle. It therefore denotes in this context a nonecstatic spoken word, which might be a word of apostolic authority (as in v 15) or a word of spiritual wisdom (as in 1 Cor 12:8) or a word lacking either authority or wisdom. Again, discrimination on the hearer's part was called for.

μήτε δι' ἐπιστολῆς ὡς δι' ἡμῶν, "nor by letter purporting to be by us." The phrase δι' ἡμῶν might denote the writers as agents of Christ or of the Spirit, transmitting his message in epistolary form (cf. the recurrent formula τὸ ῥηθὲν διὰ τοῦ προφήτου, "that which was spoken through the prophet," Matt 1:22 and frequently, or more particularly γέγραπται διὰ τοῦ προφήτου, "[that which] was written through the prophet," Matt 2:5); but there is ample attestation for διά with the genitive denoting the author or originator (cf. δι' οὗ 1 Cor 1:9; διὰ πολλῶν = ἐκ πολλῶν προσώπων, 2 Cor 1:11).

The particle ὡς does not definitely deny the writers' authorship of the epistle in question: the misunderstanding may or may not have arisen from an epistle, and if it has so arisen, the epistle may or may not be authentic. If the reference is to an authentic epistle (and the genuineness of 2 Thessalonians itself be accepted), we should have to think of a misunderstanding of 1 Thessalonians. In 1 Thess 5:1–11 it is explicitly said that the Day of the Lord will come suddenly, and it is probably implied that its coming is imminent. It is conceivable that, not long after their reception of 1 Thessalonians, something happened to make some members of the church conclude that the great Day had actually arrived. According to Lindemann ("Zum Abfassungszweck . . ."), the reference here is indeed to 1 Thessalonians, which the pseudonymous author of 2 Thessalonians wishes the readers to reject as spurious. Mearns ("Development") also takes the reference to be to 1 Thessalonians, but argues that Paul had changed his mind about the suddenness of the Day of the Lord since writing that letter and is now correcting perfectly reasonable inferences that the readers might have drawn from it.

On the other hand, the writers may have suspected that a letter falsely claiming to come from them had actually led the Thessalonians astray; this might explain the care taken in 3:17 to draw attention to Paul's signature as a token of authenticity. In any case, it is best to take ὡς δι' ἡμῶν as referring to δι' ἐπιστολῆς only; the πνεῦμα or the λόγος could have been uttered by one of the church members or by some otherwise unknown visitor.

ὡς ὅτι ἐνέστηκεν ἡ ἡμέρα τοῦ κυρίου, "to the effect that the day of the

Lord is present." Formally there is no difference between the unusual ὡς ὅτι and the simple ὡς or ὅτι but the addition of ὡς before ὅτι may here impart a subjective flavor to the clause thus introduced: the Day of the Lord is alleged to be present, the writers imply, dissociating themselves from any endorsement of the allegation.

It cannot be seriously disputed that "is present" is the natural sense of ἐνέστηκεν. This is the regular force of the perfect tense of ἐνιστάναι in NT usage. Twice Paul distinguishes ἐνεστῶτα from μέλλοντα as "things present" from "things to come" (Rom 8:38; 1 Cor 3:22). The ἐνεστῶσα ἀνάγκη of 1 Cor 7:26 is the "present distress"; the αἰὼν ἐνεστὼς πονηρός of Gal 1:4 is the "present evil age"; the καιρὸς ἐνεστηκώς of Heb 9:9 is the "present time" (whether the "time now present" or "time then present" is to be decided by exegesis). Cf. RV "the day of the Lord is *now* present"; RSV ". . . has come"; NEB ". . . is already here." But there remains considerable support for the sense of imminence (which ἐνέστηκεν does not bear) rather than actual presence; cf. AV "the day of Christ is at hand"; ASV "the day of the Lord is just at hand." Lightfoot translates ἐνέστηκεν as "is imminent" ("The Apostle then does not deny that the day of the Lord may be near. He asserts that it is not imminent"); cf. Stephenson ("On the Meaning . . .") for the argument that the rendering "is present" or "has come" is "logically impossible": it cannot be supposed that "the Thessalonians could have been misled by false letters saying that the events which Paul has described in I Thessalonians had taken place."

Aus ("Relevance," 263, 264) suggests that the severity of the Thessalonians' persecution made them think that the eschatological birth pangs had begun (cf. Isa 66:7) and that the Day of the Lord had arrived—much as, at a later date, the severity of the persecution of Christians under Septimius Severus "disturbed the minds of the many" and encouraged the opinion that the Parousia of Antichrist was then "already approaching" (Euseb. *HE* 6.7). But in the list of factors which might possibly have led the Thessalonians to their conclusion about the Day of the Lord no mention is made of the force of circumstances or the severity of persecution.

Another possibility is that the Thessalonians had recently been exposed to teaching which moved some of them to accept a realized, or even over-realized, eschatology, not unlike that with which Paul later takes issue in 1 Cor 4:8, when certain members of the Corinthian church appear to have embraced the idea that the kingdom of Christ had already been consummated and that they themselves were reigning with him. If so, the new teaching was less developed than it was to become in Corinth; the arguments used to counter it at Thessalonica are not those which Paul used in his Corinthian correspondence.

Schmithals (*Paul and the Gnostics*, 202–208) thinks that here, as in the rest of the Thessalonian correspondence, the writers take issue with a form of gnostic teaching according to which "the Resurrection is past already" (cf. 2 Tim 2:18); he compares *Gos. Thom.* 52 (51), where the disciples ask when "the rest (ἀνάπαυσις) of the dead" (the life to come) and the new world will come, and are told: "What you wait for has come already, and you have not recognized it." But if the Thessalonians had really given up the futurist eschatology of 1 Thess 4:13–5:11 for such a radical spiritualization, it would not have helped the situation for them to be given further futurist eschatology such as is presented in vv 3–8.

In fact, all that we can learn about the sense in which they thought the Day of the Lord to have come must be inferred from the counterargument of vv 3–8, and the interpretation of the counterargument is so uncertain that the wise interpreter will recognize the limits placed here on his knowledge. Probably there was no question of the Thessalonians' replacing the teaching they had already received with a completely new system. But if some of them had drawn unwarranted inferences from the statement in 1 Thess 5:5 that they were all "sons of the day" (so von Dobschütz ad loc.), or if a prophet had announced in the church that the Day of the Lord was now present, they might well have been bewildered; what had happened to the Resurrection and translation into the Lord's presence which they had been taught to expect at the Parousia? Paul and his colleagues, who knew more about their converts' problem than the exegete of today can know, judged that it would help them to be told something about the sequence of events leading up to the Day of the Lord. They had been taught about the actual events, but they needed to have them set in their chronological relationship.

3. Μή τις ὑμᾶς ἐξαπατήσῃ, "(see to it) that no one deceives you." This exhortation sums up the contents of vv 1, 2. We might have expected the imperative, μή . . . ἐξαπατησάτω ("let no one deceive you"), but βλέπετε or ὁρᾶτε may be understood before μή (ὁρᾶτε is expressed in such a construction in 1 Thess 5:15; it is left to be understood, as here, in 1 Cor 16:11; 2 Cor 11:16, μή τίς με δόξῃ ἄφρονα εἶναι "let no one think me foolish").

ὅτι ἐὰν μὴ ἔλθῃ ἡ ἀποστασία πρῶτον, "[That day will not arrive] unless the rebellion comes first." The apodosis on which the conditional clause is dependent is not expressed; it would be introduced by ὅτι but is left to be understood: "because (that day will not arrive) unless the rebellion comes first."

ἀποστασία, "the rebellion" a Hellenistic formation, corresponding to classical ἀπόστασις, denotes either political rebellion (as in Josephus, *Vita* 43, of the Jewish revolt against Rome) or religious defection (as in Acts 21:21, of abandonment of Moses' law). Since the reference here is to a world-wide rebellion against divine authority at the end of the age, the ideas of political revolt and religious apostasy are combined.

Other meanings are attested for ἀποστασία—e.g. the "departure" of the apostles with the Virgin Mary to Jerusalem from Bethlehem in the apocryphal treatise on *The Falling Asleep of the Holy Mother of God* attributed to St. John (33); cf. C. von Tischendorf (ed.), *Apocalypses Apocryphae* (Leipzig, 1866) 105; M. R. James, *Apocryphal NT* (Oxford, 1924) 206. An attempt has been made to find this meaning here and to identify this "departure" with the translation of believers at the Parousia (1 Thess 4:17); cf. English,

Re-thinking, 69–71, with refutation by Gundry, *Church and Tribulation*, 125. English argues that the article ἡ marks the ἀποστασία out as something about which the readers were already informed; true: they had been informed about it by Paul when he was with them (v 5).

A general revolt by Israel against the law of God was foretold for the end-time by some Jewish schools of thought (e.g. in Jub 23:14–23; cf. b. Sanh. 97). Davies ("Paul and the People of Israel," 8) identifies the ἀποστασία foretold here with "the refusal by Jews to receive the gospel"; this refusal is "a rejection of God's will and is the work of Satan." But if the authenticity of 1 Thess 2:15, 16 be accepted, as it is by Davies (see comment ad loc., above), it is difficult to see how the Jews could make any advance on the great refusal which had already taken place—unless 2 Thessalonians (whether itself authentic or not) represents a rather different perspective from 1 Thess 2:15, 16. In the one place in the Pauline corpus which deals specifically with the future of Israel, there is no word of an end-time rebellion but of a present partial insensitiveness (πώρωσις) to be followed by a future restoration, in which "all Israel will be saved" (Rom 11:25–27).

It appears more probable from the context that a general abandonment of the basis of civil order is envisaged. This is not only rebellion against the law of Moses; it is a large-scale revolt against public order, and since public order is maintained by the "governing authorities" who "have been instituted by God," any assault on it is an assault on a divine ordinance (Rom 13:1, 2). It is, in fact, the whole concept of divine authority over the world that is set at defiance in "*the* rebellion" par excellence.

καὶ ἀποκαλυφθῇ ὁ ἄνθρωπος τῆς ἀνομίας, ὁ υἱὸς τῆς ἀπωλείας, "and the man of lawlessness is revealed, the son of perdition." The leader of the great rebellion is described by two phrases each containing an adjectival genitive (a Semitic idiom, common in OT and taken over repeatedly into LXX and NT Greek): he is "the man of lawlessness" (cf. the more idiomatic Greek ὁ ἄνομος of v 8) and "the son of perdition," i.e. he who is destined for perdition (cf. the application of the same phrase to Judas Iscariot in John 17:12). This person is characterized by his opposition to the divine law and therefore he is doomed to destruction. The verb ἀποκαλυφθῇ ("be revealed") implies that the "man of lawlessness," like the Lord Jesus (cf. 1:7), is to have his ἀποκάλυψις (called his παρουσία in v 9). This suggests that he is in some sense a rival Messiah, the ἀντίχριστος of 1 John 2.18 ("you have heard that Antichrist is coming").

James ("Man of Sin and Antichrist") argues curiously that the sense here is that *first* the falling away takes place and "after this, the revealing of the Man of Sin" follows. But πρῶτον, "first," in reference to the coming of the ἀποστασία (AV "falling away") means that it comes before the Day of the Lord; the coming of the ἀποστασία and the revealing of the man of lawlessness are coincident. In an article ("2 Thess. ii.3") refuting James on this point, Nestle goes on to argue that "man of lawlessness" is a rendering of the OT phrase "man of Belial" (איש בליעל), pointing out that in LXX both ἀνομία (as in 2 Sam. [LXX 2 Kgdms] 22:5 = Ps 18:4 [LXX 17:5]) and ἀποστασία (as in 1 Kings 21:13 [LXX 3 Kgdms 20:13A]) appear as renderings of Heb. בליעל. This is a pointer to the origin, character and destiny of the person so described, and rules out such an interpretation of ἀνομία as that antinomians were viewed as constituting a greater danger to the church than legalists (so Stürmer, *Auferstehung* . . . , 49).

4. ὁ ἀντικείμενος, "he who opposes." The characterization of the great rebel continues. Nestle, in the article already cited, goes on to point out that ἀντικείμενος is used in LXX (1 Kings [3 Kgdms] 11:25A) as a rendering of Heb. שׂטן ("adversary"); the verb ἀντικεῖσθαι, "to oppose," is used in Zech 3:1 to render the corresponding Hebrew verb שׂטן ("oppose," "prosecute"). Cf. 1 Tim 5:14, where ὁ ἀντικείμενος is Satan, the supreme "adversary."

καὶ ὑπεραιρόμενος, "and exalts himself"; the middle voice has reflexive force here. Cf. the repeated ἵνα μὴ ὑπεραίρωμαι ("lest I should be excessively exalted, too elated") in 2 Cor 12:7.

ἐπὶ πάντα λεγόμενον θεὸν ἤ σέβασμα, "over every so-called god or object of worship." The addition of λεγόμενον before θεόν implies that the man of lawlessness elevates himself above the living and true God and every other "so-called" god. The more comprehensive σέβασμα denotes (as in Acts 17:23) any object of worship. The language echoes that in which Antiochus IV is depicted in Dan 11:36, 37: Antiochus, the willful king, is to "exalt himself and magnify himself above every god" (ἐπὶ πάντα θεόν).

ὥστε αὐτὸν εἰς τὸν ναὸν τοῦ θεοῦ καθίσαι, "so that he takes his seat in the sanctuary of God." Elsewhere Paul speaks of the believer's body (1 Cor 6:19) or (more often) of the believing community as the sanctuary (ναός) of God (1 Cor 3:16; 2 Cor 6:16; Eph 2:21), but the picture here is of a material shrine. The ναός is the sanctuary proper, the holiest part of the temple complex, the dwellingplace of the deity. The inner sanctuary of the Jerusalem temple, the Holy of Holies, was the throne room of the invisible presence of the God of Israel: there, in the house which Solomon built for him, as earlier at Shiloh (1 Sam 4:4), he was worshiped as "Yahweh of hosts, who is enthroned on the cherubim" (cf. Pss 80:1; 99:1). Although no ark surmounted by cherubim was to be found in the postexilic Holy of Holies, the God of Israel was still believed to have his dwelling there. The man of lawlessness is pictured as enthroning himself there in the place of God, in the spirit of the king of Babylon who is portrayed in Isa 14:13, 14 as aspiring to "ascend to heaven" in rivalry to the Most High. The attempt of the Emperor Gaius (Caligula) in A.D. 40 to have his statue set up in the Jerusalem temple, in assertion of his claims to divinity which the Jews refused to acknowledge (Philo, *Leg.* 203–346; Josephus, *Antiq.* 18. 261–301), provided a foretaste of what the final Antichrist was expected to do.

But which sanctuary is actually meant here? The later idea that it is in the Christian church, "God's dwelling place in the Spirit" (Eph 2:22), that

Antichrist is to manifest himself and establish his power base, is inapplicable at this early stage, when there was no united church organization which could provide such a power base. A local church, such as the church in Thessalonica, scarcely comes into consideration in this regard. One might think of the Jerusalem church, which (by some of its members at least) was viewed as the new and living sanctuary of God, with James the Just and his successors as the new high priesthood; but there is no evidence that a manifestation of Antichrist was expected within it and no hint that it is referred to in the present context.

The material temple in Jerusalem has much to be said in its favor. Not all early Christians took the negative attitude toward it that Stephen did (Acts 6:13, 14; 7:44–50)—not even Paul, if the evidence of Acts is accepted—and Jesus' words in the Olivet discourse about "the abomination of desolation standing where he ought not" (Mark 13:14, ἑστηκότα ὅπου οὐ δεῖ) are reproduced by Matthew in the form ". . . standing in the holy place" (Matt 24:15). It may be best to conclude that the Jerusalem sanctuary is meant here by Paul and his companions, but meant in a metaphorical sense. Had they said, "so that he takes his seat on the throne of God," few would have thought it necessary to think of a literal throne; it would simply have been regarded as a graphic way of saying that he plans to usurp the authority of God. This is what is meant by the language actually used here, although the sacral associations of ναός imply that he demands not only the obedience but also the worship due to God alone.

ἀποδεικνύντα ἑαυτὸν ὅτι ἐστὶν θεός, "proclaiming himself to be God." We may compare the king of Tyre, proclaiming "I am God (אל), I sit in the seat of the gods" (Ezek 28:2), or Herod Agrippa I, receiving divine honors at the Caesarean games (Acts 12:21–23; Josephus, *Antiq.* 19. 343–347). Cf. Morgenstern, "The Chanukkah Festival. . . ," 89 n. 170; "The King-God . . ."

5. Οὐ μνημονεύετε ὅτι ἔτι ὢν πρὸς ὑμᾶς ταῦτα ἔλεγον ὑμῖν; "Do you not remember that I told you these things while I was still with you?" As in 1 Thess 5:27, the first person singular suggests that here we have an insertion by Paul into the joint epistle (cf. Askwith, " 'I' and 'We'. . ."). Some instruction about the eschatological rebellion and its demonic leader had evidently been included in the teaching from which the Thessalonian converts had learned not only to worship the "living and true God" but also "to wait for his Son from heaven, . . . Jesus, our deliverer from the coming wrath" (1 Thess 1:9, 10). Since they had received this instruction by word of mouth, a general allusion was sufficient to remind them of the details. What had to be made clear to them was that the rebellion would precede (and be brought to an end by) the Parousia of Jesus on the Day of the Lord.

For πρὸς ὑμᾶς, "with you" cf. 1 Thess 3:4, with comment ad loc.

6. καὶ νῦν τὸ κατέχον οἴδατε, "and now (cf. Heb. equivalent adverb ועתה) you know what is restraining him." The RSV perpetrates a solecism by rendering, "And you know what is restraining him now" (as though νῦν

were separated from its adjunct by the definite article, like ὧδε in Mark 9:1); νῦν is to be construed with οἴδατε, not with κατέχον, and its force is probably resumptive rather than temporal: "and, as it is, you know what is restraining him." They knew because they had been told; later readers are at a disadvantage compared with them, and have to guess.

εἰς τὸ ἀποκαλυφθῆναι αὐτὸν ἐν τῷ ἑαυτοῦ καιρῷ, "so that he may be revealed at his proper time." If εἰς τό with the infinitive denotes purpose here (as in 1:5, etc.), the meaning must be: "you know what is restraining him in order that he may not be revealed before his proper time." If εἰς means "until," the meaning is: "you know what is restraining him, until he is revealed at his proper time" (but this is less probable). If purpose is indicated, the purpose is God's, to which both the man of lawlessness and the restraining power are perforce subservient. It is implied that there is a "proper time" decreed for the revelation of Antichrist as well as for the epiphany of the true Christ (cf. καιροῖς ἰδίοις, "in his own time," 1 Tim 6:15; also Mark 13:32; Acts 1:7).

7. τὸ γὰρ μυστήριον ἤδη ἐνεργεῖται τῆς ἀνομίας, "for the mystery of lawlessness is already active." The distinctive NT usage of μυστήριον relates to the hitherto concealed but now disclosed purpose of God, with special reference to the *fulfillment* of his purpose (cf. Mark 4:11; Rom 11:25; 16:25; 1 Cor 15:51; Eph 1:9; 3:3, 4). The Qumran texts use the Hebrew-Aramaic equivalent רז in a similar way (following the precedent of Dan 2:18, 19, 27, 28, 29, 30, 47; 4:9 [MT 6]); cf. 1Q27.1.2, רזי פשע ("mysteries of iniquity"), which, unfortunately, lacks sufficient context to establish its relevance, if any, to the present passage, and 1Q27.1.7, which looks forward to the time when "those who hold back the wonderful mysteries (תומכי רזי פלא) shall be no more"—but these "restrainers" are impeding the *divine* purpose. In the NT the divine μυστήριον is bound up with Christ, differing little indeed from the ἀποκάλυψις Ἰησοῦ Χριστοῦ (Gal 1:12; 1 Pet 1:7; Rev 1:1); in Col 2:2 the mystery of God *is* Christ.

The "mystery of lawlessness" (formally antithetic to the τῆς εὐσεβείας μυστήριον, "the mystery of our religion," 1 Tim 3:16) is a satanic counterpart to the mystery of God's purpose; at present it works beneath the surface but when the due time comes for its disclosure it will find its embodiment in the manifested "man of lawlessness." Until then it is under restraint; μόνον ὁ κατέχων ἄρτι—but this time the restraining agency is personal (ὁ κατέχων, masculine, as against τὸ κατέχον, neuter, in v 6). The restrainer holds the mystery of lawlessness in check "until he is removed," ἕως ἐκ μέσου γένηται. The phrase ἐκ μέσου (without further qualification of the μέσον) in itself implies removal. For other instances of ἐκ μέσου γενέσθαι in Greek literature cf. Plutarch, *Timoleon* 5.3, "he decided to live by himself, having moved away (ἐκ μέσου γενόμενος) out of public view"; Achilles Tatius, *Leucippe and Clitophon* 2.27, "when Clio has been removed (τῆς Κλειοῦς ἐκ μέσου γενομένης)"; Ps.–Aeschines, *Ep.* 12.6, "what they formerly covered up is clearly revealed, now that they have been removed (ἐκ μέσου γενομένων)"—i.e. by death or exile.

The subject of γένηται cannot be other than ὁ κατέχων. Attempts have been made to construe the clause as though the reference were to the mystery of lawlessness "coming to pass out of the midst"—i.e. emerging from its place of concealment, but that would require εἰς μέσον, not ἐκ μέσου.

Any one undertaking to identify the restraining agency must reckon with the fact that it may be viewed either personally (ὁ κατέχων) or impersonally (τὸ κατέχον). It is plain, moreover, that both the mystery of iniquity and the restraining agency are at work at the time of the writing of the epistle; the restrainer has not yet been removed, therefore the man of lawlessness has not yet appeared, and *a fortiori* the Day of the Lord has not yet arrived.

It has been argued by Cullmann ("Le caractère eschatologique . . .") and Munck (*Paul*, 36–42) that the restraint was imposed by Paul and his Gentile mission, which had to be completed before the end came (cf. Mark 13:10). It is true that Paul attached eschatological significance to his mission as apostle to the Gentiles (cf. Rom 11:13–16, 25–32; 15:15–29), but if this were the restraining agency it is strange that it is alluded to in such carefully guarded terms, with a reminder to the readers of what they had been taught orally. It is probable, too, that while the eschatological teaching of this epistle (and of 1 Thess 5:1–11) was generally current among early Christians, the teaching about the restraining agency is Paul's personal contribution. But no more convincing account of the restrainer has been suggested than that put forward by Tertullian (*De resurr. carn.* 24): "What is this but the Roman state, whose removal when it has been divided among ten kings will bring on Antichrist?" (the reference to the ten kings is an importation from Rev 17:12–14). Similarly Chrysostom (*Hom. 4 on 2 Thessalonians*) says of ὁ κατέχων, "some interpret this of the grace of the Spirit [an allusion perhaps to his rival Severian of Gabala], but others of the Roman Empire, and this is my own preference. Why? Because, if Paul had meant the Spirit, he would have said so plainly and not obscurely, . . . but because he meant the Roman Empire, he naturally glanced at it, speaking covertly and darkly. . . . So . . . when the Roman Empire is out of the way, then he [Antichrist] will come."

An attempt to do justice to both the interpretations mentioned by Chrysostom was made by Darby ("Notes . . .," 452): "the thing which restrained then is not that which restrains now. Then it was, in one sense, the Roman empire, as the fathers thought. . . . At present the hindrance is still the existence of the governments established by God in the world; and God will maintain them as long as there is here below the gathering of His church. Viewed in this light, the hindrance is, at the bottom, the presence of the church and of the Holy Spirit on the earth." It is strange that the role once filled by the Roman Empire should ultimately be filled by the Spirit in the church; however, the exegete's task is to determine what the writers meant and what the persons addressed understood. In general, Paul viewed established government as imposing a salutary restraint on evil (Rom 13:3, 4), and in his mission field established government meant effectively the Roman Empire (τὸ κατέχον), personally embodied in the emperor (ὁ κατέχων). He himself had cause to appreciate the benevolent neutrality of Roman rule; shortly after this epistle was written came his brief appearance before Gallio (Acts 18:12–17), and his consequent reflections on the divinely overruled benefits of Roman rule for the progress of the gospel could have influenced his language in Rom 13:1–7. He knew that Roman rule would not last forever, and that its benevolent neutrality could not be counted on indefinitely, but in the present situation a welcome curb was placed on the forces of lawlessness. It would be unwarranted to see here a play on the name of Claudius, the reigning emperor (as though κατέχειν corresponded to Latin *claudere* or *claudicare* [to limp], which it does not), or to suppose that, by prophetic foresight, Claudius's being succeeded by Nero was viewed as the replacement of the restrainer by the man of lawlessness (this might have seemed to be a reasonable interpretation in retrospect, but at the time of writing Nero was but newly into his teens). (For further interpretations see Excursus, p. 179.)

8. καὶ τότε, "and then"—when the restrainer has been removed.

ἀποκαλυφθήσεται ὁ ἄνομος, "the lawless one will be revealed." For the third time the passive of ἀποκαλύπτειν is used to denote the epiphany of the counterfeit Christ, lawlessness incarnate. But he is revealed only to be destroyed.

ὃν ὁ κύριος [Ἰησοῦς] ἀνελεῖ τῷ πνεύματι τοῦ στόματος αὐτοῦ, "whom the Lord [Jesus] will destroy with the breath of his mouth." This clause is based on Isa 11:4, LXX, where the coming Prince of the house of David is to "smite the earth with the word of his mouth (τοῦ στόματος αὐτοῦ) and destroy (ἀνελεῖ) the wicked one (ἀσεβῆ) with breath (πνεύματι) through his lips." There "the wicked one" is generic; here he is the particular individual (ὁ ἄνομος) in whom the mystery of lawlessness is made public.

καὶ καταργήσει τῇ ἐπιφανείᾳ τῆς παρουσίας αὐτοῦ, "and will bring (him) to an end with the dawning of his Advent." This is the only NT occurrence of ἐπιφάνεια outside the Pastoral Epistles, where it used once (2 Tim 1:10) of the first coming of Christ and four times (1 Tim 6:14; 2 Tim 4:1, 8; Tit 2:13) of his Advent in glory (παρουσία does not occur in the Pastorals). If ἐπιφάνεια ("manifestation") were synonymous with παρουσία here, the construction would be pleonastic; it more probably means "dawning," as in Polybius, *Hist.* 3.94.3, τὴν ἐπιφάνειαν τῆς ἡμέρας ("the dawn of day," "daybreak"). The bright dawn of Christ's Parousia will consume the man of lawlessness; we may compare the "flaming fire" of 1:7, 8.

This picture of the warrior Messiah has OT precedent (cf. Isa 11:4 quoted in preceding comment; Isa 66:15, 16 and Mal 4:1 quoted in comment and explanation on 1:8; also Yahweh's portrayal as a man of war in Isa 42:13, 25; 59: 15b–19; 63:1–6). It passed into apocalyptic imagery, as in the *Ascension of Isaiah* (4:14), where "the Lord will come with his angels and with the armies of the holy ones from the seventh heaven with the glory of the seventh heaven, and he will drag Beliar into Gehenna together with his armies," and in the detailed picture of Rev 19:11–21, where the "Word of God," mounted on a war-horse, smites his enemies with the sharp sword proceeding from his mouth and throws the "beast" (corresponding to the man of lawlessness) and his agent the false prophet into the lake of fire and brimstone.

9. οὗ ἐστιν ἡ παρουσία, "whose advent is"; the false Christ has his solemn Parousia or, as we might call it (remembering the title of that proto-Antichrist, Antiochus Epiphanes), his "epiphany." (From the time of Gaius Caligula onward, ἐπιφάνεια is used of an emperor's parousia, with the implication that his visit is a "manifestation" of divinity.) The use of παρουσία here probably suggests a parody of Christ's Parousia (v 8).

κατ᾽ ἐνέργειαν τοῦ σατανᾶ, "according to Satan's activity." The energizing of the man of lawlessness by Satan has its analogue in Rev 13:2, where the beast from the abyss (the persecuting empire) receives "his power and his throne and great authority" from the great red dragon.

ἐν πάσῃ δυνάμει καὶ σημείοις καὶ τέρασιν ψεύδους, "with all power and lying signs and wonders" (or "wonders of falsehood"; the adjectival genitive may qualify τέρασιν only, or (as is probable) σημείοις καὶ τέρασιν, "lying signs and wonders," or even all three datives). The three substantives are used of the works of Jesus, e.g. in Acts 2:22, where Peter speaks of him as divinely attested by the δυνάμεις and τέρατα and σημεῖα "which God did through him"; similar works, attending the proclamation of the gospel, bore witness to the authority of the risen Christ by his Spirit in the message and its preachers (as in Acts 2:43; Gal 3:5; Heb 2:4). Here again the ministry of Jesus is parodied (cf. the σημεῖα μεγάλα of Rev 13:13, by which the earth-dwellers are persuaded to worship the imperial beast). Indeed, Jesus himself foretold that false Messiahs and false prophets would appear in the interval preceding the coming of the Son of Man "and show signs and wonders (σημεῖα καὶ τέρατα), to lead astray (ἀποπλανᾶν), if possible, the elect" (Mark 13:22 par. Matt 24:24).

10. καὶ ἐν πάσῃ ἀπάτῃ ἀδικίας, "and with all deceitfulness of unrighteousness." The two phrases introduced by ἐν are parallel; ἐν here is comitative, so that the construction of the sentence is: "his parousia, according to the activity of Satan, is attended by all power and fraudulent signs and wonders and by all unrighteous deceitfulness" (ἀδικίας is another instance of the adjectival genitive). What form these seductive displays take is not said. In Rev 13:13 the false prophet persuades people to worship the beast by making fire come down from heaven, but if the elect are to be led astray, something more in the nature of healing miracles might be expected. However, it is not the elect who are led astray in the present context, but those who are on the way to perdition, whose unbelief has made them gullible. We may integrate τοῖς ἀπολλυμένοις, "those on the way to perdition," with the rest of the clause by rendering: "his parousia . . . is attended by all power and . . . deceitfulness for those who are on the way to perdition" (some such phrase best conveys the force of the present participle passive of ἀπολλύναι, for which cf. 1 Cor 1:18; 2 Cor 2:15; 4:3).

ἀνθ᾽ ὧν, a form found elsewhere in NT in Luke's writings (Luke 1:20; 12:3; 19:44; Acts 12:23), is perfectly classical ("in return for which," hence "because"); it continues into Hellenistic usage (including LXX). Cf. BDF § 208 (1).

τὴν ἀγάπην τῆς ἀληθείας οὐκ ἐδέξαντο, "they did not receive the love of the truth." Refusal of the truth lays one open to all kinds of error; cf. Rom 1:21–28, where those who reject the knowledge of God have their understanding darkened and are given over "to a reprobate mind" (εἰς ἀδόκιμον νοῦν). So, in Rev 13:8, the beast receives worship from all the earth's inhabitants except those whose names have been written in the Lamb's Book of Life.

εἰς τὸ σωθῆναι αὐτούς, "so as to be saved." This phrase goes closely with ἐδέξαντο. To receive the love of the truth is the way of salvation; to refuse it means perdition. Cf. the synonymous clause ἵνα σωθῶσιν (1 Thess 2:16; 1 Cor 10:33).

11. καὶ διὰ τοῦτο πέμπει αὐτοῖς ὁ θεὸς ἐνέργειαν πλάνης, "and therefore God sends them a working of delusion"; a power is set in operation within them which makes them prone to embrace error or be led astray. The same process of judicial blinding is traced, as has just been said, in Rom 1:21–28 (διὰ τοῦτο here may be compared with διὰ τοῦτο in Rom 1:26 or διό in Rom 1:24). Cf. Rom 11:8 where Paul, quoting Isa 29:10, tells how God has given unbelieving Israel "a spirit of torpor, to prevent eyes from seeing and ears from hearing." Here God sends "a working of delusion" in the sense that to be misled by falsehood is the divine judgment inevitably incurred in a moral universe by those who close their eyes to the truth. But the true God is not the deliberate author of this infatuation; it is, as Paul puts it in 2 Cor 4:4, "the god of this aeon" (cf. the "activity of Satan" in v 9 above) who "has blinded the minds of the unbelievers, to keep them from seeing the light of the gospel of the glory of Christ."

εἰς τὸ πιστεῦσαι αὐτοὺς τῷ ψεύδει, "that they should believe the lie"; for the articulated ψεῦδος cf. Rom 1:25, where the desperate plight of the pagan world is due to its having "exchanged the truth of God for the lie (ἐν τῷ ψεύδει) and worshiped and served the creature rather than the Creator." By "the lie" is apparently meant the denial of the fundamental truth that God is God; it is the rejection of his self-revelation as Creator and Savior, righteous and merciful Judge of all, which leads to the worship due to him alone being offered to another, such as the "man of lawlessness." We may compare the part played in Zoroastrianism by the druj ("the lie"), which comes to assume demonic proportions as the enemy of aša ("rightness"). A comparison may suggest itself also with the איש הכזב (literally "the man of the lie") in Qumran literature (e.g. 1QpHab 2.1, 2; 5.11), but he is a historical individual, an opponent of the Teacher of Righteousness.

12. ἵνα κριθῶσιν, "that they should be judged." Again, the embracing of falsehood, which leads to destruction, is the judgment divinely decreed on "all those who have not believed the truth" (πάντες οἱ μὴ πιστεύσαντες

τῇ ἀληθείᾳ), "the truth" being synonymous with the revelation of God.
ἀλλὰ εὐδοκήσαντες τῇ ἀδικίᾳ, "but approved of unrighteousness." As in
Rom 1:21–28, "truth" and "falsehood" have moral implications. To reject
the truth is to reject the will of God; to embrace falsehood is to take
pleasure in unrighteousness. A wrong idea of God means a wrong way
of life. Cf. the reference in Rom 2:8 to those who "do not obey the truth,
but obey unrighteousness"; also 1 Cor 13:6, where love "does not rejoice
in unrighteousness, but rejoices with the truth."

Explanation

Some members of the Thessalonian church had recently been persuaded
that the Day of the Lord, described in 1 Thess 5:2–6 as destined to come
when least expected and take the unwary by surprise, had already arrived.
This was causing them bewilderment and anxiety; it was difficult to reconcile
this account of the matter with the teaching they had already received
from Paul and his companions. Paul and his companions had learned of
this strange notion which their friends were entertaining, but plainly were
not sure where they had gotten it from. If they were not sure, we can
only guess. More recent analogies might suggest that an alleged prophecy
to this effect had circulated among them, just as voices are heard today
which assure people living in the closing decades of the twentieth century
that they belong to the "terminal generation."
    It is therefore explained that certain developments are bound to precede
the Day of the Lord. Even if these developments are near at hand, they
have not appeared yet, and therefore the Day of the Lord cannot have
arrived. The developments which must precede that Day are sinister
enough; they will involve a widespread rebellion against God, led by one
who is the very embodiment of lawlessness, who will try to usurp the throne
of God and claim divine honors for himself. (The readers are reminded
that Paul told them this while he was with them.)
    For the time being, this outburst of rebellion is held in check. The
"mystery" or hidden principle of lawlessness is at work beneath the surface,
but is contained by a restraining power. When that restraint is removed,
then (but not until then), in the words of W. B. Yeats:

> Things fall apart: the centre cannot hold;
> Mere anarchy is loosed upon the world,
> The blood-dimmed tide is loosed, and everywhere
> The ceremony of innocence is drowned.
> The best lack all conviction, while the worst
> Are full of passionate intensity.

In the twentieth chapter of his *City of God* (written early in the fifth
century) Augustine quotes Paul's words about the restraining power and
says, "I admit that the meaning of this completely escapes me." He mentions, however, one or two guesses at its meaning which others had made;
guesses at its meaning are all that the exegete can manage even today.

The Thessalonian Christians knew what the restraining power was, because Paul had told them; they also knew that it was operating at that time. But a certain reticence can be detected in the references made to it in the letters; this can best be explained if more explicit language was liable to cause trouble should the letter fall into the wrong hands.

In Thessalonica the missionaries had been charged with subversion, with proclaiming a rival to the emperor who ruled in Rome. It would be best not to say anything in a letter which could be interpreted as lending color to such a charge. Their opponents had tried to hinder the progress of the gospel by enlisting the aid of the city rabble. The readiness of the rabble to be used for this purpose may well have brought home to Paul and the others the ease with which the forces of anarchy might be mustered against the cause of God. In Thessalonica, indeed, the attempt to stir up trouble had less disastrous consequences than the instigators hoped, because the magistrates acted sensibly. Paul indeed had to leave the city and was prevented from returning, but public order was maintained and the progress of the gospel was not impeded, whatever the converts had to endure in the way of persecution.

Some weeks earlier, an attempt had been made to put a stop to gospel witness in Philippi. There the custodians of law and order had shown themselves weak and easily influenced by clamor, but when they were persuaded of their duty, the outcome there too had been for the furtherance of the gospel. And so long as the forces of law and order were able to maintain control, not in Macedonia only but throughout the Mediterranean world, the gospel would succeed in surmounting all obstacles in its path.

Above the praetors of Philippi and the politarchs of Thessalonica stood the power and authority of the Roman Empire. Civic and provincial authorities could function only as power was delegated to them, directly or indirectly, by the emperor. It was the imperial power that was the ultimate protector on earth of ordered life and (as it seemed in A.D. 50) of gospel progress. The protection which the Gentile mission enjoyed under the imperial administration is one of the themes of Luke's history; even more relevant to the present passage is Paul's insistence in Rom 13:1–7 that rulers are not a terror to law-abiding subjects but to criminals and should therefore receive the respect, obedience and tribute due to them, since the work they do is the work of God.

Paul was not so ingenuous as to suppose that the secular authorities would invariably protect the gospel and those who preached or practiced it. Occasions would arise when those authorities would claim more than Christians could conscientiously give; in such situations Paul would have agreed with Peter that "we must obey God rather than men" (Acts 5:29). But in his missionary experience thus far he had reason to appreciate the security afforded by the imperial organization; it had helped the gospel forward, not hindered it.

This state of affairs, however, would not last indefinitely. Paul's experience of unruly mobs in the cities of Macedonia (and earlier in some cities of South Galatia) gave him a forewarning of what would happen on a wider and more irresistible scale at the end-time. When the restraint of law and order was relaxed, the forces of lawlessness would have it all their own way, under the direction of the "man of lawlessness."

This figure has OT antecedents in such God-defying monarchs as the king of Babylon in Isa 14:12–14 or the prince of Tyre in Ezek 28:2. But these adumbrations were later filled out in the apocalyptic portrayal of the persecuting Antiochus Epiphanes (175–164 B.C.). His depiction as the "little horn" of Dan 7:8, with "a mouth speaking great things," or as the willful king of Dan 11:36–45, who "shall exalt himself and magnify himself above every god, and shall speak astonishing things against the God of gods," provides the prototype for the NT "lawless one."

Antiochus came to his end, "with none to help him," but his attempt to abolish the worship of the true God was not forgotten, and served as a precedent for later visions of the end. Jesus' Olivet discourse gave warning that, after the preaching of the gospel to "all the nations," the crisis immediately preceding the coming of the Son of Man would be precipitated by "the abomination of desolation standing where he ought not" (Mark 13:10, 14–27). The personal characterization of the "abomination" is noteworthy. Ten years later it looked as if these words were on the point of fulfillment when the Emperor Gaius (nicknamed Caligula), annoyed because his Jewish subjects would not take his divinity seriously, ordered that his statue should be set up in the Jerusalem temple. This order was countermanded at the last moment, but the consternation of those days made a deep impression on the minds of Jews (including Jewish Christians) and supplied further details for the picture of the expected Antichrist. Behind the present description of the lawless one enthroning himself in the sanctuary of God and claiming divine honors lie Jesus' words about the "abomination of desolation" and the memory of Gaius's threat to desecrate the temple.

Gaius's madness was cut short by his assassination in A.D. 41. The forces of order were powerful enough to check his insane policy. But what had happened once could happen again, and the forces of order would not always be available to hold anarchy in check. One day those forces would be removed.

With the removal of their restraint, the incarnation of lawlessness would dominate the scene, captivating the minds of the unthinking masses and leading a large-scale revolt against the authority of God. This revolt would be put down by the glorious Advent of Jesus. How the rise and fall of Antichrist are presented in later NT documents is considered in the excursus (pp. 179–188).

So far as modern literature is concerned, no more powerful portrayal of the great rebellion has appeared than Vladimir Solovyev's "Short Narrative about the Antichrist." Here the new world emperor, having established a benevolent despotism and inaugurated an age of universal peace and prosperity, convenes an ecumenical council with the object of uniting the main streams of Christianity. When he is invited to make public confession of "the name of Jesus Christ the Son of God, who was born in the flesh, who rose from the dead, and who will come again," his statesmanlike disguise is dropped and his diabolical nature stands revealed.

Excursus on Antichrist

1. *The background*

The personage called "the man of lawlessness" is certainly identical with the personage elsewhere referred to as Antichrist. The earliest literary occurrence of Greek ἀντίχριστος is in 1 John 2:18, but the word and its significance were already known to the readers of that document: "you have heard," the writer tells them, "that Antichrist is coming." The teachers against whom the writer warns were so many lesser "antichrists" who presumably were paving the way for the final Antichrist himself. It is a reasonable inference from his language that the final Antichrist would lead a large-scale departure from God. He does not say from whom or when his readers had heard of the coming of Antichrist; it was part of the common stock of early Christian eschatology (see pp. xxxvi–xxxix).

The rise and development of the expectation of Antichrist were examined in 1895 by Bousset *(The Antichrist Legend)*. He concluded, from a study of the relevant literature, that the Christian expectation was adapted from an existing Jewish conception. According to Bousset's reconstruction of the Antichrist expectation, Antichrist would appear among the Jews after the fall of Rome, proclaiming his divine status and installing his cult in the Jerusalem temple. He would himself be a Jew, born of the tribe of Dan (an idea based on Gen 49:17; Deut 33:22; Jer 8:16). Elijah would appear and denounce him, and would be put to death for his pains. Antichrist would reign for three and a half years. True believers, refusing to give him the worship which he demanded, would seek refuge in the wilderness and be pursued by him there, but when they are on the point of being wiped out, he is destroyed by the intervention of God (who may use an agent such as Michael the archangel or the Messiah of David's line).

All the details in this reconstruction are attested separately in the literature, but they do not add up to a picture which can properly be called "*the* Antichrist legend." Some pieces of evidence do point to the idea of a Jewish Antichrist, but those which point to a Gentile Antichrist are more relevant to the NT. The Antichrist expectation was held among Jews and Christians alike, but in both communities it took a wide variety of forms.

A near-synonym of ἀντίχριστος is ψευδόχριστος, which appears in the Olivet discourse of the Gospels; during the coming unparalleled time of distress, says Jesus, "false Christs and false prophets will arise and show signs and wonders, to lead astray, if possible, the elect" (Mark 13:22 par. Matt 24:24). Like the Antichrist of 1 John 4:3, these "false Christs" are linked with false prophets who, speaking by the spirit of error (τὸ πνεῦμα τῆς πλάνης, 1 John 4:6), lead their hearers astray (ἀποπλανᾶν, Mark 13:22).

The Antichrist himself does this, but he goes farther than the "false Christs" of the Olivet prophecy by claiming divine worship for himself.

The attempt by the Emperor Gaius (Caligula) to set up his statue in the temple at Jerusalem was fresh in the minds of Jews and Christians when the gospel came to Thessalonica, and would be remembered by readers of 2 Thess 2:4, which describes the leader of the end-time rebellion as "exalting himself above every so-called god or object of worship, so that he takes his seat in the sanctuary of God and proclaims himself to be God." During the critical days of A.D. 40 some of the disciples of Jesus probably thought that his words about "the abomination of desolation standing where he ought not" (Mark 13:14) were on the point of being fulfilled by Gaius, and published the discourse to which those words belonged so that Christians would know what to do when the appalling horror materialized. The parenthesis "let the reader understand," attached to the reference to the abomination of desolation, may have been a direction to the reader of this separate leaflet (which was later incorporated in the Gospel of Mark).

In any event, Gaius's statue was not set up in the temple; it proved unnecessary for the Judean disciples to "flee to the mountains" on that occasion. But the dismay and anxiety of those days remained for long in the memories of those most closely affected, and suggested to them what was likely to happen when the abomination of desolation did indeed stand "where he ought not."

The phrase "the abomination of desolation" goes back two centuries before the time of Gaius. It was the derogatory designation given by Jews to the installation of the cult of Olympian Zeus in the Jerusalem temple by the Seleucid monarch Antiochus IV toward the end of 167 B.C. It is applied in 1 Maccabees 1:54 to the altar of Olympian Zeus which Antiochus's agents erected on top of the altar of Yahweh. But in origin the βδέλυγμα ἐρημώσεως or rather its Hebrew *Vorlage* שקוץ שמם (Dan 12:11, etc.), was a mocking pun on בעל שמין ("the lord of heaven"), the name by which Olympian Zeus was known in the Aramaic-speaking parts of Antiochus's kingdom (cf. Nestle, "Der Greuel der Verwüstung").

Antiochus's title Epiphanes ("manifest") expressed his claim to be the earthly manifestation of his patron deity, Olympian Zeus. It is probably because the god whom he allegedly manifested usurped the place of the God of Israel that Antiochus is said to "exalt himself and magnify himself above every god, and . . . speak astonishing things against the God of gods" (Dan 11:36), language which anticipates what is said about the man of lawlessness in 2 Thess 2:4.

Three years after the cult of Olympian Zeus was installed at Jerusalem it was removed, and the temple was restored to its proper use (a restoration commemorated ever since then in the Jewish festival of the Dedication or Hanukkah). The picturesque wording used to describe the idolatrous installation was retained and reapplied to comparable sacrileges. Jesus, as we have seen, spoke of the setting up of the (personal) "abomination of desolation" as a future event which would launch the great tribulation of the last days. The Matthaean form of his discourse envisages the abomination as "standing in the holy place" (Matt 24:15). This has sometimes been thought to point to the Roman legionaries setting up their standards in the temple court while the sanctuary was going up in flames at the end of August, A.D. 70, and offering sacrifice to them opposite the east gate (Josephus, *Bell.* 6.316). While Josephus may have seen a fulfillment of Daniel's prophecy in this event (cf. Bruce, "Josephus and Daniel"), the Evangelists probably did not; the temple court was not "the holy place," and there was no demand that the Jews should join in the worship of the Roman standards. Besides, by the time that this act of sacrilege took place, it was too late for those in Judea to "flee to the mountains."

2. *In the Apocalypse*

Antichrist appears again in the NT in the Apocalypse, although he is not called by that name there. The beast from the abyss which kills the two witnesses of God in Rev 11:7 is introduced more formally in Rev 13. In the first ten verses of that chapter we can hardly fail to recognize a more detailed description of the man of lawlessness of 2 Thess 2, although in Revelation there is some oscillation between the antichristian power and the individual in whom that power is vested for the time being. But for John of Patmos the antichristian power is unambiguously the Roman Empire which, with Nero's assault on the Christians of Rome in the aftermath of the great fire of A.D. 64, had embarked on the intermittent course of persecution of the church which was to last for two and a half centuries.

But the fact that the imperial power persecuted Christians would not have sufficed to equate it with Antichrist in their eyes. Nero's attack on them may have been capricious, but the real issue between church and empire in the generations which followed was a religious one. The imperial power claimed divine honors which Christians could not conscientiously accord it. When the emperor claimed the title κύριος in a divine sense, they were bound to refuse it; to them there was one Lord, Jesus Christ, and to grant the title to anyone else in the sense in which they used it of Christ would have been high treason against him. The emperor's claim to the title in that sense made him Antichrist, a rival Christ, who treated the refusal of the divine honors which he claimed as high treason against *him*, or against the Roman state.

John sees this state of affairs developing until it reaches its climax in the first beast of Revelation 13, the ultimate Antichrist. The depiction of this beast represents a conjunction of ancient symbols. Some of these were of great antiquity; his seven heads, for example, link him with Leviathan, the primeval monster that symbolizes the unruly deep, curbed by the Creator's fiat. His ten horns link him with the fourth beast of Daniel's vision of judgment (Dan 7:7). (The fact that the great red dragon of Rev 12:3 also has seven heads and ten horns indicates that it is he who energizes the beast, as Rev 13:2b states in less pictorial language.) It is not only

with Daniel's fourth beast that John's beast is linked; he incorporates features of all four of Daniel's beasts, and he also takes over the functions
of the "little horn" which Daniel saw sprouting from the head of his fourth
beast; like the "little horn" (Dan 7:21), he "makes war with the saints
and prevails against them" (Rev. 13:7). Like the man of lawlessness, he
receives all but universal worship. The duration of his rule (forty-two
months) is based on Dan 7:25; 9:27; 12:7.

In the receiving of worldwide worship, John's imperial beast is greatly
helped by the "false prophet," portrayed as "another beast which rose
out of the earth" in Rev 13:11. It is this false prophet who performs the
"mighty works and signs and lying wonders" by which, according to 2
Thess 2:9, 10, people are beguiled into worshiping the man of lawlessness.
Here John may have had in mind the priesthood of the emperor-worship
which had been established as a popular cult in the province of Asia since
29 B.C.

John foresees the end-product of the beast's regime to be a social and
economic boycott of all who refuse to worship him, cutting them off from
access to the necessities of life. But, as in 2 Thess 2:8, the man of lawlessness
is destroyed by the Advent of Christ, so in Rev 19:20 the beast and the
false prophet are consigned to perdition by the victorious Word of God
at his appearing.

In Rev 17 the imperial beast reappears, serving as a mount for the
scarlet woman, the city of Rome. The beast's seven heads are interpreted
incidentally as the city's seven hills but more importantly as seven emperors,
five of whom have come and gone, one of whom is currently on the throne,
and the seventh of whom will rule only for a short time. The eighth emperor,
who will succeed the short-lived seventh, will be the demonically energized
persecuting Antichrist, but in fact he will be one of the seven, restored
to life. (He is identical with the head which, according to Rev 13:3, had
its mortal wound healed.) It has been supposed by many commentators
that this detail reflects the belief in *Nero redivivus*. The identity of this
demonic ruler is not divulged; the numerical value of his name is said
to be 666, which might point to Nero Caesar (Heb. קסר נרון, so spelled
in Mur 18.1, dated A.D. 55/56). Certainly there is clear evidence in the
generations immediately following that the last Antichrist was envisaged
by many Christians as a returning Nero.

3. *The imperial persecutor*

The *Ascension of Isaiah*, an early Christian document, incorporates a *Testament of Hezekiah*, in which the ultimate Antichrist appears as an incarnation
of Beliar (the Greek spelling of Belial, as in 2 Cor 6:15), the spirit of
evil in the world. This expected incarnation of Beliar, moreover, is identified
with the returning Nero, described by King Hezekiah as "a lawless king,
the slayer of his mother" (*Asc Isa* 4:2)—a reference to Nero's widely suspected responsibility for the killing of the younger Agrippina. This king,
Hezekiah continues, "will persecute the plant which the twelve apostles
of the Beloved have planted" (*Asc Isa* 4:3).

From about the same date (late first century A.D.) some of the *Sibylline Oracles* foretell the domination of Beliar, who will be burned up with "all men of pride, all who put their trust in him" (*Or Sib* 3.63–75), and also predict the return of Nero (*Or Sib* 5.137–154), without apparently identifying the two, for Nero is an impious tyrant while Beliar is a false prophet who leads many astray, including "many faithful and elect among the Hebrews."

Both these manifestations of Antichrist—the false prophet and the persecuting tyrant—are found in early Christian literature. But during the age of imperial repression of the church the persecuting tyrant naturally occupied a prominent place in Christian thought about Antichrist. The author of the *Ep. of Barnabas* (*c.* A.D. 90) seems to have envisaged him as overthrowing the Flavian dynasty of emperors (his interpretation of the three "horns" of Dan 7:8, 20) and ruling in their place (4:4, 5). This author was also moved to the conviction that the last days had set in by a report that the temple in Jerusalem was about to be rebuilt (inevitably, from his viewpoint, an antichristian institution). These last days would consummate the epoch of evil, controlled by the power variously called "the black one" and "the wicked archon" (2:1; 4:9, 13).

Mention has been made above (see comment on 2:2) of the opinion expressed (by a Christian named Judas, in a discourse on the seventy heptads of Dan 9:24–27) that the severity of the persecution of the church under Septimius Severus (A.D. 202) pointed to the imminent approach of Antichrist.

Christian perspective on the subject was naturally changed when the empire began to show favor to the church instead of persecuting it. On the other hand, the Jews suffered more persecution under the Christian emperors than they had done under their pagan predecessors; it is in the post-Constantinian age that Jewish literature first presents a Roman Antichrist, in the person of Armillus (probably a corruption of Romulus), who is to be slain by the Messiah (*Tg. Isa* 11:4, for example, says of the "shoot from the stump of Jesse," that "with the breath of his lips he shall slay the wicked Armillus").

4. *The false prophet*

The portrayal of the Antichrist as a false prophet and misleader of the elect rather than a persecutor is also attested in the NT writings; indeed, the only explicit NT instances of ἀντίχριστος relate to false teaching. John in his letters sees the spirit of Antichrist manifesting itself in contemporary docetic teaching which denied Christ's coming "in flesh" (1 John 4:2, 3; 2 John 7); those who misled people by such teaching he describes as "many antichrists" whose activity was a token that it was now "the last hour" (1 John 2:18).

While Jude does not use the term ἀντίχριστος, it is probable that, when he denounces certain false teachers as "loud-mouthed boasters" (v 16), he alludes to the "little horn" of Dan 7:8 with "a mouth speaking great things" and to the self-willed king of Dan 11:36 who "shall speak astonishing things against the God of gods" (the Theodotionic version calls those "astonishing things" ὑπέρογκα, the same adjective as is used of the heretics' boastful words in Jude 16 and 2 Pet 2:18).

The perspective of John's letters reappears in Polycarp's *Letter to the Philippians* (*c.* A.D. 120). "Whosoever does not confess that Jesus Christ has come in the flesh is antichrist. And whosoever does not confess the testimony of the cross is of the devil; and whoever perverts the oracles of the Lord to his own lusts and says that there is neither resurrection nor judgment—he is Satan's firstborn" (7:1).

By "the testimony of the cross" Polycarp perhaps means the witness which the passion and death of Jesus bore to his genuine manhood (cf. John 19:35; 1 John 5:6–8). "Satan's firstborn" is presumably a synonym for "antichrist"; on a later occasion, when Marcion met Polycarp and sought his recognition, Polycarp is said to have replied, "I recognize—Satan's firstborn" (Euseb. *HE* 4.14.7).

5. *In Irenaeus and his successors*

The idea that Antichrist will be a Jew is first extant in Irenaeus (*c.* A.D. 180). It may have been derived from Papias of Hierapolis, but certainty on this is unattainable because of the fragmentary preservation of his work. (Some have discerned a still earlier reference to the idea in John 5:43, where Jesus says to his critics in Jerusalem, "I have come in my Father's name, and you do not receive me; if another comes in his own name, him you will receive"—but this is very uncertain.)

According to Irenaeus, the Roman Empire is to be partitioned among ten kings (cf. Rev 17:12), in whose days Antichrist will arise and lead the final apostasy. He is identified with the man of lawlessness (2 Thess 2:3), the abomination of desolation (Matt 24:15 par.), the little horn (Dan 7:8), the "king of bold countenance" (Dan 8:23), the deceiver who is to come in his own name (John 5:43), the beast from the abyss (Rev 11:7; 17:8, etc.). His rule will mark the completion of six millennia of world history; his overthrow will be followed by the seventh (sabbatic) millennium. Irenaeus makes various attempts to solve the riddle of the number of the beast; *Euanthas*, *Lateinos* and *Teitan* are put forward as possible solutions, but he wisely refuses to dogmatize. He bases Antichrist's Jewish origin—more particularly, his derivation from the tribe of Dan—on Jer 8:16 LXX: "From Dan we shall hear the sound of the speed of his horses; at the sound of the neighing of his cavalry the whole earth shakes; he will come and devour the earth and its fullness, the city and those who dwell therein." These words, spoken by the prophet with reference to a Gentile invader, are interpreted of Antichrist; "from Dan" is understood not geographically but genealogically, and this, says Irenaeus, is why Dan is omitted from the list of tribes in Rev 7:5–8. Antichrist is thus pictured as an apostate Jew, sitting enthroned in the temple of Jerusalem, and claiming to be worshiped there as God (*Adv. Haer.* 5.25–30).

Hippolytus's treatise *On Antichrist* (*c.* A.D. 200) takes over and elaborates the ideas found in Irenaeus, including the derivation of Antichrist from the tribe of Dan. If Jacob says, "Judah is a lion's whelp" (Gen 49:9), referring to Christ as the lion of the tribe of Judah, Moses says, "*Dan* is a lion's whelp" (Deut 33:22), referring to Antichrist as a counterfeit imitation of the true Christ. And when Jacob says, "Dan shall be a serpent in the way" (Gen 49:17), the allusion to the old serpent of Eden (Hippolytus thinks) is too evident to be missed. But Jacob also says, "Dan shall judge his people" (Gen 49:16). This, says Hippolytus (who would probably have been unaware of the play on words in Hebrew), is not (as others thought) a reference to Samson, the judge from the tribe of Dan, but to Antichrist as the unjust judge, in which role he figures in one of the Gospel parables (Luke 18:2–5).

Hippolytus repeats the various identifications of Antichrist made by Irenaeus and other predecessors, but he recognizes him further in the Assyrian of Isaiah 10:12–19, the Babylonian king of Isa 14:4–21, the prince of Tyre of Ezek 28:2–10. (This joining together of distinct enemies of Israel in earlier days and giving them a unitive eschatological interpretation is similar to the method of OT exegesis attested in the Qumran texts.) Antichrist, according to Hippolytus, is also the partridge of Jer 17:11 (he adds a brief excursus on the natural history of the partridge), and the sender of ambassadors in vessels of papyrus described in Isa 18:2, carrying his directives against the saints. Exegesis has here slipped its moorings to drift in the sea of imagination (*De Antichristo* 7, 14–18, 54–58).

Victorinus of Pettau (martyred A.D. 303), the earliest Latin commentator on the Apocalypse, is important not only in his own right but also because he preserves material from earlier writers no longer extant, particularly Papias. On Rev 11:7, where the "beast that ascends from the abyss" first appears, Victorinus explains this designation in terms of the Old Latin translation of Ezek 31:3–9 LXX (which he mistakenly attributes to Isaiah, perhaps by confusion with Isa 10:34). In the Greek text of Ezek 31, Assur (the Assyrian) is a cypress in Lebanon nourished by the waters ("the many thousands of men," says Victorinus, "who will be subject to him") and caused to grow high by the abyss (which, says Victorinus, "belched him forth").

Victorinus then quotes from 2 Thess 2:7–12, saying that the statement "the mystery of lawlessness is already at work" was intended to show that the coming Antichrist was the man who was even then emperor, i.e. Nero (that Nero was not yet emperor when the letters to the Thessalonians were written would not have occurred to Victorinus).

On Satan's expulsion from heaven in Rev 12:9 Victorinus says: "This is the beginning of the advent of Antichrist. However, Elijah must first prophesy and there must be times of peace then; so it is after that, when the three years and six months of Elijah's prophesying have been completed, that Antichrist, with all the renegade angels, is to be cast out of heaven (to which hitherto he has had the right to ascend). That Antichrist is thus raised up from hell is further attested by the apostle Paul when he says, 'unless first there come the man of sin, the son of perdition, the adversary, who will exalt himself above everything that is called god or that is worshipped.' "

There is some confusion here between Antichrist, who is energized by Satan, and Satan himself; and it is curious to be told that Antichrist is both cast down from heaven and raised up from hell.

Following Irenaeus (*Adv. Haer.* 5.30.3), Victorinus dates the Apocalypse in the time of Domitian (A.D. 81–96); therefore Domitian, he reckons, is the sixth ruler of Revelation 17:10 (the "one" who "is"), while the seventh (who "has not yet come") is Nerva (A.D. 96–98). The eighth is Nero *redivivus*, the "head" of Rev 12:3, whose "mortal wound was healed."

But Victorinus's really original contribution to the understanding of Antichrist is his combining of Nero *redivivus* with the expectation of a Jewish Antichrist; Nero will come back to life as a Jew, and will indeed demand that all his subjects accept circumcision. It is the new name which he is to bear in his reincarnation that will have (in Greek) the numerical value of 666: this, says Victorinus, will enable the wise to recognize his identity when he appears. He will erect a golden image and require it to be worshiped, as Nebuchadnezzar did. This image, the "abomination of desolation," representing Antichrist himself, will stand in the temple of Jerusalem. But he will meet his doom at the Advent of Christ, and his dominion will be superseded by the millennial reign of the saints.

With the peace of the church, which dawned ten years after the death of Victorinus, the line of interpretation which he represents died out, until aspects of it were revived by Francisco Ribeira in the sixteenth century and again in a fresh form by the latter-day futurism pioneered by Manuel de Lacunza and others at the end of the eighteenth and beginning of the nineteenth centuries. But a line of interpretation which was reasonable while the Roman Empire still existed as a persecuting power loses something of its persuasiveness when it has to be stretched on a Procrustean bed to make room for a gap of many centuries between the fall of that empire and the rise of Antichrist.

6. *Later developments*

In the post-Constantinian age the form of the expectation of Antichrist was inevitably modified. He was envisaged as an enemy of the Christendom which now comprised both church and empire, but opinions continued to differ on whether he would arise from without or within. On the one hand he was envisaged as an external enemy, like Genseric the Vandal in the fifth century (whose name could be spelled in Greek so as to yield the total 666) or Muhammad in the seventh century. On the other hand he was envisaged as an apostate individual or group arising within Christendom. Such an individual was recognized by some in a pope, like John XII (955–963), or in a secular ruler, like Frederick Barbarossa (Holy Roman Emperor, 1155–90).

If an individual pope was identified with Antichrist, he was regarded as an unworthy occupant of a sacred office, a usurper "taking his seat in the sanctuary of God" (2 Thess 2:4). When Joachim of Fiore met Richard Coeur-de-Lion at Messina in the winter of 1190/91, he may have had such a development in mind when he told him that Antichrist "is already born in the city of Rome and will set himself yet higher in the see apostolic" (Reeves, *Joachim,* 136). But some of Joachim's disciples, notably Gerard of Borgo San Donnino (in his introduction to a collection of Joachim's works, published about 1254 under the title *The Eternal Gospel*), went farther and identified the Papacy itself with the Antichrist. This idea lived on in some circles throughout the later Middle Ages and was taken up by Luther, Calvin and other reformers in the sixteenth century. It attained confessional status in many churches of the Reformation; for example, according to the *Westminster Confession of Faith* (1646), "the Pope of Rome . . . is that Antichrist, that man of sin, and son of perdition, that exalteth himself, in the Church, against Christ and all that is called God" (25:6). The first Reformed exegete to abandon the identification of the Papacy with Antichrist was Hugo Grotius (1644).

On the other side, the adherents of the old religion were not slow to recognize the features of Antichrist in Luther and his followers. Luther's name could, with a modicum of ingenuity, be made to yield the sum of 666; he himself was identified by one exegete with the fallen star which is permitted in Rev 9:1, 2 to unlock the exit from the abyss, and another exegete identified the locusts which thereupon emerged from the abyss (Rev 9:3–11) with the Lutherans.

No identification of the mystery of lawlessness can be acceptable if it would not have been intelligible to the Christians to whom 2 Thessalonians was first addressed. Individuals or systems figuring in the subsequent course of Christian history cannot be considered when the primary application of the apostolic words is being decided. As for a possible further application, the best policy might be for everyone who studies the matter to ask the question which came to the lips of the disciples in the upper room when they were told that one of them was a traitor: "Lord, is it I?" The spirit of Antichrist will be strengthened if Christians allow themselves to be seduced by it and to foster it in their hearts; it will be diminished and weakened if they individually watch for every manifestation of it within themselves, cast it out and wage unceasing war against it, confessing Jesus as Lord and Christ not in word only but in deed and in truth.

7. *The restraining power*

Unlike the man of lawlessness, the restraining power does not seem to figure in any NT writing outside 2 Thess 2:6, 7. There is indeed a figure in the Apocalypse who is in a position to exercise restraint in this situation: the "angel of the abyss" whose name is Apollyon (Rev 9:11) holds the key by which he can release the demonic locusts from the abyss and lock the dragon up there (Rev 20:1–3), so that he could presumably have hindered the seven-headed beast from coming up from the abyss (Rev 11:7), but he is not said to have done so.

Since the force being restrained is evil, the restrainer might be thought to be good. God himself is not the restrainer, for the restrainer is to "be taken out of the way" (2 Thess 2:7); yet the restrainer is identified with God by F. J. A. Hort (*Life and Letters* i, 213), Strobel (*Untersuchungen*, 98–116), Ernst (*Gegenspieler*, 55–57) and Aus ("God's Plan," 544–552: God's plan is τὸ κατέχον, God is ultimately ὁ κατέχων and it is the man of lawlessness who is to 'be taken out of the way"). At the other extreme the restrainer is identified with the devil by Giblin (*Threat*, 230, 234: the neuter τὸ κατέχον denotes "satanic activity").

Among other identifications of the restraining power (apart from those referred to in the comments on 2:6, 7) may be mentioned Warfield's view that it was the continuing existence of the (second) Jewish commonwealth; "so soon as the Jewish apostasy was complete and Jerusalem given over to the Gentiles . . . the separation of Christianity from Judaism, which had already begun, became evident to every eye; the conflict between the new faith and heathenism, culminating in and now alive almost only in the Emperor-worship, became intense, and the persecuting power of the empire was inevitably let loose" ("The Prophecies . . . ," 473).

This interpretation, however, does not account for the reserve with which the restraining power is mentioned, nor does it adequately account for the personal restrainer (ὁ κατέχων). Warfield, indeed, doubts if the masculine participle "demands interpretation as a person," but if it does, "it might possibly be referred without too great pressure to James of Jerusalem" (474).

One merit of the imperial interpretation preferred in the comment above (p. 171), is that it accounts at one and the same time for the diplomatic allusiveness of the language and for the alternation between the neuter and masculine genders (τὸ κατέχον and ὁ κατέχων). It may be added that even after the Roman Empire passed away, the principle of the wording did not become obsolete, for when the secular power in any form continues to discharge its divinely ordained commission, it restrains evil and prevents the outburst of anarchy.

If, however, Paul meant that the imperial power held back the advent of Antichrist, while John the seer identified the imperial power with Antichrist, must it be concluded that Paul and John held irreconcilable positions on this matter? Not necessarily. Is it conceivable, then, that the restrainer should himself become the Antichrist? Quite conceivable—the crisis provoked by Gaius, ten years before this letter was written, showed what the imperial power itself was capable of, and what had happened then might happen again, without such timely relief as brought that crisis to an end. But while civil authority was maintained as it was during the principate of Claudius, lawlessness was held at bay and the cause of Christ advanced throughout the Roman world. Indeed, to such an extent was good order maintained even under the persecuting empire that Tertullian, a century and a half later, believed that Antichrist could not appear so long as the Roman state remained intact.

Further Thanksgiving, Encouragement and Prayer (2 Thess 2:13–17)

(a) Thanksgiving (2:13–14)

Bibliography

Ellis, E. E. "Paul and his Co-Workers." *NTS* 17 (1970–71) 437–452. **Harnack, A. von** "Das Problem des zweiten Thessalonicherbriefs." *SAB* 31 (1910) 560–578. **O'Brien, P. T.** *Introductory Thanksgivings in the Letters of Paul.* NovTSup 49. Leiden: Brill, 1977. **Schmithals, W.** *Paul and the Gnostics.* Tr. J. E. Steely. Nashville/New York: Abingdon, 1972.

Translation

¹³ *But as for us, it is our duty to give thanks to God for you always, brothers so dear to the Lord,* ᵃ *because God chose you as firstfruits* ᵇ *for salvation by sanctification of the Spirit and belief in the truth.* ¹⁴ *It was for this* ᶜ *that he called you* ᵈ *through our gospel, that you might obtain the glory of our Lord Jesus Christ.*

Notes

ᵃ For κυρίου a few witnesses (influenced evidently by 1 Thess 1:4) read θεοῦ (D* latᵇ ᵐ ᵛᵍ).
ᵇ ἀπαρχήν is read by B F G P 33 81 1739 2464 *al* latᵛᵍ syrʰᵉˡ copᵇᵒ; ἀπ' ἀρχῆς ("from [the] beginning") by ℵ D Ψ byz latᵛᵉᵗ syrᵖᵉˢʰ copᵃ Ambst.
ᶜ εἰς ὅ [καί]. καί is omitted by A B D Ψ byz latᵃ ᵇ ᵐ* ᵛᵍ.codd syrᵖᵉˢʰ Ambst.
ᵈ For ὑμᾶς ("you") ἡμᾶς ("us") is read by A B D* 1881 *pc* latᵇ ᶠ ᵛᵍ.codd

Form/Structure/Setting

The thanksgiving report in vv 13–14 is so similar to the introductory thanksgiving of 1:3, so far at least as its opening clause is concerned, that Schmithals has identified here the proem or introductory thanksgiving of a separate letter ("Thessalonians C"), which has lost its prescript and concluding salutation, but whose body has survived, displaced, as 2:1–12 (*Paul and the Gnostics*, 193, 194).

It is more satisfactory to recognize in this thanksgiving the resumption of the introductory thanksgiving of 1:3, just as 1 Thess 2:13 resumes the introductory thanksgiving of 1 Thess 1:2. Except that the customary καθώς clause (found in 1:3, καθὼς ἄξιόν ἐστιν) is missing here, this "is a complete thanksgiving with its principal verb (ἡμεῖς δὲ ὀφείλομεν εὐχαριστεῖν, 2:13), personal object (τῷ θεῷ), temporal adverb (πάντοτε), pronominal object phrase (περὶ ὑμῶν), and causal ὅτι -clause" (O'Brien, *Thanksgivings*, 167).

Comment

13. Ἡμεῖς δὲ ὀφείλομεν εὐχαριστεῖν τῷ θεῷ πάντοτε περὶ ὑμῶν, "it is our duty to give thanks to God for you," a repetition of the first clause of 1:3, introduced by the emphatic ἡμεῖς. The subject of Antichrist has been dealt with and the recipients' uncertainty about the Day of the Lord has been cleared up; now the note of thanksgiving is resumed.

ἀδελφοὶ ἠγαπημένοι ὑπὸ κυρίου. Cf. 1 Thess 1:4, ἀδελφοὶ ἠγαπημένοι ὑπὸ [τοῦ] θεοῦ. The κύριος, "the Lord," here is probably Jesus.

ὅτι εἴλατο ὑμᾶς ὁ θεός, "because God has chosen you." This is the only place in the NT where the simple verb αἱρεῖσθαι is used (in the middle voice) of God's choosing his people. The compound ἐξαιρεῖσθαι appears in Gal 1:4 (ὅπως ἐξέληται ἡμᾶς, "that he might deliver us"). But the sense of αἱρεῖσθαι here is close to that of ἐκλέγεσθαι elsewhere (as in Eph 1:4, καθὼς ἐξελέξατο ἡμᾶς); the reference, as in 1 Thess 1:4 (see comment ad loc.), is to the readers' "election" (ἐκλογή).

ἀπαρχήν, "firstfruits." The evidence (see p. 189 above) is slightly stronger for ἀπαρχήν then for ἀπ' ἀρχῆς, "from the beginning" (for which πρὸ καταβολῆς κόσμου in Eph 1:4 might provide a sense-parallel). But in what sense could the readers be called firstfruits? The Thessalonian believers could not be called the firstfruits of Macedonia (cf. the "firstfruits of Achaia" in 1 Cor 16:15 or the "firstfruits of Asia" in Rom 16:5), for the Philippian church was established before theirs. Elsewhere in the NT, believers in Christ are the firstfruits of God's creation (Jas 1:18); faithful confessors and martyrs are the firstfruits of mankind (Rev 14:4). But a more particular reference is apparently required here. Harnack ("Problem") saw a reference to the Jewish Christians of Thessalonica; according to Acts 17:4 it was members of the synagogue congregation (including, to be sure, a good number of God-fearers) who were the first converts in the city. But this understanding of ἀπαρχή would be acceptable only if there were adequate ground for the view that 2 Thessalonians was addressed to the converts from Judaism, and such adequate ground there is not. Ellis ("Paul and his Co-Workers," 450), arguing that 2 Thessalonians was intended more particularly for Paul's Thessalonian co-workers, thinks that it was they who formed the ἀπαρχή. " 'The first fruits' is a concept deeply embedded in the Old Testament cultus as the portion dedicated to God and that which sanctifies the whole. . . . The . . . Thessalonian brothers . . . are the consecrated first-born who, like the Levites, are set apart for the work of God." But the church as a whole is the ἀπαρχή of mankind to God.

εἰς σωτηρίαν, "for salvation"; this is the object for which God has chosen them. It is a matter both of present enjoyment and of future hope (for the future hope cf. 1 Thess 5:9).

ἐν ἁγιασμῷ πνεύματος καὶ πίστει ἀληθείας, "in sanctification of the Spirit and belief in the truth"; these are means by which the salvation is secured rather than attendant circumstances (i.e. ἐν has instrumental rather than comitative force). For sanctification effected by the Spirit cf. 1 Thess 4:7,

8; also 3:13; 5:23, with comments ad loc. Sanctification is the Spirit's present work in believers; it will be completed at the Parousia, when Christ is "glorified in his holy ones" (1:10). As this hope of glory (i.e. consummated salvation) is assured to the Thessalonian converts "because," as the writers have said, "our testimony to you was believed" (1:10), so here the Spirit's sanctifying work is linked with their "belief in the truth" (ἀληθείας is objective genitive). The contrast is plain between those now addressed and "all who did not believe the truth but took pleasure in unrighteousness" (v 12). The "truth" is the revelation of God and his way of salvation imparted in the gospel.

14. εἰς ὃ [καὶ] ἐκάλεσεν ὑμᾶς. For the call of God cf. 1 Thess 2:12; 4:7; 5:24, with comments ad loc.

διὰ τοῦ εὐαγγελίου ἡμῶν, "through our gospel" (for this expression cf. 1 Thess 1:5, with comment ad loc.); "our gospel" (the gospel which we preach) is identical with "the gospel of our Lord Jesus" (1:8).

εἰς περιποίησιν δόξης τοῦ κυρίου ἡμῶν Ἰησοῦ Χριστοῦ, "for the obtaining of the glory of our Lord Jesus Christ." For this sense of περιποίησις cf. 1 Thess 5:9, where God is said to have appointed his people "for the obtaining (εἰς περιποίησιν) of salvation through our Lord Jesus Christ." For δόξα in this sense cf. 1 Thess 2:12, where God is said to call them "into his own . . . glory" (see comment ad loc.). The glory is here said to be Christ's; the Christian gospel is "the gospel of the glory of Christ, who is the image of God" (2 Cor 4:4), and through it is communicated "the light of the knowledge of the glory of God in the face of Jesus Christ" (2 Cor 4:6). The glory of Christ which his people are to obtain is their sharing in his glory at the Parousia (see comment on ἐνδοξασθῆναι, 1:10).

Explanation

The writers express their thanks to God that he has chosen these Thessalonian believers—not simply that he chose them in Christ before all worlds but that his eternal choice of them has now been manifested in time by their wholehearted response to the gospel. This response was made when in due course they heard his call—"those whom he predestined he also called" (Rom 8:30)—and his call to them proved to be effectual in faith and life.

It is a travesty of God's electing grace to suppose that, because he chooses some for salvation, all the others are thereby consigned to perdition. On the contrary, if some are chosen for special blessing, it is in order that others may be blessed through them and with them. This is a constant feature in the pattern of divine election throughout the Bible story, from Abraham onward. Those who are chosen constitute the firstfruits, bearing the promise of a rich harvest to come.

The salvation for which the people of God have been chosen comprises much more than their deliverance from the wrath to come. It involves, in this life, their believing acceptance of the truth of the gospel in which

God's call was conveyed to them, together with the sanctifying ministry of the Holy Spirit within them; while in the life to come it carries the sure promise of their participation in the glory of their Lord.

These two verses, says James Denney, "are a system of theology in miniature. The apostle's thanksgiving covers the whole work of creation from the eternal choice of God to the obtaining of the glory of our Lord Jesus Christ in the world to come."

(b) *Encouragement* (2:15)

Bibliography

Bruce, F. F. *Tradition Old and New.* Exeter: Paternoster Press, 1970. **Campenhausen, H. von** *Tradition and Life in the Church.* Tr. A. V. Littledale. London: Collins, 1968. **Congar, Y. M.-J.** *Tradition and Traditions.* Tr. M. Naseby and T. Rainborough. London: Burns & Oates, 1966. **Cullmann, O.** *"Kyrios* as Designation for the Oral Tradition Concerning Jesus." *SJT* 3 (1950) 180–197. **Cullmann, O.** "The Tradition." In *The Early Church,* ed. and tr. A. J. B. Higgins. London: SCM Press, 1956, 55–99. **Hanson, R. P. C.** *Tradition in the Early Church.* London: SCM Press, 1962. **O'Brien, P. T.** *Introductory Thanksgivings in the Letters of Paul.* NovTSup 49. Leiden: Brill, 1977. **Schmithals, W.** *Paul and the Gnostics.* Tr. J. E. Steely. Nashville/New York, Abingdon, 1972.

Translation

¹⁵ So then, ª brothers, stand fast ᵇ and hold the traditions which you were taught, whether by word (of mouth) or by our epistle.

Notes

ª ἄρα οὖν (cf. 1 Thess. 5:6), a combination peculiar to Paul in the NT, is intended "presumably to provide an emphatically inferential connective" (M. E. Thrall, *Greek Particles in the New Testament,* Grand Rapids, MI: Eerdmans, 1962, 10).

ᵇ στήκετε, imperative (as in 1 Cor 16:13; Gal 5:1; Phil 4:1); cf. its use as indicative in 1 Thess 3:8 (p. 65 note c).

Form/Structure/Setting

This verse presents "a paraenetic thrust . . . in which the consequences (ἄρα οὖν) of the preceding are drawn out" (O'Brien, *Thanksgivings,* 170, 171).

Schmithals (*Paul and the Gnostics,* 193, 194) finds here the beginning of the letter-closing or "eschatocol" of "Thessalonians C" (the "body" of which, 2:1–12, has in his view been displaced from its proper position between 2:14 and 2:15). The bibliographical improbability of this analysis is such that it would be acceptable only if the evidence forced it on the reader—which it does not.

Comment

2:15. στήκετε. That their converts should "stand firm" in the Lord is the very breath of life to Paul and his colleagues, as they have already said (1 Thess 3:8); they therefore encourage them to go on doing so.

κρατεῖτε τὰς παραδόσεις. One way of standing firm in the Lord is to "hold fast to the traditions" which had been delivered to them. There is no tension between the vitality of the risen Lord and the dead hand of tradition; the traditions mentioned comprise all that is involved in the practical acknowledgment of his lordship. Their content was not only derived by transmission from the historical Jesus (cf. 1 Cor 11:23); it was continuously validated by the risen Lord through his Spirit in his apostles and their followers (cf. Cullmann, "The Tradition," 66–75). The main lines of teaching belonging to "the tradition of Christ" are indicated in the comment on 1 Thess 4:1 (καθὼς παρελάβετε); one particular aspect of this tradition is emphasized in 3:6 below.

The Thessalonian Christians were not the only ones in the Gentile mission area to be instructed in these matters; it is plain that the Corinthian church received similar instructions from Paul, and in their letter to him assured him that they maintained the traditions which he delivered to them. He replied, commending them for this (καθὼς παρέδωκα ὑμῖν, τὰς παραδόσεις κατέχετε, 1 Cor 11:2), but went on to suggest that their faithfulness to these traditions was not so complete as they supposed.

εἴτε διὰ λόγου εἴτε δι' ἐπιστολῆς ἡμῶν, "whether by word (of mouth) or by letter of ours"; ἡμῶν probably refers as much to λόγου as to ἐπιστολῆς ("whether by our oral or written teaching."). If one particular letter is in view, it is probably 1 Thessalonians (it might conceivably be 2 Thessalonians, but the aorist ἐδιδάχθητε is scarcely epistolary). There is no restriction of "tradition" to what is unwritten.

The εἴτε . . . εἴτε construction is reminiscent of that with recurrent οὔτε in v 2 above, but there is no εἴτε διὰ πνεύματος here. Schmithals thinks that the omission of this phrase is deliberate; the πνεῦμα was prone to be the vehicle of gnostic teaching, and appeal is never made to διδαχή or παράδοσις in the Pauline writings "in any context other than the anti-Gnostic battlefront" (*Paul and the Gnostics*, 209). As Paul in 1 Cor 15:1–8 appeals to the "tradition" as a weapon against the overrealized eschatology which led to the denial of the resurrection of the dead in the church of Corinth, so, Schmithals implies, appeal is made to the παράδοσις here for very much the same purpose in the church of Thessalonica. But the omission of εἴτε διὰ πνεύματος is much more simply explained. While διὰ λόγου could, in an appropriate context, include the word of prophecy, it probably does not include it here. There is a distinction in the Pauline writings between the gospel received by revelation (as in Gal 1:12) and the gospel received by tradition (as in 1 Cor 15:3), and the language of διδαχή and παράδοσις is appropriate to the latter, not to the former. Even communications made διὰ πνεύματος must be tested by their conformity to the παράδοσις and if they conflict with it they are to be refused (cf. 1 Thess 5: 19–22).

There is no possibility here (as with the construction ὡς δι' ἡμῶν in v 2) that the communications might *not* have come from the present writers; they appeal to what they were known to have taught.

Explanation

The spirit of Christian freedom and progress is by no means incompatible with loyalty to the primitive Christian heritage. Christian stability calls for the maintenance of Christian continuity, in belief and action alike, in corporate as in personal life. This maintenance of continuity is encouraged in the injunction to "hold the traditions." The Christian tradition, in all its variety, is rooted in the historical Jesus, in his redemptive work and in the way of life set out in his teaching, but as these are made good to one generation after another by the risen Lord through his Spirit, the Christian tradition remains alive and dynamic.

Other kinds of tradition are referred to with disapproval in the NT. Jesus rebuked some of his contemporaries because, as he said to them, "you leave the commandment of God, and hold fast the tradition of men" (Mark 7:8). Similarly, the false philosophy against which the Colossian Christians are put on their guard is described by Paul as "the tradition of men" (Col 2:8). But it is not tradition as such, but false, inadequate or outmoded tradition, that is deprecated. The tradition of Christ shares his truth, his adequacy and his abiding vitality.

The Jewish rabbis made a distinction between the written precepts of Moses' law and the oral "tradition of the elders." While in theory the oral law went back to Moses, who was said to have received it "from Sinai" together with the written law and delivered it to later generations through a succession of "tradents," in practice the oral tradition amplified and applied the principles of the written law. In Christianity too (especially in the Western church) the relation of unwritten tradition to canonical scripture has been ardently debated, but a widely accepted view today is that unwritten tradition performs an interpretative service for the written text and represents, in the words of Congar, "the living continuity of faith quickening God's people."

In NT times, however, the apostolic teaching was equally valid whether it was delivered by word of mouth or in written form. It was more satisfactory in general for the apostles to talk to their converts face to face; the very tone of voice they used could add something to the force of their words, as Paul confesses in Gal 4:20. But when face-to-face communication was not convenient, the teaching was imparted in a written letter. We in our day must be thankful that the latter course was so often necessary; the spoken words have gone beyond recall, but the letters remain, preserving the traditions for our instruction and obedience.

(c) *First Wish-Prayer* (2:16–17)

Bibliography

O'Brien, P. T. *Introductory Thanksgivings in the Letters of Paul.* NovTSup 49. Leiden: Brill, 1977. **Wiles, G. P.** *Paul's Intercessory Prayers.* SNTSMS 24. Cambridge: Cambridge University Press, 1974.

Translation

¹⁶ *Now may our Lord Jesus Christ himself and God our Father,*[a] *who has loved us and given us eternal encouragement and good hope by grace,*¹⁷ *encourage your hearts and establish you in every good work and word.*[b]

Notes

[a] [ὁ] θεὸς καὶ πατὴρ ἡμῶν. ὁ is omitted before θεός by BD*K 33 1739 1881 *al.* καί is inserted before ὁ πατήρ by A D² I Ψ byz lat[b d m vg] syr[hcl] (this καί would be epexegetic: "God, even our Father").

[b] ἔργῳ καὶ λόγῳ, for which the reverse order λόγῳ καὶ ἔργῳ is read by F G K *al* lat[b m] and ἔργῳ alone by 33 *pc.*

Form/Structure/Setting

Like the wish-prayers of 1 Thess 3:11–13 and 5:23, this wish-prayer begins with the emphatic αὐτός and is expressed by means of the aorist optative (παρακαλέσαι . . . στηρίξαι). Unlike those wish-prayers, however, it lacks an "eschatological climax."

The qualification of the twofold subject by the repeated definite article followed by two aorist participles (ἀγαπήσας . . . δούς) and their objects (the equivalent of an adjective clause) gives this wish-prayer something of the character of a collect in the third person (cf. the more elaborate example in Heb 13:20, 21).

Comment

2:16 Αὐτὸς δὲ ὁ κύριος ἡμῶν Ἰησοῦς Χριστὸς καὶ [ὁ] θεὸς ὁ πατὴρ ἡμῶν. . . . For the emphatic αὐτός in wish-prayers cf. 3:16; 1 Thess 3:11; 5:23. For the composite subject with singular verbs cf. 1 Thess 3:11; there "our God and Father" precedes "our Lord Jesus"; here "our Lord Jesus Christ" precedes "God our Father" (for this sequence cf. the apostolic benediction of 2 Cor 13:14). In such a context God and Christ are so completely united in action that either may be named before the other without making any difference to the sense.

ὁ ἀγαπήσας ἡμᾶς, "who has set his love on us" (so the force of the aorist might be brought out). For similar uses of the articulated aorist participle of ἀγαπᾶν cf. Rom 8:37; Gal 2:20 (with reference to Christ). Here ἀγαπήσας (like the following δούς) may agree formally with [ὁ] θεός but in sense it relates to both subjects, ὁ κύριος and [ὁ] θεός.

καὶ δοὺς παράκλησιν αἰωνίαν, "and has given us eternal encouragement." In Rom 15:5 Paul speaks of "the God of . . . παράκλησις"; cf. 2 Cor 1:3, θεός πάσης παρακλήσεως.

καὶ ἐλπίδα ἀγαθήν, "and good hope." For the collocation of encouragement and hope cf. Rom 15:4, "that by patience and by παράκλησις of the scriptures we might have ἐλπίς."

ἐν χάριτι, "by grace." The preposition ἐν might be instrumental, going closely in sense with δούς ("who by grace has given . . ."), or it might be comitative, linking "grace" with "encouragement" and "hope" ("who has given us encouragement and hope together with grace"). This latter construction, found (e.g.) in Eph 4:19 (ἐν πλεονεξίᾳ); 5:26 (ἐν ῥήματι); 6:24 (ἐν ἀφθαρσίᾳ), is less likely in the present context. Hope and grace are not natural concomitants; the grace is God's, the hope is ours, given us by his grace. It is because he gives his people "good (i.e. well-founded) hope" that he is "the God of hope" (Rom 15:13).

17. παρακαλέσαι, "encourage." Cf. 2 Cor 1:4, where God is ὁ παρακαλῶν ἡμᾶς ("the one who comforts us").

στηρίξαι, "establish." The implied object may be either ὑμᾶς or ὑμῶν τὰς καρδίας (the expressed object of παρακαλέσαι); cf. 1 Thess 3:13, εἰς τὸ στηρίξαι ὑμῶν τὰς καρδίας ("so as to establish your hearts") ἐν παντὶ ἔργῳ καὶ λόγῳ ἀγαθῷ. For the collocation of ἔργον and λόγος cf. Luke 24:19, δυνατὸς ἐν ἔργῳ καὶ λόγῳ, "mighty in word and deed" (of Jesus); Acts 7:22, δυνατὸς ἐν ἔργοις καὶ λόγοις αὐτοῦ (of Moses). Emphasis is laid on ἀγαθῷ by its repetition so soon after ἐλπίδα ἀγαθήν "good hope" in v 16. For ἔργον ἀγαθόν (ἔργα ἀγαθά) "good work(s)" cf. Rom 2:7; 2 Cor 9:8; Eph 2:10; Phil 1:6; Col 1:10, and especially the Pastorals (1 Tim 2:10; 5:10; 2 Tim 2:21; 3:17; Tit 1:16; 3:1).

Explanation

In the wish-prayer which brings this section of the letter to a close, the writers again bespeak divine encouragement and confirmation for their friends in Thessalonica, that in the hope imparted to them by God's grace they may act and speak as befits his children in their pagan environment.

On the naming of Christ before God at the beginning of this wish-prayer, in contrast to the naming of God before Christ in a similar construction in 1 Thessalonians 3:11, Neil says, "The only theological significance to be attached to the variations in order is that there is complete equality in the apostle's mind between the Father and the Son" (185). With this we may agree, bearing in mind that for Paul the equality was one of purpose and action rather than a metaphysical equality.

Further Prayer   (2 Thess 3:1–5)

(a) *Prayer Request* (3:1–2)

Bibliography

Dewailly, L. M. "Course et gloire de la parole (II Thess., III, 1)." *RB* 71 (1964) 25–41. **Funk, R. W.** "The Apostolic *Parousia:* Form and Significance." In *Christian History and Interpretation: Studies presented to John Knox,* ed. W. R. Farmer, C. F. D. Moule, R. R. Niebuhr. Cambridge: Cambridge University Press, 1967, 249–268. **Wiles, G. P.** *Paul's Intercessory Prayers.* SNTSMS 24. Cambridge: Cambridge University Press, 1974.

Translation

[1] *For the rest, brothers, pray for us, that the word of the Lord may speed on and be glorified,* [a] *as it has done among you.* [2] *(Pray) also that we may be delivered* [a] *from perverse and wicked men; for not all have faith.* [b]

Notes

[a] As in 1:11, ἵνα with the subjunctive after προσεύχεσθαι (or a verb of similar meaning) encroaches on the use of the infinitive to express an indirect request; cf. BDF § 392.1(c).

[b] οὐ γὰρ πάντων ἡ πίστις ("for not all have faith")—an instance of meiosis (understatement); cf. Rom 10·16, ἀλλ' οὐ πάντες ὑπήκουσαν τῷ εὐαγγελίῳ (where in fact only a minority had "obeyed the gospel"). The construction is illustrated in the trimeter quoted by Strabo, *Geog.* 8.6.20. οὐ παντός ἀνδρὸς ἐς Κόρινθον ἔσθ' ὁ πλοῦς ("not for every man is the voyage to Corinth").

Form/Structure/Setting

As in 1 Thess 5:25, the prayer request is emphasized by the vocative ἀδελφοί (cf. also Rom 15:30) and the intercessory aspect is indicated by the prepositional phrase περὶ ἡμῶν. Here the content of the prayer is made explicit by means of the ἵνα clauses (missing from 1 Thess 5:25). Noting that the prayer to be delivered from some peril is found also in Rom 15:31; 2 Cor 1:10, Funk adds that "it does not appear to be a constitutive element in the apostolic *parousia*" ("The Apostolic *Parousia,*" 253 n. 1).

Comment

3:1. Τὸ λοιπόν, "for the rest," "finally," an indication that the letter is drawing to a conclusion (even if the writers subsequently remember other matters which they must mention); cf. Phil 3:1; 4:8 (where the repeated τὸ λοιπόν may have belonged originally to two separate letters); also λοιπόν, 1 Thess 4:1; 13:11; τοῦ λοιποῦ, Gal 6:17.

προσεύχεσθε, ἀδελφοί, περὶ ἡμῶν; "brothers, pray for us," which is practically identical with the request for prayer in 1 Thess 5:25. Paul similarly requests his readers to pray for him in Rom 15:30; 2 Cor 1:11; Eph 6:19, 20; Phil 1:19; Col 4:3, 4.

ἵνα ὁ λόγος τοῦ κυρίου τρέχῃ, "that the word of the Lord (cf. 1 Thess 1:8) may run"; cf. Ps 147:15 (LXX 4), ἕως τάχους δραμεῖται ὁ λόγος αὐτοῦ, "his word runs swiftly." The primary object of the apostles' prayer requests is regularly the progress of the gospel (cf. Eph 6:19, 20; Col 4:3, 4). Paul sometimes speaks of his apostolic endeavors as "running" (cf. 1 Cor 9:24; Gal 2:2; Phil 2:16); here it is the message that runs rather than the messenger.

δοξάζηται, "may be received with honor" (so Lightfoot, who compares Acts 13:48, which tells how the Gentiles of Pisidian Antioch ἐδόξαζον τὸν λόγον τοῦ θεοῦ, "glorified the word of God").

καθὼς καὶ πρὸς ὑμᾶς, "even as also (it did) among you" (cf. 2:5) or ". . . (when it was brought) to you."

2. καὶ ἵνα ῥυσθῶμεν ἀπὸ κτλ, "and that we may be delivered from . . . ." Cf. Rom 15:31, where Paul asks the Roman Christians to pray for him, ἵνα ῥυσθῶ ἀπὸ τῶν ἀπειθούντων ἐν τῇ Ἰουδαίᾳ ("that I may be delivered from the unbelievers in Judea").

ἀπὸ τῶν ἀτόπων καὶ πονηρῶν ἀνθρώπων, "from the perverse and wicked men." For ἄτοπος ("out of place," "untoward," "improper") cf. Luke 23:41; Acts 25:5; 28:6. The writers have in mind here those opponents of the gospel who tried to stop its progress by stirring up attacks on those who preached it, like their enemies in Thessalonica who incited the rabble against them (Acts 17:5). The reference here is not restricted to Jews or Gentiles, to those in authority or the "rascal multitude"; it applies to all whose policy or activity hindered the spread of the saving message and worked to the detriment of the messengers.

οὐ γὰρ πάντων ἡ πίστις, "for not all have faith." The πίστις here is probably the believing response to the gospel; while some yielded such a response as soon as they heard it, others reacted with hostility. It is unlikely that in such an early document ἡ πίστις should mean "the faith" in the sense of the gospel itself or the body of Christian teaching presented to men and women for belief.

Explanation

While praying constantly for their converts, Paul and his colleagues felt the need of prayer for themselves and encouraged their converts to make the fellowship of prayer a reciprocal exercise. By praying for the missionaries, the converts were participating in the spread of the gospel. The missionaries were much more concerned that their gospel witness should not be impeded than they were for their own safety; they were expendable "earthen vessels" to which the treasure of the gospel was committed. But the enemies of the gospel tried to frustrate its progress by personal attacks on Paul and his associates, as had happened in Thessalonica and was happening right now in Corinth. Praying for Paul's preservation until his work was completed was tantamount to praying for the prosperity and accomplishment of the work which was entrusted to him.

(b) *Expression of Confidence* (3:3–4)

Bibliography

O'Brien, P. T. *Introductory Thanksgivings in the Letters of Paul.* NovTSup 49. Leiden: Brill, 1977. **Wiles, G. P.** *Paul's Intercessory Prayers.* SNTSMS 24. Cambridge: Cambridge University Press, 1974.

Translation

³ *But the Lord* ^a *is faithful: he will establish* ^b *you and guard you from the evil one.* ⁴ *And we have confidence in the Lord concerning you, that you are doing and will continue to do* ^c *the things which we charge (you to do).* ^d

Notes

^a For ὁ κύριος A D*·² F G 2464 *pc* lat^{vet vg.cl} cop^{bo.cod} Ambst read ὁ θεός (under the influence of 1 Cor 1:9, etc.).

^b For στηρίξει F G read τηρήσει ("will keep").

^c [καὶ] ποιεῖτε καὶ ποιήσετε· καὶ before ποιεῖτε is omitted by ℵ* A 6 629 1739 *pc* lat^{b d m vg.codd}; D* reads ποιήσατε (imperative) for καὶ ποιεῖτε. For the whole phrase F G read καὶ ἐποιήσατε καὶ ποιεῖτε, B lat^a cop^{sa} read καὶ ἐποιήσατε καὶ ποιεῖτε καὶ ποιήσετε.

^d ἃ παραγγέλλομεν, to which ὑμῖν is added by A D² F G byz lat^{a m} syr.

Form/Structure/Setting

The prayer request of vv 1, 2 leads into a confident appeal to the Lord's faithfulness. The expression πιστὸς ὁ κύριος (or πιστὸς ὁ θεός, as in 1 Cor 1:9; 2 Cor 1:18) could be regarded as equivalent to the "Amen" of the synagogue or to the benediction following the reading of the *haftarah* (the lesson from the prophets):

ברוך אתה . . . האל הנאמן האומר ועושה—"Blessed art thou, . . . O faithful God, who sayest and doest" (cf. 1 Thess 5:24). Like that benediction, the construction of vv 3, 4 affirms confidence in the covenant-keeping God.

Comment

3:3. Πιστὸς δέ ἐστιν ὁ κύριος, "but the Lord is faithful"; cf. 1 Thess 5:24, πιστὸς ὁ καλῶν ὑμᾶς, ὃς καὶ ποιήσει (also 1 Cor 1:9; 10:13; 2 Cor 1:18).

There is an intended contrast between the πίστις of God and the ἀπιστία of the opponents of the gospel, even if the πίστις of God is his faithfulness while their lack of πίστις is their unbelief. Those who put their faith in God can count on his faithfulness.

ὃς στηρίξει ὑμᾶς. Cf. 2:17; 1 Thess 3:13 for the wish-prayer that God may "establish" (στηρίξειν) the Thessalonians' hearts.

καὶ φυλάξει ἀπὸ τοῦ πονηροῦ, "and will guard (you) from the evil (one)." This is reminiscent of the petition ἀλλὰ ῥῦσαι ἡμᾶς ἀπὸ τοῦ πονηροῦ, "but deliver us from (the) evil" in the fuller text of the Lord's Prayer preserved in Matt 6:13. It is impossible to be sure here whether τοῦ πονηροῦ is personal (masculine) or impersonal (neuter); the latter is defended by M. Dibelius (ad loc.), but the personal "evil one" forms a more effective antithesis to the personal κύριος. Behind the ἄτοποι καὶ πονηροὶ ἄνθρωποι, "perverse and wicked men" (v 2), may be recognized ὁ πονηρός himself (for this as a designation of the devil cf. Matt 13:19, 38; Eph 6:16; 1 John 2:13, 14; 5:18, 19). The activity of Satan against the interests of the preachers and their converts has been referred to in 1 Thess 2:18; 3:5 (ὁ πειράζων); here (as in 2:9 above) there may be an allusion to Satan's intensified activity in the end-time; such an allusion is more probable than that there is a parallel here to the Jewish prayer for deliverance from the evil inclination (יצר הרע).

The adjective clause qualifying ὁ κύριος and expressing the evidence or result of his faithfulness is paralleled in 1 Thess 5:24; 1 Cor 1:9; 10:13.

4. πεποίθαμεν δέ, "and we are confident." The theme of confidence is continued; confidence is now voiced that the Thessalonians will go on living in accordance with the apostolic teaching. But it is a confidence ἐν κυρίῳ—the writers trust the Lord to maintain in those believers the good work that he has manifestly begun (cf. 1:3; 1 Thess 1:6–8; 2:13, 14; 4:9, 10a). For ἐν κυρίῳ in such a context cf. Rom 14:14; Gal 5:10; Phil 2:24.

ἃ παραγγέλλομεν, both previously (by word of mouth and in writing; cf. 1 Thess 4:11) and now afresh. Even as they express their confidence, the writers repeat their παραγγελία, especially in one particular area of community life (vv 6, 10, 12).

[καὶ] ποιεῖτε. Cf. 1 Thess 4:10 (καὶ γὰρ ποιεῖτε αὐτό, "indeed, you do it"); 5:11 (καθὼς καὶ ποιεῖτε, "as indeed you are doing").

καὶ ποιήσετε. For the combining of the future tense with the present, whether in expressions of confidence or in exhortation, cf. 1 Thess 4:1, 10.

Explanation

Whether the apostles request prayer for themselves, or pray for their converts, their confidence is firmly founded in the supreme hearer of prayer: "the Lord is faithful." "The Lord" here is the Lord Jesus; elsewhere they say "God is faithful" or "he who calls you is faithful" (1 Thess 5:24). It makes no material difference whether God or the Lord is spoken of in this regard; the faithfulness of God is secured to his people in Christ, "for all the promises of God find their Yes in him. That is why we utter the Amen through him, to the glory of God" (2 Cor 1:20). To say, while praying, "the Lord is faithful" is another way of uttering the Amen. To ask him to strengthen his people and guard them from evil is to ask in the assurance that (as Paul says to the Corinthian Christians) "it is God who establishes us with you in Christ" (2 Cor 1:21). And to exhort his people to do the things that belong to Christian living is no fruitless exercise, because it is the Lord who enables them so to do. In prayer and exhortation alike the apostles' confidence is in the Lord.

(c) Second Wish-Prayer (3:5)

Bibliography

Wiles, G. P. *Paul's Intercessory Prayers.* SNTSMS 24. Cambridge: Cambridge University Press, 1974.

Translation

> ⁵ *Now may the Lord direct* ᵃ *your hearts* ᵇ *into the love of God and into the* ᶜ *steadfastness of Christ.*

Notes

ᵃ For κατευθύναι F G read κατευθύνη.
ᵇ For ὑμῶν τὰς καρδίας D reads τὰς καρδίας ὑμῶν (G τὰς καρδίας ἡμῶν).
ᶜ TR omits τήν before ὑπομονήν.

Form/Structure/Setting

This is the simplest form of wish-prayer. The two prepositional phrases express what G. P. Wiles terms an "additional benefit" (in this case, two benefits), but only in a very technical sense, for they really belong to the main blessing sought for the people addressed. An "eschatological climax" might be recognized if ὑπομονήν τοῦ Χριστοῦ, "(the) steadfastness of Christ" could be taken to mean "patient waiting for Christ"—but this is improbable.

Comment

3:5. ὁ δὲ κύριος κατευθύναι ὑμῶν τὰς καρδίας, "now may the Lord direct your hearts . . . ." For the aorist optative κατευθύναι in another wish-prayer cf. 1 Thess 3:11. For καρδία (in the psychological sense, "mind") in other wish-prayers cf. 2:17 (παρακαλέσαι ὑμῶν τὰς καρδίας, "encourage your hearts"); 1 Thess 3:13 (εἰς τὸ στηρίξαι ὑμῶν τὰς καρδίας, "so as to establish your hearts"). The phrase κατευθύνειν τὴν καρδίαν (. . . τὰς καρδίας) is used repeatedly in 1 and 2 Chr LXX (1 Chr 29:18; 2 Chr 12:14; 19:3; 20:33) to render Heb. (ב)לבב הכין ("to incline one's heart"), where the word for "heart" with the pronominal suffix is an emphatic substitute for the simple personal pronoun (as it is here).

εἰς τὴν ἀγάπην τοῦ θεοῦ. It may be asked whether the genitive is subjective ("God's love for you") or objective ("your love for God"). Pauline usage would point to the former interpretation; in any case, Christian love is for him the effect of the outpouring of God's love into his people's hearts by the Holy Spirit (cf. Rom 5:5). The more they appreciate God's love, the more they will reflect it in their love to him and to others.

καὶ εἰς τὴν ὑπομονὴν τοῦ Χριστοῦ. The decision whether to take this genitive as subjective or objective can scarcely be avoided by the attempt (as with τοῦ θεοῦ in the preceding phrase) to combine both. The patience or stead-fastness which Christ displayed (like his other ethical graces) should be reproduced in his followers; indeed, he may be said to impart it to them. As he "endured from sinners such hostility against himself" (Heb 12:3), so should they; indeed, they were already learning to do so (cf. the commendation of their ὑπομονή and πίστις in 1:4). To take τοῦ Χριστοῦ as objective genitive, as in AV (following Geneva) "the patient waiting for Christ," chimes in happily with the emphasis on the Parousia which characterizes these two letters and could be related to the "patience (ὑπομονή) of hope in our Lord Jesus Christ" of 1 Thess 1:3; it is, however, a less natural way to construe the phrase, and sits less easily with τὴν ἀγάπην τοῦ θεοῦ.

Explanation

The writers pray that the risen Lord will lead their Thessalonian friends into a growing appreciation of God's love for them (which will inevitably increase their love for him and for one another) and into a still greater participation in the steadfast endurance of Christ. Even if there is no explicit reference to his Advent in this wish-prayer, their steadfast endurance will in any case be strengthened by their confident expectation of that consummation of their hope.

Exhortation   (2 Thess 3:6-16)

(a) On Idleness (3:6-13)

Bibliography

Bjerkelund, C. J. *Parakalô: Form, Funktion und Sinn der Parakalô-Sätze in den paulinischen Briefen.* Bibliotheca Theologica Norvegica, 1. Oslo: Universitetsforlaget, 1967. **Cullmann, O.** "The Tradition." In *The Early Church,* ed. and tr. A. J. B. Higgins. London: SCM Press, 1956, 55–99. **De Boer, W. P.** *The Imitation of Paul.* Kampen: Kok, 1962. **Ellis, E. E.** "Paul and his Co-Workers." *NTS* 17 (1970–71) 437–452. **Frame, J. E.** "Οἱ ἄτακτοι (1 Thess 5:14)." In *Essays in Modern Theology . . . a Testimonial to C. A. Briggs.* New York: Scribners, 1911, 191–206. **Moulton, H. K.** "Tired of Doing Good?" *BT* 26 (1975) 445. **Schmithals, W.** *Paul and the Gnostics.* Tr. J. E. Steely. Nashville/New York: Abingdon, 1972. **Spicq, C.** "Les Thessaloniciens 'inquiets' étaient-ils des paresseux?" *ST* 10 (1957) 1–13.

Translation

[6] Now, brothers, we charge you in the name of our [a] Lord Jesus Christ to keep aloof from any brother who conducts himself in a disorderly manner and not in accordance with the tradition which they received [b] from [c] us. [7] You yourselves know how our example should be imitated, because we did not lead disorderly lives among you, [8] nor did we eat any one's bread for nothing. We kept on working with labor and toil night and day, [d] so as not to become burdensome to any of you, [9] not because we have no right (to be supported by you); our purpose was rather to present ourselves [e] as an example for your imitation. [10] Indeed, when we were with you, we gave you this charge: "If any one refuses [f] to work, let him not eat." [11] For we hear [g] that some are conducting themselves in a disorderly manner among you, not attending to their own business but to other people's. [12] We charge and exhort such people in the Lord Jesus Christ [h] to work quietly and eat their own bread. [13] But for your part, brothers, do not give up [i] doing good.

Notes

[a] ἡμῶν is omitted by B D*.

[b] παρελάβοσαν (א* A 33 pc; cf. D* ἐλάβοσαν) illustrates the Hellenistic encroachment of the μι conjugation on the ω conjugation (cf. John 15:22, 24, εἴχοσαν). This particular encroachment may have been the more readily accepted because it removed the occasion of ambiguity arising from the identical classical forms of the first person singular and third person plural of the imperfect and second aorist active of the ω conjugation. Here παρελάβετε is read by B F G 2464 pc lat^{vg.codd} syr^hel cop^sa; the strictly concordant παρέλαβε(ν) by 1962 pc; the classical παρέλαβον by א² D² Ψ byz.

[c] For παρ' ἡμῶν B 104 630 pc read ἀφ' ἡμῶν.

^d For νυκτὸς καὶ ἡμέρας A D I Ψ byz read νύκτα καὶ ἡμέραν.

^e For ἑαυτούς as reflexive pronoun of the first person plural cf. 1 Thess 2:8 (ἑαυτῶν, 1st person); 5:13 (ἑαυτοῖς, 2nd person), with p. 118 note d.

^f εἰ τις οὐ θέλει. The negative after εἰ is οὐ, not μή, because οὐ and θέλειν are taken closely together in the sense "refuse" (cf. v 14, εἰ δέ τις οὐχ ὑπακούει).

^g ἀκούομεν, perfective present (a classical usage); the writers do not mean that the news was coming in as their letter was being dictated (cf. ἀκούω in Luke 9:9; 16:2; 1 Cor 11:18).

^h ἐν κυρίῳ Ἰησοῦ Χριστῷ, for which א² D² Ψ byz syr^{hcl} read διὰ τοῦ κυρίου ἡμῶν Ἰησοῦ Χριστοῦ (ἡμῶν is omitted by Ψ pc).

ⁱ ἐγκακήσητε, for which ἐκκακήσητε is read by D² F G Ψ byz.

Form/Structure/Setting

This subsection forms one sustained hortatory period exhibiting the pattern outlined by C. J. Bjerkelund (*Parakalô*, 125–140), with the verb of exhortation (here the stronger παραγγέλλομεν in place of παρακαλοῦμεν) followed by a vocative (ἀδελφοί), a prepositional phrase (ἐν ὀνόματι τοῦ κυρίου ἡμῶν Ἰησοῦ Χριστοῦ), and an injunction in the infinitive (στέλλεσθαι ὑμᾶς). The pattern is repeated in briefer compass in v 12, without the vocative and with the injunction expressed by ἵνα and the subjunctive (ἵνα ἐσθίωσιν).

Comment

3:6. Παραγγέλλομεν δὲ ὑμᾶς, ἀδελφοί, "Now we charge you, brothers." The following charge is no doubt included in ἃ παραγγέλλομεν (v 4), but is now set out more explicitly. As in 1 Thess 5:14, the question arises whether the ἀδελφοί here are the Thessalonian believers as a whole or a particular group within their fellowship. Ellis ("Paul and his Co-workers," 450, 451) thinks of "a group of Christian workers" as addressed not only here but in 2 Thessalonians generally. So far as the present context is concerned, he points to vv 7–9, where the persons addressed "are commanded to imitate Paul in one specific respect, that is, in forgoing the Christian workers' right to unqualified support," and to v 10, where "these persons are receiving financial support or, at least, communal meals" (although in v 10 it is not the persons addressed who are admonished to work for what they eat, but the ἀτάκτως περιπατοῦντες, "those leading disorderly lives," who require discipline at their hands). In any discipline which is exercised by the church, it is the προϊστάμενοι who must take the initiative.

ἐν ὀνόματι τοῦ κυρίου [ἡμῶν] Ἰησοῦ Χριστοῦ, "in the name of [our] Lord Jesus Christ." Apostolic authority is essentially the authority of Christ, received by delegation from him and to be exercised only in accordance with his will. The apostles are his accredited representatives. For the use of the phrase in relation to church discipline cf. 1 Cor 5:4.

στέλλεσθαι ὑμᾶς, "that you keep aloof from"; for στέλλεσθαι (middle) in this sense cf. the only other NT instance of the simple verb: 2 Cor 8:20, στελλόμενοι τοῦτο, "avoiding this." Cf. Mal 2:5 LXX, where it occurs in synonymous parallelism with φοβεῖσθαι and means "to stand in awe of" (ἀπὸ προσώπου ὀνόματός μου στέλλεσθαι αὐτόν).

ἀπὸ παντὸς ἀδελφοῦ ἀτάκτως περιπατοῦντος, "from every brother who conducts himself in a disorderly manner." The warning against living ἀτάκτως is fuller and more peremptory than in 1 Thess 4:9b–12; 5:14. Perhaps the gentler admonition given in the earlier letter had not been effective in checking tendencies to unruliness in the congregation. The nature of the unruliness can be inferred only from the detailed wording of the charge as it is developed in vv 7–13.

καὶ μὴ κατὰ τὴν παράδοσιν ἣν παρελάβοσαν παρ' ἡμῶν, "and not according to the tradition which they received from us." The "tradition," which had been delivered to them orally (v 10) and in writing (1 Thess 4:9b–12), covered matters of faith and conduct alike; cf. 2:15; 1 Thess 4:1, 2 (with comments ad loc.). It is the tradition relating to conduct that is primarily in view here. For a similar admonition relating more to matters of faith see Rom 16:17, 18, where the Roman Christians are urged to "avoid" (ἐκκλίνετε ἀπ' αὐτῶν) people "who create dissensions and difficulties, in opposition to the doctrine which you have been taught (παρὰ τὴν διδαχὴν ἣν ὑμεῖς ἐμάθετε)."

7. Αὐτοὶ γὰρ οἴδατε πῶς δεῖ μιμεῖσθαι ἡμᾶς, "For you yourselves know (cf. 1 Thess 2:1, with comment) how our example should be followed." If the "brothers" addressed are the responsible group of co-workers, then those who ought to imitate Paul and his colleagues (while including the co-workers) constitute a wider circle, the whole church. The tradition had been delivered by example as well as by precept. The missionaries' conduct during their stay in Thessalonica is recalled in 1 Thess 2:3–12, mainly by way of apologia but also in order that their converts might learn from them "to lead a life worthy of God." The "imitation of Paul" is a recurring theme in his letters; cf. 1 Thess 1:6 (with comment ad loc.); 1 Cor 4:16; 11:1; Phil 4:9.

ὅτι οὐκ ἠτακτήσαμεν ἐν ὑμῖν, "that we did not lead disorderly lives among you." The verb ἀτακτεῖν (lit. "to be out of order") appears in Xenophon (*Cyr.* 7.2.6) and Demosthenes (*Third Olynth.* 11) of military indiscipline or desertion (cf. the adverb ἀτάκτως in Thuc. *Hist.* 3.108, of the defeated Peloponnesians trying to hasten back to their camp ἀτάκτως καὶ οὐδενὶ κόσμῳ, "in no order"), and then in various writers of undisciplined or irregular conduct in general. (See Milligan, 152–154, Note G: "On ἀτακτέω and its cognates.")

8. οὐδὲ δωρεὰν ἄρτον ἐφάγομεν παρά τινος, "nor did we eat any one's bread for nothing," "nor did we eat bread at any one's expense without payment." The adverbial accusative δωρεάν, "freely," "for nothing," appears in the Matthaean account of Jesus' commissioning of the twelve (δωρεὰν ἐλάβετε, δωρεὰν δότε, Matt 10:8), in a context not irrelevant to the present passage (see the reference to ἐξουσία in v 9). "The laborer deserves his food," said Jesus to the twelve when sending them out (Matt 10:10), but Paul and his companions, for reasons which they state below, preferred to earn their food by manual work.

ἐν κόπῳ καὶ μόχθῳ νυκτὸς καὶ ἡμέρας ἐργαζόμενοι πρὸς τὸ μὴ ἐπιβαρῆσαί τινα ὑμῶν, "with labor and toil night and day we kept on working so as not to become a burden to any of you." This is practically a repetition of what they had said in 1 Thess 2:9 (see comment ad loc.).

9. οὐχ ὅτι οὐκ ἔχομεν ἐξουσίαν, "not because we have not authority"; cf. 1 Cor 9:4, 5, μὴ οὐκ ἔχομεν ἐξουσίαν . . . ; There Paul affirms that he has the right to eat and drink and be generally supported at his converts' expense, but goes on to say (1 Cor 9:15) that he has availed himself of none of these privileges for reasons of apostolic policy and pastoral concern. Here he and his companions make much the same point. The ἐξουσία was that bestowed by the Lord himself when commissioning his disciples (Matt 10:9, 10; Luke 10:7, 8), "that those who proclaim the gospel should get their living by the gospel" (1 Cor 9:14).

ἵνα ἑαυτοὺς τύπον δῶμεν ὑμῖν, "in order to present ourselves to you as an example" (cf. Phil 3:17, καθὼς ἔχετε τύπον ἡμᾶς, "live as you have an example in us").

εἰς τὸ μιμεῖσθαι ἡμᾶς, "so as to imitate us." Cf. v 7, with comment ad loc. It would have been more difficult for the church to discipline its members who lived ἀτάκτως, at the expense of their fellows, if they could have pleaded that this was what the missionaries did. But if those who were entitled to be supported by others chose rather to support themselves, how much more should those who had no such entitlement earn their own living! In his dealings with the Corinthian church, Paul's purpose in forgoing the right to be supported by it was "to undermine the claim of those who would like to claim that in their boasted mission they work on the same terms as we do" (2 Cor 11:12)—a reference to intruders into his mission field who had no scruples about living at the expense of *his* converts.

10. καὶ γὰρ ὅτε ἦμεν πρὸς ὑμᾶς, "indeed, when we were with you." Cf. 2:5; 1 Thess 3:4. The writers repeat instructions which they had given by word of mouth (τοῦτο παρηγγέλλομεν ὑμῖν).

ὅτι εἴ τις οὐ θέλει ἐργάζεσθαι, μηδὲ ἐσθιέτω. This is an instance of ὅτι recitantis, introducing direct speech: "If any one refuses to work, neither let him eat," or "let him not even eat" (cf. 1 Cor 5:11, μηδὲ συνεσθίειν). This may have been a proverbial saying based on Gen 3:19 ("in the sweat of your face you shall eat bread"); it has become a proverbial saying from its occurrence here. This charge to their converts would have been less persuasive if the missionaries had not confirmed it by their own practice.

It is *refusal* to work that is reprobated here (*"nolle* vitium est," says Bengel). Comparable sayings are quoted from Jewish and early Christian literature. Rabbi Abbahu is cited as saying, "If I do not work, I do not eat" (*Gen. Rab.* 2.2 on Gen 1:2). In a non-Pauline area of the early Christian world the *Didache* instructs its readers how to deal with visitors who come to them in the Lord's name: "If he who comes is a traveler, help him as much as you can, but he shall not stay with you more than two days or, if necessary, three. If he wishes to settle down with you and has a craft, let him work for his bread (τεχνίτης ὤν, ἐργαζέσθω καὶ φαγέτω). But if he has no craft, make such provision for him as your intelligence approves, so that no one shall live with you in idleness as a Christian. If he refuses (οὐ θέλει) so to do, he is making merchandise of Christ (χριστέμπορός ἐστι); beware of such people" (12:2–5).

11. Ἀκούομεν γάρ, "for we hear" (cf. 1 Cor 11:18). This information presumably came to them together with the news about the misunderstanding with regard to the Day of the Lord.

τινας περιπατοῦντας ἐν ὑμῖν ἀτάκτως, "some are conducting themselves in a disorderly manner among you." Cf. v 6, where the same adverb and participle are used.

μηδὲν ἐργαζομένους ἀλλὰ περιεργαζομένους, "busybodies instead of busy" (J. Moffatt), "neglecting their own business to mind other people's" (R. A. Knox), "minding everybody's business but their own." These are attempts to convey the nuance of the Greek play on words, the *figura etymologica* (for which cf. Acts 8:30, ἀρά γε γινώσκεις ἃ ἀναγινώσκεις; Rom 12:3, μὴ ὑπερφρονεῖν παρ᾽ ὃ δεῖ φρονεῖν ἀλλὰ φρονεῖν εἰς τὸ σωφρονεῖν, 2 Cor 3:2, γινωσκομένη καὶ ἀναγινωσκομένη).

For the sense cf. 1 Thess 4:11, πράσσειν τὰ ἴδια (and the warning in 1 Pet 4:15 against a Christian's getting into trouble as an ἀλλοτριεπίσκοπος, a meddler in other people's affairs). The tendency to mind other people's business might simply be an example of the principle that "Satan finds some mischief still/ For idle hands to do"; it might, however, be a symptom of that religiosity which must always be prying into the private lives of others. Schmithals compares Irenaeus's description of the Marcosians (*Adv. Haer.* 1.13) and Origen's account of gnostic prophets (*Cels.* 7.8, 9); he also mentions an entry in the minutes of a West German presbytery (*c.* 1770), where some pietists are reported to be "very negligent of their business at home . . . and give occasion to general nuisance" (*Paul and the Gnostics,* 199). But there is nothing peculiar to Gnostics in conduct of this kind. Whatever occasions it, it is the kind of conduct which gives a community a bad name, and the interests of the community, as well as of the offenders themselves, require that they be disciplined.

12. τοῖς δὲ τοιούτοις παραγγέλλομεν καὶ παρακαλοῦμεν, "we charge and exhort such"; the combination of the two verbs (cf. 1 Thess 4:1, ἐρωτῶμεν . . . καὶ παρακαλοῦμεν) adds emphasis to the injunction, as does the invocation of the Lord's authority: ἐν κυρίῳ Ἰησοῦ Χριστῷ (cf. v 6, ἐν ὀνόματι τοῦ κυρίου . . .). The wording may indeed convey more than the invocation of his authority; as in 1 Thess 4:1 (ἐρωτῶμεν ὑμᾶς καὶ παρακαλοῦμεν ἐν κυρίῳ Ἰησοῦ), it may imply Christ's personal involvement in the situation (see comment ad loc., with quotation from Dunn).

ἵνα μετὰ ἡσυχίας ἐργαζόμενοι τὸν ἑαυτῶν ἄρτον ἐσθίωσιν, "that they work quietly and eat their own bread" (i.e. eat bread which they have earned, as distinct from δωρεὰν ἄρτον φαγεῖν, v 8). With μετὰ ἡσυχίας cf. 1 Thess 4:11, ἡσυχάζειν . . . καὶ ἐργάζεσθαι ταῖς [ἰδίαις] χερσίν, "to lead a quiet life . . . and to work with your own hands." Such "quiet" behavior is the antithesis to interfering in other people's affairs and being a general nuisance. Neil sums up the injunctions thus: "Stop fussing, stop idling, and stop sponging."

If Paul did not impose law on his converts, he (and his associates) certainly gave them guidelines within which their personal and communal life should be conducted. Here these guidelines are part of a common Christian tradition; at other times Paul had to express his own judgment (γνώμη) which, while he reckoned it advantageous to his converts, could not be binding on them (1 Cor 7:25–38; 2 Cor 8:10). But the traditions had the force of a "commandment of the Lord" (1 Cor 7:10, 11; 14:37).

13. Ὑμεῖς δέ, ἀδελφοί, μὴ ἐγκακήσητε καλοποιοῦντες, "But for your part, brothers, do not give up doing good." The emphatic ὑμεῖς δέ contrasts those addressed with the ἄτακτοι. Cf. Gal 6:9, τὸ δὲ καλὸν ποιοῦντες μὴ ἐγκακῶμεν, "let not be weary in doing well." Exhortations to perseverance are common in Paul's writings (cf. 1 Cor 15:50, 58; 16:13; Phil 1:27, 28; 2:15, 16; 4:1; 1 Thess 3:5, 13; 5:23). The Hellenistic verb ἐγκακεῖν ("give up," "slacken") is preceded by a negative in all its NT occurrences (cf. Luke 18:1; 2 Cor 4:1, 16; Eph 3:13). Doing positive good to others for the love of God is a very different matter from idly interfering in their affairs, although a certain type of "do-gooder" is more prone to the latter activity than to the former. Cf. Eph 4:28, where the converted thief no longer robs others but helps them: "let him labor, doing honest work with his hands, so that he may be able to give to those in need."

Explanation

At the end of the previous letter (1 Thess 5:14) the Thessalonian church, and probably its leaders in particular, received a charge to admonish those of its members who were idlers, leading unruly and undisciplined lives. It does not appear that any admonition of the kind had made much impression on those people, for in this letter a fuller and more serious charge is given about the way to deal with them. It was important that the other residents in the city should not look at those idlers and conclude that their mode of behavior was characteristic of Christians in general. The church and its leaders are therefore instructed to dissociate themselves from those of their number who refuse to work for their living.

Paul and his companions remind the Thessalonians again how they themselves worked for their living while they were with them, forgoing the right to live by their ministry, in order to set their converts a good example. Their maxim, taught by precept and by action, "If any one refuses to work, let him not eat," need not be taken as a summary of the Christian doctrine of labor, but it does teach that it is scandalous for those who profess and call themselves Christians to lead idle lives and look to others for support if they themselves have opportunity and strength for working to maintain themselves and to help others who are less fortunate.

The idlers were evidently interfering in other people's business, rather than profitably employing their time. Nothing is more certain to get oneself disliked, and the dislike is apt to rub off on those who are thought to be associated with the busybody. Hence the call to keep aloof from such troublemakers.

As in 1 Thessalonians, so here no clear indication is given of the reason for those people's idle ways and intrusion into the affairs of others. It may have been a conviction that the Day of the Lord was imminent, if it had not indeed already arrived; it may have been a belief in their own superior spirituality, which exempted them from such mundane concerns as earning an honest living and entitled them to pry into other people's personal affairs; it may have been a combination of those or other factors. But the vice to which they were prone is familiar enough for us to be thankful that it is so severely condemned in the apostolic teaching.

(b) *On Discipline* (3:14–15)

Bibliography

Moffatt, J. "2 Thessalonians iii.14, 15." *ExpTim* 21 (1909–10) 328.

Translation

> ¹⁴ *But if anyone disobeys* ᵃ *our* ᵇ *word (conveyed) by this epistle, take note of this person, so as not to associate* ᶜ *with him, in order that he may be ashamed.* ¹⁵ *And do not count him as an enemy, but admonish him as a brother.*

Notes

ᵃ εἰ δέ τις οὐχ ὑπακούει, with οὐ, not μή, after εἰ, because οὐχ is so closely joined to ὑπακούειν (cf. v 10, εἰ τις οὐ θέλει).

ᵇ For ἡμῶν B 81 326 2464 *pc* have the misreading ὑμῶν.

ᶜ For the infinitive construction μὴ συναναμίγνυσθαι ("not to associate") D² byz syr have the imperative preceded by καί (καὶ μὴ συναναμίγνυσθε, "and do not associate").

Form/Structure/Setting

This note of warning and disciplinary direction at the end of a letter is paralleled in Rom 16:17; 1 Cor 16:22 (in the latter of these, beginning εἰ τις, as here, the anathema called for is incomparably more severe than the restorative discipline recommended for the Thessalonians).

Comment

3:14. Εἰ δέ τις οὐχ ὑπακούει τῷ λόγῳ ἡμῶν διὰ τῆς ἐπιστολῆς, "But if any one disobeys our word (conveyed) by this epistle." Again the note of apostolic authority is struck. The only "word" calling for obedience in this letter is the call to "hold fast the traditions" in 2:15, which is later given a specific application in the more peremptory charge to the church regarding idlers (3:6) and addressed directly to the idlers themselves (3:12).

τοῦτον σημειοῦσθε, "take note of this man." This is the only NT instance of σημειοῦν, found usually (as here) in the middle voice (cf. Ps 4:6 LXX, ἐσημειώθη ἐφ' ἡμᾶς τὸ φῶς τοῦ προσώπου σου, "the light of your face has been set as a mark on us"; 1 Clem 43:1, Μωϋσῆς τὰ διατεταγμένα αὐτῷ πάντα ἐσημειώσατο ἐν ταῖς ἱεραῖς βίβλοις, "Moses noted down in the sacred books all the injunctions given to him"). The force of the verb here is similar to that of σκοπεῖν in Rom 16:17, "keep an eye on (σκοπεῖτε) those who create dissensions and stumblingblocks . . . ; avoid them (ἐκκλίνετε ἀπ' αὐτῶν)."

μὴ συναναμίγνυσθαι αὐτῷ, "do not associate with him," "have nothing to do with him." The verb (in the middle, as here) is used in 1 Cor 5:9, 11, where Christians are instructed to withhold social contact from those who profess the faith but are guilty of fornication and similar vices. But the words which follow here suggest a less severe degree of dissociation than that laid down in 1 Cor 5:9, 11.

ἵνα ἐντραπῇ, "in order that he may become ashamed of himself." For this sense of the passive of ἐντρέπειν cf. Tit 2:8, ἵνα ὁ ἐξ ἐναντίας ἐντραπῇ ("that the opposing party may be put to shame"). The withholding of fellowship is designed to bring the offender to a better frame of mind, to make him realize that his conduct is unworthy of the name of Christ.

15. καὶ μὴ ὡς ἐχθρὸν ἡγεῖσθε, ἀλλὰ νουθετεῖτε ὡς ἀδελφόν, "and do not count him an enemy, but admonish him as a brother." The use of καὶ rather than an adversative conjunction before μὴ . . . ἡγεῖσθε may imply that, once a sense of shame has been awakened in him, he is to be treated as a member of the Christian family. With νουθετεῖτε cf. 1 Thess 5:14, νουθετεῖτε τοὺς ἀτάκτους. The person in question is still to be regarded as a true believer, though temporarily under discipline. The situation is different from that envisaged at Corinth, where "someone who is *called* a brother" (ἐάν τις ἀδελφὸς ὀνομαζόμενος . . .) lives and acts in such a way as to give the lie to his Christian profession; that person is to be treated as an unbeliever, with no entitlement to the privileges of Christian fellowship (1 Cor 5:11).

Moffatt ("2 Thessalonians iii. 14, 15") compares the observation of Marcus Aurelius (*Med.* 6.20), that if someone behaves roughly and rudely in the gymnasia we simply "avoid him, yet not as an enemy" (φυλαττόμεθα, οὐ μέντοι ὡς ἐχθρόν), and so in life, when we meet people of this character, it is proper "to avoid them (ἐκκλίνειν, as in Rom 16:17, quoted in comment on v 14) and not look at them askance or conceive hatred for them." Moffatt points out that Marcus Aurelius shows no concern for the improvement of the offender and "recognizes no duty of remonstrance ὡς ἀδελφόν." But he may build too much on the emperor's silence when he concludes that "the Stoic individualism and the Christian sense of obligation towards a brother are thrown into sharp contrast by the very similarity of the phrase [ὡς ἐχθρόν] . . . and of the situation under review."

Explanation

Membership in a Christian church in a pagan city imposed serious obligations. Christians were an unpopular minority and those who disliked them or wished to counter their influence lost no opportunity to spread unfavorable rumors about their conduct. It was most important that Christians should live in such a way as to provide practical refutation of such rumors. This was one reason for the emphatic ethical injunctions so characteristic of the NT letters, including 2 Thessalonians. The ethical injunctions of this letter are aimed mainly at those members of the church who were giving it a bad name by living as idlers and busybodies. Such a person, while not guilty of the kind of conduct which called for outright and formal excommunication, must nevertheless be treated in a way that might bring him to his senses and teach him to live as a responsible member of the believing community. He is not to be banished from communion as if he were an enemy—"a pagan and a tax-gatherer," in the language of Matt 18:17—he is to be acknowledged as a brother (even if, for the present, he is one of the black sheep of the family), who will be responsive, it is hoped, to brotherly reproof and instruction.

(c) Third Wish-Prayer (3:16)

Bibliography

Gamble, H., Jr. *The Textual History of the Letter to the Romans.* SD 42. Grand Rapids, MI: Eerdmans, 1977. **Robinson, J. A. T.** "The Earliest Christian Liturgical Sequence." In *Twelve New Testament Studies.* SBT 34. London: SCM Press, 1962, 154–157. **Wiles, G. P.** *Paul's Intercessory Prayers.* SNTSMS 24. Cambridge: Cambridge University Press, 1974.

Translation

[16] *Now may the Lord of peace himself give you peace at every time in every way.* [a] *The Lord be with you all.*

Notes

[a] For τρόπῳ ("way," "manner") A* D* F G 33 *pc* lat read τόπῳ ("place").

Form/Structure/Setting

This verse contains two simple wish-prayers, both having ὁ κύριος as subject (strengthened with αὐτός in the former; cf. 2:16). The optative is, as usual, expressed in the former (δῴη); it is understood (εἴη, optative of εἶναι) in the latter. The former is an expansion of Paul's regular peace benediction.

J. A. T. Robinson ("Liturgical Sequence," 156 n. 5) suggests that the frequent occurrence in the closing greetings, and nowhere else, of the formula "the God of peace" (here "the Lord of peace") may point to a liturgical origin. "It looks as if these phrases may originally have formed the words introducing the kiss of peace itself" (cf. 1 Thess 5:26, with comment ad loc.).

Comment

3:16. Αὐτὸς δὲ ὁ κύριος . . . Cf. 2:16 (in an earlier wish-prayer); 1 Thess 4:16 (not in a wish-prayer); also αὐτὸς δὲ ὁ θεός, 1 Thess 3:11, 5:23 (both in wish-prayers).

ὁ κύριος τῆς εἰρήνης. This is the only NT instance of this designation, but cf. the common ὁ θεὸς τῆς εἰρήνης, found in wish-prayers and similar constructions (1 Thess 5:23; Rom 15:33; 16:20; Phil 4:9; also Heb 13:20; cf. ὁ θεὸς τῆς ἀγάπης καὶ εἰρήνης, "the God of love and peace," 2 Cor 13:11).

δώῃ ὑμῖν τὴν εἰρήνην. The wish that the readers may enjoy peace is found not only in the regular prescript of Pauline letters (cf. 1:2; 1 Thess 1:1), χάρις ὑμῖν καὶ εἰρήνη, but also frequently near the end. Sometimes it takes the form of a wish-prayer or an assurance that the God of peace will be with them or do something for them (cf. also Rom 15:13, where peace is the gift of "the God of hope"); at other times εἰρήνη itself is the subject, as in Gal 6:16; Eph 6:23; Phil 4:7; Col 3:15. The only letters among the Pauline *homologoumena* which lack such a prayer or assurance are 1 Corinthians and Philemon. (See Gamble, *Textual History*, 67–68.) Here "the Lord of peace" is asked to give the readers peace—the article τήν before εἰρήνην points to the peace as *his* peace (cf. Col 3:15, ἡ εἰρήνη τοῦ Χριστοῦ, and Phil 4:7, ἡ εἰρήνη τοῦ θεοῦ).

It is noteworthy that in Rom 16:20; 2 Cor 13:11; Gal 6:16, the peace-wish follows on a warning passage, as also here.

There is an echo here of the priestly blessing in Num 6:26 LXX, . . . κύριος . . . δώῃ σοι εἰρήνην, "the Lord . . . give you peace."

διὰ παντὸς ἐν παντὶ τρόπῳ, "continually and in every way." For διὰ παντός (? *sc.* καιροῦ), sometimes written as one word, διαπαντός, cf. Matt 18:10; Mark 5:5; Luke 24:53; Acts 2:25 (in a quotation from LXX); 10:2; 24:16; Rom 11:10 (in a quotation from LXX); Heb 9:6; 13:15. The multiplication of expressions containing πᾶς or its derivatives is a common rhetorical figure in Greek literature (cf. Acts 24:3); Paul is prone to use it in words of prayer or assurance (cf. especially 2 Cor 9:8).

ὁ κύριος μετὰ πάντων ὑμῶν, probably a liturgical benediction; cf. Rom 15:33; Phil 4:9 (where "the God of peace" is the subject); also 2 Tim 4:22a (ὁ κύριος μετὰ τοῦ πνεύματός σου). We may compare the assurance of the risen Lord to the disciples in Matt 28:20, "Behold, I am with you all the days (πάσας τὰς ἡμέρας)." This clause contains a further form of πᾶς to stand alongside the two in the preceding wish-prayer.

Explanation

In praying for the blessing of peace on their converts, the writers ask that it may be bestowed by "the Lord of peace." The repetition of "peace" adds emphasis to their prayer. The substitution of "the Lord of peace" for the more frequent "the God of peace" may suggest that the risen Christ shares with God the prerogative of being "the author of peace and lover of concord." Elsewhere in the Pauline writings we are told that Christ has "made peace" (Col 1:20); more than that, "he is our peace" (Eph 2:14).

Letter Closing   (2 Thess 3:17–18)

Bibliography

Askwith, E. H. " 'I' and 'We' in the Thessalonian Epistles." *Expositor*, series 8, 1 (1911) 149–159. **Champion, L. G.** *Benedictions and Doxologies in the Epistles of Paul.* Oxford: published privately, 1934. **Eschliman, A.** "La rédaction des épîtres pauliniennes." *RB* 53 (1946) 185–196. **Gamble, H., Jr.** *The Textual History of the Letter to the Romans.* SD 42. Grand Rapids, MI: Eerdmans, 1977. **Lake, K.** *The Earlier Epistles of St. Paul.* London: Rivingtons, ²1914. **Lindemann, A.** "Zum Abfassungszweck des Zweiten Thessalonicherbriefes." *ZNW* 68 (1977) 35–47. **Lyonnet, S.** "De arte litteras exarandi apud antiquos." *VD* 34 (1956) 3–11. **Roller, O.** *Das Formular der paulinischen Briefe: Ein Beitrag zur Lehre vom antiken Briefe.* BWANT 4/6 (58). Stuttgart: Kohlhammer, 1933.

Translation

[17] *The greeting in my own hand—Paul's—which is my token in every letter; this is how I write.*
[18] *The grace of our Lord Jesus Christ be with you all.*[a]

Notes

[a] ἀμήν is added after the benediction in ℵ² A D F G Ψ byz lat syr cop[bo]. It represents the congregational response when the benediction was read at the end of the letter in the course of a church service. See p. 133 note d.

Form/Structure/Setting

This brief letter closing consists of two elements: (1) the attention drawn to Paul's autograph and (2) the grace-benediction. Both elements conform to a recurring pattern. The former appears in identical words in 1 Cor 16:21 and Col 4:18 (ὁ ἀσπασμὸς τῇ ἐμῇ χειρὶ Παύλου); cf. also Gal 6:11 and Phlm 19 (τῇ ἐμῇ χειρί). The grace-benediction appears, with variation of wording, in all the Pauline letter closings.

Comment

3:17. Ὁ ἀσπασμὸς τῇ ἐμῇ χειρὶ Παύλου, "The greeting in my own hands— Paul's." The same formula is used in 1 Cor 16:21; Col 4:18; cf. also Gal 6:11, "see in what large letters I am writing with my own hand (τῇ ἐμῇ χειρί)," and Philem 19a, where Paul signs his IOU (ἐγὼ Παῦλος ἔγραψα τῇ ἐμῇ χειρί).

It was no uncommon thing in ancient letter-writing for the sender, having dictated the bulk of the letter, to write the last sentence or two in his own hand. This is the best explanation of the change of script at the end of several papyrus letters which have been preserved. This practice would help to authenticate the letter (for readers who recognized the sender's writing); a more general purpose would be to make the letter look more personal than one written entirely by an amanuensis. Cicero seems commonly to have written his letters himself, but where he uses an amanuensis, he indicates that the letter-closing is in his own hand (cf. *Ad Att.* 13.28: *hoc manu mea,* "this in my own hand"). In another letter he quotes a sentence from one which he himself had received from Pompey and says that it came *in extremo, ipsius manu,* "at the end, in his own hand" (*Ad Att.* 8.1).

Paul, it appears, regularly used an amanuensis when sending a letter, like Tertius (Rom 16:22). Sometimes the amanuensis may have been one of his own associates, like Timothy; we cannot be sure. This letter, like 1 Thessalonians, is ostensibly sent from Paul, Silvanus and Timothy (1:1); the fact that Paul expressly adds his autograph and signature shows that, whether he was directly responsible for the wording or not, he approves of the substance and underwrites it with his apostolic authority.

It was not usual for the sender of an ancient letter to append his signature; its appearance in the prescript was sufficient. Paul's "mark in every letter" (σημεῖον ἐν πάσῃ ἐπιστολῇ) was not his signature but his autograph. In the three extant letters where he does append his signature, drawing attention to the fact, there was probably some special reason for doing so. The reference in 2:2 to "a letter purporting to come from us" (ἐπιστολῆς ὡς δι' ἡμῶν) perhaps indicates what that special reason was in this letter; the name as well as the autograph would make the authentication doubly certain. On the assumption that 1 Thessalonians was the earlier of the two letters, there had presumably been no reason for suspecting the circulation of a forgery when that letter was sent. There is no ground for concluding, with Roller (*Das Formular,* 187–191), that Paul's drawing attention to his autograph and signature means that the *whole* of 2 Thessalonians (as of Galatians, 1 Corinthians and Philemon) was written in Paul's hand.

Lake (following Harnack, and unconvincingly) suggested that Paul drew attention to his signature because the Jewish Christians to whom (*ex hypothesi*) this letter was sent would be "suspicious of anything coming from the Gentile community" (*Epistles,* 90). Even less convincing is the argument of Lindemann that the pseudonymous author of 2 Thessalonians signed the letter in Paul's name in order to cast doubt on the genuineness of 1 Thessalonians, which lacked this σημεῖον ("Zum Abfassungszweck . . . ," 38).

οὕτως γράφω, "this is how I write." For the present γράφω rather than the epistolary aorist ἔγραψα (as in Gal 6:11; Philem 19) cf. 1 Cor 4:14; 14:37; 2 Cor 1:13; 13:10; Gal 1:20; 1 Tim 3:14.

18. Ἡ χάρις τοῦ κυρίου ἡμῶν Ἰησοῦ Χριστοῦ μετὰ πάντων ὑμῶν, "the grace of our Lord Jesus Christ be with you all." Apart from the addition of πάντων before ὑμῶν this benediction is identical with that of 1 Thess 5:28

(see comments ad loc.); it is totally identical with that of Rom 16:24, which indeed is textually doubtful (see, however, H. Gamble, *Textual History,* 129– 130).

Explanation

As the writers take their leave of the Thessalonian Christians, Paul takes up the pen on behalf of all three, pointing out that his personal handwriting at the end authenticates this and other letters and praying (as at the beginning of the letter) that the grace of Christ may be with them all.

Index of Ancient Authors

Index of Modern Authors

Index of Subjects

Index of Biblical Texts
Old Testament